The Legal Environment of Insurance

Volume I

The Legal Environment of Insurance

Volume I

JAMES J. LORIMER, J.D., CPCU
Government Relations Officer
Nationwide Mutual Insurance Company

HARRY F. PERLET, JR., J.D.
Attorney-at-Law
Retired Assistant General Counsel
Insurance Services Office

FREDERICK G. KEMPIN, JR., J.D., O.L.B.
Professor and Chairman
The Wharton School Legal Studies Department
University of Pennsylvania

FREDERICK R. HODOSH, Ph.D., J.D., CPCU
Secretary and General Counsel
Director of Legal and Claims Education
American Institute for Property and Liability Underwriters

Second Edition • 1981

AMERICAN INSTITUTE FOR
PROPERTY AND LIABILITY UNDERWRITERS
Providence and Sugartown Roads, Malvern, Pennsylvania 19355

Foreword

The American Institute for Property and Liability Underwriters and the Insurance Institute of America are companion, nonprofit, educational organizations supported by the property-liability insurance industry. Their purpose is to provide quality continuing education programs for insurance personnel.

The Insurance Institute of America offers programs leading to the Certificate in General Insurance, the Associate in Claims (AIC) designation, the Associate in Management (AIM) designation, the Associate in Risk Management (ARM) designation, the Associate in Underwriting (AIU) designation, the Associate in Loss Control Management (ALCM) designation, the Associate in Premium Auditing (APA) designation, and the Accredited Adviser in Insurance (AAI) designation. The American Institute develops, maintains, and administers the educational program leading to the Chartered Property Casualty Underwriter (CPCU) professional designation.

Throughout the history of the CPCU program, an annual updating of parts of the course of study took place. But as changes in the insurance industry came about at an increasingly rapid pace, and as the world in which insurance operates grew increasingly complex, it became clear that a thorough, fundamental revision of the CPCU curriculum was necessary. This text is the second edition of one of those which were written for, and published by, the American Institute for use in the revised ten-semester CPCU curriculum which was introduced in 1978.

Throughout the development of the CPCU text series, it was—and will continue to be—necessary to draw on the knowledge and skills of Institute staff members. These individuals will receive no royalties on texts sold and their writing responsibilities are seen as an integral part of their professional duties. We have proceeded in this way to avoid any possibility of conflicts of interests. All Institute textbooks have been—and will continue to be—subjected to an extensive review process. Reviewers are drawn from both industry and academic ranks.

We welcome criticisms of our publications. Such comments should be directed to the curriculum department of the Institutes.

Edwin S. Overman, Ph.D., CPCU
President

Preface

The two volumes composing the text, *Legal Environment of Insurance*, have been designed to fill two major educational needs of the person preparing for the Chartered Property Casualty Underwriter examinations or who is otherwise interested in the interaction of the law and insurance. The chapters in Volume I deal primarily with what traditionally has been referred to as insurance law. This specialized field of the law evolved from the application of general legal principles to factual patterns common in insurance transactions. The result of this process is the gradual emergence of a body of special legal rules invoked by the courts in insurance litigation.

To enable the student to grasp the basic principles of insurance law, the first part of each chapter is devoted to the discussion of general legal concepts, followed by the examination of their applicability—or nonapplicability—in an insurance context. This approach is used in Chapter 1 by describing first the nature and sources of law, then the legal characteristics and features of the insurance product. In each of the next four chapters, there is a detailed discussion of basic contract rules and of the application of these rules to insurance situations. Similarly, in Chapters 6 and 7, the principles of general agency law are explained together with their interpretation in an insurance environment.

Volume I concludes with a distinctive area of insurance law that has developed to regulate the rights and duties the parties may have contrary to policy provisions.

The chapters in Volume II deal with legal topics the knowledge of which is essential for minimum "legal literacy" for most people, including persons active in the insurance mechanism. These are primarily subjects involving the legal problems of the business-consumer relationship. In preparing this material, special efforts were made to convey only the most basic rules in each of the topics; nevertheless, a certain amount of technical detail had to be included in such areas as the law of corporations, partnerships, property, and the

Uniform Commercial Code. The text exposes the student to sufficient familiarity with these legal fields to recognize the legally significant events in everyday business and personal affairs and thereby avoid potentially serious mistakes or pitfalls. Chapter 14 summarizes largely statutory developments designed to grant new rights to consumers in a business context, while Chapter 15 outlines the basic rules of administrative law, reflecting the growing importance of this area in light of increased regulatory activity, especially in the field of insurance.

The authors' task was made easier by the knowledge that their manuscript would be reviewed by a group of reviewers who are not only acknowledged experts in the subject matter, but who also for many years have played important roles in the field of insurance education. These reviewers, we feel, being our first and most critical readers, have given us a certain peace of mind by insuring that the final product is reasonably close to the mark both from the legal and the educational standpoint. Thus, we are most grateful to Joseph P. Decaminada, CPCU, CLU, Sr. Vice President, Secretary and Counsel, The Atlantic Companies; B. David Hinkle, LL.B., Senior Vice President and Director of Human Resources, Crawford and Company; Dugald W. Hudson, J.D., LL.M., CPCU, CLU, Professor of Business Law and Insurance, Georgia State University; Roger W. Penner, CPCU, Griffin, Dysart, Taylor, Penner & Lay, P.C.; and C. Graham Stillings, CPCU, CLU, Vice President, Associate Counsel, Michigan Mutual Insurance, for the invaluable help they gave us by their thoughtful comments and suggestions.

Of course, the burden of any error of omission or commission rests firmly and solely on the authors who encourage constructive criticism aimed at the improvement of future editions.

James J. Lorimer
Harry F. Perlet
Frederick G. Kempin, Jr.
Frederick R. Hodosh

Table of Contents

Chapter 7—Agency—Liability to Third Parties

Chapter 8—Extra-Contractual Rights and Obligations

CHAPTER 1

Introduction to Insurance Law

THE NATURE AND SOURCES OF LAW

The Aim of Social Justice

Necessity of Law   There are few human activities that are not affected by law. In today's society, the simple act of transporting oneself from place to place is surrounded by a large body of civil and criminal law. Such law spells out in detail the standards of conduct that individuals are expected to recognize and are obliged to follow. For the law-abiding person who learns early in life that ignorance of the law is no excuse, the challenge of knowing the law can be one of the more unsettling requirements of modern life.

Although we cannot escape the effect of the law upon our lives, in a civilized society escape is neither possible nor desirable. We know that, as the result of laws, individuals are able to go about their business and regulate their lives with greater certainty and safety. Laws are simply rules that society adopts to govern itself. Without such rules, society could not exist. Through laws, people express principles of order to which they believe they must conform as members of society. Laws provide a framework for harmony in society.

Knowing the Law   Although it is required that we be familiar with the law, the average citizen is not expected to have the knowledge of a lawyer. The more accurate and reasonable expectation is that each person possess knowledge in those areas of law that most directly affect his or her life. Since individuals necessarily come in contact with each other, knowledge concerning the basic legal rights, duties, and obligations between persons must be developed. Whether confronting a

1

difficult neighbor, entering a contract for the purchase of goods or services, undertaking a new employment or business venture, contemplating marriage or divorce, or planning the eventuality of death, each of life's activities and goals involve many legal considerations.

In like manner, the occupation one pursues will often require knowledge of specialized branches of law which have particular application to that field or profession. Those engaged in business pursuits should have some understanding of contract law, the law of agency, and the law relating to business associations. If one is engaged in a specialized type of business, such as the field of insurance, still more detailed knowledge of the law, regarding special features of insurance contracts and insurance agency, is necessary.

Whether in the area of individual rights and liabilities or in the field of one's employment, knowledge of legal ground rules is essential. These rules provide the necessary guides for conduct, and provide the base of certainty in human dealings that life in a complex society requires. Each society thus recognizes the necessity of law, as well as the requirement that its members know and conform their conduct to that law.

Development of the Law

Early Legal Systems. When people first gathered in groups, they found it necessary to adopt rules to govern their relations with one another. In the beginning, these rules were handed down from one generation to the next by word of mouth. As people developed the ability to record their thoughts, laws began to be written. An interesting example of one such early code was developed around 1700 B.C. by Hammurabi, a Babylonian ruler. His famous code contained some 300 laws which dealt with business and family relations. A main principle of Hammurabi's Code was that "the strong shall not injure the weak," a principle that is still observed in modern law.

A well-developed legal system was one of the great contributions of the Roman Empire to western civilization. Today, concepts of the Roman law form the basis of civil law in several European and Latin American countries. Some principles of Roman law have also become part of English and American common law. A noteworthy weakness of the Roman legal system was its attempt to establish two standards of law: one which applied only to citizens of Rome, and another which applied to all conquered peoples. Such double legal standards enjoyed little more acceptance in the Roman Empire than they would in the United States today.

The Common Law. At the basis of both English and American law is the so-called common law. Beginning as unwritten customs which were recognized and enforced by local courts, the system came into being in England following the Norman conquest in 1066 A.D. The law common to all England developed out of a constantly expanding number of cases involving actual disputes decided by the English royal courts and tribunals. Cases dating back to the fifteenth century are still cited in English and U.S. courts today.

When English colonists settled in North America, they brought with them the English common law. By then the common law had become a well-developed body of principles. It subsequently served as the legal foundation for the United States of America.

The Constitution, Statutory, and Common Law. The adoption of the U.S. Constitution in 1789 provided this country with the basic law of the land by establishing the form of government, and by assuring through the first ten amendments the fundamental rights and liberties of the people. Since those early days of the republic, the Constitution, the statutory law adopted by the federal and state governments, and the common law have all undergone considerable amendment, change, and interpretation. The U.S. Constitution is today the oldest constitution in the world, having managed to survive the most significant social and economic developments in history. The requirements of stability, certainty, and flexibility have been met within the framework of our constitutional, statutory, and common law system.

Law Not an Absolute While the law provides a framework for stability in society, the law cannot and does not stand still—it is a continually evolving process. The law is a reflection of society's common convictions at a given time, and these convictions change as society changes. One need only witness the stresses involved in the human rights movement in recent decades to understand the difficulties society experiences at each step as it adjusts its attitudes and its laws.

Evolutionary Process. The law, therefore, should not be viewed as an absolute, but as part of the evolution of society. What was considered good law in the United States a century ago would, in many instances, be considered bad law at present. In the 1880s, in most jurisdictions in this country, there were few restrictions on the use or abuse of child labor. Less than half the population enjoyed the right to vote, since all women and nearly all blacks were disfranchised. Married women did not enjoy full legal rights, inasmuch as their legal identities became merged with their husbands'. The rule of the marketplace was that of "caveat emptor," or "let the buyer beware." Labor unions were just beginning, and workers were at the mercy of employers. Industries were unhampered in their efforts to crush or wipe out competitors. In the yet-to-be-controlled insurance industry, it was not uncommon to find policies containing so many conditions and exceptions that payment of benefits would be made only under the most unusual circumstances.

While the law of a century ago may have seemed adequate to most citizens at the time, it would appear unjust by today's standards. Thus, changes in social and economic life, along with changes in the basic attitudes of people, have resulted in new laws which make the law of the 1880s seem primitive by comparison. In each of the areas mentioned, the law has evolved to a position clearly different, if not completely opposite, than that which previously existed. Such an evolution can be seen in virtually every field of the law.

Laws of the Future. History demonstrates that the law of the year 2080 A.D. will make present law appear as inadequate as the law of the past century seems now. It is challenging to contemplate what form laws of the future might take. To the extent that experience provides a guide, it appears likely that major changes will continue in the field of human rights. Increased socialization of all aspects of life might be seen, with government becoming more and more involved in the daily lives of citizens. As people live longer, significant changes can be expected in laws relating to older citizens. Laws affecting retirement, assuring the pursuit of several careers, providing for serial marriage, and increasing the means of caring for the aged are among the few directions that might be hypothesized. In like manner, conflicts between a depersonalized computer age and the rights of the individual will have to be resolved with increasing frequency. New concepts regarding the rights of privacy and individual security will necessarily evolve. Whatever direction the law of the future takes, it must continue to reflect a principle of growth.

Certainty Versus Flexibility. The fact that laws evolve as the needs of society change does not mean that reasonable certainty is not possible under the law. A major function of the law is to provide just such certainty. This need is especially apparent in the field of business law, where the requirements of economic life dictate that activities in the commercial realm have definite legal meaning. Certainty as to what constitutes a binding agreement, and the conditions under which such agreement will be enforced, is essential to the success of an advanced economy in which millions of such transactions are finalized daily.

The need for certainty also exists in many other fields of law, such as property and inheritance. In countries like the United States, where ownership of private property is a basic characteristic of the economy, the certain and effective transfer and inheritance of property is of great importance. In nations such as the Soviet Union, where the institution of private property has less significance, laws relating to private ownership of property are of lesser importance. The basic philosophy of a society will thus affect not only the substance of its laws, but also the extent to which it must develop and provide certainty in specific fields of the law.

While certainty of result is considered important in many areas of the law, more flexible standards may be found in others. For example, in the law of torts, which involves wrongs between persons, standards of conduct impose liability for negligence if the individual has failed to exercise the care which a reasonably prudent person would use under the circumstances. The law thus recognizes a standard with some flexibility that may be applied to an unlimited number of situations. A judge or jury sitting as the trier of fact will apply the standard to the actions of the individual. A guideline is thereby provided for both the individual and the judge or jury, although the standard is necessarily made flexible.

Doctrine of Stare Decisis.   At the foundation of the common law process lies the inclination of courts to follow established *precedent*. Once a court has decided a dispute, that decision serves as authority for the solution of similar cases in the future. The doctrine of *stare decisis* is generally adhered to by the courts, and it means "to stand as decided." The strength of the doctrine is that it affords certainty to the law; it rests on the principle that law should be fixed, definite, and known so that people may govern their affairs accordingly. Thus, if previous cases involving similar circumstances are found, a court will be strongly inclined to decide a present dispute in the same way. This does not mean that all questions will be decided exactly the same way, but rather that strong reasons will be required to cause the court to depart from the rules of law set forth in a previous case.

The doctrine of *stare decisis* has not been applied in a manner which has made the law rigid and inflexible. If American courts find that a prior decision was clearly wrong, they will not adhere to the doctrine and will proceed to overrule the previous holding. Much of the strength of our common law rests with the fact that no decision will be followed when it has lost its usefulness or when the reasons for it no longer exist. Thus, just as legislatures change the law by new legislation, so our courts change the law from time to time by overruling former precedents. Courts are subject to social forces and changing circumstances just as are legislatures. Still, *stare decisis* continues to serve the valuable function of removing the capricious element from the law, and of giving stability to society and to business.

The Law's Primary Aim—Social Justice   Justice is one of the more elusive goals of humanity. The social, political, and economic histories of a people give shape to their concepts of justice. In the field of human rights, for example, the rights to criticize government, to own property, to travel freely, and to publish one's beliefs would be viewed differently by persons accustomed to democratic government than by citizens of nondemocratic societies. In an age of increasing international commerce, such differences must be clearly recognized. Because of differing perceptions of law and order, justice in one society may be considered injustice in another.

As a society pursues its various social and economic objectives, such objectives will be expressed and will find support in laws. Very often the objectives of these laws come in conflict. It is then that society must make a choice. For example, an objective of society might involve the right of individuals to own property and to use that property freely in furtherance of their own profit-making interests. At the same time, the objective of furthering trade in the entire economy may be an aim of society. If an individual entrepreneur uses property in a way that results in restraint of trade in the general economy, a conflict is created. The challenge for society then becomes one of choosing between the socially desirable objective of promoting individual rights and the interests of the whole society in furthering trade. The choice will ultimately depend on society's concept of justice. It is desirable, of course, that the choice conform to the concept of right that the people hold. To the extent that it does, greater support for the decision will result.

Society is thus continually obliged to weigh competing objectives and to make effective choices which conform to generally held concepts of social justice. The estimate of the comparative value of one social or economic interest with another, when they come in conflict, is made by the citizenry through the political process and by the courts which interpret the law. These decisions are shaped by the experiences of society, and by its understanding of the prevailing canons of justice and morality. If social justice, as perceived by the mass of citizens, is not given effect by law and action, then society and government will likely experience conflict and disorder. Social justice, then, must be the primary aim of the law. The success of any society depends in no small measure on how effectively it strives toward and reaches that goal.

The Lawmakers

There are fifty-one basic legal systems in the United States: that of the federal government and those of the fifty states. While these systems are similar in many ways, they also have important differences. The law is found in four forms:

1. the constitutions of the United States and of the fifty states
2. the statutes enacted by our elected representatives
3. case law, as expressed in court decisions

4. administrative law adopted by various administrative agencies

Treaties made with other countries also have the force of law.

Constitutional Law A constitution is a body of basic principles stating the powers and limitations of a government and the way those powers are to be exercised. Most constitutions in democratic societies not only establish the form and powers of government, but also limit those powers and define the rights of individual citizens. While the United States Constitution is the basic law of our land, it is important to remember that each state constitution sets forth the form of government of that state, as well as the rights of its citizens. In the event of conflict between a state constitution and the federal Constitution, the latter would prevail. In like manner, any law that violates a provision of the federal Constitution is unconstitutional and therefore void. The Constitution of the United States and the constitutions of the various states are operative in their respective spheres; taken together, they provide the broad fundamental principles on which our government is based.

Source and Scope of Constitutional Guarantees. As far as the structure of the U.S. Constitution is concerned, the various clauses that guarantee the basic personal, property, and political rights of the individual do not all spring from the same source. Some of the clauses are found in the Constitution proper; some in the first ten amendments—the Bill of Rights—and some in the later amendments, particularly the fourteenth. In general, the first ten amendments place certain limitations upon the power of the federal government, while the Fourteenth Amendment imposes many of these same limitations upon state governments.

Express and Implied Powers of Congress. The powers of the United States Congress are specifically set forth in Article I, Section 8 of the Constitution. They include the power to regulate commerce, to lay and collect taxes, to borrow money, and to establish uniform laws on bankruptcy, as well as other specifically enumerated powers. In addition to the stated powers, Section 8 also provides that Congress be empowered "to make all laws which shall be necessary and proper for carrying into execution the foregoing powers and all other powers vested by this Constitution" (Section 8, Clause 18). Such is the implied power of Congress. It is further provided that the powers not given to the federal government by the Constitution, nor prohibited by it to the states, are reserved to the states, or to the people.[1] For a person engaged in business, there are several clauses in the Constitution that merit particular attention.

Commerce Clause. The commerce clause of the U.S. Constitution gives Congress the power to regulate commerce with foreign nations and among the several states. It provides the basis for determining those aspects of commerce that the federal government and state governments may regulate and tax. "Commerce" has been broadly construed under this provision to include any commercial activity, whether interstate or intrastate, if it has any appreciable effect upon interstate commerce, whether that effect is direct or indirect. Federal antitrust laws have been upheld by the U.S. Supreme Court as an exercise of the commerce power. Trade or commerce as used in these laws is held to include the distribution of movies, real estate, gathering of news, professional sports (except baseball), and insurance underwriting. The modern view of the commerce clause would apply the power of the federal government to any commercial activity that has an effect on interstate commerce, and this construction is referred to as the *Affectation Doctrine.*[2]

Insurance and the Commerce Clause. The early U.S. Supreme Court case of Paul v. Virginia, held that insurance policies did not involve transactions in interstate commerce, and that the business of insurance was therefore not subject to federal regulation.[3] This decision continued in force until 1944, when the Supreme Court reversed its previous position by holding that insurance did involve interstate commerce.[4] The insurance industry thereby became subject to federal regulation, and doubt was cast on the then well-established state regulatory system. In the following year, 1945, Congress enacted the McCarran Act, often referred to as Public Law 15, which permitted the continued regulation of insurance by the states.[5] The act left open the possibility of federal regulation to the extent that the states did not adequately regulate the insurance business. Numerous state laws were immediately passed in the areas of rate regulation, fair trade practices, and stock acquisitions by insurance companies, to assure that the insurance business was regulated by state law.

Due Process Clause. The most famous constitutional clause is found in the Fifth Amendment which provides, among other things, that no one may be deprived of life, liberty, or property "without due process of law." This amendment places the due process obligation on the federal government, and the Fourteenth Amendment places the same obligation on the states. Federal courts may step in if any state or local government body or official disregards the requirements of due process. The U.S. Supreme Court has stated:

> Due process of law implies at least a conformity with natural and inherent principles of justice, and forbids that one man's property, or right to property, shall be taken for the benefit of another, or for the

benefit of the state, without compensation, and that no one shall be condemned in his person or property without opportunity of being heard in his own defense.[6]

The guarantee springing from this clause extends both to criminal and civil proceedings.

Equal Protection Clause. The Fourteenth Amendment provides that no state shall deny any person within its jurisdiction the equal protection of the law. This clause prohibits the making of any laws that are discriminatory, and provides protection to both natural persons and to private corporations. It does not afford protection to municipal corporations, which are considered creatures of the state itself.[7]

The purpose of the equal protection clause is to assure that all persons will be treated alike under like circumstances and conditions, both in privileges conferred and in the liabilities imposed.[8] Equal protection clauses are also found in many state constitutions, and form the basis for many insurance rating classification laws. Other examples of the application of this clause to the business of insurance may be seen in court decisions holding state "guest statutes" unconstitutional. Such statutes normally require the guest in a vehicle to establish that the driver thereof was guilty of willful and wanton misconduct, rather than ordinary negligence, in order to recover damages from the driver. Imposition of such a special burden of proof on guest passengers has been held in some jurisdictions to result in discrimination against guests and failure of equal protection of the law. Such so-called invidious discrimination is not permitted by the Constitution.

Legislatures In nearly all states, a two-chambered, or bicameral, legislative body is established by the state constitution. Just as at the federal level, state senates and a state house of representatives, or an assembly, have been established. These legislative bodies attempt to clarify or change the common law of their respective states, and may do so to the extent that such enactments are not contrary to federal or state constitutions.

At the city or local level, thousands of town and village councils also enact various ordinances that specify standards of conduct for the community and provide for the operation of the governmental unit involved.

The U.S. Congress and the state legislatures enact laws which are called statutes. Statutory law generally declares, commands, or prohibits something. Because of differences among the laws of the several states, especially as applied to business, confusion may arise when persons accustomed to the laws of one state do business in another. To minimize such difficulties, many states have adopted certain "uniform laws," which are essentially the same from state to state. The Uniform

Commercial Code (UCC), which has been adopted in all but one state, regulates the sale of goods and other commercial transactions. The UCC has resulted in much uniformity in commerce throughout the country.

In the areas of powers specifically granted to the federal government by the U.S. Constitution, the Congress of the United States alone may act. In the areas that are primarily the concern of the individual states, the legislatures of the respective states may enact legislation. If it is claimed that Congress or the state legislatures did not have the right to legislate in a given area, the question may be referred to an appropriate court for the necessary decision. This is true also of questions regarding the interpretation of statutes. If there is a question, it is decided by a court.

Courts A court is a tribunal established by government to hear and decide matters properly brought before it. Generally the agency or instrument through which legal rights are enforced is a court. There are two systems of courts in the United States. One is maintained by the states, and the other by the federal government. While courts are charged with the responsibility of applying and interpreting law, such efforts often do, in effect, result in law making. So-called *case law* is found in the decisions and opinions of judges. Legislative bodies can modify or suspend common-law rules as announced by courts, if such modification does not violate a basic constitutional right. Until such court-made law is changed by statute, however, it is just as binding upon the people as law in any other form.

Federal Courts. The Constitution provides that "the judicial power of the United States shall be vested in one Supreme Court, and in such inferior courts as Congress may from time to time ordain and establish" (Article III, Section 1). The Supreme Court is thus the only federal court specifically provided for by the Constitution. Congress has since provided for courts of appeal in eleven judicial circuits, as well as for many U.S. district courts. In addition to such constitutional courts, various legislative courts have been created to hear cases involving particular types of disputes, such as the U.S. Customs Court, Tax Courts, Patent Appeals Court, the Court of Military Appeals, and the Court of Claims.

Federal Court Jurisdiction. Federal courts handle cases involving the Constitution, federal laws, and cases in which the United States is a party. Original jurisdiction rests with federal courts where civil suits are brought against or by the United States, in cases involving admiralty and maritime jurisdiction, in actions brought by citizens of different states claiming land under grants by different states, or in cases involving $10,000 or more that arise under the Constitution between citizens of different states or between citizens of one state and of a foreign state. The latter is called *diversity jurisdiction.*

State Courts. Every state has one or more courts of original jurisdiction in which suits may be brought. Some of these courts, such as justice of the peace courts, mayors' courts, municipal courts, county courts, probate courts, and the like, are termed courts of limited jurisdiction because the kinds of cases they are authorized to decide are limited. For instance, a justice of the peace court may handle only minor violations of a community's ordinances that fall under the heading of misdemeanors. While such a court would have original jurisdiction to hear traffic violation cases, the decisions rendered would be subject to appeal to and review by a court of more general jurisdiction. The case might be taken on appeal to a Court of Common Pleas, a Circuit Court, or a District Court. In most states, just as in the federal system, the court system is structured on at least three levels: courts of limited jurisdiction, courts of general jurisdiction, and appellate courts. The latter are Superior or Supreme Courts, and they may have some original jurisdiction in cases involving state agencies or state officials. However, appellate court duties primarily involve hearing of disputes that have been appealed from lower court decisions. Appeals may be taken from the state supreme court to federal courts only if a violation of the Constitution or a federal statute is alleged. In each instance, the appellate court determines whether it will hear the case appealed or whether it will let the decision of the inferior court stand as made.

Conflict of Laws. Since we have fifty state court systems and the federal court system, questions frequently arise concerning which law will be applied in a given case. The body of law known as *conflict of laws* answers such questions.

There are many situations in which the law of several jurisdictions might be applicable. This is especially true in the field of insurance agreements, which often involve parties living or traveling in different states. For example, a person living in State X might obtain insurance with a company in State Y to cover property located in State Z. Recognizing that the law of each state may differ to some extent, which state's law would be applied in the event of loss to the property? Similarly, a person may purchase automobile insurance while living in State X, which has a comparative negligence law. While driving in State Y, which has a no-fault law applicable to automobile accidents, the policyholder may be involved in an accident that results in injury to another. Which state's law would apply to such a loss?

While conflict of law rules in the various states differ to some extent, there is general agreement in some areas. Thus, in the field of torts, which would be applicable to the automobile accident, the law applied would generally be that of the state where the injury occurred. If the policyholder was sued in State X, where he or she resides, the courts in State X would apply the tort law of State Y. It should be noted that State X courts would apply their own procedural law, described more fully later, but would determine the substantive rights of the parties according to the tort law of the jurisdiction where the accident occurred. A qualification to this rule is found in some jurisdictions where the court feels its own state has the "most significant contacts" with the action. The qualification is seen most frequently in cases involving transportation, where both parties are citizens of one state and the accident occurs in another state. In this situation, if suit is brought by the parties in their state of residence, the local court may apply the substantive tort rules of the state in which the action is brought. This concept of the state which has the most contacts with the event applying its own law is referred to as the "center-of-gravity rule." The rule has been used with greater frequency in contract cases.

In the field of contract law, there is not as much uniformity in conflict of law rules among the various states. As noted, a strong trend is found toward using the "center-of-gravity" test. In jurisdictions adopting this view, courts consider where the parties to the contract reside, where the contract was entered into, where it is to be performed, and similar matters, in determining which state has the greatest contact with the contract. The law of that state would then be applied to disputes involving the contract.

Our dual system of federal and state courts also creates conflict of law problems. Federal courts will apply their own procedural law in every case, and will also apply federal substantive law in matters involving federal law dispute. In cases that reach federal courts as the result of diversity of citizenship between the litigants, the federal court will apply the substantive law of the state in which it is sitting, but in such cases, the federal court will still require that its own procedural law be followed.

The trend toward adoption of uniform statutes and codes, such as the Uniform Commercial Code, has tended to decrease conflict-of-law problems in the fields in which uniformity has been pursued. Many disputes still arise, however, and it is important to know that such a problem and such a body of law exist.

Administrative Agencies and Administrative Law   With the growth of government came the realization that many functions could not be performed by the legislative or executive branches. The complexity of society and of government required that legislatures create, by statute, certain administrative agencies to carry out some of government's diverse functions. As various administrative agencies were thus established, authority was delegated to them to control and regulate specific areas. Although agencies vary greatly in the scope of their functions, purposes, and powers, they generally have in common the right to make rules, establish rates, and determine the rights of parties in areas falling within their jurisdictions. Such general regulations and specific rulings have the force of statute, and are known as *administrative laws*. This delegation of rule-making power to an administrative agency has been held to be a constitutional delegation of legislative authority, so long as the scope of the delegated power is carefully defined, the rule-making power is exercised within the scope of delegation, and the rules that are made are subject to judicial review.

Tremendous growth in the number of administrative agencies and in the rules they promulgate has been experienced at federal and state levels. There are few, if any, businesses that escape the supervision of administrative agency regulations. This is particularly true in the field of insurance, which is subject to both federal and state regulation. For an insurance company that does business in a number of states, care must be taken to comply with the rules and regulations of the insurance department of each state. In addition, many other regulatory agencies promulgate rules that have application to the business of insurance. For instance, employment practices, matters of unfair competition, postal regulations, tax matters, and the issuance of securities are all matters that fall within the scope of administrative regulation at federal and/or state levels.

The Executive Federal and state constitutions, along with charters of most municipalities, provide for a chief executive who shares the responsibilities of government equally with the legislative and judicial branches. A system of checks and balances, which includes the executive's power to veto legislation, has been established to assure that no one branch of government shall become too powerful.

Whether the chief executive officer is the President, a governor, or a mayor, the obligation to recommend and approve laws generally exists. At the same time, the executive branch uniformly has delegated to it the responsibility for appointing the heads of the various administrative agencies. The power of appointment affords the opportunity for giving direction to the numerous rules and regulations adopted by such agencies.

While the executive function is not primarily one of lawmaking, the responsibility to recommend legislative programs, the obligation to enforce the law, the power to approve or veto legislative proposals, the supervision of administrative agencies, and the position of leadership in the political system all tend to make the executive an integral part of the lawmaking process.

Classification of Law

The study of law encompasses a very broad field. It includes not only rules for proper conduct, but also the means for enforcing these rules. The most important classifications of law involve several basic distinctions.

Civil and Criminal Law Civil law refers to the rights and duties of individuals and governments. When legal rights are violated, as when one fails to fulfill a contractual obligation, the matter is governed by civil law. In such cases, the person or government whose rights have been violated may bring an action for damages directly against the wrongdoer. Civil law is designed to protect rights and to provide remedies for breaches of duties.

Criminal law deals with acts that society deems so harmful to the public welfare that the government takes the responsibility for prosecuting and punishing the perpetrators. Under criminal law, society prescribes a standard of conduct to which all people must adhere. A criminal act may involve a major crime such as murder, or a minor crime or misdemeanor such as a traffic violation. But all criminal offenses are alike in that the offenders are prosecuted in the name of society, whether or not the victim of a crime comes forward to demand prosecution. Under criminal law, it is the government that controls legal proceedings and seeks redress; under civil law it is the individual who does so. The prosecution in a criminal action must establish proof of its case beyond a reasonable doubt, while in civil actions the injured party may establish the case by a preponderance of evidence only.

Penalties. In a civil action, the injured party generally requests payment of damages as reimbursement for the harm done. The court may also be requested to direct the wrongdoer to perform in a certain manner, such as transferring real estate that had been the subject of a contract to sell. Where a violation of criminal law is involved, the penalty is prescribed by the statute or ordinance. Such penalties take the form of a fine and/or a term of imprisonment, depending on the severity of the offense.

One Act Both a Crime and a Civil Wrong. Many times the same conduct can constitute both a crime and a civil wrong. One person's striking or assaulting another is considered both a civil wrong, for which damages may be awarded, and a criminal act, which may result in prosecution by the government. Both remedies might be sought; in such case they would be the subject of separate trials. In a civil action, the injured party would sue the wrongdoer for damages sustained, and the case would have to be established by a preponderance of the evidence. In a criminal action, the government would bring the action against the wrongdoer; and if the case was established beyond a reasonable doubt, a fine or imprisonment could result.

Law and Equity Trial courts in the United States have been frequently divided into courts of law and courts of equity. The term "equity" is unique in English-American law. Courts of equity arose because of the failure of law courts to give adequate remedies in some cases. Thus, while the law refers to the usual body and remedies of law, courts of equity were established to afford special remedies where the legal remedy was not felt to be adequate. Courts of equity supplement law courts and recognize many rights that are not recognized in common law courts. For example, in a contract for the sale of a unique item such as a one-of-a-kind antique, the usual legal remedy for breach of the contract would be money damages. A court of equity would consider the fact that money damages might be inadequate as a remedy, since the more important question is the right to possess the antique. A court of equity might then direct specific performance of the contract by decreeing that the antique must be transferred to the new owner as agreed.

Courts of equity are still found as separate courts in some jurisdictions. In most states, however, the courts have been combined in a single system although the court may sit as a court of equity on one occasion and as a court of law on another. In some jurisdictions, such as the federal system, law and equity are merged and both are applied in the same court. Even then, however, the distinction is needed because although one is entitled to trial by jury on questions of law, jury trial is unknown in equity.

Whether the case is heard in equity or in law is determined by the remedy desired. Courts of equity often use maxims instead of strict rules of law. The decision in equity is based upon moral right, and a court of equity will require a party coming into court to "have clean hands"—that is, to have done no wrong with respect to the transaction in question. Likewise, "delay defeats equity" and an equity court will dismiss a claim it considers to be stale.

Substantive and Procedural Law Substantive law defines the rights and liabilities of citizens. It is the result of legislative and judicial actions, which define legal relations between persons and between individuals and the state. Substantive law includes rules of law that specify what constitutes an enforceable contract, who may own and transfer property, what standards of conduct are expected of the individual in society, and many other legal rules. The definition of "the law" understood by most people probably would equate with the definition of substantive law.

Procedural, or adjective law, specifies the methods used to enforce substantive law. While substantive law spells out legal rights, procedural law sets forth the means for enforcing those rights. Different procedures are required in criminal and civil actions. In the case of civil actions, such as breach of contract, the law will be quite specific about procedures which must be followed. Such procedures will generally require the filing of certain pleadings with the appropriate court having jurisdiction of the matter. The party against whom the action is commenced, the defendant, must then be properly served with a summons or court order and a copy of the complaint. The form and method for filing such pleadings, and those rules that prescribe the means by which courts apply substantive law to resolve conflicts, fall under the classification of procedural law.

Substantive rights have little meaning unless there are procedures that provide a means for enforcing them. The practicing attorney is particularly concerned with the procedural means for enforcing individual and business rights.

Public and Private Law   Some branches of the law deal more directly than others with the relationship that exists between the government and the individual. On the basis of the degree to which this relationship is involved, the law is sometimes classified as public or private. Public law is concerned with the organization of government and the relationship between government and the individual. Administrative law, which is comprised of the principles which govern procedures of governmental boards and commissions, is within the public law sector since it is concerned with the enforcement of laws against individual citizens and organizations.

Private law deals with the relationship between individuals or between individuals, corporations, partnerships, and other legal entities in the private sector. Private law includes the subjects of contracts, property, and tort law.

Common-Law System and Civil Law System   Our common-law system contains "civil" and "criminal" law, as has been discussed. The term "civil law *system*," however, refers to the legal system of continental European nations and others that have adopted it. Those nations have comprehensive codes to cover all law, and rely on scholarly interpretations of their codes, rather than on prior cases, for interpretations of the law.

Subject Matter Classification   A means frequently used to classify law, particularly for the purpose of study, is by subject. On this basis, there are several branches of law that relate to specific subject areas, and have developed their own body of rules and precedents.

Administrative Law. Relates to the delegation of legislative power to administrative agencies, statutory and constitutional controls on such delegation, administrative proceedings, right to notice and hearing, adequacy of findings, and procedure for obtaining judicial review of administrative action.

Agency. Relates to the creation and termination of agency, rights and duties which exist between agent and principal, third persons in agency relationships, and rights surrounding employment.

Commercial Paper. Relates to the requisites and the consequences of negotiability, the forms and consequences of various types of endorsements, the requisites of a holder in due course, and the liabilities of various parties to commercial paper.

Constitutional Law. Relates to powers delegated to the national government, powers of the states as affected by the delegation of powers to national government, constitutional limitations, due process and equal protection of the law, privileges and immunities of citizens, and judicial review.

Contracts. Relates to formation of contracts consideration, beneficiaries, assignments, the statute of frauds, performance and breach, illegal contracts, discharge of contracts, and the parol evidence rule.

Corporation Law. Relates to nature and the classes of corporations, creation and termination, corporate powers, corporate stock, rights of shareholders, and management of corporations.

Criminal Law. Relates to the nature and sources of criminal liability, mental conditions requisite to responsibility, specific crimes and defenses.

Evidence. Relates to competency of witnesses, examination of witnesses, attendance of witnesses, depositions and discovery, privilege of witnesses, presumptions, and burden of proof.

Family Law. Relates to law of marriage, divorce, and alimony, relationships between parent and child, husband and wife.

Partnerships. Relates to creation and termination, authority of partners, duties, rights, and liabilities, and special partnerships and associations.

Property Law. Relates to personal and real property, nature and transfer, bailments, leases.

Sales. Relates to passage of property under various types of sales agreements, documents of title, financing, performance of sales contracts, warranties, and remedies.

Torts. Relates to wrongs between persons, intended interference with persons and property, unintended interference, negligence, contributory negligence, liability without fault, defamation, and interference with advantageous relations.

Wills and Estates. Relates to testate disposition of property, testamentary capacity, execution and revocation of wills, and intestacy.

These are but a few of the subject areas that might be made the specific objective of a course study. The subjects of agency, contracts, and torts are essentially common law in origin, while the subjects of corporations, criminal law, sales, and wills are controlled almost entirely by statutes in the various states.

Legal Procedure

The Lawsuit Most disputes between people are settled without resort to the courts. In many instances the sums involved are too small to justify legal action, and in others the parties are able to reach a satisfactory compromise. Still, hundreds of thousands of cases reach the courts each year, and it is through the adjudication of these controversies that our system for administering justice is tested.

As previously noted, the rules for instituting a lawsuit are controlled by the procedural law of the jurisdiction involved. While there is some variation in terminology between jurisdictions, the following pre-trial, trial, and post-trial procedures represent a general statement of the legal requirements found in most states.

Pre-Trial Procedure. In the trial of a civil action, the typical suit is commenced by the injured party, the plaintiff, filing a *complaint* with the court having jurisdiction of the case. The complaint is usually filed by an attorney representing the plaintiff, although procedures in many courts, particularly small-claims courts, make it possible for an individual to file a complaint without need for an attorney. At the time the complaint is filed, the court will issue a *summons* to the person against whom the complaint is made, the defendant, notifying him or her of the action. Such defendant then has a period prescribed by law in which to file an *answer* to the complaint.

If the defendant does not wish to file an answer, either admitting or denying the allegations of the complaint, then an *entry of appearance* may be filed. It is a simple acknowledgment of the complaint and an indication of intention to be present at the time of trial. An answer will put in issue all allegations of the complaint that are denied. A simple entry of appearance is not an admission of the truth of allegations in the complaint. The entry becomes part of the record and subjects the respondent to the jurisdiction of the court.

An answer may also contain affirmative defenses that, if proved, will defeat the plaintiff's claims. If the defendant has a cause of action against the plaintiff, these may be set forth in the answer as *counterclaims*. After receipt of the answer, the plaintiff may file a *reply*, which may admit or deny the allegations of the answer. The complaint, the answer, and the reply make up the typical pleadings in a civil case. Their main purpose is to permit the court and the parties to ascertain the questions that will be at issue in the trial.

Various motions may be made before trial. The defendant may admit, for the purpose of argument only, that the statements in the complaint are correct, but deny that they state a ground for recovery. This is often called a *motion to dismiss* the action for failure to state a claim upon which relief may be granted, and is commonly called a *demurrer*. Or, one party may believe that the only question in the case is one of law since the facts are not in dispute and ask the judge to rule on the legal question by filing a *motion for judgment on the pleadings* or a *motion for summary judgment*. Only when the facts are in dispute is a trial necessary. Upon request, the court may call a pre-trial conference at which the parties may agree on some facts and establish those matters in dispute that must be decided at a trial.

During the pleading stage, the law also provides for *discovery* procedures that are designed to permit the opposing parties to have the advantage of pertinent information possessed by the other. The availability of such evidence prior to trial is felt to further clarify the issues, and proof, which are involved in the case. Discovery practice assures that each side may be fully aware of all facts in the case, so that settlement of suits prior to trial will be encouraged. Upon request for information, each side is required under discovery rules to correctly and fully inform the other party of the proof available in the case.

Trial Procedure. Unless a suit is decided on the basis of a pre-trial motion, or unless the parties elect to settle out of court, the case will eventually be set for trial. The litigants may elect to have the case tried without a jury, in which event the judge decides questions of fact as well as questions of law. If the parties do not agree to waive a jury trial, the court will then proceed to impanel a jury.

In selecting a jury, the names of prospective jurors, usually twelve, are drawn from a list and each person is questioned by the attorneys in an effort to determine the juror's possible bias or partiality. If bias is felt to be present, either party may *challenge the juror for cause* and that person will be dismissed. All jurisdictions also permit a specified number of *peremptory challenges*, which allow a prospective juror to be removed without the need for giving a reason therefor.

After the jury has been selected and sworn in, the plaintiff's attorney in a civil suit makes an *opening statement* to the jury. This statement sets forth the basis upon which the claim is made and what the plaintiff intends to prove. The case is then presented to the jury through the means of testimony of witnesses and documentary evidence. Each witness is subject to direct examination or questioning by the party introducing that witness. The other party then has the right of *cross-examination* of that witness, in order to clarify or challenge statements made during direct examination.

The rules of evidence provide that evidence cannot be introduced unless it is competent and relevant to the issues raised in the pleadings. Testimony must bear on a fact at issue in the trial. If it does not, then counsel should object to its admission, and the court should sustain the objection by excluding the testimony. *Hearsay evidence,* which consists of what someone said or wrote outside of court, introduced for the purpose of proving the truth of what was said or written, is also normally excluded from the hearings. The reason for excluding such evidence is that the person making the statement is not available for cross-examination. In like manner, the opinion of a witness who is not an expert, concerning what the witness believes to be true, but has no personal knowledge of, is generally not admissible. *Opinion evidence* is not excluded in every case, however, and where technical matters are involved the opinion of a properly qualified expert is often admitted as an aid to the jury in reaching its decision.

After all the evidence has been introduced, each attorney may summarize it and make a closing argument to the jury. The judge then instructs the jury concerning the law applicable to the case, and the jury retires to reach its verdict. The court may decide to take the case from the jury at any time by *directing a verdict* in favor of one party, by declaring a *mistrial,* or by declaring a *nonsuit* if the plaintiff failed to present a sufficient case. Any of these actions by the judge is subject to review by an appellate court.

In many jurisdictions, provision is made for two kinds of verdict: general and special. A general verdict is one in which the jury makes a complete finding and a single conclusion on all issues presented to it. In a special verdict, the jury makes only findings of fact. It then becomes the duty of the court to apply the law to the facts as found by the jury.

Post-Trial Procedure.   Either the plaintiff or defendant may allege errors at the trial that constitute grounds for appeal to a higher court. The person who appeals is called the *appellant,* and the other party is called the *appellee.* It is uniformly required that the appeal be made to the appropriate court, and that such appeal be made within the prescribed time period.

A transcript of the lower court proceedings will be filed with the appeals court, which will rely on the transcript, along with additional briefs and arguments made by counsel, in reaching its decision. After the appeals court has held the hearing and its members have deliberated, an opinion will be written setting forth the law involved and the reason for the court's decision. The court may affirm or reverse the decision of the lower court, or it may send the case back to the lower court for a new trial.

In general, one has a right to a first appeal but a second appeal, to the highest court, often requires consent of the highest court. In the U. S. Supreme Court, for instance, in most cases a *writ of certiorari* must be granted, and it will be denied if the Court believes that the issue presented is not sufficiently important.

If final judgment is for the defendant, the matter is ended except for payment of court costs, usually by the plaintiff. If the plaintiff wins, the defendant must comply as by obeying an equitable order to do or not to do something, or by paying a money judgment. Failure to obey an equity court order is *contempt of court,* and an order to pay money damages may be enforced by a *writ of execution* levied against the judgment debtor's property to satisfy the judgment.

Arbitration While thousands of disputes are handled within the judicial system or through administrative agencies, by far the greatest number of controversies are resolved between parties by compromise or settlement agreements. Such out-of-court settlements have the advantages of economy, greater speed of resolution, less hostility between the parties, and some degree of privacy. One important method of resolving disputes without referring the matter to courts or administrative agencies is known as *arbitration.* Arbitration involves the submission of a controversy to a private body for decision. It has become a major means of dealing with controversies in contract disputes, labor-management relations, and insurance settlements.

Arbitration most frequently results from an agreement between the parties. Either as part of the initial contract or upon confronting a dispute, an agreement may be made to submit the matter to an arbiter or to an arbitration panel. In some instances, such as workers' compensation disputes, state statutes may require submission of controversies to binding arbitration. Most states have enacted general arbitration laws that cover all aspects of arbitration procedures. At common law, it was considered that agreements to arbitrate future disputes were contrary to law since they were viewed as attempts to oust the jurisdiction of the courts. Even under common law rules, the parties could agree that after a dispute had arisen the matter would be submitted to arbitration. In most states, statutes have modified this common law view by making contracts to arbitrate valid and enforceable. Even in those states that have comprehensive arbitration statutes, parties are still permitted to pursue common law arbitration procedures. In most states, if common law methods are followed, the agreement to arbitrate is usually revocable by the parties. Where statutes are involved, arbitration agreements are not revocable.

While procedures vary under arbitration statutes, they do involve *submission* of an existing dispute to arbitration and an *award* or decision being made by an arbitrator. Both the Uniform Arbitration Act, which has been adopted in nearly twenty states, and the Federal Arbitration Act provide specific remedies if one of the parties refuses to arbitrate or denies the existence of an arbitration agreement. The parties may provide that an arbitrator be selected in accordance with rules prescribed by the American Arbitration Association. Under those rules each party is sent a list of proposed arbitrators, and each is given ten days to cross off any objectionable names and to number the arbitrators according to its preference. The Association then appoints an arbitrator acceptable to both parties. Another alternative method of selecting an arbitrator involves each party appointing an arbitrator and those arbitrators in turn appointing a third arbitrator.

Strict rules of evidence and procedure are generally relaxed in arbitration proceedings. The power to subpoena witnesses exists under most statutes. Once the award or judgment of the arbitrator has been rendered, it is filed with a clerk of court. There are very few grounds for appealing an arbitrator's award. If the appeal is not taken within the period prescribed by law, the arbitrator's finding is treated the same as a judgment of a court, and may be executed upon just as any court judgment.

Arbitration as a means of settling insurance disputes is employed with increasing frequency. A great many insurance policies specifically provide for arbitration. Uninsured motorist coverages in automobile policies uniformly include an arbitration provision in the event of dispute under the policy. Close to 600 insurance companies participate in the Nationwide Inter-Company Arbitration Agreement, which binds the companies to arbitrate physical damage claims that do not exceed $5,000. A special arbitration agreement is also widely used to allocate costs of settlements between companies where co-insurers are involved, along with difficulties of overlapping coverages. Increased use of arbitration has also resulted from provisions in various no-fault statutes recently adopted in half the states. Under these acts, persons involved in automobile accidents look to their own insurance carriers for payment of benefits. Where disputes arise as to payment of first-party benefits or where subrogation problems arise between insurers, some no-fault laws provide for submission to arbitration. As an effective method of settling disputes in all commercial undertakings, arbitration gives promise of even greater use in the future.

CHARACTERISTICS OF THE INSURANCE PRODUCT

Regulation of Business

Federal-State Network Regulation of business in the United States involves a highly complex system. At the federal level more than sixty regulatory agencies have been created, affecting hundreds of thousands of companies. This system exists side by side with regulatory activity in the fifty individual states and hundreds of local municipalities. The combination has produced an increasingly pervasive bureaucracy that touches virtually every aspect of business activity.

The roots of the federal regulatory system are embedded in the nation's past industrial development and the evolution of "regulated" industries — railroads, banks, utilities, communications companies, and airlines. The emergence of new federal agencies designed not for particular industries but for particular functions of all industries — equal employment, financial disclosure, worker health and safety, environmental pollution among them — has considerably complicated the regulatory web in ways that could not be foreseen.

Right to Regulate The federal constitution provided for a central government that was vested with limited and designated powers. One of the specific grants of power to the federal government was the authority "to regulate commerce ... among the several states. ..."[9] An implied power that has been held to accompany this grant is the power to regulate matters that affect commerce.

There are no significant constitutional limitations on the power of government, federal, state or local, to regulate business. Generally, regulation of business is considered valid so long as such regulations apply uniformly to all members within the same class. The federal government may impose any regulations upon any phase of business required by the economic needs of the nation.[10]

Similarly, the states, by virtue of their police power (i.e., the power inherent in the state to act in protection of the public health, safety, and morals), can regulate business in all of its aspects so long as they do not impose unreasonable burdens on interstate commerce or on any activity of the federal government.

These broad powers of government to regulate business have been utilized with increasing frequency in recent years. The accompanying impact on the commercial legal environment has been substantial and often impeding. Much political and legal emphasis in the 1980s will center on reforming the relationship between government and business in this country.

Insurance Regulation   There is no industry in the United States more closely regulated than the insurance industry. While the business of insurance has remained unique as a large industry subject primarily to state regulation, its activities have been increasingly affected by federal regulatory processes. In 1945, Congress passed the McCarran Act, Public Law 15, authorizing the continued regulation and taxation of insurance by the states. Certain federal laws were to be applicable to the business of insurance only to the extent the states did not adequately regulate the insurance industry in the public interest. With this proviso still the law, the specter of federal regulation remains with the insurance industry today.

Although regulation by fifty state insurance departments continues as the basis mode of industry regulation, a system with many aspects of dual, state-federal regulation has evolved. Many federal agencies exercise oversight of activities of insurance companies. The Internal Revenue Service, Securities & Exchange Commission, U.S. Labor Department, the several offices investigating equal employment opportunity, the Federal Trade Commission (which in the early 1980s had restrictions placed on its right to investigate the insurance industry), are but a few of the important agencies that review industry activities on an ongoing basis.

Virtually every aspect of insurance companies — licensing, rating, claims handling, underwriting, policy forms, investments, employment practices — is carefully regulated by state and/or federal government agencies. The fear of being controlled by a monolithic federal bureaucracy has caused most insurance industry representatives to prefer continuation of the present system that relies primarily on multistate oversight and compliance rather than face the unknowns of federal control.

A Common Agreement

The insurance contract is perhaps the most common and least understood agreement in use in modern society. No contract is entered into more and read less than the insurance contract. As will be seen, it is unique in that it is an agreement that the law seldom requires the purchaser to read or understand. The reasons for this special treatment by the law are reflected in the insurance contract's history and in the unusual function it is designed to perform in society.

The Earliest Contracts

Origins. Measured against human history, the insurance contract is of recent origin. The practice of insurance was first seen in the mutual agreements among merchants engaged in shipping enterprises. Extensive use of such contracts was found in the medieval maritime states of Italy. The word "policy" itself is a reflection of the Italian origin of insurance, being derived from the Italian word *polizza*.

From Italy, the practice of insuring commercial ventures against disaster extended to other maritime states in Europe. Lombard merchants from northern Italy went to London during the thirteenth century, and took with them the custom of insuring against the hazards of trade. Questions relating to insurance were determined in accord with the custom of merchants, by tribunals established by the merchants themselves. The so-called law of merchants, or *law merchant*, was thereby developed.

The Father of Insurance Law. It was not until the middle of the eighteenth century that the English Chief Justice, Lord William Mansfield, encouraged the incorporation of the law merchant into English common law. Mansfield sought out the merchant courts, became familiar with their law and procedures, and encouraged them to refer their disputes to the customary courts. Lord Mansfield thus earned recognition as the father of both commercial law and insurance law. While merchant courts had been little more than arbitration committees, the application of the rules and authority of the common law courts added much to the stability of insurance contracts which were an important part of the merchant's agreements.

Early Loss Exposures Assumed. For the 100 years following its introduction in England, insurance contracts were confined largely to marine perils and hazards. In fact, marine insurance remained the most important branch of insurance law until comparatively recent times. At the time of the Great Fire of London in 1666, only slight progress had been made in the writing of fire insurance. During these early years, loss exposures were underwritten mostly as a sideline by merchants, bankers, and moneylenders in private offices. Interestingly, it was the introduction of coffee in the middle of the seventeenth century that resulted in a leap forward in the organization of the insurance enterprise. The business of underwriting insurance received its greatest impetus in the coffee houses that sprang up at the time, the most famous being founded by Edward Lloyd in 1687.

Lloyd's of London. The coffee shop of Edward Lloyd was a favorite meeting place for shipowners and marine underwriters. Those persons willing to underwrite or assume all or part of a particular loss exposure could come to Lloyd's Coffee House and enter into such agreements. Lloyd's today is an association of individual underwriters who will underwrite all types of insurable loss exposures.

Fire Insurance.   The first regular office writing fire insurance was established in London in 1681. The coverage was written with much greater frequency following the Great Fire of London, but the early scope of the business did not begin to approach that of marine insurance. Benjamin Franklin assisted in the formation of the oldest fire insurance company in continued existence in America, established in 1752. A common method of encouraging fire insurance business at the time was to give the policies away in the hope that as their merit was felt, the premium would be forthcoming.

Life Insurance.   Theological groups at first denied all types of insurance as an interference with God's plan for salvation through hardship and testing of the human race. Life insurance was condemned as an immoral wager. It was not permitted in France until 1820. In the mid-eighteenth century in England, the practice of insuring the lives of well-known persons by others who had no interest in their lives became a growing business. Word that one's life was being insured in the "alley" at 90 percent was often enough to resign the ill party to an early demise. Such wagers on human life were later outlawed by specific acts of the English Parliament, although not before they had become a source of great concern to those underwriters who were attempting to establish the legitimate use of life insurance.

Accident Insurance.   The first company to issue contracts providing indemnity for accidental injury was the Railway Passengers' Assurance Company of London, which was formed in 1849. Its early policies provided coverage for railway accidents only, but were later extended to include accidents of all kinds. The first accident insurance company in the United States was formed a short time after, in 1863, with the chartering of Travelers' Insurance Company of Hartford, Connecticut. The first accident policy issued by Travelers' was purchased in 1864 by James Bolter to cover the period he spent walking between his home and the post office. Premium for the policy was two cents.

Automobile Insurance.   The Travelers' Insurance Company also issued the first automobile policy in 1898. Dr. Truman Martin of Buffalo, New York, paid a premium of $11.25 to obtain $5,000 to $10,000 liability insurance. The growth of the casualty insurance field, along with the tremendous increase in use of the automobile, has been one of the most significant developments in the insurance field.

Starting with the early marine insurance contracts, and progressing through the development of fire insurance, life insurance, accident insurance, and casualty insurance, the nature and scope of the insurance business has changed dramatically during the last century. Thus, while the insurance contract had its origins fairly early in history, the most significant developments have occurred within a relatively brief period.

The Insurance Agreement as a "Flood of Darkness"

The insurance contract is intended to provide protection if specified losses occur. In the attempt to define and delimit those losses, certain conditions, limitations, and exceptions become part of the agreement. Creating a contract which adequately defines the assumed loss exposure and at the same time can be understood is a challenge which has troubled insurance underwriters and purchasers since such agreements were first entered. Shortcomings in this area have resulted in much public criticism, restrictive legislation, and many adverse court rulings. Again, the problem is not of recent origin.

In reviewing the language of a fire insurance policy in 1873, the New Hampshire Supreme Court stated:

> Men have a right to be dealt with some regard for the state of mind and body, of knowledge and business, in which they are known actually to exist. Whether they ought to be what they are, or not, the fact is, that in the present condition of society, men in general cannot read and understand these insurance documents. . . . Forms of applications and policies, of a most complicated and elaborate structure, were prepared, and filled with covenants, exceptions, stipulations, provisos, rules, regulations, and conditions, rendering the policy void in a great number of contingencies. . . . The study of them was rendered particularly unattractive, by a profuse intermixture of discourses on subjects in which a premium payer would have no interest. The compound, if read by him, would, unless he were an extraordinary man, be an inexplicable riddle, a mere flood of darkness and confusion. . . . As if it were feared that, notwithstanding these discouraging circumstances, some extremely eccentric person might attempt to examine and understand the meaning of the involved and intricate net in which he was to be entangled, it was printed in such small type, and in lines so long and so crowded, that the perusal of it was made physically difficult, painful, and injurious. Seldom has the art of typography been so successfully diverted from the diffusion of knowledge to the suppression of it. There was ground for the premium payer to argue that the print alone was evidence, competent to be submitted to a jury, of a fraudulent plot. . . .[11]

While considerable effort has been expended to simplify the language of insurance contracts, there is some question as to how much progress has been made. In a recent Ohio Court of Appeals case the court held that the holders of an insurance policy were not bound by its provisions because its printing was of "a size type that would drive an eagle to a microscope."

The court stated:

> It cannot be reasonably assumed that the insured having average sight of a human being would be aware of the content of the questioned clause, at least in the absence of special optical equipment. . . . It should not be necessary for the insured to provide himself with a microscope in order to inspect the small print contained within his insurance policy. Neither should it be necessary for an insured to provide himself with an insurance policy to protect himself against the provision to be found within such small print of his insurance policy.[12]

Still another evaluation of the readability of insurance policies was made by the Pennsylvania Insurance Department. In this study,[13] the standard automobile policy was measured by the Flesch Readability Scale, which is a method for testing the readability of documents by assigning point values for length and complexity of sentence structure. It was reported that on the Flesch Scale, the Bible received a readability score of 66.97, Einstein's Theory of Relativity scored 17.72, and the standard automobile policy 10.31.

While such evaluations may be overly harsh, it is a matter of continuing concern to insurers that their products receive such criticism and that they are not better understood by the public. The task of creating agreements that will cover the perils intended, under conditions that make a reasonable premium possible, and at the same time produce documents that may be understood, is far from being accomplished. In recent years, attempts to simplify the language of automobile policies are felt to represent steps in the right direction. Current trends in insurance policy construction are toward more simplified language. It is recognized that such language will require new interpretations by the courts, and how successful efforts at clearer expression will prove remains to be seen.

DISTINCTIVE FEATURES
OF INSURANCE CONTRACTS

General

There is a legal aphorism that asks: "What do they know of the law of insurance contracts who only the law of contracts know?" The inference is that the insurance contract is in some way unique among contracts, or that courts treat it differently than other contracts. As will be seen, the insurance contract has the same basic requisites as other contracts. There is a need for an agreement, consideration, genuineness of assent, competent parties, and a legal purpose. At the same time, there are distinctive features of the insurance contract which courts have recognized with sufficient frequency to make their consideration essential to a proper understanding of the contract and to its likely interpretation by the courts.

While the insurance contract might not stand alone as the only or best example of these features, in combination they provide a valuable insight into the nature of these special agreements that make up the insurance product. The rationale for judicial decisions in cases involving insurance contracts will almost invariably be stated in terms of one or more of these characteristics.

Aleatory Contracts

Protection for Uncertain Events   While most contracts involve an exchange of money for goods or services, under the insurance contract the money will buy indemnity and/or protection upon the occurrence of an uncertain event. The contract is thus referred to as an aleatory contract, since its performance depends upon the happening of a fortuitous event. Such an event is the insured peril. If the peril does not occur, then no obligation of performance will be required.

Not Wagering Agreements.   While insurance is an aleatory contract, care must be taken to distinguish it from a wagering agreement. Insurance is not a contract of chance, but a contract under which some of the rights of the parties are contingent upon certain events. In wagering contracts the parties contemplate gain through mere chance. The gambler can experience either gain or loss. In the insurance contract, the parties seek to distribute the loss caused by fortuitous events. Provision is made through insurance for indemnity in the event of loss, and no gain is possible. Insurance is a device to reduce uncertainty—the hazard is present, and the insured is trying to protect against it. Gambling, on the other hand, creates or increases uncertainty. In insurance, the insurer takes the chance of being compelled, if the contingency occurs, to pay the sum agreed upon; and the insured takes the chance of parting with a premium or consideration without receiving anything for it if the contingency does not happen.

Protection Afforded.   It is not entirely correct to say, however, that if the peril does *not* occur the insured has received nothing. The insured has received the protection of the insurance coverage. This means the insured has been free to take part in the activities which expose him or her to a given peril, with the assurance that any loss suffered will be shifted by the contract to the insurer, and will not result in financial ruin for the insured. The premium paid by the insured for protection may be grossly unequal to the amount the insurer may have to pay if the uncertain event takes place. The condition under which the performance of one party is contingent upon some event which may or may not happen renders the insurance contract aleatory.

Other Aleatory Agreements There are several contract devices in addition to the insurance contract by which persons seek protection against future events. Large bodies of law have been developed around contracts of suretyship, in which one party is obligated to pay the debt of another if the principal debtor defaults. The surety is bound with the principal as a primary undertaker of the obligation. Thus, where a performance bond is obtained to assure the performance under the terms of a construction contract, the surety providing the bond is bound as a primary obligor under the agreement. Contracts of guarantee also involve an undertaking to pay the debt of another. Where the owners of a closely held corporation personally guarantee the contractual promise of the corporation itself, such a promise is incidental to the original contract of the principal-corporation. It does not impose any primary liability on the owner-guarantors. They will not have to respond under their collateral agreement unless the principal debtor (i.e., the corporation) defaults, and they are given notice of that default by the party to whom the guarantee was made. So, too, pledges in which there is a bailment of goods to a creditor as security for some debt or engagement are devices designed to protect against the happening of some future event, namely default on the debt. It should be noted, however, that each of these security devices involves some forfeiture of performance rather than the problem of meeting some peril. They are thus distinguishable from the insurance contract.

Contract of Adhesion

Insurer Prepares Agreement The insurance contract is recognized by the courts as a contract of adhesion. Contracts of adhesion are drawn up by one party, with another party simply entering into the agreement and assenting to the terms already established. The concept of adhesion had its origin in the law relating to treaties between nations; a nation wishing to join in a treaty drawn by other nations would sign the treaty and would *adhere* to its provisions.

Insurance contracts are seen as contracts of adhesion since the insurer generally prepares the contract and offers it to the insured, who has little opportunity to alter its words or terms.

Rule of Strict Construction. The hallmark of the contract of adhesion is the so-called rule of strict construction. Under this rule, any doubt or ambiguity found in the document is construed against the party who drew it up. Since the insurer prepared the contract, all questions concerning its meaning are resolved against the insurer.

This rule of construction is based on the premise that since one party to the contract, the insurer, selected the language and terms of the agreement, it must be assumed that the insurer had every opportunity to serve its own best interests. The insured, on the other hand, usually without benefit of legal counsel and usually without having read the policy, has merely adhered to the agreement without understanding or reading its terms. Consequently the insurer must pay the penalty for any ambiguity it creates, and all such doubts are resolved in favor of the insured.

Ordinary Meaning Given Terms. As noted, if there is ambiguity the courts will interpret the contract against the party who drew it up. Still, contracts of insurance, like other contracts, are construed according to the terms that the parties have used. These terms are taken and understood, in the absence of ambiguity, in their plain, ordinary, and popular meanings. As one learned justice stated: "Insurers who seek to impose upon words of common speech an esoteric significance intelligible only to their craft, must bear the burden of resulting confusion."[14]

Application of Adhesion Doctrine Courts have shown little reluctance in finding ambiguity in insurance contracts. The court interprets the form contract to mean what the reasonable buyer would expect it to mean, and thus protects the insured's expectations with respect to that agreement.

For example, take the case of New York Life Insurance Company v. Hiatt,[15] in which the insured's death resulted from inhalation of carbon monoxide. This was one of nine causes of death excepted from the double indemnity rider to the policy. The company, in an attempt to comply with a California requirement to print a brief description on the front page of the policy, had stamped in purple ink, "DOUBLE INDEMNITY FOR FATAL ACCIDENT." This was their undoing. In deciding in favor of the beneficiary, the court held that recovery for double indemnity benefits must be allowed. The stamped writing superseded the printed rider, and the conflict between the two must be resolved in favor of the insured. The court said:

> To the lay mind the phrase represents the concise expression of a readily comprehensible thought. To him the term comprehends all forms of death suffered accidentally. Not inconceivably, the presence of the stamped matter was the decisive factor in effecting the sale of the policy.

The court found ambiguity because the stamped material on the face of the policy was in apparent conflict with the exclusions contained in the policy rider. Under the rules of construction applicable to a contract of adhesion, this ambiguity was resolved against the party drawing the contract, the insurer.

Adhesion Doctrine Today. Courts continue to refer to the insurance contract as a contract of adhesion that must be strictly construed against the insurer. This is true even though some may argue that since the law now compels insurers to use many standard policy forms and language, the insurer can no longer be regarded as having selected the contract terms entirely on its own. Policies are subject to many statutory requirements regarding content, and state regulatory authorities closely scrutinize all policy language and forms. Under these conditions, it would seem that some support for the rationale of strict construction against the insurer would be weakened. To date, however, the rule of strict construction against the insurer remains the law.

Contract of Indemnity

Indemnity Purpose of Property Insurance

Gain Not Permitted. An insured is entitled to be compensated or indemnified only to the extent of the loss he or she sustained. The primary purpose of property insurance is to provide reimbursement. An insured is not entitled to make a financial gain or to be placed in a better position than before the loss. This same principle of indemnity is applicable to liability insurance, which also does not contemplate that an injured party should make a profit from a loss which is experienced. Indemnification is to be for the estimated amount of the loss. If gain is possible, then the contract is essentially a gambling transaction, and therefore is contrary to public policy.

Insurance involves the transfer of loss from the insured to the insurer. Implied in the transfer is the concept that the value of the benefit to be received will not exceed the loss incurred. Property insurance is aimed at reimbursement, but no more than reimbursement. If the insured can be placed in a substantially better position after the loss than before, the principle of indemnity has been violated. The principle of indemnity is the most basic principle of property insurance.

Moral Hazard. The possibility of making a gain from a property loss leads to the evils of wagering and inducements to destroy property. If property worth $5,000 could be insured for $10,000, the temptation for an owner to destroy the property, and thereby obtain double its value, would be very great. Such "moral hazard" refers to any condition, other than a physical one, which increases the likelihood that the insured property will be destroyed. Where an insured can destroy property and obtain an amount greater than its value, the moral hazard will be the possibility of deliberate harm caused by the insured to obtain the policy proceeds.

Valued Policy Laws. In most states, valued policy laws have been passed, under which the value of real estate stated in the policy controls the amount paid if the property is totally destroyed. Such laws are followed even if it is shown that the amount paid is more than the property's actual value at time of loss. Such laws are not considered contrary to the principle of indemnity since the amount of insurance is established beforehand with an eye toward the true value of the property. The purpose of valued property laws is to encourage the insuring parties to correctly value the property, as well as to avoid unnecessary disputes concerning property values in case of total destruction. The value under such statutes is conclusively presumed to be the value set by the parties in the policy.

Similar qualification to the principle of indemnity is seen in various inland marine policies where specific values are fixed for designated items of personal property. The stated values of such items as jewels and furs will be paid in the event of total loss, even though it might be shown that the items had depreciated in value. Again, where the parties to an insurance contract have actually agreed upon the value of the property insured, courts will consider indemnity in that amount even if the real value subsequently changes.

Insurable Interest Requirement An important corollary to the principle of indemnity is the legal requirement that no person may secure insurance on property or life in which he or she has no insurable interest. Unless an individual stands in some relation to property that would result in economic loss to him or her upon its destruction, then no insurable interest exists and coverage will not be properly obtainable. To hold otherwise would be to permit a person to insure a neighbor's property and then collect for its later destruction. Such an arrangement would be violative of the principle of indemnity, would create a moral hazard, and would involve a substantially gambling type contract. All of these are violative of law and public policy.

Contract Affected with a Public Interest

A Necessary Contract The insurance contract is seen by the courts as essentially different from contracts found in ordinary commercial transactions. In modern society, insurance has become more a matter of necessity than a matter of choice. The many loss exposures that threaten the security of life, family, and property make it improvident not to obtain insurance. In some activities, such as driving an automobile, the law may require that insurance be obtained.

If the insurance is liability insurance, it involves both the interests of the insured and of the general public in having a fund available from which to obtain recovery for injury. Our society recognizes that the business of insurance is a business affected with a public interest, and this recognition is reflected in the decisions of legislative bodies and courts.

Such recognition carries with it both burdens and benefits. While the benefit is readily apparent to those in the insurance industry from the large demand seen for the insurance product, the burden results from the special regulation and attention given the product in the public interest. Legislatures and courts alike view the business of insurance as one that must be regulated for the public benefit, and considerable law reflects this viewpoint.

Public and Industry Attitudes Notwithstanding the often stated opinion that the insurance contract is a contract affected with a public interest, insurers often view their policies as simple contractual obligations between parties. While an insurance policy does represent a contractual commitment, the attitudes of the general public, the legislatures, and the courts make clear that the insurance agreement is viewed as having broader ramifications than a mere contract. The public has a definite interest in the reliability of the insurance product. Insurance involves an obligation that affects the public interest as well as the policyholder, and, therefore, is necessarily subject to certain restrictions. The extent to which these differing views of the insurance contract are not harmonious increases the possibility of further restrictive legislation, adverse court decisions, and perhaps a greater assumption of the insurance function by government.

Legislative Response. While some insurers insist that they should have the rights to insure only persons they wish to insure and to cancel their contract obligations under the usual rules of contract law, the law of nearly all states clearly restricts such ordinary contractual rights. Legislation restricting the right of insurance companies to consider the race, religion, or sex of an applicant for insurance in determining the acceptability or rate classification of that person is now the law in most states. In like manner, many jurisdictions have adopted legislation that limits the right of insurers to reject or cancel certain types of insurance.

Each new session of the state legislatures brings forward a large number of new proposals, some of which are adopted, restricting in some material way the rights of insurers with respect to their contractual obligations. The right of the states to regulate the business of insurance has long been affirmed by the U.S. Supreme Court. The Court has recognized that the business of insurance is "clothed with a public interest" and accordingly that its activities merit special scrutiny.[16]

Personal Contract Requiring the Utmost Good Faith

Disclosure Requirement It has long been recognized by the courts that the insurance contract is a personal contract requiring the highest degree of good faith between the parties. The character, credit, and conduct of the parties to this personal contract are highly important. Failure to disclose vital information, or dishonesty or fraud on the part of either party, will result in the courts' declaring the contract voidable at the election of the innocent party. Depending on the type of fraud, the contract might also be declared void and of no effect whatever.

Ordinary Contract Rule. Most contracts entered into in the marketplace involve relationships in which the courts declare the parties are "dealing at arm's length." No duty is generally owed by one party to the other to reveal facts that might prove helpful in evaluating the merits of the bargain being entered into. Thus, the fact that a large harvest is going to cause the price of wheat to drop in the near future need not be revealed to the buyer in a contract for the sale of wheat at a presently higher price. The requirements of modern economic life are such that courts will not place themselves in the position of having to remake a multitude of bad bargains that might be alleged if another rule of law were adopted.

Situations Where Duty Found. The general rule that we are not our brother's keeper in the marketplace has been qualified where a special relationship exists between the contractual parties. Those who serve in fiduciary or confidential capacities, such as agents, trustees, or guardians, whose positions involve unique elements of trust and confidence, owe a duty of full disclosure to the principal beneficiary or ward in all contractual and other dealings. In cases other than those involving a fiduciary relationship, even though there is no duty to advise the other party of all information we possess, we may not actively misrepresent or defraud the person with whom we deal under any circumstances.

Duty in Insurance Contracts. The declaration that the insurance contract is a personal contract requiring the highest degree of good faith places upon the parties the same duty of full disclosure of material information as is found in fiduciary contracts. The highly personal nature of the insurance contract, in which both parties must rely on each other to a considerable extent, is felt to require such a duty.

Property Insurance Does Not Run with the Land

Fire Insurance. Because of the personal nature of the insurance contract, certain rules of construction have been established by the courts. Thus, in the case of property insurance, it is well established that the insurance contract does not "run with the land." That is, a fire insurance contract issued to a property owner to cover a specific property will not, upon a fully completed sale of that property to another, extend the policy's protection to the new owner of the property. The insurance policy is a personal contract with the party to whom it is issued. The insurer based its judgment in agreeing to assume the possibility of loss on elements such as the character, reputation, and occupation of the insured. To permit the policy to pass along with the land as part of the sales transaction would require the insurer to assume the loss possibilities, not bargained for, presented by the new owner. Accordingly, the new owner must apply for his or her own insurance, and thereby must permit an evaluation to be made of his or her own reliability.

In like manner, items of personal property, such as one's car or furniture, are insured on the basis of the personal record, credit, conduct, and standing in the community of the applicant for the insurance. An insurer will not generally enter into a contract of insurance without first establishing these basic facts of insurability. In keeping with that general rule, if an insured obtains coverage on personal property that is later sold, the policy of insurance will not pass to the new owner. An insurance policy may not be assigned to another upon the transfer of one's property. Certainly, the new property owner may negotiate a contract of insurance with the insurer which previously provided coverage, but then a new contract is entered into and new parties are involved. The insurer is thus afforded an opportunity to evaluate potential loss-exposure characteristics of a new applicant for insurance.

Qualifications to Rule that Insurance Contracts Are Not Assignable

General. The law recognizes some situations in which insurance contracts are assignable. Either the purpose for which the policy is sold or the economic requirements of the relationship in question, make some qualifications necessary. In such cases, the personal nature of the insurance contract is still present, but other factors are considered that outweigh the normal restrictions against assignability.

Marine Insurance. In marine insurance contracts, it has long been the established custom to permit assignment of the policy. Normally, in the absence of any specific restriction on assignability, the marine policy may be assigned to a successor in interest in the chain of transportation and ownership. The special rule relating to marine insurance recognizes the fact that goods subject to such coverage are frequently transferred in distant ports under circumstances that would make the obtaining of new coverage in transit most difficult. Once issued, the marine policy may normally be assigned to the insured's successor in title without any agreement or assent on the part of the insurer. Delays that might otherwise be experienced in transporting the insured cargo are thereby avoided. The commercial necessity of making the marine policy more readily assignable is thereby acknowledged. As noted, it is still proper for the parties to expressly forbid assignment of the marine policy, but such a restriction is the exception rather than the rule.

Life Insurance. The life insurance policy is another policy that is readily assignable by its owner. While the life insurance contract is a personal contract requiring the highest degree of care on the part of both parties, the investment characteristic of life insurance requires that such interests be readily assignable. A life insurance policy is considered a kind of property, and the basic investment character of this property dictates that it shall be freely assignable.

The owner of a life insurance policy, either taken out on his or her own life, or on the life of someone on whom the owner has an insurable interest, may freely assign that policy to another person without the consent of the insurer. A specific provision may restrict such assignment without the consent of the insurer or the beneficiary, but in the absence of such a restriction the life policy owner may freely assign the interest. Such assignment acts as a transfer of all ownership rights under the life policy.

The transfer of a life policy to a new owner may take place as the result of a contract, an assignment, or as a simple gift. In any case, the new owner becomes entitled to all rights of ownership and may borrow against the policy, cash it in, change the beneficiary, transfer it to still another owner, or do any of those acts that the owner of property may normally perform.

Executory and Conditional Contract

Insurance Contract Is an Executory Agreement Although an insured carries out his or her part of an insurance contract by paying the premium, the contract remains executory on the part of the insurer. Executory means that some act prescribed in the contract remains to be performed by one of the parties, namely the insurer. Naturally, the insurer will not execute its part of the agreement until a specified event occurs.

Insurance Contract Contains Many Conditions

Main Condition. The insurance contract is not only executory as to the insurer, but is also subject to numerous conditions. The principal condition is the occurrence of the insured event. Until that event occurs, no obligation to perform exists on the part of the insurer.

Other Conditions. Policies necessarily spell out the various conditions of the insurer's promise, the conditions of settlement, and the obligations of the insured. The insured is normally required to give notice of a loss within a specified period of time or as soon as practicable following the loss. In the case of the fire insurance policy, an additional "Proof of Loss" statement may also be required and provides some itemization of loss. Most liability policies also stipulate that the insured must cooperate with the company in the investigation and settlement of the case. If the duties of notice and cooperation are not fulfilled by the insured, loss of policy protection may result. The insurer is normally empowered to make decisions regarding settlement of the case without consent of the insured. The insurer assumes several duties in liability policies to investigate the occurrence, to make settlement, and to defend any actions that are instituted.

Effect of Policy Standardization—Examples

Attempts on the part of insurers to limit and define the loss exposures that will be assumed have resulted in the developing of many conditions and exceptions over the years. This is not to suggest that insurance contracts are deceptive or arbitrary. The insurance contract is one of the most important legal inventions of modern times. While many insurance contracts can be phrased mostly in lay language, nearly all of them require either some terms which are unique to the insurance business or, what is more likely to mislead, some special meaning given to normally simple terms. The total is likely to add up to an involved contract that few insureds can understand.

The number of conditions and special phrasings required in those conditions have thus led to rules of construction of insurance contracts under rules that are highly favorable to the insured. All doubts with respect to meaning are resolved in favor of the policyholder.

Over the years many policy forms and conditions have become highly standardized. Legislatures and regulatory agencies alike require certain policy conditions in specific types of contract, and will permit only the prescribed language to be used. These restrictions have tended to limit the number of policy conditions that may be grafted onto coverages.

A review of modern automobile policies indicates that many conditions and definitions are set forth in nearly identical language. This is due in large measure to legislative and regulatory fiat, and affords the advantage of a large number of court interpretations concerning the meaning of such standard provisions. Thus, the definition of an insured, the circumstances under which the vehicle must be used, and the policy exclusions are quite similar in automobile insurance. The same is true of the New York Standard Fire Insurance Policy of 1943, which has been adopted in nearly all states in identical form. Such uniform usage has contributed greatly to a general understanding of the policy conditions in fire insurance policies. The modern life insurance policy also contains very few exceptions, since regulatory authorities will refuse to approve policy language that is considered unnecessarily restrictive.

The fact does remain, however, that policy conditions and exceptions are intended to, and do, define and delimit the coverage of the insurance policy in a manner selected by insurers. The courts recognize this fact and interpret such provisions restrictively against the insurer.

Honoring Reasonable Expectations

The complexity of the modern insurance policy, the fact that most policyholders do not read their policies, or if they read them do not fully understand the terms, and the fact that the insured usually relies on the knowledge and ability of the agent, have given rise to a principle that goes beyond the doctrine that an insurance contract is a contract of adhesion. This emerging principle is called the principle of reasonable expectations. Under this principle, policies can be construed to include coverages that the average person would reasonably understand them to include, and insurers will not be permitted to enforce limitations and exceptions inconsistent with those reasonable expectations.

The principle has, as yet, no clearly defined limits, and is not sufficiently structured to be called a doctrine. Nevertheless the principle has been sufficiently applied by courts to spur insurers to even greater efforts to carefully define coverages, to clearly indicate conditions and exceptions, and to inform insureds of policy provisions that might bear on their expectations.

Other Equitable Principles

The ultimate aim of the courts is to achieve a fair and just decision in the difficult context of a very technical contract that is basic to the economic well-being of individuals and of the nation. On the one hand, courts must guard against the cupidity of policyholders, and on the other hand, must assure that insurers are not permitted to deny liability on tenuous and technical bases.

This problem leads the courts to rely heavily on general maxims of equity. Equitable maxims are necessarily vague, so that their nets can expand or contract as the court thinks necessary. There are no well-defined limits to the principle, for instance, that one cannot take unconscionable advantage of another, or that equity will not permit one to be unjustly enriched at the expense of another. Unconscionable bargain, undue delay, or denying relief to one who enters the court with unclean hands are terms equally subjective and arguable.

Supporting this approach, of course, is the fact that a cunning cad can skillfully evade a well-drawn, clear, and definite rule. It is difficult, however, to evade a general principle that we should live honestly, should hurt nobody, and should render to everyone what he or she is due.

Chapter Notes

1. 10th Amendment, U.S. Constitution.
2. National Labor Relations Board v. Jones & Laughlin Steel Corporation, 301 U.S. 1, 57 S.Ct. 615, 81 L.Ed. 893 (1937).
3. Paul v. Virginia, 8 Wall 168 (1868).
4. U.S. v. South-Eastern Underwriters Association, 322 U.S. 533, 64 S.Ct. 1162, 88 L.Ed. 1440 (1944).
5. McCarran-Ferguson Act, 59 Stat. 33-44 (1945) 15 U.S.C.A. Sections 1011-1015.
6. Holden v. Hardy, 169 U.S. 366 (1898).
7. Williams v. Baltimore, 289 U.S. 36, 53 S.Ct. 431, 77 L. Ed. 1015 (1933).
8. Old Dearborn Distributing Company v. Seagram Distillers Corporation, 299 U.S. 183 (1936).
9. Section VII, Art. 3, U.S. Constitution.
10. American Power and Light Company v. SEC, 329 U.S. 90, 91 L.Ed. 103 (1946).
11. Delancy v. Insurance Company, 52 N.H. 581 (1873).
12. Drake v. Globe American Casualty Company, Ohio 10th Circuit Court of Appeals, Unreported case No. 74AP-472, March 11, 1975.
13. Pennsylvania State Insurance Department press release February 23, 1973.
14. Justice Learned Hand in Gaunt v. John Hancock Mutual Life, 160 Fed. 2nd 599 (1947).
15. New York Life Insurance Co. v. Hiatt 140 F. 2d 752, 9th Circuit (1944).
16. German Alliance Ins. Co. v. Lewis, 34 S.Ct. 612 (1913).

CHAPTER 2

Law of Contracts—The Agreement

FORMATION OF CONTRACTS

Contract Defined

Introduction A great many of the daily activities that form the routine of our lives involve contract obligations. While the vast majority of these commitments are performed voluntarily and are seldom thought of as contracts, occasions arise when parties fail or refuse to perform as promised. It is then that the question of whether there was a binding contract becomes crucial. Agreements involving the purchase of food or clothing, rental of housing, employment arrangements, acquisition of insurance, enrollment in a course of study, entrance into marriage—all these involve contractual undertakings which may be enforced by the courts. At the same time, promises to take a vacation with a friend or to attend a social function as a guest are not the type of promises that the law recognizes as being enforceable. An understanding of the conditions that give rise to binding contracts can be of great practical importance to the individual, and such understanding is at the heart of contract law.

Legally Enforceable Promise A contract is a binding agreement that creates an obligation. The Restatement of Contracts defines a contract as "a promise or a set of promises for the breach of which the law gives a remedy, or the performance of which the law in some way recognizes as a duty."[1] In other words, a contract obligation is a legally enforceable promise.

The law of contracts is concerned with the creation, transfer, and disposition of property and other rights through promises. A promise is an undertaking, however expressed, either that something will happen, or that something will not happen in the future. When parties enter into a contract, they fix their own terms and set limits on their own liabilities. To create a valid contract, the terms of the agreement must be in compliance with law. The form of the contract, the age of the parties, the subject matter of the contract, and related matters must be considered in determining the validity of the obligation the parties would like to assume.

The parties to a contract mutually agree to undertake obligations that did not exist before. If these obligations are not performed, then resort may be had to the courts which will normally assess a penalty consisting of monetary damages. Under some circumstances, as when a unique item is the subject of the contract, the court may direct the parties specifically to perform their obligations by transferring the property in question. When the contract involves the performance of personal services, the courts will generally not require the performance of those services since it is impossible for a court to supervise the performance that it may order. However, monetary damages may still be obtained from the party failing to perform.

Parties to the Contract. Since a contract involves a legally enforceable promise, the party making the promise is referred to as the *promisor*. The party receiving the promise is the *promisee*. Where there is a mutual exchange of promises, each party to the contract is both a promisor and a promisee with regard to the respective promises made.

It should be noted that throughout the language of the law, the party on the receiving end will be identified with the "ee" suffix. Thus, the *promisee* of a contract is the person to whom the promise is made. A *vendee* in a sales transaction is the person who will receive the goods. A *bailee* is a person who receives in his or her possession the property of another.

The interests of *third parties* are also frequently involved in contracts. The promisor and promisee may agree that the benefits of a contract are to accrue to the advantage of a third person. Such a third party is referred to as a *third-party beneficiary*. Where the intention of the contracting parties is to confer a benefit on a third party in discharge of some obligation which previously existed to that third-party, then the third-party beneficiary will have a legally enforceable right under the contract in the event it is later breached.

In most cases, where two or more parties enter into a contract, there is said to arise a *privity of contract* between these parties that imposes special obligations upon them with respect to performance in accord with their promises. Privity of contract refers to the connection or relationship between parties to a contract. Some such relationship, or privity, is generally essential in order that one be able to sue under the contract. A third party who is not a third-party beneficiary and not in privity of contract with the contracting parties usually has no right to sue under the contract if the contract is breached.

Classification of Contracts

For the purpose of clearer understanding of contractual relationships, it should be noted that contracts may be classified in a number of ways.

Bilateral and Unilateral Contracts In a *bilateral contract,* one promise is given in exchange for another promise. Most contracts involve the exchange of mutual promises, with their actual performance to occur at some later time. Thus, the promise to pay someone $50 in exchange for that person's promise to paint your garage gives rise to a bilateral contract—mutual promises have been made. Each party has both made and received a promise, and each thus becomes both a promisor and a promisee. In the event of default, either may enforce the promise of the other in an action at law.

A *unilateral contract* involves the exchange of a promise for an act. For example, if a person promises to pay $50 when the garage has actually been painted, then the performance of an act is required in exchange for the promise. No binding contract arises until the act is actually performed, and a simple return promise to paint the garage will not give rise to a contract. The promise to pay $50 is conditional on the performance of the act of painting the garage, and the promise to paint will not create either a unilateral or bilateral contract.

Executed and Executory Contracts An *executed contract* is a contract that has been completely performed—nothing remains to be done by either party. Thus, where a suit of clothes is bought, delivered, and paid for, the contract is said to be executed. In an *executory contract,* something *does* remain to be done. If a tailor contracts to make a suit of clothes for a certain price, the contract is executory since the tailor must make the suit and deliver it for that price; i.e., something remains to be done and the contract is therefore considered executory. As noted in the preceding chapter, the insurance contract is an example of the executory contract since the promise to perform on the part of the insurer is an executory promise made conditional on the happening of the event insured against. An executed contract is one that has been completely performed by both parties. An executory contract is one in which performance by either or both parties is incomplete.

Express and Implied Contracts *Express contracts* are those in which the parties have made oral or written declarations of their intentions and of the terms of the transaction. Such contracts arise where the manifestation of agreement of the parties is by written or spoken words. Such contracts exist in the majority of cases where the parties have specifically agreed by words or in writing to do certain things. Thus, where the parties have agreed either orally or in writing on the sale of an automobile for $1,000, such a contract is an express contract.

Implied contracts may be either implied in fact or implied in law. A contract is said to be *implied-in-fact* when there is assent between the parties, evidenced by other than written or spoken words. Such contracts may arise where a person performs services for another and the latter has the opportunity to reject those services and fails to do so. For instance, should a doctor find a person injured and administer medical services, the injured person accepting the services without comment will be liable for the reasonable value of those services under a contract implied in fact. In similar manner, if a person having an account in a store picks up an item, shows it to the store owner without comment, and then walks out of the store with it—a contract implied-in-fact to pay for the item will be found.

Contracts implied in fact often arise through and are governed by customs of trade, by prior relations between the parties involved, and by community custom of which all concerned parties are aware.

Contracts *implied-in-law*, sometimes referred to as *quasi-contracts*, arise where (because of the special relationship of the parties or unusual circumstances of the case) a contractual obligation is found to exist, even though the parties have not in fact approved such an agreement. A quasi-contract is not really a contract, but is a fictitious promise implied by the law to take care of certain situations where it is felt that a remedy is needed. Such obligations are not based on the apparent intentions of the parties concerned, but are imposed for reasons of justice. If a wife or child is not being provided with the necessities of life (e.g., food, clothing, shelter, or education, befitting someone in this station of life), and some other person provides those necessities, then the husband or father will be held liable to that third person under a contract implied in law for the reasonable value of those necessaries. Similarly, where a doctor renders professional services to an unconscious person who cannot assent to or refuse such services, a contract will be implied-in-law to pay the reasonable value of such services. A quasi-contract is thus an obligation that the law creates, even in absence of a specific agreement, where a benefit has accrued to another under conditions which in good conscience and equity require that reimbursement be made. It is, in effect, not so much a contract as a duty imposed by law.

Void Agreements and Voidable Contracts *Void agreements* are those without legal effect. It is not logical to call such agreements void contracts, since they are not legally enforceable or binding in any way. No liability is imposed in such situations. They represent simple events rather than contracts. Agreements to commit a crime are thus void and completely unenforceable. In like manner, a contract made by one who has been judicially declared insane is void since one of the contracting parties lacked contractual capacity.

A *voidable contract* is a contract that for some reason can be rejected, or avoided, at the option of one or both of the parties; i.e., some circumstance surrounding the execution of the contract gives the right of avoidance. A contract entered into by one who is not of legal age may normally be avoided by the minor any time during minority or within a reasonable time after reaching majority. If both parties to the contract are infants, then either or both may avoid the obligations of the contract. It is important to note that such contracts are only voidable and not void; hence, the contract will continue in force and may be completely executed unless avoided by one of the parties.

A contract may be rendered voidable as the result of the fraud of one of the parties; e.g., where there is an intentional misrepresentation of a material fact relating to the contract. If the contract is entered into as the result of duress, as where a salesperson will not permit a prospect to leave the room until a contract is signed, such contract may be avoided by the injured party if such avoidance is undertaken within a reasonable time.

A voidable contract can later be ratified by the injured party. Thus, in the case of either fraud, duress, or mistake by one of the parties, the innocent party may later elect to be bound by the agreement and may hold the other party to the contract. The right of avoidance is available *only* to the innocent or injured party.

Simple and Formal Contracts The distinction between simple and formal contracts has much less significance now than it did in the early history of contract law. The majority of contracts, both written and oral, are *simple contracts*. At common law, certain contracts were raised to the status of *formal contracts* by placing a seal or raised imprint on the written contract. In such cases, the need for establishing the existence of *valuable consideration* (a contract requirement to be discussed later) was not necessary.

Although seals are still affixed to many documents, their legal significance has been reduced under the law in most states. The Uniform Commercial Code (UCC), which applies to the sale of goods and other commercial transactions, has abolished the use of seals in such business transactions.[2] Contracts of record—such as judgments of courts, recognizances, and appearance bonds—still contain seals and fall within the category of formal contracts. In most cases, the seal represents an attestation to the truth of the facts sworn to in the document in question.

Elements of a Contract

General Each of the following six elements must be present for a binding and enforceable contract to exist. (These elements will be discussed in greater detail in this and subsequent chapters.)

1. *An agreement.* One party must make an offer which is accepted by another.
2. *Competent parties.* The legal capacity of the parties must not be restricted because of minority, insanity, or intoxication.
3. *Consideration.* It must appear that there was a legal benefit received by the promisor or a legal detriment suffered by the promisee. Consideration refers to the price paid by each party to the other, or to what each party receives and gives up in the agreement.
4. *Genuine assent.* There must be real assent between the parties which was not affected by fraud, duress, concealment, or mistake.
5. *Legal purpose.* The contract must not be tainted by illegality. It must have a lawful object that is consistent with sound public policy.
6. *Form required by law.* Some contracts are required by law to meet formal requirements; e.g., the Statute of Frauds requires that certain contracts be evidenced by writing.

THE AGREEMENT

The Offer

General The first requirement of an enforceable contract is that there be an *agreement* between the parties. An agreement consists of an offer and an acceptance of that offer. The parties to a contract must at some time mutually assent, or agree, to the same bargain. Over the years, a considerable body of law has been developed concerning the exact circumstances under which an agreement may be found to exist.

An *offer* is a particular kind of promise that is conditioned upon an act or return promise given in exchange for the promise. It may be conditional upon the other party's giving a promise in return, in which case there exists a bilateral contract if the return promise is made; or it may be conditional upon performance of some act, in which case a unilateral contract exists once the act is performed.

An offer has been made if the recipient (the offeree) can reasonably construe the communication as a proposal to enter into an agreement on the terms stated, to become binding on both parties immediately upon acceptance.

An agreement arises when one person (the offeror) makes an offer and that offer is accepted by the person to whom it was made (the offeree). In every case, there must be both an offer and acceptance, or no contract will be found.

Meeting of the Minds   Although reference is sometimes made to a need for a "meeting of the minds" before an agreement will be found, the law does not impose such a requirement. The real test of an agreement is not whether the parties had a meeting of minds but whether, under the circumstances, one party was reasonably entitled to believe that an offer was made and the other party to believe that there was an acceptance. It is the manifestation of mutual assent that is the controlling factor.

Thus, if a party offers "to sell my library for $3,000," and the library contains a rare book which the offeror did not intend to sell, but forgot to mention, an acceptance of the offer will result in an agreement to sell the entire library, including the rare book. If the offeree was reasonably entitled to believe the offer included the sale of all books in the library, acceptance of the offer would bind the offeror to sell the entire library even though the subjective intent was not to sell the rare book. A meeting of minds is not required—it is what the parties were reasonably entitled to believe that determines the existence of an agreement.

In a case where the offeror promises to sell a book in return for the offeree's promise to pay $30 and both parties think such a promise is not binding unless made in writing, there nevertheless will be an agreement. In this instance, although neither party believed the contract to be binding, their respective manifestations of assent, if reasonably believed by the other party, would be sufficient to give rise to a binding offer and acceptance. Generally, mental reservations will not prevent a person from being bound by conduct that is reasonably understood by others.

Elements of Offer   The essential elements of an offer are: (1) an expression of present contractual intent, (2) definite terms, and (3) communication to the offeree. The presence of these three elements will give the offeree a power of acceptance to thereby create a contract.

Intent to Contract. The offeror must intend, or must appear to a reasonable person to intend, that the proposal made will create a legal obligation if it is accepted. The language used by the offeror becomes the most important factor in determining whether a particular communication is actually an offer. An offer is a promise, and if words of promise are not used, the communication will be treated as a general statement of intention or, at best, an invitation for an offer.

GENERAL STATEMENTS OF INTENTION. Statements that contain nothing from which a promise may be inferred do not constitute offers. If *A* says to *B*, "I am going to sell my car for $1,000," and *B* replies, "All right, I'll pay $1,000 for your car," no contract is created. The test is whether, under the circumstances, a reasonable person would conclude that *A* intended to make a promise to sell. Clearly, *A* can only be said to have stated a future intention to sell the car.

Similarly, if *A* advises *B*, "I will not sell my property for less than $20,000," and *B* replies, "I accept your offer," no contract will result. The mere statement of a figure below which *A* would not sell does not provide a reasonable basis for implying that *A* is promising to sell at the figure mentioned. All that may be inferred is a general statement of intention to sell at or about the figure mentioned. No present contractual intention may be inferred.

INVITATIONS. Many communications are sent for the purpose of inducing the recipients to respond with an offer. Most advertisements, catalogues, and circular letters are seen as invitations to negotiate or to make an offer. They are not considered offers in themselves, since no present contractual intent may be found. The parties to whom such proposals are directed are expected to realize this due to the circumstances under which the statements are made.

If a store advertises a certain stereo at $495, it is simply inviting offers which it may later accept at that price. If the store runs out of the stereos or if the goods were mistakenly advertised for an incorrect price, the store would not be bound by a customer's acceptance. No power of acceptance is created in the usual advertisement or catalogue situation. Advertising, however, with no intention to sell at the price stated is illegal by statutes.

In some cases it is possible for an advertisement to constitute an offer that may be accepted. Where an advertisement indicates that the goods will be sold at a specific price to the first person who enters the store, the conditions of acceptance are spelled out and a unilateral contract will be created when the first person actually agrees to buy the goods. Where advertisers use words of promise or specify circumstances that will give rise to unilateral contracts, the courts may find a contractual intention exists and may then hold the advertiser liable.

Usually, however, advertisements are viewed as mere solicitations for the prospective purchaser to make an offer.

INVITATIONS TO SUBMIT BIDS.   As in construction and sales, contracts are also viewed as calling for offers that may or may not be accepted. The party asking for bids may elect to accept one or to reject all of them. Anyone making a bid may withdraw the bid at any time prior to its being accepted. In the absence of special statutes, which sometimes exist in connection with public construction contracts, the party calling for the bid may accept any bid, whether or not that bid is the lowest.

SOCIAL INVITATIONS.   Social invitations are not construed as creating binding legal obligations. Invitations to attend a party or a wedding are not considered offers under the law. If an invitation that has been made is withdrawn, or if the party is called off, no legal remedy would exist. The courts recognize the difficulty of attempting to enforce invitations in the social realm, so such offers are not viewed as involving contractual intent.

EXPRESSIONS OF OPINION.   When a statement represents a prediction or an expression of opinion, no offer or intent to contract will be found. If an individual makes a prediction as to the weather conditions or amount of rainfall that will occur, and on the strength of such statements another person undertakes a certain course of action that results in a loss due to bad weather or lack of rainfall, no contractual intention or binding offer concerning such prediction will result. Similarly, where a doctor predicts that a patient will be in the hospital "only a few days" and the period of hospitalization proves much longer, no contractual intent exists and the doctor will not be held liable for having made a promise or offer that was enforceable at law.

OFFERS MADE IN EXCITEMENT OR JEST.   If a reasonable person would recognize that a statement was made in jest or in the heat of anger, the statement cannot be turned into a contract by an acceptance. This is so because the person who made the statement did not intend to be bound by it. Also, the person to whom the statement was made should have known that an offer was not intended, and should recognize that the person making the statement was joking or giving vent to emotions. Care must be taken in this area to distinguish cases in which statements made in excitement or jest can be reasonably interpreted as intending an offer. In such situations, a binding contractual obligation may arise. For example, A may offer to sell B a farm for $50,000 in jest for the purpose of embarrassing B into admitting he doesn't have $50,000. If B thereupon accepts the offer and has both parties sign a writing, A will be bound by his offer if B is reasonably entitled to believe an offer was made. A's secret intention will not be controlling.

The objective manifestation of A's intent as viewed by a reasonable person will be the crucial consideration.

Consider a situation in which A cries out in excitement, "Save my child from that burning building and I'll give you $1,000." In response, B runs into the building and saves A's child. If B could reasonably have construed A's statements as an offer, then the actions taken would give rise to a binding unilateral contract upon B's saving the child. If A's statement had been, "I'll give you a million dollars," then the statement would likely be viewed as the result of excitement, and a reasonable person would not be entitled to rely on or enforce such a promise. In each case, however, the entire set of circumstances must be considered in determining whether the statement could reasonably be construed as intending a binding offer to contract.

OBJECTIVE TEST APPLIED. The central question in each case involving contractual intent is whether, by words or conduct, the party manifested an intent to be presently bound. If the objective manifestation of such intention is not found, then a communication cannot be treated as an offer nor as a basis for an acceptance by an offeree. The *subjective* intent of the party whose conduct is being examined is normally of no importance. What is controlling is the manner in which the average reasonable person would interpret the party's *external* expressions of intent. The objective theory of contracts controls all rules of construction of communications between parties.

REASONABLE PERSON TEST. It will be noted that a great many of the rules relating to formation of contracts require that the actions of the parties be viewed from the standpoint of a reasonably prudent person. The purpose of this requirement of the law is to provide some standard which may be applied to the conduct of people in general. Thus, a judge or jury must weigh all the circumstances of a case being tried and make a determination of how a reasonable person acting under the same or similar circumstances would react in this situation. The decision in each case will depend in the final analysis on the subjective judgment of the judge or jury.

OFFERS AT AUCTIONS. The law of offer and acceptance may be seen in action at public auctions. When goods are sold at public auction, the seller is held to be inviting offers from those present and bidding. The announcement of an auction in a newspaper is not an offer. If nothing is stated in the advertisement or at the auction, which is usually the case, the auction is considered to be *"with reserve."* At an auction with reserve the public is invited to make offers or bids for the items put up for sale. The auctioneer is not making offers, but is merely soliciting offers by holding up items for bidding.

Each new bid is a new offer that the auctioneer may either accept or reject. A bid or offer is finally accepted and the agreement concluded by the fall of the hammer or by some other sign given by the auctioneer, such as saying "sold." The auctioneer can withdraw the item prior to the time the hammer falls, even though the bidding has started. Until the hammer falls or other concluding signal of acceptance has been given, the bidder may retract a bid. The withdrawal of a bid does not have the effect of reviving previous bids. If the hammer is falling when a new bid is made, it is up to the auctioneer's discretion whether to accept the previous offer or reopen the bidding.

In an auction announced to be *"without reserve,"* once the bids have been called for, the goods must go to the highest bidder. The seller in such a case has given up the right to withdraw an item when it has been put up for sale. Each item held up for sale is being offered to the public, and each new bid constitutes an offer at a higher level. An anomaly in the law of auctions should be noted. The bidder is entitled to withdraw his bid, even in an auction without reserve, any time prior to the hammer's falling. As will be seen later, an acceptance is normally effective to bind the parties immediately upon being made, but in an auction without reserve, the bid—acceptance may still be withdrawn prior to the hammer's dropping.

Unless otherwise announced prior to the auction, the seller has no right to bid at his own sale. For the seller to bid or to have an agent bid on the seller's behalf would amount to fraud. If this rule is violated, the buyer has the option of avoiding the sale upon learning of the improper bidding.

The Uniform Commercial Code (UCC) (2-238), which has been adopted in every state except Louisiana, sets forth the above rules in some detail. The language of the UCC represents a statement of the common law rules relating to auctions.

Definite Terms. To be considered an offer, a communication must be sufficiently definite or certain in its terms. Such certainty is required to make any agreement enforceable and any damages subject to calculation. The terms of the agreement must be definite enough to enable a court to determine whether the parties have lived up to their promises.

REASONABLE CERTAINTY. An offer must state its terms with at least a reasonable degree of certainty before a power of acceptance can exist. While essential terms would involve the identification of the parties, the subject matter, the price, and the time of performance, the absence of one or more of these terms may not prove fatal to the offer. The test increasingly applied by the courts is whether the offer is clear enough in its terms to provide a reasonably certain basis for affording a remedy in the event of default. Thus, such missing terms as price or time of performance will be supplied where possible. In the absence of designated time for performance, courts will normally find that an implied part of the agreement was that performance was to occur within a reasonable time considering the subject matter involved. Inability to identify the parties to an agreement or the subject matter of the offer would ordinarily create sufficient uncertainty to render the offer indefinite and therefore not susceptible to acceptance. If the offer is sufficiently definite to permit the court to determine what the parties intended, then it will be enforced even though it may become necessary to imply some terms. The requirement of reasonable certainty is thus relative, and therefore dependent upon the circumstances of each case.

ILLUSORY PROMISES. In many situations, a statement creates the illusion of being a promise but does not, in fact, promise anything specific. Thus, A's promise to B to pay a "fair share of the profits" if B works for A is too indefinite to be enforced. Similarly, a promise to "take care of" an employee who has been injured will generally be found to be too vague to afford a reasonably certain basis for giving a remedy. Such indefinite language creates the illusion of obligation but provides no means of determining the true intention of the parties. If, however, in the first case B actually goes to work for A, B will be entitled to the fair value of the services rendered under the theory of implied-in-fact contract, even though the promise to pay a fair share of the profits is unenforceable.

REQUIREMENT CONTRACTS. Agreements to deal with one supplier are generally held enforceable even though the possibility exists that no goods may be "required." A's promise to buy all steel requirements from B is generally held sufficiently definite to be enforceable. Obligations are being created on both sides, since A promises to buy any steel requirements from B, and B promises to sell A the steel needed according to the terms of the agreement. If the language of the agreement involved B's promise to sell "all such coal as I wish to supply you," then the agreement is again illusory and not definite enough to afford a basis for giving a remedy. B may not wish to supply any coal, and such vagueness will not give rise to a valid offer.

CERTAINTY UNDER THE UNIFORM COMMERCIAL CODE. Although missing terms in usual contract law may be implied by ascertaining what the parties actually intended at the time of contracting, the UCC goes farther by providing, for sales of goods contracts only, that the parties may agree in a binding contract to set terms in the future.[3] These so-called "open terms" may even include the price, if it is found that the parties intended to be bound. In usual contract law it is essential that the price mutually intended be ascertained as of the time the contract was made, unless the goods are actually delivered and accepted in which case a "reasonable" price is implied. The code thereby rejects the usual rule that "an agreement to agree is unenforceable."

Communication of Offer. An offer has no effect until it has been communicated to the offeree by the offeror (or an agent of same), and the offeree cannot accept a proposal before having knowledge of it. To illustrate, assume that X offers to sell his library to Y for $1,000 and sends Y a letter to that effect. Prior to receiving the letter and without knowledge of the proposal, Y sends a letter to X stating that he will buy X's library for $1,000. Y's letter is not an acceptance of X's offer, since it was not made with knowledge of that offer. The second letter was simply an offer of its own, and no contract arises since neither communication related to the other. Mere cross-offers are involved, and no acceptance occurs until a reply is made in response to one of the two offers.

Similarly, a newspaper advertisement is placed that offers "$100 to anyone who will enter the 100 yard dash on July 4th and beat X." Y, having no knowledge of the advertisement or offer, enters the race and beats X. There is no contract, as Y could not accept an offer of which she had no knowledge.

Note, however, the entire performance that constitutes acceptance need not be performed prior to learning of the offer. Consider the case in which an offer is made for information leading to the arrest and conviction of a person responsible for a particular crime. P made prior investigation and determined that D had committed the crime. Then, upon learning of the reward, P turned D in to the authorities. If D is subsequently convicted, P may collect the reward even though part of his effort was made prior to learning of the offer. The crucial fact is that the culprit was turned in with knowledge of the offer.

An offer is normally effective when delivered to the offeree or when the offeree gains knowledge of the offer. Still, the law does require communication of the offer from the offeror to the offeree. Thus, where a friend learns of the offeror's intent to offer a certain item for sale and so advises P of the forthcoming offer, P may not accept the offer until it is tendered to him or to the public at large. The law holds that a person is master of his or her own offer, and someone simply learning that an offer is to be made may not seize upon the offer and insist that the item be sold to him or her.

Duration and Termination of Offers The length of time during which an offer is binding depends upon several considerations.

Lapse of Time. An offer will cease to be binding upon the expiration of the *time specified* in the offer or after the lapse of a *reasonable time.* Such a requirement is imposed to avoid the possibility of offers remaining open indefinitely. What is reasonable time depends on such considerations as the subject matter of the contract and the general commercial setting of the transaction. In every case, the offeree has a continuing power of acceptance until the offer is terminated. Acceptance attempted after the offer has terminated becomes a counteroffer which may be either accepted or rejected by the original offeror.

By Operation of Law. The occurrence of any one of several events automatically terminates an outstanding offer. If, for example, an *offeror or the offeree dies* or is adjudicated insane, the law deems the offer to be terminated automatically. It should be noted, however, that if a contract has actually been entered into, i.e., the offer has been made and accepted, such a contract will not be terminated by reason of death or insanity, unless, of course, the contract involved the rendering of a personal or professional service which would excuse the performance of the contract. Otherwise, the agreement would be enforceable against the estate of the deceased party.

Where the *subject matter* of the contract is *destroyed* prior to the offer being accepted, the offer is deemed to have terminated upon such destruction. The fact that the offeree did not know of the destruction prior to acceptance does not affect this result. The offer is terminated by operation of law.

If *performance* of the contract is made *illegal* after the offer has been made, the offer is deemed to terminate. Thus, where a statute is passed that makes it unlawful to deal in certain types of goods, an offer that had been made to sell such goods is automatically terminated.

Rejection by Offeree. Rejection of the offer by the offeree results in termination of that offer. A rejection occurs when the offeree notifies the offeror that he does not intend to accept. As in the case of the offer itself, the rejection by the offeree is not effective until actually communicated to the offeror, or offeror's agent. After the rejection has been made, the offeree may not then change his or her mind and attempt to accept the offer. Such attempted acceptance after a rejection at best amounts to a new offer by the offeree.

The only qualification to this rule may be seen in the case of *option contracts.* In such contracts the offeror has agreed, for a consideration, to hold an offer open for a specified period of time. Thus, where a sum of money or other consideration has been given by the offeree to hold the offer open for a period of time, courts will generally permit the offeree who has rejected the offer to later make a valid acceptance if such acceptance is made within the original option period, unless the offeror has substantially changed position in reliance on the rejection.

An offeree may reject an offer either by an express refusal to accept or by making a counteroffer.

Counteroffers. A proposal made by the offeree to the offeror that varies in some material respect from the original offer is a *counteroffer*. A counteroffer is considered a rejection of the original offer and constitutes an offer by the offeree. A distinction must be drawn between counteroffers and mere inquiries that request further information. In the latter case, no rejection occurs. For example, *X* offers to sell *Y* a television set for $200. *Y* replies, "I'll give you $150 for it." Such reply is a counteroffer that has the effect of rejecting *X*'s original offer, and *Y* cannot later accept the original $200 offer. Note, however, if *Y* had replied to *X*'s offer by inquiring, "Will you accept $150?", such question would not constitute a counteroffer and would not result in a rejection. If *X* indicated that the lower figure was unsatisfactory, *Y* could still accept the $200 offer.

The offer will also remain open if the offeror makes an offer and adds, "This offer will remain open beyond any counteroffers." A counteroffer by the original offeree would in such case not constitute a rejection. Similarly, an offer also continues if the counteroffer provides that such counteroffer will not constitute a rejection of the original offer.

Revocation by Offeror. A *revocation* is a withdrawal of the offer by the offeror. As a general rule, an offeror may revoke an offer at any time prior to its acceptance by the offeree. As in the case of the original offer, the revocation is effective only when it has been communicated to the offeree. A letter or telegram revoking an offer is not effective until actually received by the offeree. Thus, if the offeror mails a revocation but receives the offeree's acceptance by telephone before the revocation is received, a contract does exist.

Offers made to the general public must be revoked through use of the same means of communication used in making the original offer. An advertisement offering a reward may be revoked only through a like advertisement. Such revocation by advertisement will effectively revoke the offer even though it is not seen by a party who tries to accept the original offer.

The mere statement on the part of the offeror that the offer made will remain irrevocable for a period of time will not be sufficient to take away the right of revocation. The general rule is that the offeror may revoke an offer even though it has been stated that the offer will remain open. There are some important qualifications to this rule. An *option contract* is a contract to keep an offer open for a stated period of time. The promise to hold the offer open is supported by consideration; once that consideration has been given, the offer may not be revoked within the prescribed period. Such option contracts are frequently seen in real estate transactions, where an amount of money (i.e., a consideration) is given to obtain a binding option to buy. The offeror thereby agrees to hold the offer open for a period of time and cannot revoke that offer within the option period.

Under the provisions of the UCC, if a merchant makes a *firm offer* in writing to buy or sell goods and states that the offer is to be irrevocable for a stated period, such offer may not be revoked even in the absence of any consideration up to a maximum period of three months.[4] The UCC does require that the offer be in writing and be signed by the merchant.

In the situation where a *unilateral contract offer* has been made and the offeree has made partial performance of the acts requested, most courts hold that such offer is irrevocable after such performance. If *P* promises to pay *X* $2,000 if *X* will dig an excavation of a certain size on *P*'s property, and *X* has completed one-third of the excavation when *P* attempts to revoke the offer, such revocation is ineffective. Most courts do require that some substantial start in the performance requested must have been made. If so, then the offeree must be given a reasonable time to perform the entire acceptance before revocation will be permitted. The question of whether substantial performance has begun is one of fact, to be determined by the trier of fact under the circumstances. The mere gathering of tools in preparation for performance has been held *not* sufficient to constitute a substantial start.

The Acceptance

General An *acceptance* occurs when a party to whom an offer has been made agrees to the proposal or does what was proposed. If the acceptance is to result in an enforceable agreement, it too must meet certain requirements. An acceptance must be:

1. made by the person to whom the offer was made;
2. unconditional and unequivocal; and
3. communicated to the offeror by appropriate word or act.

An acceptance is an expression on the part of the offeree which indicates that the offeree consents to be bound by the terms of the offer. While the offeree may state that the offer is "accepted," it is not necessary that this particular term be used. Any language that shows the offeree is assenting to the proposal is sufficient. Whatever language is used, it is necessary that these three conditions be met in order for a binding agreement to be formed.

Acceptance by Person to Whom Offer Was Made An offer may be accepted only by the person or persons to whom it is made. The offeror has the right to choose with whom a contract will be made. If *A* makes an offer to *B*, who dies after receiving it, *B*'s executor cannot accept.

An offer may be made to one person, to a group or class of persons, or to the public at large. The identity of the offerees will be determined by the language and circumstances of the offer. For example, if *A* promises to sell and deliver a set of books to *B* if *B*'s father will promise to pay $100 for the set, *B*'s father is the offeree. Only *B*'s father can accept the offer by making the return promise.

When an offer is made to a particular group, then any member of the group may accept. Thus, where a form letter containing an offer is sent to many persons, any recipient may accept the offer in accord with its terms. If an offer is made to the public at large, as in the case of a reward advertisement, it may be accepted by any member of the public who has knowledge of it. Once the reward offer has been accepted, no one else may accept.

Acceptance of Option Contracts. As previously noted, an option is an offer that remains open for a specified time because it is supported by consideration. The option is thus a contract and, as will be seen later, contracts may normally be assigned to another party. Hence, offers contained in option contracts are assignable and may be accepted by the assignee of the contract, unless the option is for a personal service contract. It should be noted that the offeree normally does not have the power to make an assignment of the right of acceptance. Only in the situation where the offer has been confirmed by a binding option contract does this right of assignment exist.

Unconditional and Unequivocal As a general rule, an acceptance to be effective must conform to the terms of the offer. If there is a deviation from these terms, the purported acceptance will be construed as a counteroffer. Provisions in an offer relating to time, place, or manner of acceptance must be strictly complied with by the offeree.

Conditional Responses. While the acceptance must not deviate from the basic terms of the offer, the law recognizes that customary business practices may not in the acceptance reflect a word-for-word response to the offer. Some terms or words used in the acceptance will not render the acceptance conditional if such terms would be *implied by law* in any event. For example, an acceptance in a real estate sale that states, "Good title must be passed," would constitute an unconditional acceptance, since such an understanding would be implied by the law in such transactions. Similarly, where the purported acceptance is made subject to *"details being worked out,"* whether such a reply results in an unconditional acceptance will depend on the nature of the details referred to. If the details involved are mere *clerical matters,* then an unconditional acceptance would result. A reply that is made subject to "details to be worked out between you and my attorney" would constitute a valid acceptance if the details related to such matters as the form of the agreement, title search, or similar matters. If, however, the offer related to the building of a house and the reply purported to accept "subject to details to be worked out," too many essential elements would be missing and the response would not produce an unconditional acceptance.

Equivocal Responses. While an equivocal response will not result in a valid acceptance to an offer, neither will it result in a counteroffer or in outright rejection. Where the offeree replies that the offer "will receive our immediate attention," such a reponse does not manifest a clear intent to contract and would be considered too equivocal to constitute an acceptance. Similarly, mere expressions of hope such as "I hope to have the cash for you next Friday morning" would not reflect an unequivocal acceptance and no contract would result.

Under Uniform Commercial Code. When the contract offer relates to the sale of goods, the UCC provides that a variance between the acceptance and the offer is not necessarily fatal to the formation of a contract. Under the provisions of the code, "A definite and seasonable expression of acceptance or a written confirmation which is sent within a reasonable time operates as an acceptance even though it states terms additional to or different from those offered or agreed upon, unless acceptance is expressly made conditional on assent to the additional or different terms."[5] The code goes on to specify the following:

> The additional terms are to be construed as proposals for addition to the contract. Between merchants such terms become part of the contract unless: (a) the offer expressly limits acceptance to the terms of the offer; (b) they materially alter it; or (c) notification of objection to them has already been given or is given within a reasonable time after notice of them is received.

It should be carefully noted that, under the UCC provisions, if both the offeror and offeree are not merchants, the additional terms do not become part of the contract unless mutually agreed upon. The crucial point is that the proposal of additional terms in sales contracts involving goods does not render the acceptance conditional and thereby result in rejection of the offer. Such terms are simply proposals for addition to the contract. If the offeror fails to object to such proposed addition within a reasonable time, assent to its inclusion is inferred and it becomes part of the contract. Thus, if the buyer's acceptance states "inspection of goods will be allowed prior to their acceptance," such addition will become part of the contract unless objected to by the original offeror. The other remaining terms of the contract will remain as accepted.

Where the purported acceptance of an offer for the sale of goods states terms that *materially vary the agreement,* such response constitutes a counterproposal and rejection of the original offer. In such a case no notification by the offeror of objection to the added terms is necessary. To make the added terms a part of the contract, the offeror's express assent and acceptance of the counteroffer are required. For example, if the purported acceptance would change the quantity to be delivered or the unit price to be paid, such material change would constitute a counteroffer and a rejection of the orginal offer. Only by inquiring whether the offeror would consider the new terms and by stating the original proposal is not to be considered rejected, could the offeree avoid the result that such material change proposals constitute a rejection.

Communicated to Offeror by Appropriate Word or Act An acceptance must involve more than a mere mental resolve on the part of the offeree to accept; it must be communicated. The nature of the communication required depends on the contract offer. In a unilateral contract offer, the acceptance occurs upon completion of the act requested by the offeror. In a bilateral contract offer, in which there is a request for a return promise, acceptance is accomplished by communication of that return promise. Most offers are bilateral in that they contemplate a return promise to perform. Where it is not clear as to whether the parties intended a unilateral or a bilateral agreement, courts will favor the construction that a bilateral contract was intended. In any event, the law requires that the mutual assent of both parties be outwardly manifested, either by words or by conduct.

Manner of Acceptance. An acceptance must conform to the terms of the offer. If certain means of acceptance are specified by the offer, those means must be used. If no method of acceptance is indicated, those means which are customary in similar transactions or that are reasonable under the circumstances will be permitted. The UCC provides that in the sale of goods, an offeree may accept in any commercially reasonable manner.[6] If an offer requires that acceptance be "by return mail," an acceptance mailed the same business day the offer is received is generally required. If no time for acceptance is set, then acceptance must be within a reasonable time. The circumstances of each case will determine what constitutes a reasonable time. If the offer involves the sale of highly perishable goods, such as strawberries, the reasonable time for acceptance would obviously be much shorter than in the case of nonperishables.

Where the offer prescribes a particular mode of acceptance, such as a requirement that the acceptance be "in writing" or "by telegram," an attempted oral response to such offers would be ineffective as an acceptance and would not give rise to a contract. The express directions of the offeror regarding the method of acceptance will always control.

Notice of acceptance may be dispensed with entirely. If an offer to sell contains the words, "This proposal becomes a contract when accepted and approved by an executive officer of the company," the acceptance will occur when an executive officer indicates such acceptance on the document. Thus, there is no need to send notice of acceptance to form a contract. Some courts would still impose a duty on the offeree in this situation to inform the offeror of an acceptance within a reasonable time.

The Complaining Acceptance. Where the offeree replies to the offer by stating, "Your price is extremely unfair, and if I didn't need the property so badly I would never accept at this figure. Enclosed is my check for the amount you so unreasonably demand. . . ," a contract still results. The acceptance is considered unequivocal even though the offeree may complain about the price.

Silence as Acceptance. Silence on the part of the offeree will not be held to operate as an acceptance. Some actual response, some overt act, is generally required for an acceptance to occur. Thus, one person may not impose on another the duty to respond to an offer. If *A* offers an item for sale to *B* by stating in a letter, "If I do not hear from you within ten days, I will assume the offer is accepted," no acceptance will occur if *B* simply remains silent. A qualification to this rule may be found in the case where *prior dealings* between the parties have imposed a duty to reject the current offer. Thus, if the parties have been dealing for some time on the basis of sending goods and then paying for them at a later date, the party receiving an additional shipment may be required to reject them on this occasion if there is no wish to accept. In absence of a pattern of prior dealings, the person receiving unrequested goods owes no duty to reply or maintain such goods. The UCC is in accord with this view.[7]

The Federal Postal Reorganization Act of 1970 specifically provides that a person receiving unordered merchandise has the right to ". . . retain, use, discard, or dispose of it in any manner he sees fit without any obligation whatsoever to sender."[8] This broad language is applicable to any case in which the mails are involved.

Acceptance of Unilateral Offers. In the case of unilateral contracts, the offeror is interested in obtaining the performance of an act or the forbearance of the offeree to perform an act. When such act or forbearance is performed with knowledge of the offer, then an acceptance is made. There is generally no requirement that the offeree actually communicate the fact that the act has been performed, since it is assumed that the offeror will learn of the performance. Where the terms of the offer specify that notice of completion be given, then such notification will be required.

The most difficult problems have arisen where the offeree begins to perform the act requested and the offeror then elects to revoke the offer prior to completion of the entire performance. As noted under the discussion of revocation, most courts hold that a *substantial perfor-mance* begun by the offeree will suspend the right of the offeror to revoke his offer. The unilateral contract offer is said to include the understanding that if substantial part performance is accomplished, the offeree will be permitted to complete that performance within the prescribed time. No contract is formed until all work has been completed, but the right of the offeror to withdraw the offer is at least temporarily suspended. What constitutes substantial part performance sufficient to suspend the offeror's right of revocation is a question of fact for the trier of fact to determine. Generally, mere preparations for performance will not suffice as substantial performance.

Acceptance of Bilateral Offers. In the case of a bilateral offer, the acceptance is not complete until the offeree communicates assent by giving the offeror the return promise bargained for. The offeror may revoke the offer anytime until the return promise is communicated. The communication, in every case, may be to the offeror or to an agent of the offeror who is authorized to accept such communications.

While the usual bargained-for exchange in a bilateral contract offer is a return promise, the offeree may elect to perform the act requested rather than give a return promise. For example, if A writes to B, "I'll pay you $200 if you'll promise to paint my house by June 1," and B does not reply to the letter but proceeds to paint A's house and completes the work prior to June 1, a contract will result. The reasonable construction of the parties' conduct is that, by commencing the work, B implied acceptance of A's offer and thereby agreed to be bound by its terms. A acquiesced in this form of acceptance and a bilateral contract resulted.

When Acceptance Takes Effect. An acceptance that is made in a manner invited by an offer is effective as soon as it leaves the offeree's possession, without regard to whether it ever reaches the offeror. It is still necessary, however, that the communication be directed to the offeror. If the offeree simply makes a statement to a third person to the effect that the offer is accepted, such purported acceptance will be ineffective.

In all contract communications other than acceptance, actual delivery to the other party or an agent of that party must be accomplished. Where an acceptance by mail or telegraph is an approved mode of response to an offer, the acceptance becomes effective when the letter is mailed or the telegram is handed to the telegraph clerk. Mailed and telegraphed acceptances give rise to a legally binding contract when they are put out of the offeree's possession. While the principal application of this rule applies to mail and telegraph, the rule would apply equally to other service instrumentalities that are not controlled by the offeree. Thus, delivery of the acceptance to a private messenger service will give rise to a contract immediately upon such delivery. Such acceptances are considered operative to create a contract when they are out of the possession and control of the offeree. The rationale of this rule—which is unique to the communication of acceptances—is that the rule is conducive to contract finality and formation. The offeree is not obliged to prove that the acceptance was actually received by the offeror.

Acceptance Must Be Properly Dispatched. In order for the acceptance to be effective upon dispatch, it must be properly addressed to the offeror. The offeree may meet this requirement by using the return address indicated in the offer, whether in a letterhead or otherwise. If, however, the acceptance is sent to the wrong address, it is then effective only upon receipt by the offeror. For example, if an offer is received on stationery indicating a business address and the offeree mails the acceptance to the offeror's home address, no contract will result until the acceptance is actually received.

Loss or Delay of Acceptance. If acceptance is made in a manner authorized by the offeror, then the acceptance is effective when it leaves the control of the offeree even though such acceptance never reaches the offeror. If, however, the offer is made conditional upon receipt of the acceptance, then the acceptance is not effective when sent. For example, *A* mails an offer to lease land to *B* that states, "Wire me a yes or no answer. If I do not hear from you by noon this Wednesday, I shall conclude your answer is no." *B* duly telegraphs, "Yes," but the telegram is not delivered until after noon on Wednesday. No contract is formed by this telegraphic acceptance, since the acceptance was not received within the time period prescribed.

Revocation of Acceptance. An acceptance once made cannot be withdrawn or revoked by the offeree. The fact that the offeree may be able to reclaim the acceptance from the post office or from the telegraph service will not prevent the acceptance from taking effect when it was dispatched. The moment such letter or message is delivered to the postal department or telegraph company, the acceptance becomes effective. Attempts to revoke acceptances by retrieving them are legally ineffective.

Effect of Conflicting Communications. While the majority of communications leading to the formation of contracts are handled in routine fashion, it sometimes becomes crucial to determine the exact time a particular action was taken. Unless otherwise provided by the parties, contract communications are not effective until actually delivered to the other party or to an agent authorized to accept such delivery. The only qualification to this rule is in the case of the acceptance. If mailing the acceptance is the method expressly or impliedly authorized, then the acceptance becomes effective when mailed. To illustrate these rules, consider the following fact patterns:

SITUATION ONE.
May 3—*A* mails offer to *B*
May 4—*B* receives offer at 11:00 A.M.
May 4—*A* mails revocation at 3:00 P.M.
May 4—*B* mails acceptance at 6:00 P.M.
May 5—*B* receives revocation at noon
May 5—*A* receives acceptance at 2:00 P.M.

In Situation One the contract became effective at the time of mailing of the acceptance on May 4, at 6 P.M. Since *A* had mailed the offer, acceptance would be authorized by mail. *A*'s earlier revocation was not effective until received, while *B*'s acceptance was effective when mailed.

SITUATION TWO.
May 6—*A* mails offer to *B*
May 7—*B* receives offer at 11:00 A.M.
May 8—*B* mails letter of rejection at noon
May 9—*B* telegraphs acceptance at 2:00 P.M.
May 9—*A* receives rejection letter at 3:00 P.M.
May 9—*A* receives acceptance telegram at 4:00 P.M.

In Situation Two, no contract was formed. Acceptance is normally effective immediately upon leaving control of offeree, but when the offeree takes the conflicting actions of first mailing a rejection and then following with an acceptance, it becomes a race between the two communications. The first communication received by the offeror will have binding effect. In this situation, most courts will apply a construction more favorable to the offeror and will hold no contract was formed since the rejection first reached the offeror. The attempted acceptance may, however, be treated as a counter-offer.[9] Note that, if the offeree had first mailed the acceptance and then telegraphed a rejection that is received first, the acceptance would have been effective when mailed and a contract would result. But if the offeror substantially relies on the rejection while unaware of the acceptance, the offeree may not enforce the contract.

FORMATION OF INSURANCE CONTRACTS

Elements of Insurance Contracts

To be enforceable, the insurance contract must have the same essential elements as any other contract. It must appear that the parties entered into an *agreement* consisting of a legally binding offer and an acceptance of that offer. The agreement must have been entered into between *parties* who are *competent* to contract. There must have been legally sufficient *consideration* to support the agreement. The parties must have given *genuine assent* to the contract, and the contract must have a *lawful object.* The requirement that the contract be in writing, found in some contracts, does not apply to the insurance contract.

The need for a binding agreement will be the focus of this discussion. The nature of the agreement in insurance contracts will be considered in the next section, while the other elements of binding contracts mentioned in the preceding paragraph (including special emphasis on their application to insurance contracts), will be considered in Chapters 3 and 4.

Agreement in Insurance Contracts

Role of Agent The business of insurance is handled almost exclusively through agents. Insurers rely on agents to solicit business, take applications, and sometimes issue policies. Such agents can create contract liability for their insurer-principals, notwithstanding the intent of the insurer not to be bound until a final underwriting decision is made in the home or regional office. Commitments made by insurance agents are binding on the insurer if a rule of agency law imposes such liability. In the formation of the insurance contract, the law of agency is thus superimposed on the law of contracts in determining whether an agreement binding on the insurer has been reached. Agency law is discussed in Chapters 6 and 7, but some preliminary considerations regarding the role of the insurance agent should be mentioned.

Agency forces of insurance companies are highly varied as to organization, degree of specialization, and authority to act for an insurer. Some insurance companies employ their own agents as exclusive representatives and vest these agents with varying degrees of authority. Other companies employ independent agents who may represent several insurers and who will also have varying degrees of authority to bind these insurers for particular coverages. Whatever type of agency relationship is employed, the insurance agent is the crucial legal intermediary between the insurer and the insured. When an insurance agreement is purportedly entered into or some claim for benefits arises under an insurance contract, legal questions concerning the existence of the agency relationship, the nature of the representation, the extent of authority vested in the agent, the type of coverage involved, and the circumstances surrounding the agreement itself must all be considered in evaluating the liability of the parties.

As has been seen, it is a general requirement of all contracts, including the insurance contract, that an agreement be reached between the parties. Again, the agreement consists of an offer and an acceptance. The problems of offer and acceptance as they relate particularly to the contract of insurance will now be considered.

Offer and Acceptance   When an agent contacts a prospective insured for the purpose of selling an insurance policy, is the agent making an offer to contract or merely soliciting offers? As a general rule, the selling efforts of the agent are viewed as merely soliciting offers. The application for insurance that the applicant signs and sends to the insurance company through the agent is the offer. A policy of insurance later issued strictly in accordance with such offer is the acceptance that consummates the agreement. If, on the other hand, the policy issued by the insurer does not conform to the application (or initial offer), then the policy is considered a counteroffer which requires specific acceptance by the applicant. It should be remembered, however, that in the first instance the agent is considered to be merely soliciting offers that may or may not be accepted by the insurer.

The Policy as an Offer.   In many insurance transactions, the applicant does not make an offer but merely invites the insurer to make an offer. Thus, where the applicant has not definitely decided to take the insurance but submits an application without payment of premium in order to determine whether the risk will prove acceptable to the insurer, no offer can be said to have been made by the applicant. In such case, when the policy is issued by the insurer and accepted by the insured with payment of the premium, then an offer and acceptance will have been concluded. Similarly, where the policy issued by the insurer does not comply with the coverage or rates requested by the proposed insured, such policy constitutes a new offer that must then be accepted by the applicant. Where the policy issued is merely an offer, the person named as insured is in no way bound to accept it. To avoid the potential for litigation in such cases, the agent is well advised not to deliver the policy to the proposed insured until the premium has been paid. When the policy is simply mailed to the insured, no premium may be paid for a considerable time and the status of the contract will be in question throughout that period. While no contract will in fact exist, the possibility of dispute with respect to validity of the contract, and dispute regarding alleged promises to pay the premium, may provide grounds for litigation.

Communication of the Offer. As with contracts in general, the communication of the offer to the offeree is essential. One cannot accept an offer of which one has no knowledge. Thus, when the policy issued is merely an offer, it cannot become binding as a contract until it is actually communicated to the offeree or the offeree's agent, who is authorized to accept such offers. No one other than the person to whom an offer is addressed, or that person's duly authorized agent, can accept an offer. For example, if the proposed insured died before taking action to accept the policy (offer), the widow or other survivors would have no legal power to accept the offer.

In accord with the general rule of contracts, the mailing of an acceptance, where mailing is a permitted mode of acceptance, will bind the insurance contract when the acceptance is actually mailed. This is true without regard to whether the mailed acceptance is received. Thus, where the issuance of a policy by the insurer constitutes the offer, the act of mailing the premium in response to that policy (offer) will constitute the binding acceptance.

Oral Contracts of Insurance. Insurance contracts that are entirely oral may be as fully binding as written insurance policies. In situations in which the insurance agent has authority to enter into oral agreements to bind coverage, the offer and acceptance will be governed by the words and conduct of the parties as in any contract. Generally, any acts or words that reflect an intention to make an offer and give an acceptance of that offer will suffice to establish a binding insurance contract. To determine the circumstances under which binding oral contracts of insurance might arise, it is necessary to consider the different types of coverage involved in insurance transactions. Different rules and practices have arisen in different branches of insurance. In the field of property and liability insurance, oral applications and contracts are common. In life insurance, written applications and contracts are universally required.

In Property and Casualty Insurance. The individual and business requirements of modern commercial life have given rise to the need for immediate insurance coverage in many situations. A person who enters into a binding contract to purchase property may thereupon assume the risk of loss in the event the property is destroyed. Such potential loss results in the practical necessity of obtaining insurance coverage without delay. In the case of property and casualty insurance, then, authority is most frequently given the agent to immediately bind the insurance company.

For example, *B* telephones agent *A* and asks for "immediate fire insurance coverage on my home in the amount of $30,000." *A* replies, "You are now covered." The fire insurance company which *A* represents will be bound by this oral agreement to provide fire insurance protection. The need for such instant coverage is recognized by insurers and the courts. In absence of some limitation on the agent's authority which was known to the prospective insured, an oral contract of insurance entered into by the agent will prove binding until actually rejected by the insurer.

No Agreement for Immediate Coverage. In cases where the insurance agent and the prospective insured have not agreed that there will be immediate coverage for property or liability insurance, it becomes necessary to examine the conversations between the parties, as well as the agent's authority, to determine when the policy does become effective. If the agent simply obtained an application for fire insurance from the insured without any assurance the coverage would take effect immediately, then the rule stated above applies and the application will be considered an offer that may later be accepted by the insurer issuing a policy in conformity with that offer. The prospective insured and the insurance agent may agree that coverage will be effective immediately or may make no reference to the effective date. In the latter situation, the effective date of coverage might be delayed until issuance of the policy by the insurer.

Time When Acceptance Takes Effect. Unless otherwise agreed between the parties, an acceptance made in the manner requested will complete the agreement as soon as the acceptance leaves the offeree's possession. Thus, where agent *A* offers to insure *B*'s house against fire with the insurance to take effect upon actual payment of the premium, and *B* is requested to mail the check for the amount of the premium, the coverage will become effective upon *B*'s mailing the check. If the house burns while *B*'s letter is in transit, benefits will still be payable. It should be noted that this result is in keeping with the usual rule of contract law concerning the time when acceptance becomes effective.

In Life Insurance. The life insurance contract differs from the property insurance contract in several important ways. Long periods of coverage are involved (i.e., the life of the insured), very large amounts of coverage are often agreed upon, and highly specialized underwriting considerations regarding medical history, life expectancy, and so on must be considered. These factors have led insurers to proceed with caution in extending authority to insurance agents to enter such contracts. In the life insurance contract, it is generally held that the offer to contract is made by the prospective insured in filling out and submitting the application. Acceptance of the offer and formation of the contract do not become effective under the language of most life insurance policies until the policy is actually delivered to the insured and the first premium is paid. If the insurer does not accept the original application with the coverage and rate offered, a counterproposal becomes a counteroffer that the prospective insured may thereby accept or reject.

In absence of a specific policy provision or agreement to the contrary, the life insurance contract will become effective in accord with the usual contract rules of offer and acceptance. For example, if X applies to the Y insurance company for a policy of life insurance and pays the first premium on an understanding that the insurance must be approved at Y's home office, Y's notification of approval becomes effective as an acceptance when mailed without regard to whether the acceptance is actually received by X.

Insurance to Take Effect on Approval of Application. Where X applies in writing for life insurance to the Y insurance company, pays the first premium, and is given a receipt that states, "this insurance shall take effect on the date of approval of the application," subsequent approval at the home office will be considered an acceptance of X's offer even though no action is taken by Y to notify X of the approval. The parties have agreed that acceptance will occur upon approval, and actual notification to the offeror (X) is not essential to an acceptance. The offeree (Y) has performed its part of the bargain sufficiently to give rise to a binding contract when approval of the application is given.

Other Types of Coverage. Offer and acceptance of *accident and health insurance* policies are generally subject to the same rules found in life insurance agreements. It is understood by the parties that the application for coverage will require examination and approval in the home office or regional office of the insurer. There, an underwriter will consider the special risk factors involved in the employment and health history of the applicant before any final decision is made to accept; then, as in the case of most life insurance policies, the coverage becomes effective upon delivery of the policy to the insured and payment of first premium.

In *group insurance* coverages, the policy of insurance is issued to a group policyholder which may be an employer, labor union, or some other association. The agreement becomes binding when the insurer accepts the application of the group policyholder following the registration of the required number of certificateholders. It is generally provided in such agreements that the group policy will become effective on a specified date, provided a certain percentage of eligible members of the group have agreed to accept the coverage and to become certificateholders under the coverage of the policy. Once the group policy becomes effective, individual certificateholders may generally obtain coverage automatically by making application to the plan and being approved by the group policyholder. If the plan requires underwriting of individual certificateholders, then coverage must await such underwriting approval.

Air terminal insurance is frequently offered through machines that are located throughout the airport. In such cases, forms are provided by the insurance company for completion by the traveler. Such forms constitute an offer by the insurer that the prospective insured may accept by completing the form and mailing the application. This type of insurance provides still another situation in which the mailing of the acceptance by the offeree gives rise to an immediate contract even though the mailed acceptance may never be received.

Effective Date of Insurance Contracts The ability to determine the exact moment insurance contract coverage begins and ends is of crucial importance. Unless a loss can be shown to have occurred within the policy coverage period, no benefits will be payable. As previously noted, the general rules of contract law concerning the time when acceptance becomes effective are also applicable to the insurance contract. Frequently the date and time when the insurance contract is to become effective will be specified in the policy itself. The law with respect to the effective dates of insurance contracts has been both aided and complicated by the use of so-called "binders" and "conditional receipts." Binders are found most frequently in property and liability insurance. Conditional receipts are used in life insurance.

Binders in Property and Casualty Insurance. The "binding slip" or "binder receipt" is of considerable practical importance in insurance. Such "temporary binders" are intended to provide evidence of insurance and interim coverage until the actual policy is approved and is issued to the insured. They are informal written contracts that provide a memorandum of the basic coverages and terms of the insurance agreement. They meet the requirements of modern business in that they provide evidence of immediate, although temporary, protection. The binders frequently provide that coverage is being extended for a period of thirty days, pending the issuance of the actual insurance policy. They have the additional sales advantage of binding the agreement at that moment without waiting for a later delivery of the policy and for the possibility the insured may have a change of mind in the interim.

Binders have long been in use in insurance. Even though the issuance of a binder is usually conclusive evidence of a preliminary contract of insurance, the insurer may still show that the binder was delivered with the oral understanding that it was not to take effect until the happening of some later condition. For instance, the condition might be imposed that the temporary coverage was not to become effective until another insurer had agreed to assume part of the risk. Such an oral condition may be shown to defeat the coverage if not complied with. In any event, cancellation of a binder by the insurer must be made in accordance with the same prescribed methods called for in the policy itself. All the provisions of the policy are considered in force the moment the binder is issued. The binder continues in effect until actual notice of cancellation is given or until the binder is superseded by issuance of a policy.

In the property and liability insurance field, binders have uniformly been held to provide immediate coverage when issued by an authorized agent. They meet the individual and commercial requirements of immediate coverage. The actual policy coverage that is agreed upon is controlled by the language of the policy that the insurer would customarily issue in such a case.

Basic Elements Agreed Upon. While the binder is a brief document, it must contain the basic information needed to reach an agreement and indicate the types of coverage purchased in order that the events insured against can be determined. If an object is to be insured, such as an automobile, the binder should briefly describe the vehicle and indicate the name of the insured and the identity of the insurer. The amounts of coverage involved also must be reflected in order that policy limits may be established. With agreement on these basic points, the more detailed policy provisions may be determined by reference to the policy to be issued. Exhibit 2-1 reflects a typical binder receipt used to bind automobile insurance coverages.

Premium Receipts in Life Insurance. It is in the field of life insurance and accident and health insurance that most litigation has arisen concerning temporary contracts of insurance. Insurers generally attempt to phrase the premium receipt in life insurance to avoid affording immediate coverage to the applicant. Companies do not wish to be bound while they are still attempting to learn whether the applicant is in fact insurable. Again, the long periods of policy coverage, the large amounts of money often involved, and the need for highly specialized underwriting regarding health history force insurers to be cautious in binding this type of insurance, even temporarily.

Insurance companies are careful not to use language in the premium receipts given in life and accident and health insurance that

Exhibit 2-1
Binder Receipt

BINDER RECEIPT

The undersigned Company agrees to extend the following coverages as are indicated by the mark ☒ as respects the described automobile for a period of 30 days from the effective date indicated, pending the issuance of an automobile insurance policy. This extension of insurance shall be in accordance with the terms of the Company's auto insurance policies and manual of rates and classifications applicable in the state on the effective date of this agreement. This agreement may be cancelled by the Company by mailing written notice to the applicant stating when in accordance with any applicable statutes or policy terms such cancellation shall be effective.

Applicant _____

COVERAGES: | A – Comprehensive ☐ ACV less $............ded. | B – Collision ☐ ACV less $............ded. | C – Property Damage ☐ $............000

| D – Bodily Injury ☐ $............000 ea. person, $............000 ea. accident/occurrence | E – Med. Pay. ☐ $............ ea. person Less............Ded.

| F – Fam. Comp. ☐ | G – C. Fam. Liab. ☐ $............000 ea. occurrence, and Med. Pay ☐ $............ ea. person | H – ☐ UMC

Pers. Inj. Prot. ☐ Less $............Ded.   Add. or Excess Pers. Inj. Prot. ☐ $_____ | Loss of Use ☐   T & L ☐

Insurance to apply on: Automobile _____

Year _____   Trade Name _____   Identification Number _____

Receipt of $ _____ Cash ☐   Check ☐ is hereby acknowledged; Balance of $ _____ due _____

Effective date: _____, 19____ Date remittance received _____, 19____

Lienholder and Address: _____

Date Lien Expires _____   Month _____ Day _____ Year _____

_____

$_____ premium pays for Coverage ☐ A and ☐ B

_____

If marked ☒ to _____   Month _____ Day _____ Year _____

The right of any refund during the encumbrance period is hereby assigned to the Lienholder named herein ☐ Yes ☐ No

CHECKS AND DRAFTS ARE RECEIVED SUBJECT TO COLLECTION ONLY

Agent _____   Institute Insurance Company

refers to a "binder." Instead, the receipts are generally called "conditional receipts," and great effort is expended to make it clear that the receipt is not intended to provide immediate coverage. Such attempts to issue a "receipt" without admitting at the same time that a contract has been temporarily bound have met with limited success. The decided case law in this area reflects the history of a continuing struggle to create receipts that provide evidence of the agreement, but that bind the insurer *only if* the applicant is subsequently found to be in fact insurable. Trying to keep a contract in force without at the same time admitting a contract exists is a challenge that continues to confront insurance attorneys.

Major Kinds of Premium Receipts. While the binders seen in property and liability insurance have remained relatively stable in their form and content, the life insurance receipt has been seen in at least three major forms:

1. *Binding receipts,* much the same as used in property insurance, are used by a few life companies. Such receipts do provide coverage on the date of the receipt and continue such coverage until a specified time or until the company disapproves the application. The customary practice, however, is for insurers to issue some form of conditional receipt.

2. *Approval receipts* reflect the intention of the insurer not to be bound by a receipt until approval is actually given by the insurance company. Such approval is viewed as a necessary condition precedent to the existence of coverage. Where the conditional intention of such approval receipts is clearly stated, most courts have given effect to the condition and have permitted coverage to be suspended until approval is given. Other courts have taken the position that the applicant in such cases is paying for a period of coverage that is never actually received. The insurers are held to be collecting premium and at the same time attempting to give little more coverage than if no premium had been paid. Thus, courts have construed approval receipts as expressing a condition that afforded insurance coverage as of the date of the receipt but subject to later determination of insurability. Such interpretations have led to the more extensive use of still a third type of conditional receipt, the insurability type.

3. *Insurability receipts* are the most frequently used life and accident and health receipts. The typical language of such receipts stipulates that the insurance will become effective on the date of the receipt or on the date of the medical examination, provided the proposed insured is found to have been *insurable* on that date. Under such receipts, even though the insurance is not effective unless the applicant is later found to be insurable, the applicant's insurability on a

specific date can still be determined even after the applicant's death. Should the applicant die after the issuance of the receipt and it is found that he or she would have been insurable on the date of the receipt, by applying the objective underwriting standards of the company, then the coverage would exist. Following are two examples:

● *A* applies for life insurance and is given an insurability receipt dated May 1. *A* is found to be insurable by the insurer's home office but is hit by a car before the policy is actually issued. Since *A* was insurable on the date of the receipt, coverage would be afforded even though *A* was killed before the policy was issued.

● Again, *A* applies for life insurance and is given an insurability date of May 1. This time, *A* is found uninsurable by the application of the insurer's objective underwriting standards (i.e., those usually applied in such cases by this company). If *A* is killed by a car before a rejection of the application has actually been issued, there would still be no coverage. *A* did not meet the insurability standards of the company. Exhibit 2-2 is a typical example of the insurability receipt currently in use in the life and accident and health field.

Present Status of Conditional Life Receipts. The variety of conditional receipts and the complexity of their language have led some courts to view them as "instruments of confusion" that must be construed strictly against the insurer. Such courts readily find "ambiguity" in the receipt and construe such doubt against the insurer (since the documents are prepared by the insurer) by holding that the conditional receipt does provide immediate interim coverage. A majority of courts, however, give validity to the provisions of clearly drawn conditional receipts, and find no life insurance in force until the condition (i.e., determination of insurability) has been met. When insurability is determined, the effective date of the insurance will revert (or be retroactive) to the date of the receipt. If the insurability has not been determined at the time of death, the insurer is required to evaluate it later. Such evaluation must be made in good faith using the normal underwriting standards of this insurer. If the company does not make the decision or is believed to have made an incorrect decision, a judge or jury must decide what insurability finding the company should reasonably have made.

Effect of Silence or Delay The law of contracts requires that the mutual assent of both parties be unequivocally manifested either by words or by conduct. At common law, silence or delay on the part of either party was considered equivocal and therefore not a sufficient manifestation of acceptance to give rise to a contract. This rule was subject to the qualification that if a prior course of dealings had indicated silence was to be taken as acceptance, then such prior

Exhibit 2-2
Conditional First Life Premium Receipt

This receipt must not be detached unless settlement of the first full premium has been made by the Applicant at the time of application and such premium amount meets the Company's minimum Premium rules.

CONDITIONAL FIRST LIFE PREMIUM RECEIPT: NO INSURANCE WILL BECOME EFFECTIVE PRIOR TO POLICY DELIVERY UNLESS THE ACTS REQUIRED BY THIS RECEIPT ARE COMPLETED. NO AGENT OF THE COMPANY IS AUTHORIZED TO CHANGE ANY ACT REQUIRED.

No. 114514

Received from _____ this _____ day of _____, 19___,

the sum of _____ Dollars ($ _____) in connection with an

application for Life Insurance in Institute Insurance Company which application bears the same date and printed number as this receipt.

If the sum indicated above equals the first full premium on the premium payment basis selected in the application for the insurance applied for and if the following acts are completed: (a) receipt by the Company of a fully completed application and amendments thereto, if any, which includes fully completed medical examinations if required by published underwriting rules because of the age of the Proposed Insured, the amount of insurance applied for or because of the Proposed Insured's past medical history or current condition and (b) completion of all investigation by the Company and the Company is satisfied that the Proposed Insured and (without prejudice to the Proposed Insured) each person proposed for coverage under the Family Rider or the Children's Rider (whichever is applicable and if applied for) is insurable and qualified under the Company's established rules, limits and standards on the plan and for the amount applied for and at the premium specified herein, the said insurance shall take effect and be in force subject to the provisions of the policy applied for from the date of the application or the last medical examination, whichever is later, or if no medical examination is required, the insurance shall take effect on the application date. Unless all acts required are completed, no insurance shall take effect nor be in force under the application or this receipt unless and until a policy has been manually delivered to and received and accepted by the Applicant and the full first premium specified in the policy has actually been paid to and accepted by the Company during the continued insurability of the Proposed Insured and (without prejudice to the Proposed Insured) during the continued insurability of each person proposed for coverage under the Family Rider or the Children's Rider (whichever is applicable and if applied for). Insurance under the Family Rider or the Children's Rider (whichever is applicable and if applied for) shall take effect at the same time and under the same conditions as the insurance on the Proposed Insured.

In any event, the amount of insurance becoming effective under the terms of this receipt is hereby limited to the extent that in the event of the death of the Proposed Insured the total liability of the Company shall not exceed $150,000, said amount to include any life insurance then in force with the Company and any benefits payable by the Company as a result of accidental death.

If the application is declined, the amount evidenced by this receipt shall be refunded.

_____
(Agent must sign here)

NOTICE: This receipt is not valid for any premium for the insurance applied for except the first full premium thereon which in no event shall exceed one annual premium for such insurance together with the premium for interim term insurance, if any.

_____ Agent

dealings would control. For example, agent A has for years insured B's property against fire under annual policies. At the expiration of one policy and in accord with prior practice, A sends B a renewal policy and a bill for the premium. B retains the policy for two months, remaining silent, and then refuses to pay the premium on demand. B will be held liable for the premium that accrues prior to his rejection. In the example, the course of prior dealings between the parties gave the offeror (A) reason to understand that silence would constitute acceptance.

By contrast, where agent A directs a letter to B indicating, "Your fire insurance policy will be renewed for another three years unless I hear from you to the contrary," there being no prior course of dealings to indicate that acceptance by silence may be inferred, and the insured fails to reply, continued coverage will not automatically result. By simply remaining silent, no unequivocal promise has been made by B to accept the promise of A to renew. The offeror, A, cannot dispense with the basic legal requirement that mutual assent be manifested by some overt act. B's silence under these conditions is not sufficient for acceptance.

Another reason for the general rule in contract law that mere silence is not an acceptance of an offer involves the nuisance of unsolicited offers. If silence could be taken as acceptance of an offer, those who sell goods or services could flood the country with offers that recipients would be obligated to reject or otherwise be bound by a contract to buy. The law will not permit a seller to force on a prospective buyer the obligation of rejecting or returning offered goods or services. The enterprising insurance agent who mails policies to everyone in the area advising, "unless I hear from you in a week it will be assumed you agree to accept this coverage," imposes no duty to respond on those receiving such offers.

Delay in Acting on Insurance Applications. When an application is made to an insurance company for a specific coverage and the company fails to act within a reasonable time, many courts continue to adhere to the general rule that no acceptance of the application may be inferred from mere silence or delay. A majority of courts, however, now hold the insurer will be liable under its contract where it negligently delays in acting on an application within a reasonable time. In adopting this qualification in the case of insurance applications, the courts apply the rationale that insurance is a business affected with a public interest. Since the insurers will generally have solicited these offers, and since the applicants will frequently have paid premium in advance, the insurer has a duty to act promptly in accepting or rejecting the offer.

The insurer also is in a better position to spread the risk of harm from delay in acting on applications from the general public.

The duty of affirmative action on the part of the insurer when considering applications for insurance is imposed because of the special nature of the insurance business. Some courts refer to the obligation in terms of an "implied contract," while others assert that the insurance company should be estopped or prevented from claiming that the application was not accepted after the lapse of a reasonable time. Most courts, however, base recovery on the tort theory that the insurance company is guilty of negligence. The majority of courts impose a duty upon the insurer to act upon the application, either by acceptance or rejection, without unreasonable delay. If such duty is found to have been breached, and loss results to the applicant, then liability should be imposed on the negligent insurer. Recovery thus rests upon negligence rather than upon contract law.

It should be noted that a substantial minority of jurisdictions continue to apply the general contract rule that no matter how long the insurer delays, its silence will not give rise to a binding contract. An illustration of the difficult decisions that must be made in such cases may be seen in Patten v. Continental Casualty Company.[10]

- Facts: Patten made an application for a poliomyelitis policy on August 30. He paid a $10 premium, and there was dispute in the testimony as to whether the agent said, "You are insured now." The application provided that "protection becomes effective noon on the date of the policy." On September 7, which was eight days later, the applicant's two daughters and a son came down with polio. The policy was issued dated September 8, which was one day after the illness struck and nine days after the application.

- Decision: While the courts are split on this point, imposing a duty to act upon an application within a reasonable time is entirely inconsistent with elementary principles of common law in Patten's state (Ohio). The insurer was under no duty to accept the application and owes no duty to act thereon. The insurer is not liable for damages resulting from the fact that the disease was contracted before the policy became effective. If the insurer did not accept the offer within a reasonable time, then it could not have been accepted since offers lapse after reasonable time. Let not hard cases make shipwreck of the law.

Unreasonable Delay. What constitutes unreasonable delay under the majority view is a question of fact for the trier of fact, either judge or jury. Among those facts that will be considered are the distance of the home or branch office where the application is considered from the place where the application was made; whether there were any special difficulties involved in underwriting this particular risk; what the seasonal or other workload problems of the insurer were; or what type of coverage was involved.

In some states, statutes have been adopted that prescribe the reasonable time within which action must be taken on an insurance application. One of the more restrictive of such statutes is found in North Dakota, where insurers are required to act within twenty-four hours in response to applications for hail insurance. This statute was declared constitutional by the U.S. Supreme Court as not imposing an unreasonable burden on the insurer. The effect is, of course, to require phone handling of hail insurance applications, which would be an entirely untenable procedure in the case of many types of insurance, such as life coverage.

The problem of unreasonable delay can arise notwithstanding the immediate coverage afforded by binders in property and casualty insurance or by conditional receipts in life insurance. Binders in property insurance often stipulate that coverage is provided for "30 days" only. As has been seen, conditional receipts in life insurance may be so carefully drawn as to be conditional and not provide interim coverage. In either of these events, an unreasonable delay in acting on the application could result in the imposition of coverage.

The clear tendency of modern law, which insurers must live with, is to impose responsibility on the business enterprise for the carelessness or incompetence of its representatives in dealing with the public. The imposition of liability for negligent delay is a manifestation of this principle.

Incomplete Agreements Contracts of insurance may be oral or written. They may also be evidenced by a preliminary agreement in the form of a binder or conditional receipt. Even though courts will give effect to oral contracts of insurance, there are strong reasons for preferring written contracts to oral or partially complete agreements. Oral agreements present very real potential for suit. An alleged insured, either as the result of honest exaggeration or dishonest falsification, may distort the terms of oral agreements and persuade a jury to accept an incorrect version of the agreement. Lawsuits that turn upon oral agreements often come down to one person's word against another's, with the jury having the last word. The insured, too, should prefer a written contract. The insured may be unable to recall the oral conversation with sufficient surety to persuade a jury that an oral contract was actually made.

Oral Insurance Contracts. Oral contracts to write property and liability insurance are frequently entered into. As previously noted, the exigencies of modern commercial life require the ability to obtain insurance coverage "now." In life and accident and health insurance, the oral contract is not found as frequently. In the life and health fields, conditional receipts providing evidence of interim coverage represent the prevalent practice. In all oral contracts of insurance, as well as in the case of informal written contracts (i.e., binders and conditional receipts), the contract is generally put in writing in the form of the policy itself. The crucial question becomes this: what contract language is in force from the time of the original oral agreement or informal written contract, until the insurance contract is actually put in writing?

Terms of Preliminary Agreements. One needs only to read a policy of insurance to recognize that it would involve an unusually long and legalistic conversation to embody all its terms in an oral agreement. It is unlikely that anyone would have the patience to go through such a procedure. If oral insurance contracts or even informal written contracts are to be made, some procedure must be established whereby the terms and conditions of the contract can be determined. The question of which terms or elements of the contract must be specifically agreed upon and which will be implied must be resolved.

Terms Which Must Be Agreed Upon. Certain basic elements of the insurance contract must be settled upon before there can be an agreement to insure. Thus, the oral statements or informal written contract must indicate the types of coverage sought. First, what are the risks or *events insured* against? Was fire, accident, liability, or life insurance purchased? Second, what *object* or premises, if any, are to be insured? If liability insurance in connection with ownership of property is involved, what is the address of the premises involved? A reasonable identification is necessary. If reference is made only to "my residence" and the proposed insured has several residences, such identification may be fatally ambiguous and result in no coverage existing. Third, the *amount* of insurance must be agreed upon in order to establish policy limits and the liability of the insurer. Fourth, the *name of the insured* must, of course, be known, although it is not necessary that the identity of the insurer be established at the moment of the agreement. (Problems relating to identification of the insurer are considered in detail later.) It is also desirable that the parties indicate the *duration* of the coverage, although this may be implied from past usage between the parties.

Terms Which Will Be Implied. If the foregoing elements are agreed to, then the parties and the courts may turn to several other sources to establish what terms may be *implied* from the oral or informal written agreement.

PREVIOUS DEALINGS BETWEEN PARTIES. Such dealings provide the strongest basis for implying terms of an insurance contract. If an agent is requested to "renew my fire policy," all the terms of the previous policy, including the amount of coverage and amount of premium, will be assumed or implied in the renewed policy. Provisions of renewal contracts will be implied to be the same as those of an existing policy.

CUSTOMARY USAGES. The usage of an insurer affords another important source for establishing the terms not mentioned by the parties. What type of policy does a particular insurer normally issue in a given situation? What type of policy do insurers in general normally issue? The policy language and conditions set forth in the insurance contracts of this particular insurer will be the first usage source relied upon. If no provision is found relating to usage by this particular insurer, the policy will be deemed to contain the provisions of policies customarily issued for this type of coverage. The burden of proof or responsibility for establishing the existence of such customary provisions is always on the party alleging their existence. Where the parties have failed to specify the amount of premium to be charged and there have been no previous dealings between them, the court will imply the rate that has been filed by the insurer with the insurance regulatory authorities or the rate usually charged by this insurer for this type of risk. Finally, the courts will consider the insurance needs and usages of this particular insured and of those engaged in similar occupations. While such usages will have some bearing on the terms implied, practices which are peculiar to this particular insured will not normally result in provisions being implied in an insurance contract to cover such unusual needs.

STATUTORY REQUIREMENTS. In many lines of coverage, various statutory requirements and administrative regulations have prescribed the policy language that must be included. In nearly every state, the language of the New York standard fire policy of 1943, with its "165 lines" of standard policy provisions, is required to be included in all fire and homeowners policies. Where an oral contract or a binding receipt for fire insurance is involved, the basic language that will be applicable is contained in the statutory provisions. Many similar provisions involving definitions of terms, right to convert group life insurance to other types of coverage, life insurance coverage in the event of suicide, and so on, are found in the laws of various states. When it is necessary to establish the terms of oral or incomplete agreements, reference must be made to such statutory requirements.

Designation of Insurance Company. It is not uncommon for an insurance agent, who is licensed to represent two or more companies, to agree to provide coverage to a proposed insured without at the time designating the identity of the insurer. In the event of a loss prior to the time a policy has been issued, the problem of which of the companies represented by the agent will be required to cover the loss has led to many interesting cases.

Where an insurance agent has placed previous business or oral renewals for this insured with one company, there is little dispute that an agent in accepting an oral agreement on this occasion will make that same company liable as the insurer. The previous dealings between the parties would provide the basis for implying such a result. Where, however, there have been no previous dealings between the parties or where the agent had switched companies several times in making renewals, more difficult problems arise.

If the agent has made some kind of note or memorandum indicating the company that was intended to be bound, such note will be sufficient to bind that company. Some act external to the agent is required, for instance, dictation into dictating equipment will suffice as a record. A mere mental resolve on the part of the agent to place this business with "Company X tomorrow" will not be sufficient to bind Company X if the loss occurs prior to some actual notation being made. The rationale for requiring that some external record be established is to avoid the possibility of an insurer's being designated after a loss has occurred. While difficult questions of proof are obviously involved in such cases, it must appear that the agent in fact made a record designating a specific insurer prior to the loss. In absence of such a designation or prior usage between the parties, no insurer will be on the risk. In such case, the recourse of the proposed insured would be against the agent for breach of a contract to procure insurance.

In the case of Julien v. Spring Lake Park Agency, the facts were as follows:[11]

- Facts: The president of an insurance agency was requested to place builders' risk insurance on two properties owned by the applicant, one property on Quincy Street and another on VanBuren Street. The agreement was oral and the president made a cryptic note to place the coverage with Ohio Farmer's Insurance Company. An application for insurance was later submitted for coverage on the VanBuren Street property, but no coverage was requested for the Quincy Street property. A tornado

damaged the Quincy Street property before a policy was
actually issued.

● Held: The oral binder obligated the Ohio Farmer's to provide
the coverage that had been requested. While the oral
binder was sufficient to bind coverage, it must also appear
the insurance agency designated a company to assume
the coverage. Here a choice was clearly indicated by the
agent, although through inadvertence the Quincy Street
property was omitted from the actual application. The
exigencies of modern business require and justify reliance on oral agreements of insurance entered into by
agents acting within their apparent authority. Agents
have considerable latitude in granting oral binders, and
here the obvious intent was to bind Ohio Farmer's.

It is thus possible for an insured to have a policy of insurance with
a company the insured has never heard of, if the selection has been left
to the agent. There must, however, be a selection of a company prior to
the occurrence of a loss. If that selection is not manifested in some
external way (such as by note, memorandum, or dictation on transcrib-
ing equipment), then the loss will likely be borne by the agent charged
with the responsibility of obtaining the coverage. If an insurer has in
fact been designated, then the agent will no longer be liable even
though the insurer received no notification of the insurance. In such an
event, there may be a violation of the agent's duty to the insurer in
disregarding instructions, but the responsibility to the insured remains
the same.

Failure to Read the Policy in Incomplete Agreements. It is a
generally accepted rule of contract law that a party to a contract is
charged with knowledge of that contract's provisions. In the ordinary
contract, a person will be bound by the written contract terms whether
the terms were read and understood or not. While this rule has not been
completely disregarded in the case of insurance contracts, the courts
have demonstrated a reluctance to hold insureds responsible for
knowing, or having read, the insurance policies to which they are a
party. As noted in Chapter 1, to impose upon insureds the obligation to
read and understand their policies is not in keeping with the realities of
what occurs in the commercial market place.

While the customary duties concerning knowledge of the contents
of one's contract do not fully apply to the insurance agreement, it
should be noted that all duties are not removed in this area. The insured
is still bound by the terms of the insurance contract. In order for some
other obligation to exist, special circumstances involving mistake,

misrepresentation, fraud, and so on must be shown. While these matters will be considered later, it should be noted that in the case of oral and incomplete agreements the courts have demonstrated a greater willingness to impose duties on the insured to review the policy coverages actually received. In the Julien v. Spring Lake Park Agency case mentioned earlier, a strong argument could have been made to defeat the coverage on the Quincy Street property if the policy had actually been issued to the insured without any reference to that property. While the requirements of modern business do involve the necessity of reliance on oral agreements, the insured would have received notice that the oral agreement (to insure the Quincy Street property) had not in fact been implemented, and a much better argument for nonliability of the company could have been made. Had the insured simply filed the policy among his papers without reading it and noting the lack of coverage for one of the properties, it is possible, although by no means certain, that recourse would have had to be against the agent who omitted the coverage rather than against the insurer who issued the policy.

Delivery of Insurance Policies In general contract law there is no requirement that the contract be delivered in order to be enforceable. Delivery involves the intention of the parties that the contract shall not become effective until the subject matter of the agreement has been delivered. In most bilateral contracts involving the exchange of promises, delivery is not essential to completion of the agreement. In many unilateral contracts, involving the performance of an act on the part of the offeree, delivery of goods or services may be required as acceptance.

In the case of insurance contracts, there is no common law or statutory requirement that an insurance policy be delivered prior to the formation of a contract of insurance. Still, in cases where there is no oral agreement, binder, or other written memorandum, the insurer will not usually be bound by the contract until the policy has been delivered and the first premium has been paid. Delivery provides evidence of the making of the contract and communication of the insurer's acceptance of the insured's offer. The insurance policy becomes binding only when it has been delivered and all conditions precedent mentioned in the offer and acceptance have been met.

In property and liability insurance, the requirement of delivery is rarely in dispute. The wide use of preliminary oral agreements and written binders gives rise to effective dates of policy coverage that seldom involve the question of policy delivery. It is in the field of life insurance that the issue of policy "delivery" has been the subject of much litigation. It is customary in life insurance applications, as well as in some life policies, to provide that coverage will not become effective until the policy has been delivered and the first premium has been paid.

The life policy preconditions of delivery and payment of premium are intended to make it clear that no coverage exists until the policy is actually delivered to the insured. Delivery of the policy of life insurance is generally taken as clear evidence of the insurer's intent to be bound. Notwithstanding the life application requirement of delivery, courts have been most liberal in their interpretation of what constitutes delivery. It is generally found that delivery refers to the mental attitude of the insurer and not to the physical instrument itself. A "constructive delivery" is held to be valid, even in absence of actual physical delivery of the policy. When it comes to delivery, courts will consider the substance rather than the form of what is being done.

For example, Y insurance company mails a life insurance policy to its agent A with a letter stating, "This policy is to be effective when you physically deliver it to X." Y also writes a letter to the applicant, X, stating, "Your policy has been mailed to A, and this policy will become effective when A physically hands the policy to you." After the letters and policy are mailed, but before they are received, X is killed in an accident. Under these circumstances, X's beneficiary will be permitted to recover notwithstanding the expression of intention that actual physical delivery will be required. Where no other decision or act remains to be performed other than the mere physical handing-over of the policy, courts consider that a constructive delivery has been made. The mere failure to physically deliver the policy will not preclude the formation of the insurance contract.

On the other hand, where delivery is required under the life insurance policy, it can be shown that the delivery was made subject to a condition. If Y insurance company mails a life insurance policy to X accompanied by a letter stating, "this policy will become effective when you pay $100 to agent A," and X is killed in an accident *after* receipt of the letter and policy, but *before* paying the $100 to A, Y will not be liable under the policy. Delivery was made subject to a condition, and that condition was not met. Delivery involves a question of fact wholly outside the policy itself, and evidence may be introduced to show the policy was placed in X's possession subject to the condition that the premium be paid.

Conditional Receipts and Delivery. Although conditional receipts in life insurance may be found to provide interim coverage, the significance of the requirement of delivery still continues. If delivery is actually made, courts tend to view this as communication of the insurer's acceptance of the insured's application. If the conditional receipt gives the insurer the right to refuse to deliver a permanent policy, the actual delivery or declination of delivery will bear decisively on the question of whether the policy became effective.

The clauses relating to delivery of life insurance policies, inserted in both policies and applications for life insurance, are thus valid and enforceable. The increased use of conditional receipts has to some extent lessened the significance of delivery, and some courts have applied the concept of "constructive delivery" broadly enough to further impair the effectiveness of the requirement. Still, the requirement continues in most life policies and remains the subject of litigation in cases in which death occurs prior to actual delivery of the policy.

Payment of the First Premium. As in the case of policy delivery, the parties to an insurance contract may stipulate that the policy will not become effective until the first premium has been paid. In the absence of an express agreement, it is generally understood that payment of the first premium is not necessary to the validity of an oral preliminary contract, but that payment will be made upon delivery of the policy. As will be discussed in Chapter 3 under contract consideration, even in the absence of an express promise to pay a premium, an implied promise to pay a reasonable premium will be sufficient consideration to support an insurance contract. If, however, it is expressly provided that no contract shall arise until the first premium has been paid, then no contract will be complete until such prepayment has been made.

Chapter Notes

1. Restatement, Contracts 2nd, Section 1, American Law Institute Publishers, 1973.
2. Uniform Commercial Code, Section 2-203.
3. Uniform Commercial Code, Section 2-204(3) and Section 2-305.
4. Uniform Commercial Code, Section 2-205.
5. Uniform Commercial Code, Section 2-207(1).
6. Uniform Commercial Code, Section 2-206(1)(a).
7. Uniform Commercial Code, Section 2-208.
8. Federal Postal Reorganization Act, Section 3009.
9. Restatement, Contracts, Section 39.
10. 120 NE 2nd 411 (1954).
11. 166 NW 2nd 355 (1966).

CHAPTER 3

Making of the Contract

CAPACITY TO CONTRACT

General

An essential element of an enforceable contract is the requirement that the parties involved have legal capacity to contract. Persons who have capacity to contract are known as *competent parties*, and contracts made by them may be enforced against them. Contracts made by persons lacking such competency (*incompetents*) generally may be avoided by the incompetent parties.

Incompetency to contract, or legal incapacity, may result if one or both parties are:

1. underage,
2. insane,
3. under the influence of alcohol or drugs, or
4. artificial entities (such as corporations which may lack capacity to enter certain contracts).

The law favors the protection of incompetents who are often unable to protect themselves from exploitation, and as such are given the opportunity to disaffirm contracts entered into while incompetent. At the same time, the law has an interest in enforcing the justifiable expectations of parties and in the security of transactions in general.

Minor's Contracts

Definition of Minor At common law, any person under the age of twenty-one was considered a minor, or infant. Since the courts do not like to deal in fractions of a day, minority was held to end at the first moment of the *day before* the minor's twenty-first birthday. A few states provided by statute for a lower age, particularly for women. The fact that the minor may have become emancipated (that is, entitled to keep one's earnings) by leaving home, marrying, or being orphaned did not affect the minor's capacity to contract, and no such capacity existed until the age of majority was reached. The contracts of minors were not void, but rather were voidable at the option of the minor. An adult dealt with the minor at his or her peril since the minor could enforce the agreement against the adult—the right of avoidance rested *only* with the minor.

After the adoption of the Twenty-sixth Amendment to the U.S. Constitution, which lowered the voting age in federal elections to age eighteen, most states proceeded to enact statutes lowering the age of majority to eighteen. A few states lowered the age to nineteen and one (Delaware) lowered the age of majority to twenty. These enactments lowered the age of capacity to contract to the new age of majority. In many states some limitations were retained regarding the age of majority for purchasing alcoholic beverages, holding public office, becoming a law enforcement officer, tort and criminal liability, and similar matters. It thus is necessary to consult the statutory law of each state to determine the age of majority for contracts. The rule that minority actually ends on the day before the minor reaches the legal age of majority is still in force.

Avoidance of Contracts by Minors   The law protecting minors from the immature disposition of their property reflects public policy. As a general rule, a minor may always assert minority as a defense against liability in contracts that do not involve the purchase of necessities, and no consideration is given to whether the contract was beneficial to the minor, as was the case at early common law. The minor still retains the right to avoid a contract for nonnecessities at any time during minority or within a reasonable time after reaching majority.

The minor may avoid the contract by any expression of intention to repudiate the agreement. No particular form of disaffirmance is required, and any act inconsistent with the contract will constitute avoidance. Thus, if a minor enters into a contract to convey property but conveys the property to another immediately after reaching the age of majority, such conveyance is considered an avoidance of the minor's original agreement. In the event the minor elects to avoid the contract, the entire contract must be repudiated. The minor may not affirm some parts and seek to avoid others.

It should be noted that if a parent or adult joins in the contract of a minor, such adult will be required to perform the contract even though the minor can and does avoid the contract. An adult may not assert the minor's incapacity, unless acting on behalf of a deceased minor as administrator of the minor's estate or in a similar capacity.

Time for Avoidance. A minor may avoid a contract at any time during minority or within a reasonable time after reaching the age of majority. The trier of fact must, in each case, determine what constitutes "reasonable time." If a minor has not avoided the contract within a reasonable time after coming of age, most courts hold that the minor has ratified the contract by failure to avoid. While a minor may avoid a contract during minority, a contract may not be ratified by a minor during minority.

In general, courts limit the right of minors to avoid contracts for the sale of their real estate until the minor reaches legal majority. In order to protect a minor's interests, some courts give the minor the right to repossess the real estate until reaching the age of majority, but the minor may not disaffirm until that event occurs. If the adult purchaser remains in possession of the real estate, the minor on disaffirmance at majority is entitled to the rents and profits for the period the adult was in possession.

In a number of jurisdictions, the courts will consider whether the contract is executory or executed in determining the right of avoidance after reaching majority. In such states, the courts hold that *executed* contracts (i.e., those that have been fully performed by both parties) will be binding on the minor unless actually disaffirmed after reaching majority. *Executory* contracts (i.e., those that have not been fully performed by both parties) will not be binding unless actually ratified by conduct of the minor after reaching majority. Executed contracts are valid until rescinded, and executory contracts are invalid unless ratified. In any case, the courts attempt to avoid construing the law in a way which would allow the exploitation of a minor.

Minor's Duty to Make Restitution. Most courts require a minor to return any goods obtained before a contract can be avoided. The reason for this rule is variously stated as, "One who seeks equity must do equity," or, "A minor may use minority as a shield, but not as a sword." A minor may not disaffirm the contract and at the same time retain the benefits received under the contract. If the minor has the consideration (or some form of it) received, such consideration must be returned upon disaffirming the contract. Thus, if a minor has purchased a car and later traded the car for something else, the minor is bound to return whatever consideration is available upon disaffirming the contract.

The minor is required to make only that restitution which can be made. In those cases in which the minor has spent or damaged the consideration received under the contract, most states will permit the minor to avoid the contract, notwithstanding the inability to make full restitution. If the minor purchases an automobile and demolishes it, most courts will permit the minor to disaffirm the contract by returning the wreckage. A full refund of the purchase price may thus be obtained upon disaffirmance. Courts in some jurisdictions consider this rule too harsh and require that some allowance for the depreciated value of the property returned be made before disaffirmance will be permitted. In the case of the demolished car, for instance, such courts would order the return only of its salvage value. A majority of courts continue, however, to assert that "one deals with a minor at his or her peril," and these courts permit the minor to avoid the contract and return whatever remains of the money or other consideration the minor received. The minor is thus required to make restitution only to the extent the contract consideration, or its substitute, remains in the minor's possession.

Minor's Misrepresentation of Age. Misrepresentation of age by a minor in order to induce the other party to enter into a contract will not, in most states, prevent the minor from avoiding the contract on the grounds of minority. The other party to such a contract, however, can avoid it on the grounds of misrepresentation.

If the minor elects to avoid the contract, some courts will permit recovery of the full purchase price of the article purchased by the minor, but other courts will deduct depreciation and damage to the article from the price paid, and award the minor only the value of the returned item. The other party will not be permitted to collect damages under the contract since to permit such recovery would be to permit indirect enforcement of the contract against the minor.

Contracts for Necessaries. The law recognizes that certain transactions are clearly for the benefit of the minor and, thus, should be binding on the minor. The term *necessaries* is used to describe the subject matter of such contracts, and includes anything related to the health, education, and comfort of a minor. Courts uniformly hold that a minor is liable for the reasonable value of necessaries. Liability is based not upon the actual contract, but upon a quasi-contract requiring payment of the reasonable value of necessaries rather than the agreed contract price of the goods or services supplied the minor. The minor may avoid payment of the actual contract price but will still be liable for the reasonable value of the necessaries supplied.

The reason for this special rule of law relating to necessaries is to assure that minors will not be deprived of the necessities of life because others refuse to deal with them. Public policy favors the protection of minors. If the rules of law relating to dealing with a minor "at one's peril" were applied strictly to include necessaries, then such items might not be as readily available to minors.

Necessaries include anything befitting the mind and body of a minor in that minor's station of life. Thus, this is one area in which the law is not entirely democratic. What constitutes a "necessary" for a child in a relatively wealthy family might not be construed as necessary for a child of an underprivileged family. The question of whether a particular item is a necessary is a question for the trier of fact.

If a minor is residing with parents who are willing and able to supply the necessities of life, he or she will not be personally liable for necessaries. If, however, the parents have refused or are unable to supply such necessaries, the minor will be liable for the reasonable value of necessaries supplied. Thus, in a case in which a wealthy minor bought clothing on credit that he or she in turn sold, no collection could be made from the minor since such items were not necessaries.

The question whether an automobile is a necessary is more and more answered affirmatively. The classic and still majority view is that an automobile is not a necessary. However, the increasing use of the automobile and the fact that in many areas public transportation is not available to get to school or to work, have induced a number of courts to permit the question to be answered as a question of fact in each case as it comes up.

The concept of "necessaries" is not usually extended to items used for business purposes. Generally, the thing supplied must relate to the person of the minor and not to the minor's estate. Similarly, a minor has been held not liable under contracts of fire and life insurance. Those courts that have considered the matter have held that contracts of insurance do not involve contracts for "necessaries."

While a minor is liable for the reasonable value of necessaries actually furnished, there is no liability for the value of necessaries not actually received. If a minor bought and received a suit of clothes, the minor would be obliged to pay the reasonable value of such clothing if the parents were unwilling or unable to provide the needed suit. If, however, the contract were executory and the seller had simply agreed to make a suit for the minor, then such executory agreement would not be enforceable against the minor or the minor's estate. A contract to deliver or to make necessaries may be avoided by a minor. Only when the necessaries have been provided to the minor does an obligation to pay the reasonable value thereof arise.

Where money is loaned to a minor to permit the purchase of necessaries, most courts would permit the enforcement of the lending agreement against the minor. Some courts have held that this is true even though the minor elected to squander the money on something other than necessaries. The purpose of the view is again to encourage people to make available to minors the necessities of life or the means to purchase such necessities without fear that such obligation will later prove unenforceable. Note carefully, however, that if a loan to a minor is *not* for the purchase of necessaries, even though it may be used in that manner, the loan contract may be avoided just as any minor's contract not involving necessaries.

Other Contracts Which Minors Cannot Avoid. In addition to contracts involving necessaries, the law recognizes several other situations in which the minor may not avoid contractual obligations. Thus, if the minor has married, has enlisted in the armed services, has assumed the obligation of a bail bond, or has the duty of child support, there are felt to be overriding public policy considerations that require the minor to be bound by such commitments. Similarly, where a court has approved a contract for the performance of services by a child, such as a child actor, such a contract may then be enforced against the minor.

In some jurisdictions, special statutes provide that if minors are actively engaged in business pursuits, they should be held to contracts which involve the conduct of those pursuits. Likewise, statutes in some states impose normal liability on minors in matters involving stock transfers, handling of bank accounts, and obtaining loans for higher education. In absence of some overriding public policy or the existence of special statutes, however, the rule remains that a minor may avoid any contract not involving necessaries.

Liability of Parents for Minor's Contracts. A parent is generally not liable for the contracts of a minor child. To hold otherwise would be to permit indirect enforcement of a minor's (perhaps improvident) agreement. Thus, where a minor contracts to purchase a boat and a parent does not become a party to the agreement by signing or otherwise promising to assume the obligation, then no liability will rest with the parent upon the minor's default.

There are situations in which the law will impose liability on a parent for the contracts of a minor child. For example, if the child acted as an agent for the parent in the transaction, then liability will be imposed on the parent as a principal under the normal rules of agency. (Agency law is discussed in detail in Chapters 6 and 7.) Similarly, if a parent has neglected or refused to pay for necessaries for a child, then most jurisdictions will permit a contract for necessaries actually supplied to be enforced against the neglectful parent. In such cases, the party dealing with the minor has the option of proceeding for the reasonable value of the necessaries against the minor or against the parent. Finally, in those cases in which the parent has acted as a cosigner for the minor's contract, the parent will be personally liable in the event of default by the child. This liability is the same as that imposed on any cosigner who assumes liability for default of another.

Rights of Third Parties. An adult dealing with an infant obtains only a voidable title to goods. If the infant elects to disaffirm the contract, the adult must surrender the goods to the infant. Special problems arise when the adult has sold the goods to a third party who purchased the goods in good faith without any knowledge of the minor's prior ownership or interest. At common law, the minor's rights would prevail, even against an innocent third party, and a minor could repossess goods in possession of a third party.

Under the Uniform Commercial Code (UCC), which applies to the sale of goods, a person with a voidable title, such as a party dealing with a minor, has the power to transfer a good title to a good-faith purchaser for value.[1] Thus, a person who purchases goods in good faith which were in turn purchased from a minor is immune from a minor's later decision to reclaim the title to those goods. It should be noted, however, that the UCC covers only personal property and therefore the common law rule is still applicable to real property. The minor may reclaim real property upon disaffirmance of a contract, even though such property has been transferred to a third person.

Contracts of Insane Persons

Insanity Defined In regard to contractual liability, two classes of insane persons are recognized by the law. Some people have been "adjudicated insane" by being declared insane by a court of law. An agreement entered into by such persons is completely void; the act of a person who has been adjudicated insane is without any legal effect.

The more troublesome problems involve persons who have not been adjudicated insane, but who attempt to avoid liability under their contracts on the ground that they were actually insane or mentally incompetent at the time the contract was entered into. The contracts of such people, not having been adjudicated insane, are considered voidable, although such contracts do remain in full force and effect until actually avoided by the insane party. The other party to the agreement has no right of avoidance.

In order that such insanity will permit avoidance of a contract, it must be shown that the person was so mentally deranged that:

1. the person did not know a contract was being made, or
2. the person did not understand the legal consequences of what was being done.

The incapacity might result from insanity, from idiocy, from senility, or any other mental defect. Mere mental weakness, whatever the cause, is not sufficient to permit avoidance of the contract unless one of the above two tests are met. The fact that a party suffers from delusions, has insane intervals, or is eccentric will not affect the contract in absence of one of these two conditions. It is not necessary to show that a person is permanently insane; it is sufficient if the individual was insane at the time the contract was entered into. Contracts made by mentally ill persons during lucid intervals would be binding.

The fact that a person is confined to or being treated in a mental institution does not mean that the person is incompetent to contract. In absence of an adjudiction of insanity by a court or of a finding that the person did not know a contract was being made or did not understand the legal consequences of what was being done, the contract of an individual will be enforceable notwithstanding confinement for treatment of mental or emotional illness. The burden of proving that a person is insane or otherwise incompetent is upon the party asserting such incompetency.

Avoidance of Insane Persons' Contracts As in the case of minors' contracts, the power of avoidance or ratification of contracts is reserved only to the incompetent or insane party. If a guardian has been appointed for the insane party, then such guardian may avoid the agreement. At the time the insane party regains competency and the disability has been removed, then the contract may be affirmed by the previously disabled individual. In most jurisdictions, however, if the insane party or his or her guardian elects to avoid the contract, full restitution must be made provided the other party acted in good faith and was unaware of the insanity. In a minority of jurisdictions, the insane person does not need to return the consideration if unable to do so even if the contract was made in good faith in ignorance of the insanity.

Insane Persons' Contracts for Necessaries. Contracts for necessaries result in the same quasi-contractual liability applicable to minors. Thus, the insane person must pay the reasonable value of necessaries received. Neccessary goods and services for minors are the same as those for insane persons. The station in life of the individual is considered, and the need for nursing and medical attention would be considered necessities. Legal services needed to procure release from custody would also be considered necessary, as would be money advanced to obtain necessities. In addition, necessaries provided to the incompetent's spouse and family are included in the obligations binding on the insane person's estate. The concept of "necessaries" is extended to include items needed for preservation of the insane person's estate, rather than being limited (as in the case of minors) to things that relate to the personal maintenance of the individual. Thus, repairs to the insane person's home would be included in the category of necessaries. The public policy favoring such insane persons thereby recognizes that their protection involves protection of their families and personal estates as well. Exploitation of such individuals and their families is not permitted by law.

Beneficial Contracts and Knowledge of Insanity. Most courts hold that if the agreement entered into is found to have been beneficial to the insane individual, and if the other party to the contract acted in ignorance of the infirmity, then the contract may still be enforced against the insane party, and if the contract has been performed the insane party may not disaffirm it.

If, however, one knows, or reasonably should know, of the insanity of the other party to a contract, the insane party will not be held liable if the contract is executory, and may disaffirm without making full restitution of the consideration received upon offering to return what is left from an executed bargain, if anything.

Therefore, the sane party to such a contract can either enforce it or successfully resist disaffirmance by showing *both* a lack of knowledge of the insanity of the other party and that the bargain was beneficial to the other party.

Contracts of Intoxicated Persons

Intoxication Defined As a general rule, the fact that a person was intoxicated at the time of entering a contract will not permit avoidance of that contract. The rationale for this rule is that the courts do not wish to protect persons from their own follies. If an individual was so foolish as to become drunk and thereby permit his or her judgment to become impaired, the consequences must normally be suffered. While most cases continue to express some degree of moral indignation, several qualifications to this doctrine have developed.

If the person can be shown to have been so under the influence of intoxicants or narcotics as not to understand the consequences of what was being done or that a contract was being made, then the contract may be avoided. Thus, the same tests applied to the determination of insanity are generally applied to determine whether a contract entered under the influence of liquor or drugs may be avoided. The test is a severe one. Unless that degree of disability can be shown by the person alleging such disability, the contract will be enforced even though the party may have been acting under the influence of alcohol.

Other Qualifications. If it is shown that one party to a contract purposely caused the other party to become drunk in order to obtain a contract advantage, then the innocent party will be permitted to avoid the contract. Likewise, under the law of most states, persons may be adjudicated habitual drunkards, just as they may be adjudicated insane. If such adjudication is made, it becomes a matter of public record and contracts subsequently made by such persons are completely void and of no effect. In any other case, the other party to the transaction must know, or have reason to know, that the person being dealt with is intoxicated or under the influence of drugs. For example, X, while in a state of extreme intoxication or while greatly influenced by drugs, signs and mails a written offer to Y, who has no reason to know of the intoxication or drug influence and who thereby accepts the offer. X will have no right to avoid the transaction under these circumstances.

Avoidance of Intoxicated Person's Contract A person who was intoxicated or under the influence of drugs when the contract was entered into, and whose mental impairment was sufficient to meet the tests just discussed, may either avoid or ratify the contract upon becoming sober. The right of avoidance exists only for the party so intoxicated. Once the contract is later ratified or avoided, such an act cannot then be retracted. Upon avoidance, the party avoiding must return the consideration received, although if the consideration was wasted prior to becoming sober, this would probably not be required. A drunken person will be liable on contracts for necessaries, just as in any other case involving incompetency.

Contracts of Corporations

Corporations, as artificial creations of the state, are persons in the eyes of the law. Therefore, they can hold property, sue and be sued, commit crimes and torts, and enter into contracts. The extent of their competency to enter into contracts depends upon the scope of the power granted to the corporations by their charters.

At one time all charters contained some limitation on the powers of corporations. With the rise of modern diversified business, that rule became anachronistic. Consequently an increasing number of states permit a corporation to be incorporated without restriction, enabling it to engage in any lawful business. Corporations, consequently, which are expressly incorporated to engage in "any lawful business," are not restricted in the types of contracts they may make. Not among these, of course, are specially licensed and controlled businesses such as insurance, banking, and transportation.

Under the older rule, however, an attempted contract that is not within the powers of a corporation is said to be *ultra vires*, that is, literally, beyond its power. Under the strict form of that doctrine a corporate contract beyond the scope of its charter authority is voidable by either the corporation or the other party if it is fully executory (still unperformed by both parties). In general, if either party has performed its part of the bargain, the other party must perform. If the contract is fully executed, neither party will be able to avoid the agreement even though an *ultra vires* act was involved.

At least half the states have adopted statutes which provide that the defense of *ultra vires* can no longer be used. In such states the significance of the doctrine is merely that stockholders of a corporation may sue, on behalf of the corporation, the officers or directors who authorized an *ultra vires* agreement if there is a loss, and may petition a court for an injunction against the officers and directors to stop the practice in the future.

Capacity to Enter into Insurance Contracts

Capacity of Insurers At common law, either a corporation, an association, or a natural person could be an insurer. In modern times, due to statutory requirements, corporations have been the principal conductors of the insurance business. As a legal entity, the life of a corporation extends beyond that of its owners or management. Such continued existence is considered necessary to the protection of the long-range security interests frequently involved in insurance.

Insurance companies obtain their legal capacity and authority to do business from the state in which they are incorporated, but also they must normally be licensed to conduct business in each state in which they operate. The financial requirements to become incorporated to engage in the insurance business, as well as the requirements to become licensed to write insurance in states other than the state of incorporation, are closely controlled by statute and regulatory authorities in each state. Conditions on the right to conduct the business of insurance, on the types of contracts that may be entered into, and on the nature of the language in such agreements, are imposed and controlled in the public interest. A state may refuse to grant a license or may withdraw it if all legal requirements are not met.

The statutory law and state insurance department regulatory requirements of each state must be considered in determining the qualifications necessary to engage in the business of insurance. Such laws and regulations similarly affect the nature and scope of insurance contracts. Insurance policy (contract) language must normally be approved by the regulatory authorities before such contract can be entered in a given state.

As with the contracts of any corporation, an insurance contract that exceeds or is different from the authority granted the insurer may still be enforced against the insurer. Action may be taken by the regulatory authorities to revoke the insurer's license, and the other party may proceed to enforce the contract as written. The insurer will not be permitted to set up its own wrongdoing as a defense to an action on the contract.

Contracts of Nonadmitted Insurers. The contracts of insurers that have not been licensed to do business in a state are nonetheless enforceable against such insurers. For example, if insurance Company X is duly licensed to write health insurance in State A and also solicits applications by mail from residents of State B, the contracts entered into may be enforced in either state. Such contracts must also conform to the law of the state in which they are issued. While recourse may be had to the courts, some difficulty is presented for regulatory authorities in states in which the nonadmitted insurer is doing business. Such regulatory agencies make every attempt to enforce such agreements and will communicate with regulatory authorities in the insurer's state of domicile (i.e., state in which the insurance company was incorporated) in order to achieve compliance with state law.

Capacity of Insurance Agents   The capacity of an individual to act as an insurance agent is controlled by state statute and administrative regulation. Each state administers tests to prospective insurance agents before issuing licenses in order to assure a certain degree of competency. When issued, such licenses grant the recipient the privilege of writing a particular type of insurance for a designated company. However, one agent may be licensed to write business for more than one company.

As the result of the licensing requirements for insurance agents, few cases have arisen concerning the legal competency of agents. As will be seen in greater detail in the discussion of agency in Chapters 6 and 7, the legal capacity of the principal to contract is more important than that of the agent; the agent merely acts on behalf of the principal. Since the act of the agent is considered to be the act of the principal, it is not necessary that the agent have contractual capacity. Thus, a contract completed by an agent who is a minor or who is incompetent because of mental disability cannot be avoided at a later date by a principal so long as the incompetent has the ability to carry out instructions. It is the responsibility of the principal (insurer) not to place an incompetent in the position of representing the company.

Capacity of Insureds   While the capacity of insureds to enter into insurance contracts has seldom become a legal issue, the facts of such cases are subject to the same general rules of law which apply to contracts. Unless the insured is shown to have been incompetent by reason of insanity, under age, or intoxication, insurance contracts may not be avoided by reason of incapacity. Thus, if the insured was so insane at the time of making the agreement that he or she did not know a contract was being made, such contract would then be voidable at the election of the insured. There are few such cases since the insured, or a legal representative of the insured, may always avoid a contract of insurance by the simple expedient of ceasing to pay insurance premiums. The contract is then canceled by the insurer, with some adjustment being made in the case of life insurance for payment of any existing cash values due under the policy. In any insurance contract, the insured is at liberty to terminate the agreement by ceasing to pay premium, or by cancellation.

In a number of jurisdictions, persons as young as fifteen years of age may obtain policies of life insurance on themselves. The possible right of a minor to seek to avoid life insurance contract and to obtain a refund of all premiums paid during minority would thus be precluded in such states for the period after fifteen years of age. In the few cases that have arisen concerning the capacity of insureds, those who were judged incompetent for any reason generally could obtain return of the full amount of paid premium when the insurance contract was avoided for reasons of incompetency.

CONSIDERATION

General

A third major requisite of an enforceable contract, in addition to an agreement (offer and acceptance) and competent parties, is the element of *consideration*. Most contracts involve agreements in which one party is saying to another, in effect, "If you will do this for me, I will do that for you." The thing that one person asks another to do in return for the promise is that person's consideration. The consideration necessary to make a promise enforceable may consist of (1) a return promise, (2) an act performed, or (3) a forbearance to act on the part of the promisee.

Consideration is what the promisor demands and receives as the price for his or her promise; it is the "bargained-for exchange." To constitute consideration, a performance, a forbearance, or a return promise is bargained-for if it is sought by the promisor in exchange for his or her promise and is given by the promisee in exchange for that promise.[2] A promise is binding on a person only when consideration has been received in return for the promise.

The fact that a promise was made does not mean that a contract was made. A promise to make a gift or a promise to do something without receiving consideration is not enforceable. The statement, "I'm going to give you this ring" simply involves a promise to make a gift and is not binding on the promisor. Once a gift has been made of the ring, however, such an executed gift or completed performance cannot be rescinded for lack of consideration. Consideration is needed only to make a promise legally enforceable. Lack of it will not afford a basis for avoiding promises already performed.

Types of Consideration

Valuable Consideration   The consideration needed to support a valid contract is referred to as a *valuable* consideration. The law draws a distinction between a "good" consideration and a valuable consideration, and holds that the former is not valid and sufficient to support a contract. For example, a parent signs a writing in which it states, "For and in consideration of the love and affection I have for my son, I will convey my property Whiteacre to him on November 1, 1981." Such expression of love and affection involves "good" consideration, but not a valuable consideration of the type which will give rise to an enforceable promise. Good consideration is only a reason for making a promise, and the other party has not responded to any request by the promisor since no request was made. Note that if the property were actually conveyed by the parent to the son, then the transaction would be completely executed and would not be subject to attack for lack of consideration. "Good" consideration is said, therefore, to be sufficient to support an executed gift. The transaction is unenforceable for lack of consideration, however, if it has not been performed.

Gratuitous promises made for whatever reason are not binding. While love and affection form the basis for many such promises, the promisor may be motivated merely by a desire to obtain the friendship or good will of the promisee. Whatever the motivation for a promise, unless the promisor receives valuable consideration there will not be a binding contract.

Forbearance   Giving up or promising to give up a right to do what one is legally entitled to do (forbearance) may constitute consideration. Forbearance is commonly the consideration in cases of compromise. For example, if a person has been injured in an automobile accident a right to sue for damages may arise. A promise to refrain from bringing suit in return for the promise of the other party to pay a specified sum of money will constitute valuable consideration for the promise to pay. If, however, the particular claim involved had no basis either in fact or in law, then a promise to forbear in bringing such a suit would not involve valid consideration. Under such circumstances, a suit brought upon the claim would be solely for the purpose of vexation and harassment, and forbearance to institute such an action would be ineffective as consideration. One has no right to bring a baseless suit, and therefore a promise not to bring a baseless suit is not surrendering a right.

A forbearance may constitute valuable consideration even though the act requested may be for the good of the party being asked to make the promise. The consideration will still be valid if that party has given up some right of action. Thus, it was held a century ago that forbearance to exercise the right to smoke or drink constituted sufficient forbearance to exercise legal rights (legal detriment) to support the promise to pay the money, if someone had promised to pay a sixteen year old the sum of $1,000 if he or she refrained from smoking or drinking until reaching age twenty-one. Similarly, an agreement by the seller of a business not to compete with the person who has bought the business would involve forbearance. Mutual promises to forbear are sufficient consideration to support each other.

Present Versus Past Consideration In order to constitute valuable consideration, the act or promise must involve a present or future commitment. Past consideration is not valid consideration. Thus, if a person cuts another's lawn or paints another's house without the knowledge of the property owner, a subsequent promise of the owner to pay for such work is not enforceable. The actions of cutting the lawn or painting the house did not meet the requirement of being what the promisor (owner) demanded as the price for his promise. No demand for the performance was made, and such performance cannot later become the bargained-for exchange. Similarly, if one finds a wallet or watch and returns if to the rightful owner who then promises to pay a reward, the consideration for the owner's promise (the return of the lost item) represents a past consideration and is not sufficient to support the promise to pay a reward. The promise of the reward made after the return cannot be enforced.

Exceptions to the rule concerning past consideration have been created by statute and court ruling in many states. If a person promises to pay a debt that has been unenforceable because of (1) the minority status of one of the parties, (2) bankruptcy, or (3) because the statute of limitations has run out, most jurisdictions hold the renewal promise to pay such obligations binding. The new promise to pay the obligation that has been barred is not supported by any new consideration. Still, no new consideration is necessary and the new promise is a waiver of the bar to suit that existed. Some courts state that the new promise in such cases couples itself to the preexisting debt and is, therefore, founded on valuable consideration. Other courts find such renewal promises enforceable on the ground that there is a preexisting moral obligation sufficient to support the new promise.

To illustrate, X, a sixteen year old, promises to pay Y \$200 for a car; as the promise was made by a minor, it was not enforceable. Upon reaching the age of majority (eighteen in most states), and having paid none of the purchase price, X promises to pay \$100 for the vehicle. Although X could have disaffirmed the contract entirely and owed no duty of performance, the renewal promise to pay \$100 would be enforceable. Y could not, however, collect the price agreed upon initially.

A promise to pay a debt that has been barred by the statute of limitations (i.e., failure to bring the action within the period prescribed by law) or by bankruptcy is also enforceable without any additional consideration. The promise to pay must be clearly expressed, and some states require that such renewal promises be expressed in writing. A mere acknowledgment of the debt or part payment thereof, without an actual promise to pay all or part of the preexisting obligation, is not sufficient to give rise to a binding renewal promise to pay.

Promise Must Be Binding To constitute valid consideration, the promise made must give rise to a binding obligation; illusory promises do not create such obligations. Thus, the promise of one party to, "make certain payments to you for such work as I request you to do" creates the illusion that a promise has been made when, in fact, no binding obligation has been assumed. No work may be requested by the promisor, and hence no obligation would then exist. In like manner, a promise "to stay in business as long as it is profitable" is an illusory promise that does not constitute valid consideration. A promise "to buy all the coal we may order" is similarly illusory, since the party making such a promise is not promising to buy any coal. No binding obligation is created.

Courts have generally taken a different position if the promise involved *requirements* or *output contracts*. Thus, where the promisor agrees to buy all the coal he or she needs or will require during a given period from the promisee, then a binding obligation will normally be found. Similarly, a promise to sell all of the coal produced to a particular promisee will create a binding obligation. In each case, however, it is necessary to inquire whether any requirements or output are in fact involved. If some level of previous or expectant need, or output, is present, then the obligation to continue meeting those needs, or providing the output, to just one party, will create a sufficient consideration to support the agreement. If no such needs (for coal, etc.)

were actually anticipated, then the promise would again be illusory and insufficient to constitute consideration.

Promise to Perform Existing Obligation A promise to perform a duty which the promisor is already legally obligated to perform, is insufficient consideration. In such case, the promisee receives nothing in return for his or her promise since the performance promised is required by another obligation, and does not constitute promising to do something that one has no legal duty to do. Thus, the promise of a police officer to arrest a violator for a breach of the law is not enforceable since the party to whom the promise is made received only that which he or she had a right to demand (i.e., arrest of a wrongdoer). Note, however, that if a public officer goes beyond the area of legally imposed duty, then consideration will have been given that will support a promise. If a fire fighter is offered a reward to run into a burning building to retrieve property at great risk to life, such service beyond the requirements of duty will support a claim for the reward.

Cases frequently arise in which a contractor refuses to complete the construction of a building in accord with the original agreement unless an additional payment is made. If the other party promises to pay an additional amount if the contractor will complete the project as originally promised, the promise to pay a greater consideration is not enforceable. Promises to abide by one-sided modifications of existing contracts are purely gratuitous and not supported by additional consideration. If, however, the contractor promised to do some additional work, even though the work was not commensurate with the added compensation requested, then some modification or change in the agreement would exist on both sides and the promise to pay more would be enforceable.

Two qualifications to the rule with respect to one-sided modification of contracts should be noted. First, if extraordinary circumstances cause entirely unforeseen difficulties in construction, then a promise of additional compensation may be enforced. For example, if the contractor had no reason to expect the presence of a large body of quicksand under the construction site, or an earthquake changed the conditions expected in performing the agreement, then a promise to pay additional compensation will be considered valid even though the contractor is agreeing to simply complete the building as agreed. It is considered that an implied condition of the contract was that the facts would continue as supposed by the parties. Second, under the provisions of the UCC, agreements between parties that modify a contract for the sale of goods need no consideration in order to be binding[3] It is thus possible for both parties to sales contracts involving goods to make one-sided modifications of those agreements that will be binding on both parties.

The purpose is to facilitate the making of agreements with respect to the sale of goods.

Compromise and Release of Claims As a general rule, *partial payment* of an amount of money owed by a debtor is not sufficient consideration to discharge the original obligation. Where a debtor owes $100 and promises to pay $50 if the creditor will accept that amount in full payment, the creditor's promise to do so is not binding. An agreement to take less is not supported by additional consideration, and such a one-sided modification is not binding. There are situations, however, in which a promise to take less than the original amount of the debt may be binding.

Bona Fide Dispute as to Amount Owed. Many claims between parties involve good faith disputes about the amounts of money owed. The debt is then said to be *unliquidated* (not certain). Tort claims involving damage to property or injury to persons often involve such unliquidated amounts. Settlement agreements with respect to such indefinite amounts may be subject to compromise between the parties and the promise of each party to surrender a claim that the amount is more, or less, is sufficient consideration for the return promise. A similar finding would result where the parties to a construction contract disagreed in good faith concerning price. In the latter case, a compromise agreement reached concerning the extent of the debt will be binding on both parties.

Payment Before Debt Is Due. Where the obligation is not due until a certain date and prior to that date the debtor pays an amount which is less than that agreed upon with the understanding that such payment will discharge the entire obligation, the promise to accept the lesser amount will be binding on the creditor. In this situation, the debtor has changed the performance by paying prior to due date. Such a modification of performance by the debtor will be sufficient consideration to support the creditor's promise to accept a lesser amount. Both parties have agreed to a different performance involving some legal detriment to each. The changed consideration by each makes the promises mutually binding. Similarly, an offer to pay the debt at a different place from that specified in the original agreement will be binding on the parties if the creditor agrees. In this situation, also, a change is found on the part of both parties.

Payment of Part of the Debt Plus Any Additional Consideration. If the debtor makes part payment and also offers additional consideration in some form other than money, the creditor's agreement to accept will be binding. For example, where the original debt involves a $100 obligation, and the debtor promises to repay $50 plus a book, the creditor's assent to such agreement is binding, notwithstanding the value of the book. Agreements to take part payment and something else of value (however slight that value may be), are sometimes referred to, as are other compromises which are carried out, as an *accord and satisfaction.* In this case the accord and satisfaction involves an agreement to substitute a different performance for the one called for in the contract (i.e., accord), and the performance of that substitute agreement (i.e., satisfaction). Such agreements are binding on the parties.

Composition of Creditors. Where a number of creditors combine and each expresses a willingness to take a certain percentage of the original obligation owed them, such agreements are binding on the assenting creditors. The mutual assent of each creditor to take a percentage of the full debt is sufficient consideration for the same promise of the other creditors and makes their assent to receive a lesser amount binding upon each of them. In a composition agreement, the original debt is extinguished altogether. If, following such an agreement, a debtor promised to pay one of the creditors 100 percent of the obligation owed, such renewal promise would not be binding on the debtor. This result should be distinguished from the bankruptcy situation, mentioned previously, in which a promise of a debtor to make good on the debt discharged by bankruptcy will be binding on the debtor without need for additional consideration. The reason for the distinction is the fact that debts are considered extinguished by composition agreements, but only the remedy to sue is barred or removed by bankruptcy. The remedy may be revived by a renewal promise to pay made by the bankrupt party which waives the bankrupt person's right to defend on the basis of bankruptcy.

Adequacy of Consideration Courts will not generally inquire into the adequacy of consideration. Attempts to weigh the fairness of the innumerable bargains made in business could result in an inordinate amount of litigation. The fact that a person was willing to pay $50 for a book worth only $5 is a matter beyond the province of the courts. They will not attempt to unravel or remake agreements by inquiring into the adequacy of the consideration passing between the parties.

For example, *A* writes a novel and gives it to *B* to read. *B* concludes that it could be published and offers *A* $500 for the manuscript, which *A* accepts. Before paying the $500 to *A*, *B* attempts to find a publisher unsuccessfully and concludes that the manuscript is completely worthless. In a suit for the $500 brought by *A*, *B* attempts to assert the defense that no consideration was received since the manuscript was without value. In this case, such a defense is not valid. The mere giving of the manuscript was sufficient consideration; the fact that it proved valueless is immaterial. *B* will be required to pay the $500 and the court will not consider the inadequacy of the consideration.

There are some situations, however, in which the court will review the question of value.

Fraud Indicated. If the smallness of the consideration is so greatly disproportionate to the value of the property involved as to clearly indicate the existence of fraud, then the court will inquire into the transaction. For example, if a nurse for a sick patient produces a bill of sale for the patient's new car for an amount of $10, the likelihood of fraud will cause the court to inquire into the adequacy of the consideration.

Exchange of Identical Units. In transactions involving the exchange of goods, it is sometimes found that there has been an exchange of different quantities of identical units. Where such disproportionate obligations appear, the courts may take jurisdiction to inquire into the reason for the exchange, especially if the disproportion is of a flagrant nature.

Unconscionable Agreements. Unconscionable agreements may be found in situations where a very large supplier is found to have charged an excessively high price to a small buyer who had no alternative but to deal with the seller, or where the price of goods sold on credit is exorbitantly higher than the cash price. The court may inquire into such transactions to determine if the consideration insisted upon is fair and reasonable.

Exceptions to Requirement of Consideration

To the rule that a contract is enforceable only if supported by consideration, certain well-established exceptions and qualifications have been developed.

Promissory Estoppel It has been noted that promises to make a gift, that is, gratuitous promises, are generally unenforceable. Since nothing is given in exchange for such promises, no consideration is present. In many cases, however, the application of this rule led to inequities. The doctrine of promissory estoppel is sometimes applicable when there is in fact no consideration. It permits the enforcement of a promise even in the absence of consideration where (1) a party makes a promise which he or she should reasonably expect to induce the other party to act or forbear to act in some specific way in reliance on that promise; (2) the other party justifiably relies on the promise by acting or forbearing to act; and (3) injustice can be avoided only through enforcement of the promise.

For example, *A* promises to give his son, *B*, $5,000 in the event *B* purchases a house. Reasonably relying on that promise, B purchases a house. The promise of A to pay $5,000 becomes enforceable without consideration because of B's reliance upon that promise. Under the doctrine of promissory estoppel, A will not be permitted to avoid his obligation to pay B $5,000.

To consider another example, X says to his granddaughter, G, "None of my other grandchildren has to work in a factory like you do. I'm going to give my promissory note for $20,000 so that you will not have to do factory work if you do not wish to." G later quits her job, acting in reliance on her grandfather's offer. Since X made a promise that reasonably induced G to quit her job, and since it is likely that injustice can be avoided only if the promise is enforced, X will be held to his promise under the doctrine of promissory estoppel. It should be carefully noted that if X had made the offer to G "if she would quit her job" or "in consideration of G quitting her job," then G's act of quitting would have involved real consideration in the form of a detriment suffered by the promissee, G. In the above example, however, X's gratuitous promise was not offered as a bargain in exchange for G quitting her job; it was an unconditional promise made "in the event" that she left her job. Reliance on such a promise resulting in detriment will result in application of promissory estoppel. The party making the promise (X) will not be permitted to deny (will be estopped from denying) that the promise was made or that there was no consideration given in support of that promise.

Each of the elements of promissory estoppel give rise to a question of fact to be determined by the trier of fact, either judge or jury. Generally, a substantial economic loss is required to be shown before it will be determined that injustice can be avoided only through enforcement of the promise. Under the doctrine of promissory estoppel, the remedy granted is whatever the court thinks is necessary to avoid injustice. It may include enforcement of a promise to waive the statute of limitations or the statute of frauds, enforcement of a promise to make a charitable contribution, and may require the granting of a franchise or the promised establishment of a pension plan or, if damages are sought, at least the recovery of out-of-pocket losses that result from reliance on the promise.

Charitable Subscriptions. Whenever a person makes a subscription or otherwise pledges money to a church, a united appeal or community chest, a nonprofit college, or other charitable organization that depends on voluntary contributions, such obligation involves more than a gratuitous promise to make a gift. The commitment will be as fully binding on the party pledging as if it had been supported by consideration. In this situation, some courts make reference to the doctrine of promissory estoppel, finding that the charity had relied to its detriment (by undertaking the projects for which support was sought and promised) and that injustice would result if the promise was not enforced.

Uniform Commercial Code The UCC provides that consideration is not necessary to make a contract enforceable in contracts involving the sale of goods where:

1. a party has given a written waiver or discharge of a claim involving an alleged breach of a commercial contract;[4]
2. there is an agreement to modify a contract for the sale of goods;[5] or
3. a merchant has made a firm written offer for goods that was stated to be irrevocable for a fixed time, not to exceed three months.[6]

The UCC thereby reflects the commercial need to provide additional certainty of result in contracts involving the sale of goods.

Commercial Paper The lack of consideration given for commercial paper, such as a check or promissory note, may be raised as a defense against an ordinary holder of such paper. A person who enjoys the preferred status of a holder in due course may bring an action on the instrument notwithstanding the earlier lack of consideration. As discussed in greater detail in Chapter 12, a holder in due course is an individual who has taken the instrument for value, in good faith, in ignorance that the paper was overdue or dishonored, and in ignorance of any defenses or adverse claims against the instrument. The result is that in the hands of a holder in due course, commercial paper may be enforceable even though no consideration was given.

State Statutes The Model Written Obligations Act and similar statutes have been adopted in many states. In those states, if a person signs a writing indicating an intention to be legally bound by the promise contained therein, the defense of lack of consideration cannot later be asserted by the person signing the instrument.

Sealed Instruments At common law, a promise under seal was enforceable without the necessity of consideration. During the time when many people could not read or write, a person wishing to be bound to some act would affix a seal to a writing. That individual was then bound, even though no consideration was involved. The existence of consideration was either presumed or the seal was viewed as a substitute for consideration. A *seal* could and does consist of any impression on a writing indicating an intent that it shall be a seal. Thus, an imprint affixed to a writing, the word "Seal" or the letters "L.S." (an abbreviation for the Latin words meaning "place of the seal") may be used as a seal.

In most states today the seal is no longer considered a substitute for consideration. Those states hold that an instrument under seal must, like other contracts, be supported by consideration in order to be binding. The UCC specifically negates the effect of seals in contracts involving the sale of goods.[7] Seals are currently used primarily in connection with the execution of documents that have the special attestation of a sworn statement. The seal of a notary or other official authorized to administer oaths is frequently used to certify that a statement was affirmed under oath. Such certification does not affect the need for consideration in order to make the agreement enforceable.

Consideration in Insurance Contracts

The insurance contract, like any contract, requires the support of a valuable consideration. The contract is not enforceable until each party has given value or has assumed a duty to the other. The consideration given by the insurer is its promise to indemnify the insured upon the occurrence of the situation insured against. The value given by the insured is the payment of a premium or the promise to pay a premium. Some differences should be noted with respect to the obligation of the insured to pay the premium for property and casualty insurance as distinguished from payment of the premium in life insurance.

Property and Casualty Insurance Premiums In property and casualty insurance, prepayment of the premium is not strictly required as a condition to the validity of the contract. An implied promise to pay such premium will readily be found by the courts. Hence, failure to pay the premium at the outset of the policy period will not result in a successful defense of failure of consideration. The contract of property and casualty insurance is usually deemed to be for the entire period of the contract coverage, whether that be for six months or for one, two, or three years. The whole premium becomes an obligation as soon as the risk attaches. Thus, the entire premium is considered due and payable even though the insurance may terminate before the expiration of the coverage period agreed upon. It is possible, of course, for the parties to agree that a three-year policy will be paid on a year-to-year basis. Whatever the premium payment arrangements, the consideration is generally due and payable at the beginning of that period. The premium owed then becomes a debt of the insured that must be met to the extent that policy coverage for a period was actually granted. In the event the policy is canceled during the period of coverage, an appropriate adjustment is made for a premium refund, depending on whether the cancellation was instituted by the insurer or the insured.

With most property and casualty coverages the risk attaches immediately. With direct writers, which are represented by their own agency forces, payment of the premium is usually handled on a cash basis though credit may be extended. Under the general agency system, where business is written for a number of companies by independent agents, insurers often do not require the agent to pay the premium to the company for a period of thirty to sixty days. The agent in turn may extend credit for the premium to the insured for lesser periods. If credit is extended to the insured it is done at the risk of the agent, who must settle with the company within the fixed thirty-day or sixty-day period. Where the risk has attached, the insured is obligated to the agent to pay the premium for the policy. The implied obligation to pay the premium arises out of the acceptance of the policy, even in the absence of an express agreement.

Life Insurance Premiums   In life insurance it is almost invariably provided in the life application or life policy that the insurance shall not take effect until the first full premium is paid. Life insurance is essentially a cash transaction. There is usually no duty asssumed by the insured to pay any premiums subsequent to the first. Nonpayment of premiums may result in forfeiture of rights under the policy, but no duty to pay premiums is imposed. If premiums have been paid for a number of years, then certain cash values may have accumulated under the policy and the insurer may be obligated to return those values to the insured upon termination of the policy. Refusal to pay a premium will normally result in the right of the insurer to avoid the life policy. In life insurance the premium becomes a debt only when, in the case of the first premium, the contract has become binding.

Since the law generally looks with disfavor upon forfeiture of life insurance coverage, policies frequently contain provisions for extended insurance in the event of nonpayment of premiums. Under such provisions, the policy may be extended for as long as its cash value will suffice to purchase extended term life insurance or such paid-up insurance as could be purchased by a sum equal to the cash value of the policy. At the inception of the life policy, the insured generally can choose to receive either the cash value of the policy or a paid-up policy (using policy cash values), in the event of later termination of the policy.

FORMALITY OF CONTRACTS

General

Most contracts are oral. Although many people believe that a contract must be in writing to be enforceable, most oral agreements are readily proved and may be enforced in court. There are, however, situations in which the law requires that a contract be in writing in order to be enforceable. Such requirements are created by statute and are referred to as *statutes of frauds.*

At early common law, there was no requirement that contracts be evidenced by a writing. All contracts were valid and enforceable so long as their terms could be established in a court of law. It became increasingly apparent in the seventeenth century that some modification of the law was necessary with respect to establishing the existence of certain agreements. The rules of evidence in English courts prevented a party from testifying in his or her own behalf, and many persons were defrauded of their property as the result of perjured testimony concerning the existence of oral contracts. Thus, witnesses could testify falsely that a person had orally agreed to sell a particular property, and the alleged seller was then placed in the position of having to prove that no agreement had, in fact, been made. Producing other witnesses to testify that an oral agreement had not been made resulted in a most difficult burden of proof. To deal with this problem of fraud and perjury in connection with certain types of contracts, the most famous act in English commercial law was adopted by Parliament in 1677.

The Statute of Frauds

The "Act for the Prevention of Frauds and Perjuries," commonly known as the Statute of Frauds, was adopted in 1677, just over three centuries ago. It provided that contracts which were particularly susceptible to perjury had to be in writing to be enforceable in a court of law. All states of the United States have since enacted statutes of frauds using essentially the same format as the early English statute. The purpose of each of these statutes is to provide certainty with respect to the obligation undertaken and to reduce the possibility of fraud. While state statutes sometimes include additional provisions, most statutes (and the original English Statute of Frauds) set forth six situations in which the contract must be evidenced by a writing in order to be enforceable:

1. contracts involving the sale of land or any interest therein;
2. agreements that cannot be performed within one year;
3. promises to answer for the debt of another;
4. promises made in consideration of marriage;
5. promises made by executors of decedents' estates to pay debts of estates from executors' own funds; and
6. contracts involving sale of personal property in which the sales price is $500 or more.

Contracts Involving the Sale of Land   A most important provision of the Statute of Frauds relates to the sale of real estate or interests in real estate. Oral contracts for the sale of such interests are unenforceable. The requirement extends to all interests in land, including mortgages, easements, and leases. If a transfer of an interest in land is made for the life of the transferee, a life estate is created and such transfer must also be made by a writing.

While it is not difficult in most cases to determine that a transfer of an interest in land is involved, problems of interpretation sometimes arise in sales of minerals, timber, and growing crops. Do contracts involving the sale of such items involve the sale of real estate or of personal property? Generally, if title to such property is to pass along with the real estate itself there is little dispute; the property is part of the realty. Where a growing crop is to be severed by the seller and sold to a buyer, then the contract is considered to involve personal property and need not be evidenced by a writing unless the value reaches or exceeds $500. The UCC provides that a contract for the sale of timber, minerals, and so on is a contract for the sale of goods if such goods are to be severed from the property by the seller.[8] If the buyer is to sever them, the contract involves land and is subject to the land provisions of the Statute of Frauds.

Part Performance of Real Estate Contracts.   Where the purchaser of real estate has taken possession of the property and made substantial improvements to it in reliance upon an oral agreement to sell, most courts consider it unfair to permit the seller to then avoid the agreement. Under these conditions, the case is said to be taken "outside the Statute of Frauds" and the contract may be enforced notwithstanding the absence of a writing. The trier of fact must decide what constitutes substantial performance. Where the buyer simply takes possession of real property without making substantial improvements, such act generally is not considered sufficient performance to avoid application of the statute. Payment of the purchase price alone does not satisfy the statute.

Executed Agreements.   The Statute of Frauds is not applicable to executed agreements. A party who has purchased or sold land under an oral contract cannot obtain a refund of money or cannot obtain a return of the deed to land. The Statute of Frauds does not allow rescission; it only serves as a defense to a suit for breach of an executory contract. The usual Statute of Frauds provision states that "no action shall be brought unless the agreement, or some memorandum or note thereof, shall be in writing, and signed by the party to be charged therewith...." Lack of compliance with the statute may be raised as a procedural defense between the parties, but when no defense is raised the agreement may be carried through to completion. Oral contracts that do not comply with the Statute of Frauds are not void; they are merely voidable. Third parties who are not participants in an agreement may not raise the defense of lack of compliance with the Statute of Frauds.

Agreements That Cannot Be Performed Within One Year Disputes over the terms of long-term oral contracts are very likely to arise. For this reason, Statutes of Frauds frequently include provisions that make unenforceable those contracts which cannot be performed within one year from the date of their making. In computing this one-year period, since the law does not consider fractions of a day, the day the contract was made is excluded.

Very Strictly Construed. Courts have not looked with favor upon the one-year requirement of the Statute of Frauds. It generally is held that the provision is not applicable if it was possible to perform the agreement within one year. A promise to perform a particular act "on the death of X" does not have to be evidenced by a writing, even though X may not die for many years. Since it is possible that performance will be required within one year (i.e., that X will die within a year), the one-year provision is not applicable. Similarly, a fire insurance contract written for a period of three years need not be evidenced by a writing in order to be enforceable, since the contract could be performed upon the occurrence of a fire within a one-year period. The possibility of performance is what controls the application of the one-year provision.

Where a contract for personal services is entered into, if the agreement calls for a period of services longer than one year, then the agreement must be evidenced by a writing in order to be enforceable. An oral contract under which A agreed to work for B for a period of two years would not be enforceable, since it violates this provision of the statute. Similarly, an oral contract involving the sale of a business and an agreement not to compete for three years would not be enforced, since the period of the agreement exceeds one year.

Unilateral Contracts Where Performance Is Completed on One Side. Another situation in which most courts have restricted the application of the one-year provision involves unilateral contracts where one party has fully performed. For example, where X sells and delivers a car to Y for a price of $400 and Y orally promises to pay for the car eighteen months after delivery of the car, such agreement will be enforceable. Here, X has completely performed his side of the agreement, and such performance made the promise of Y unilateral. Hence X can recover the $400 from Y on the oral promise. The one-year provision is thus applicable only where mutual promises to perform (i.e., bilateral contracts) are involved.

Provision for Cancellation of Contract. Courts are split on the question of enforceability of an oral contract that extends for a period of more than a year but which also contains provisions which permit cancellation by one or both parties within a year. Some courts hold that such an oral contract is not enforceable. The majority hold that such an oral contract is enforceable, because there is a possibility of discharge within one year.

Promises to Answer for the Debt of Another Where A promises C to pay B's debt to C if B does not do so, A's promise must be in writing to be enforceable. It should be noted that A's obligation is secondary to B's. A is promising only to pay C if B defaults upon the obligation to C. The promise of A is made to the creditor (C) and not to the debtor (B). The promise must involve the discharge of an obligation owed by someone other than the promisor (A). If the debt is either directly or indirectly that of the promisor (A), then the provision of the statute is not applicable and no writing is necessary.

Where the main purpose of the promisor in making the promise is not to answer for the debt or default of another but to secure some personal business purpose, then the case is not within the Statute of Frauds and no writing is necessary. In each case, two obligations must be found in order for the statute to be applicable. A primary obligation must have been assumed whereby a new promisor has agreed to pay the debt in the event the primary obligation is in default. The primary agreement need not be evidenced by a writing, but the secondary agreement must be so evidenced if it is to be enforceable. In a case where A promises to pay C for such clothing as B may purchase from C, the promise need not be evidenced by a writing. A is promising to pay for B's purchases and is not promising to answer for B's debt or default. Only one obligation exists in such a case, the obligaton of A to pay for clothes that B obtains from C. A has assumed primary liability and cannot assert the lack of a writing as a defense.

Similarly, where a prime contractor makes an oral promise to the supplier of a subcontractor that the supplier will be paid by the prime contractor if the subcontractor does not pay, such oral promise will be enforceable. In this case the promise to pay the debt of the subcontractor is made primarily for the benefit of the prime contractor, who wishes to keep the work progressing. Since the objective of the prime contractor is to accomplish a business purpose of his own, the case is not within the Statute of Frauds and no writing is necessary.[9]

Promises Made in Consideration of Marriage Another area that was found subject to some fraud and abuse at common law involved promises that were made in consideration of marriage. The Statute of Frauds now requires that promises to pay money or property in the event someone marries or promises to marry another, must be evidenced by a writing in order to be enforceable. While the Statute of Frauds is not applicable to mutual promises to marry, it does apply to the situation in which one party promises to give $10,000 to another if that other will marry either the promisor or a third party. Thus, where *A* orally promises $5,000 to *B* if *B* will marry *C*, and *B* accepts the offer by marrying *C*, there will be no recovery unless the contract is evidenced by a writing. It should be noted that marriage is not considered sufficient substantial performance to take the case outside the requirements of the Statute of Frauds under this provision.

Application of Two Provisions of the Statute of Frauds. Where *A* promises to marry *B* on condition that *B* transfer a house to *A*, and the marriage takes place in reliance on *B*'s promise to transfer the house, the promise is not enforceable. The provision of the Statute of Frauds relating to transfer of real property, as well as the provision relating to promises in consideration of marriage, would each prevent an oral agreement from being enforceable.

Promises Made by Executor to Pay Estate Debts Most contracts made by an executor or administrator in a representative capacity in the course of settling a decedent's estate do not require a writing. Where, however, the executor promises to pay a debt of the estate from the executor's personal funds, such a promise must be evidenced by a writing in order to be enforceable. The rule is further limited to promises made to pay debts against the decedent's estate that were incurred while he lived.

Where the decedent had owed *P* an obligation of $2,000, and the executor of decedent's estate orally promises to pay *P* the money from his personal funds, no collection can later be obtained from the executor upon such an oral promise. Such promises must be in writing in order to be collectible.

To consider another illustration, assume that *D* dies and that *E* qualifies as executor of *D*'s estate. *E* then orally promises personally to pay *P* the general legacy of $1,000 that had been provided under the will if the estate of *D* runs out of money. Such a legacy is normally payable only if funds remain in the estate after all obligations are met.

Assume that after *D*'s estate expenses are met, no money remains to pay the legacy to *P. P* then sues *E* under the oral promise to pay. A legacy is not a debt that was owed by *D* while he lived, and this provision of the Statute of Frauds is applicable only to debts incurred during the decedent's lifetime. Thus, the promise of *E* may be oral, and its enforceability will depend on ordinary rules of contract law. In this case consideration is lacking.

Contracts Involving Sale of Personal Property The original English Statute of Frauds contained a provision requiring a writing as evidence of a contract for the sale of goods. The UCC provides that a contract for the sale of goods for the price of $500 or more is not enforceable, unless there is some writing sufficient to indicate that a contract has been made.[10] The writing must be signed by the party against whom enforcement is sought or by that party's authorized agent.

The limitation of enforceable oral contracts to those under $500 applies only to the sale of goods. Whether the $500 limit has been reached depends upon the total price of all the goods sold under the contract. Thus if several items, each with a value under $500 but totaling over $500 are the subject of one contract, then the contract must be in writing to be enforceable. If several contracts were intended by the parties, then no writing would be required if the price or value of the goods to be exchanged did not exceed $500 in any one of the contracts.

Liberal Code Provisions. The UCC provides that the writing required need not set forth all the material terms of the contract in order to be binding. It can omit some terms and incorrectly state others. The only term that is required is that relating to the quantity of goods to be sold, and that term need not be stated accurately. The contract will not be enforceable, however, beyond the quantity shown in the writing. The plaintiff or party bringing the action need not have signed the writing. Only the person against whom the contract is being enforced need sign.

Merchants' Contracts. Merchants who deal in goods of a particular kind are treated specially under the UCC. In the interests of furthering trade and of providing certainty of obligation between merchants, the Code provides that one merchant can satisfy the requirement of a writing by sending a written confirmation of a transaction to another merchant within a reasonable time following the oral agreement. Unless the merchant receiving such communication responds within ten days with a written notice of objection, the confirmation will satisfy the requirements for a writing. In order to be valid, such confirmation must also be sufficient to bind the sender (merchant).[11]

Part Performance of Sales Contracts. Other situations in which the UCC provides that oral contracts for the sale of goods are enforceable involve (1) acceptance and receipt by the buyer of part of the goods, or (2) part or full payment of the price of the goods by the buyer. Each of these conditions reflects an admission by the parties that a contract, in fact, exists. There is no need, therefore, to produce a writing to establish the existence of the agreement that has been manifested by the conduct of the parties. Part performance, either by acceptance of goods or payment of a portion of the price, is effective to bind the parties only to the extent the goods were actually accepted or paid for.[12]

Specially Manufactured Goods. Still another situation in which an oral contract for the sale of goods may be enforceable involves goods that are manufactured specifically for the buyer. Under the UCC, (1) if such goods are not suitable for resale to others in the ordinary course of business, and (2) the seller has either made a substantial beginning in their manufacture or has made commitments for their procurement, then the contract will be enforceable even though there was no written agreement.[13] Thus, where the manufacturing process has begun in accordance with the buyer's specifications and the goods are not of the type that can be readily resold in the seller's business, then the requirement of a writing is dispensed with. It will be necessary, of course, for the seller to establish the terms of the agreement as part of the proof of the claim.

There are two types of personal property. The first type, goods, has been discussed. Goods are tangible, and their existence does not depend upon law. The second type is an intangible claim or right created by law, such as a claim arising out of a contract, out of ownership of a bond, or a right to intangible property such as a patent or copyright. Because goods can physically be possessed they are called "*choses* (things) in possession." Because legal claims or rights cannot physically be possessed, but can only be enforced by a legal action, they are called "*choses* (things) in action." A promissory note, for instance, is not the debt; it is merely evidence of the debt. The destruction of the note will not destroy the debt, but the existence of the debt will then have to be proved by other legally acceptably means.

The UCC requires a writing for the enforceability of all sales of investments securities, such as stocks and bonds.[14] A writing is also required in secured transactions, such as credit sales or secured loans that provide special protection for the seller or lender.[15] Oral contracts in both cases are not enforceable regardless of amount. Thus an agreement to sell a share of stock for ten dollars must be evidenced by a writing in order to be enforceable under the UCC.

A special section of the UCC covers all other types of *"choses* in action." Sales of contract rights, royalty rights, notes, insurance policies, and similar intangibles are not enforceable "beyond five thousand dollars. . .unless there is some writing which indicates that a contract for sale has been made between the parties...."[16] Although oral assignments of such contracts are enforceable if the amount is below $5,000, the difficulties of proof are such that a written agreement, signed by the party against whom enforcement is sought, is very desirable.

Form of Memorandum Required

The writing required as evidence of the contract under the Statute of Frauds may be a simple note or memorandum. No formal written contract is required. The agreement may be in any form and may consist of several communications, so long as it provides evidence of the existence of a contract. A written memorandum made some time after the original negotiations may be sufficient to satisfy the requirement. This is true even if the writing purports to avoid the original agreement. For example, where D writes a letter to P stating, "I don't want to go through with our contract to sell Blackacre to you for $5,000," signed *"D,"* the contract can still be enforced against D. The essential elements of the agreement, including the parties, subject matter, and price, are reflected in the communication. Such a writing would be sufficient to satisfy the requirements of the Statute of Frauds.

The various Statute of Frauds provisions require that the writing be signed by the party against whom the agreement is to be enforced. Such signing can consist of a signature, initials, typewritten signature, telegraph signature, or any mark that appropriately identifies the party acknowledging the memorandum or communication as his or her writing. Similarly, the signature of an agent who is authorized to execute such contracts on behalf of the principal will satisfy the Statute's requirements of a signed writing.

Need for Writing in Insurance Contracts

It is well established in the law that oral contracts of insurance are valid and enforceable; the insurance contract will be binding, notwithstanding the fact that no written policy has actually been issued. The customary Statute of Frauds provisions have been held not applicable to insurance agreements. Thus while it is highly desirable that insurance contracts be in writing, the hardship of enforcing such a requirement would fall upon the insured, and courts do not require a writing. Of the six basic Statute of Frauds provisions, only two present potential for application to contracts of insurance. Courts have considered whether the requirement for a writing in contracts that cannot be performed within one year and of promises to answer for the debt of another should be applied to insurance agreements.

Performance Within a Year The Statute of Frauds provision requiring a writing for contracts that cannot be performed within a year is not applicable to contracts of insurance. As previously noted, an oral contract of fire insurance for a three-year term would be enforceable since the agreement might well be performed at any time upon the happening of a loss. This provision of the Statute of Frauds is strictly construed, and the possibility of performance within one year takes such policies outside the Statute of Frauds.

Broker's Agreements Where an insurance broker enters into an agreement with a property owner to procure yearly renewals of insurance upon property for a definite future period beyond one year, then a contract to procure insurance exists. Such an agreement would not be enforceable unless it was evidenced by a writing. Since the agreement cannot be performed within a year and since it involves an agreement to procure insurance rather than an agreement of insurance, the usual Statute of Frauds requirement for a writing is applicable. Some courts hold in this situation that if the insured has reserved the right to terminate the agreement with the broker, then an oral agreement would be enforceable also. The option to terminate by the insured would, in the view of some courts, take the agreement outside the one-year provision.

Promise to Answer for Debt of Another The Statute of Frauds provision that requires a written memorandum of contracts of guaranty, involving agreements to answer for the debt, default, or miscarriage of another, has no application to insurance contracts.

The agreement of guaranty whereby *A* promises *C* to pay for the debt of *D* to *C*, if *D* does not pay, is covered by this Statute of Frauds provision. The purpose of the requirement is to protect the uncompensated surety or guarantor (*A*) from being defrauded by perjury and made to pay an obligation not assumed. It should be carefully noted that the promise in such case is made to the creditor (*C*), and not to the debtor (*D*).

Surety and Guaranty Agreements When surety and guaranty companies began to replace private sureties, it was first thought that the Statute of Frauds might apply to such contracts. The prevailing view today is that such agreements are not contracts to perform the original debtor's obligation, but contracts to indemnify the creditor against loss or damage as the result of the debtor's default or nonperformance. Thus, the view is uniformly held that oral contracts of guaranty insurance are not subject to the requirements of the Statute of Frauds.

Statutes of frauds are thus held inapplicable to the creation of insurance contracts. While a small minority of states do have specific legislative requirements that contracts of fire or life insurance must be in writing (Georgia requires a writing for both types of coverage), most jurisdictions hold oral contracts of insurance valid and enforceable. In fire and casualty insurance, oral contracts are quite common. In life and health insurance, as has been seen, oral contracts are not customary, but temporary written receipts provide evidence of interim coverage. In virtually all contracts of insurance, the contract is eventually reduced to writing in the form of the policy itself. Generally, the policy then stands by itself as the best evidence of the agreement between the parties.

Assigning Insurance Policies   Once created, insurance policies are choses in action. To the extent permitted by law, therefore, any assignment of an insurance policy or of rights under the policy for an amount over $5,000 must be in writing and signed by the party against whom enforcement is sought.

PAROL EVIDENCE RULE

Defined

The parol evidence rule was designed to limit the terms of a contract to those expressed in it. As such it is a rule of substantive law that tells us what the contract is, and is not a rule of evidence that tells us what evidence we may introduce to prove the terms of the contract. Unlike an ordinary rule of evidence which is waived if not raised at the trial, it may be raised on appeal. The rule assumes that all prior negotiations, conversations, and agreements were merged into the final written contract, and that the final contract is the complete statement of their agreement.

The parol evidence rule therefore prevents the introduction of any oral or written evidence of an agreement to contradict or vary the terms of the final written contract. Words that may have been spoken by the parties prior to or at the time of contracting, and letters that may have been written or memoranda that may have been prepared prior to the drafting of the final contract, may not be introduced to alter its written words. The written contract is the only admissible evidence of the agreement.

For example, D sells a car to P and orally warrants during their dealings that the car will develop no mechanical defects within six months of the date of sale. The parties then sign a written agreement regarding the sale, but no warranty is contained in the writing. P may not later introduce evidence concerning the oral warranty. All the negotiations of the parties are considered to have been merged in the written contract, and evidence of the oral warranty would be excluded under the parol evidence rule.

For another example, D sells a power boat to P. The bill of sale indicates the make, model, and year of the boat and the make and model of its compass. P later claims that D had promised to include other equipment such as a marine radio-telephone, and wants to introduce into evidence in support of the claim a letter written and signed by D prior to the date of the final bill of sale, promising to include the claimed items. If the court finds the bill of sale to be the final, integrated, contract of the parties, the letter will not be admitted into evidence because its terms were not part of the final contract, and because they vary the terms of the final contract.

A contract, of course, may consist of a series of letters or other documents. In such a case a group of documents may, together, constitute the final and integrated contract. This can give rise to uncertainty concerning its terms. Consequently one should make sure that the entire agreement is included in the final contract, and not rely on other documents or conversations.

The parol evidence rule applies only to prior or contemporaneous statements and is not applicable to oral or written agreements made subsequent to the written contract. Such evidence is admissible, therefore, to show that after entering into the written agreement the parties agreed to in some way modify, or even cancel, their written contract.

Exceptions to Parol Evidence Rule

A number of exceptions to the parol evidence rule have become well established in the law. The requirements of equity dictate that oral evidence or prior or contemporaneous agreements will be admissible in the following situations.

Incomplete Contracts Where some essential term of the agreement between the parties is missing, such term may be shown by parol evidence. For example, D orally agrees to sell Blackacre and Whiteacre to P, and they agree that they will execute a written agreement to that effect. *D* prepares the contract, which they both sign, but no reference is made to Whiteacre in the written contract. In an action to reform the contract, *P* may show that the contract was incomplete by introducing evidence of their oral agreement regarding both properties.

Ambiguity Exists If the written contract contains ambiguous language, oral evidence will be admitted to clarify the intention of the parties. Thus, where provision is made for payment of money "to my nephew, Bill" and the party in question has two nephews named Bill, parol evidence may be used to determine which nephew was intended. The testimony is not used to change the wording or intent of the agreement, but rather to establish the true intent of the parties.

Where ambiguity is found in an insurance policy, such as where the policy purports to cover "property of the Binney sisters," evidence may be admitted to establish whether the intention of the parties was to provide coverage for property owned by the Binney partnership and/or property owned individually by the sisters.

Fraud, Accident, Illegality, or Mistake Where the transaction is tainted by fraud or illegality, such wrongdoing may be shown by introduction of oral evidence. If one of the parties substituted the wrong document while obtaining the signature of the other party, such fraudulent conduct may be shown. Similarly, if guns are sold under illegal circumstances, such illegality may be shown by oral testimony, even though the writing itself does not reflect the wrongful nature of the transaction. Where by accident or mistake a copy of a contract is not a true copy of the agreement, such mistake may be shown by the parties. Errors made in reducing the contract to writing may also be shown by oral testimony of the parties.

Condition Precedent Not Met Parol evidence is admissible to show that a written document that apears to be a contract in fact never became such because of failure of some condition precedent to the agreement. Nondelivery or conditional delivery of the contract reflect conditions that may be shown orally. Where the contract was delivered to one of the parties with the understanding that it was not to take effect until certain conditions had been met, then the nonoccurrence of such conditions can be shown by parol evidence. Similarly, where the agreement was not to take effect until the contract had been delivered to one of the parties, and such delivery is obtained without the intent of the party alleged to have made the delivery, the fact of nondelivery can be shown. As with other exceptions to the parol evidence rule, no attempt is made to vary the written agreement of the parties. The objective is to permit the true intent of the parties to be shown.

To further illustrate, take the case in which a writing provides that the construction of a building shall be completed by December 1, 1981. The written agreement does not include the time when work was to begin. Oral evidence is offered to show that work was not to begin until the mortgage held by the new owner of the property was recorded. This is not evidence as to time of performance but rather speaks to the question of whether a condition precedent to performance was complied with. The offered evidence does not tend to vary or contradict the terms of the writing and does not contravene the parol evidence rule. A written promise may be conditioned by oral agreement on an event not set forth in the writing, and oral evidence is admissible to prove the condition.

UCC Qualifications The UCC specifically recognizes the parol evidence rule. It provides that "Terms . . . set forth in a writing intended by the parties as a final expression of their agreement . . . may not be contradicted by evidence of any prior agreement or of a contemporaneous oral agreement. . . ."[17] It goes on to state that a written contract may be explained or supplemented by a prior course of dealings between the parties, by usage of the trade, or by the course of performance.[18] It also allows evidence of consistent additional terms to be introduced unless the court finds the writing to have been intended as a complete and exclusive statement of the terms of the agreement.[19] Again, these provisions are designed to ascertain the true intent of the parties. The assumption is that prior dealings and usages of the trade were taken for granted when the contract was worded.

Scope of the Rule

The parol evidence rule has application to all written documents. In addition to ordinary contracts, it applies to such writings as deeds, wills, leases, insurance policies, releases, and similar legal instruments. The purposes of the rule, which apply equally to all written agreements, are (1) to carry out the presumed intention of the parties, (2) to achieve certainty and finality as to the rights and duties of the parties, and (3) to exclude fraudulent and perjured claims.

The exceptions to the parol evidence rule have done much to lessen the harshness of the doctrine. The rule has been liberalized to produce a better understanding of what the parties actually meant by their written contract. Oral evidence is always admissible to interpret or explain a writing but not to alter its terms.

LEGALITY OF CONTRACTS

General

Still another requirement of an enforceable contract is that it must have a lawful object. A contract is illegal when either the formation or performance of the agreement constitutes a crime or a tort. Ordinarily an illegal contract is void, and neither party can sue the other under the contract. The law takes the position that it will not aid parties to an illegal agreement. It will leave the parties as it found them, since the parties are considered beyond the pale of the courts and not entitled to their aid.

The result of this rule is that the parties to an illegal agreement cannot recover damages for its breach. Neither can damages be recovered for the value of any partial performance that may have been made. Although this may result in the unjust enrichment of one wrong-doer, the law imposes this harsh result in order to deter parties from entering illegal contracts. The liberty to contract is thus made subservient to the public welfare.

Types of Illegal Contracts

Contracts may be found to be illegal either because they are contrary to constitutional or statutory law, or because they are against public policy as defined by the courts. A contract that is illegal when made does not become enforceable by a subsequent change in the law that makes similar contracts legal. Conversely, if a contract is legal when made but subsequently becomes illegal as the result of statute or court decision, the parties are excused from further performance. In the latter situation, called "supervening illegality," the parties may be able to recover the value of any performance while the contract was still lawful. A party may not continue to perform, however, since no recovery will be permitted for acts done after the declaration of illegality.

Contracts to Commit Crimes or Torts Any agreement between parties whereby one is to commit an act that would constitute a crime or other wrongful act would be illegal and void. Thus, contracts to obtain the injury or death of another, to slander or libel someone, to induce a breach of contract, or to accomplish the infringement of a patent would be illegal and unenforceable agreements. In such cases, a breach of the agreement by one of the parties, such as failure to pay

in the event of any such breach, the Corporation may, in addition to the other remedies which may be available to it, file a suit in equity to enjoin me together with all those persons associated with me from the breach of such covenants.

5. I understand that this Agreement shall be binding upon and shall inure to the benefit of the successors and assigns of the Corporation and my heirs, executors and administrators.

EXECUTED this _____ day of _____, 19 ____.

_____

FRANK B. AUBREY, II

the agreed fee for such illegal acts, would not give rise to any remedy enforceable in a court of law.

Contracts Harmful to the Public Interest A number of agreements have been found illegal by the courts because they tend to be injurious to the public interest. Among such agreements are contracts involving injury to the public service, such as offers to buy or sell public offices. Similarly, agreements for illegal procurement of government contracts, agreements to contribute more than the amounts permitted by law to political campaigns, and illegal lobbying agreements are contrary to public policy and void.

Agreements designed to interfere with or obstruct legal processes are also illegal. Thus, agreements to bribe a witness, to obtain the dropping of a criminal charge, or to suppress lawful evidence would be considered harmful to the administration of justice and against the public interest. Likewise, agreements tending to stir up unnecessary litigation, such as agreements between lawyers to find claimants against a particular party and split the contingent fees they might thereby earn, would be illegal and unenforceable.

Usury Agreements The law of each state provides limits on the amount of interest that may be charged for the loan of money. Any contract under which the lender is to receive more than the maximum interest allowed by statute is usurious and illegal. In most states the lender is denied the right to collect any interest on the principal sum if an illegal rate of interest has been agreed upon. The lender may still obtain the principal amount loaned in all but a very small minority of states. A substantial number of states permit the recovery of the legal rate of interest only, construing the agreement to permit recovery up to the maximum legal rate. Reference must be made to the statutes of each state to determine the legal rates of interest permissible on various types of loans, as well as the penalties involved in the event a usurious rate is provided for.

Loans may be divided into three general classifications, each of which is treated differently under the usury statutes. The first are loans to corporations and to individuals who borrow large sums of money for business purposes or on the security of very large mortgages. These are not subject to usury statutes. Presumably such borrowers are sufficiently financially sophisticated to bargain effectively. The second are loans by the usual lending institutions such as banks, insurance companies, and private persons in intermediate amounts on personal credit or on security. These loans are subject to state-imposed maximum interest rates which vary with time and place. The third are small consumer loans and retail credit transactions. These loans are made by a wide variety of institutions including licensed small loan companies, credit unions, by banks on bank credit cards, and by pawnshops, to name a few. Retail credit is extended by the retailer.

Because of abuses that have taken place in the third class of loans, legislation aimed at the protection of the consumer has multiplied in recent years. The best publicized statute is commonly known as the "Truth in Lending Act," passed by Congress in 1968 as the Consumer Credit Protection Act (CCPA). It does not provide for maximum interest rates, but does provide for an explicit statement of the true interest rate on lending agreements, for instance, that the true annual interest on a 6 percent loan that is to be repaid in monthly installments is 11.08 percent. A less well-known provision makes extortionate credit activities a federal crime. An extortionate credit activity is one in which both parties understand that failure to repay may result in the use of violence or other criminal means to harm the debtor, generally known as "loan-sharking." The CCPA provides for both civil and criminal sanctions on offenders. "Truth in Lending" and related consumer-oriented legislation is discussed in more detail in Chapter 14.

Wagering Agreements   Most states have statutes which make gambling contracts illegal. Betting or gambling transactions cannot, therefore, be enforced in the courts. In most cases there is not much difficulty involved in determining whether an agreement is a wager. Clearly, a bet placed on the outcome of a sporting event constitutes a wager. It is the essence of a wager that neither party has any interest in the contingent event except that which they create by their agreement. The gambling agreement thus has the effect of creating or increasing a risk to which the parties would not otherwise be subject.

It is important to distinguish contracts of insurance from wagering agreements. In the insurance contract, the risk involved is being shifted or reduced by obtaining insurance to protect against the possibility of loss. The hazard, such as fire, is already there. The insured, who has an interest in a particular property, is simply trying to protect against the hazard. In the gambling contract, on the other hand, the gambler is creating a risk that did not otherwise exist. For this reason, the law does not permit a person to obtain insurance coverage on property, or on the life of another, where no insurable interest in the property or life exists. Thus, unless the insured stands to suffer some financial loss as the result of destruction of property, no insurable interest exists; the insurance contract in such case would be considered essentially a gambling transaction and would not be enforceable. Insurance contracts obtained to cover property or life in which no insurable interest exists are gambling transactions and are therefore void.

Other types of contracts present even more difficult questions in determining whether the transaction involves gambling and is therefore illegal. "Futures" agreements in the commodity markets are an example. Under such contracts, a seller promises to sell a quantity of goods, generally some agricultural product, that are not presently owned by the seller. These future contracts generally involve "hedging" transactions, which entail the making of simultaneous contracts to purchase and to sell a particular commodity at a future date with the intention that the loss on one transaction will be offset by the gain on the other. Such agreements are designed to protect against the fluctuation in market prices and are not considered gambling transactions, since they are designed to protect legitimate business profits.

License Requirements   Numerous state statutes require that a license be obtained before persons may engage in particular trades or occupations. These statutes are intended to protect the public against unqualified and incompetent individuals who perform the specialized callings. Thus, statutes require that lawyers, doctors, dentists, and similar professionals be licensed to practice. Many careers involve special licensing or certification by the state before the occupation may be legally pursued. Typical state statutes require licensing of barbers, pharmacists, insurance salespersons, real estate brokers, surveyors, architects, stockbrokers, and so on. If a person engages in any of these occupations without the necessary license, then people receiving the benefit of such services may later refuse to pay for such services on the ground the contract was illegal because it was performed by an unlicensed practitioner. Thus, an unlicensed surveyor may not suc for work done under contract as a surveyor. This is true even though the person was licensed as a surveyor in another state and, in fact, did the work correctly. Compliance must be made with the licensing laws of the state in which the services are performed.

Many difficult problems arise in the area of violating licensing requirements, such as the practice of law by unauthorized persons. People who practice law without a license are not entitled to a fee for their services and are subject to criminal prosecution for such actions. Since legal practice involves the giving of advice, special problems arise when advice is given by such specialists as insurance brokers, real estate salespersons, bankers, and accountants. Distinguishing between advice given by lawyers and by the professionals in these other fields presents some difficult ethical questions. Rules on what constitutes the practice of law differ among the states. One state may permit a real estate broker to draft a deed or lease in a transaction negotiated by the broker, another may require such drafting to be done by a lawyer, and still another may permit the broker merely to fill in blanks on a printed form that has been drafted by a lawyer. An accountant is permitted to file an income tax, but not a refund claim based on an intricate question of law. Persons specializing in various business areas must be aware that the giving of legal advice and the preparation of legal documents may result in lost compensation, and the possibility of criminal violations must also be considered.

In addition to licensing requirements for particular occupations, most states also regulate dealings in certain articles of commerce. Such statutes are also designed to protect the public against fraud or the sale of improper articles. Licenses are often required for the sale of intoxicating liquors, firearms, poisons, and other potentially harmful goods. People selling goods in violation of such licensing requirements are engaging in illegal transactions and may not have recourse to the courts to enforce such agreements.

It is important to note that some statutes involving licensing requirements are designed primarily to raise revenue rather than to protect the public against practice by unauthorized persons. As previously indicated, if the licensing requirement is for the protection of the public, then agreements entered into by unlicensed persons would be illegal and void. If, on the other hand, the purpose of the statute is simply to raise revenue, then the protection of the public interest is not the primary motive and the contract may still be enforced. A builder who failed to obtain a required building permit under an ordinance designed primarily as a revenue measure may still collect under a contract for construction. Similarly, contracts of a business that failed to pay a license tax for sale of oleomargarine are enforceable.

Sunday Laws   Most states have enacted legislation that prohibits the transaction of certain kinds of business on Sunday. These "blue laws" were generally enacted during the nineteenth century in keeping with the Biblical proscription to keep the Sabbath day holy. There is great variety of language in such statutes and an even greater variety of attitude with respect to enforcement in various localities.

Under traditional Sunday laws, some type of contracts entered into on Sunday or contracts that require performance of work on Sunday are illegal and void. No enforcement of such contracts can be obtained, and no recovery can be had for work performed under such agreements. Where the contract is negotiated on Sunday, but actual acceptance does not occur until a secular day, then such contracts are generally considered to have been "made" on the day of acceptance and are therefore enforceable.

Nearly all the Sunday laws have an exception relating to works of necessity and charity. Thus, acts necessary to preserve life, health, or property may still give rise to an enforceable contract even though performed on Sunday. If a property is in great danger, work done to protect or save it may form the basis of a contract. However, where the Sunday work is performed merely as a matter of convenience to avoid having to close the business on a weekday, such work is not considered a matter of necessity, and no recovery may be had for such Sunday performance. The courts are not in agreement with respect to what constitutes works of necessity and charity.

Contracts in Restraint of Marriage   Agreements that restrain the freedom of marriage are generally considered contrary to public policy and therefore illegal. Agreements between two persons to obtain or prevent the marriage of a third person are illegal and void, as are marriage brokerage contracts which restrain the freedom of choice in entering into marriage. A promise to pay a father a sum of money in consideration that his daughter marry is also illegal.

Some limited restraints on marriage that are incidental to some other legitimate purpose may not prevent recovery. Thus, the promise of a housekeeper or teacher not to become married while employed may form the legitimate basis for discharge from employment, if the person later marries during the employment period. So, too, the promise of very young persons not to marry until age twenty-one are generally enforceable by them against parties who have promised to pay a certain consideration in the event marriage is delayed until such age. Refraining from marriage for a limited period of time is seen as valuable consideration and sufficient to support a contract. Agreements not to marry that are not limited as to time are entirely unenforceable.

Just as agreements purporting to restrain the freedom of marriage are discouraged on social and public policy grounds, so are agreements that seek to obtain the dissolution of marriage. A promise to pay a woman a certain sum of money if she will divorce her husband would clearly be illegal and void. Under statutes in most states, property settlement agreements between a husband and wife in contemplation of divorce will be enforced.

Contracts Relating to Liability for Negligence   A provision of a contract that purports to relieve a party of liability for negligence is called an *exculpatory clause*. Such disclaimers of liability are generally looked upon with disfavor by the courts. They are construed strictly against the party that attempted to limit its liability and are often declared illegal by the courts as being contrary to public policy, especially where the other party is at a bargaining disadvantage.

Bailments are found among the more common situations in which attempts at limiting liability for negligence are found. Where the owner of personal property temporarily relinquishes its control to another, as by entrusting car keys or a coat to an attendant, the transaction generally involves a bailment. A duty to exercise reasonable care under all the circumstances is usually imposed on the bailee, or receiver of the goods, in such cases. Bailees frequently attempt to limit their liability for negligence in such places as parking lots or hat check rooms by placing some notice that disclaims liability for lost or damaged property on the receipt for the goods. Such clauses are held by some courts to be illegal since to permit such limitations would result in all bailees attempting to restrict their liability contrary to public policy, while other courts allow such limitations if fairly agreed upon by bailor and bailee.

It is clear that in cases involving attempts of common carriers (such as trains, airplanes, and buses) to restrict their liability for negligence, as well as in cases involving the supply of services by public utilities and other situations involving monopoly and lack of equality of bargaining power, such institutions may not limit their liability for ordinary negligence except as permitted by statute, the appropriate regulatory authority, or an international agreement.

Contracts in Restraint of Trade The public policy of the U.S. favors free competition. A large number of statutes, most notably the Sherman Antitrust Act of 1890 and the Clayton Act of 1914, make it unlawful to unreasonably restrain trade or to engage in acts that tend to lessen competition. The rule of both common and statutory law is that contracts which unreasonably restrain trade are illegal and void.

Agreements involving potential restraint of trade are seen very frequently in connection with the sale of a business and in employment contracts. All such agreements are not illegal. If the restrictions imposed are reasonable and do not impose any undue hardship on the party restricted, they will be upheld by the courts. The limitations agreed upon must be necessary for the protection of the parties and must be reasonable as to time and distance.

A common provision in contracts involving the sale of a business is that the seller will not open a new business to compete with the buyer within a certain distance and for a certain period of time. Thus, someone buying an insurance agency or a barbershop would have a legitimate interest in wishing to be protected against the seller's setting up a new business nearby and retaining the customers of the business that was sold. Whether the restriction will be held valid depends upon the extent of the limitation. Clearly, if the provision stipulates that the seller may never again compete in this line of business or in this city, then the limitation would be unreasonable and invalid. If the restriction held there could be no competing by the seller for one year and for a distance of two miles from the place of the business sold, then such restriction would likely be held reasonable and enforceable. The tests are whether the restriction was necessary to protect the interests of the buyer and whether such restriction was then reasonable as to time and distance. These issues involve questions of fact for determination by the trier of fact, a judge or a jury.

Similar restrictions are frequently seen in employment contracts. A prospective employer may wish to impose on the employee the obligation of not competing in the same line of business for a reasonable period following the termination of employment. Again, if such restriction is necessary for the protection of the employer and is reasonable as to the time and distance constraints placed on the employee, it will be enforced by the courts. An agreement by a prospective insurance agent that, upon later termination of the employment contract, the agent will not compete for a period of one year within a radius of ten miles would likely be held reasonable and enforceable. Attempts to violate such an agreement could result in a court action to restrain the agent from competing and would also constitute a breach of the employment agreement, justifying forfeiture of rights to commissions and so on under the employment contract.

If agreements not to compete are found to constitute an unreasonable restraint of trade, then most courts will strike out the entire provision and will not attempt to reform the contract to apply only to a reasonable restriction. A few courts do attempt to apply the so-called "Blue Pencil Rule," whereby the court would give effect to such agreements for a reasonable time and distance. Courts generally look more favorably upon agreements not to compete which are connected with the sale of business interests than upon those which apply to employment contracts. There is felt to be a greater equality of bargaining power in contracts involving the sale of business than in the usual employment contract.

Unconscionable Bargains At common law, courts of equity would not enforce contracts that contained provisions so harsh and unfair that the party resisting performance would be unduly oppressed. The UCC contains a provision relating to sales contracts and incorporating the common law viewpoint. It also provides that if a court finds a contract or clause is unconscionable at the time it is made, the court may refuse to enforce the contract or unconscionable clause or may limit the application of the clause to avoid any unconscionable result.[20] The UCC does not define "unconscionable," but the comments contained in the section indicate an intent to prevent oppression and unfair surprise. The court is thus empowered by the UCC to apply the "Blue Pencil Rule" to sales agreements by revising them to more reasonable standards at the election of the court.

Qualifications to Rules Relating to Illegal Contracts

A contract which might be considered illegal may still be totally or partially enforceable under a number of conditions. In each of these situations some overriding considerations of equity or public policy are involved, which the courts consider in determining that the agreement should be enforced.

Where Law Was Intended to Protect Party Seeking Redress In some cases a contract will be illegal because of a legislative enactment designed to protect a specific group of persons. Courts will generally interpret such contracts so as to fully protect the rights of such persons. Thus, where a corporation is prohibited by statute or charter from issuing a certain type of stock and nonetheless contracts to sell such prohibited stock, the purchaser may still sue to collect money paid in pursuance of such illegal transaction. The restriction against such sale is deemed to be for the protection of potential stockholders, and the provision will not be construed to prevent such persons from obtaining redress of wrong done them. Similarly, an insurance company that issues a policy of insurance in violation of statutory or regulatory requirements will not be able to assert its own wrongdoing in an action to collect benefits under the policy by an insured. Restrictions with respect to policy issuance are imposed for the protection of the insuring public, and the illegal nature of a policy contract will not prevent a member of the public from asserting the right to protection under the policy.

***Parties Not in* Pari Delicto** The concept of *pari delicto* is concerned with whether the parties to a transaction were equally at fault. Where one of the parties was induced by fraud or duress to enter an illegal agreement, the courts may still permit that innocent party to obtain relief under an otherwise illegal agreement. Thus, where a weak father was talked into transferring property to his son in order to perpetrate a fraud on creditors, the father may be permitted to sue under the illegal agreement to recover that which he transferred. Similarly, where a woman was induced to enter unknowingly and innocently into an illegal marriage brokerage contract, the party knowingly and wrongfully causing the contract to be entered into may be sued for recovery of money paid. It should be carefully noted that the concept of *pari delicto* will be applied by the courts only when there is a clear disparity of guilt between the contracting parties. In most cases, the general rule continues that the parties to an illegal agreement will be without remedy in the courts.

Illegality Is Incidental Only Where the agreement involved is merely incidental to some other illegal transaction, then the courts will not generally consider the incidental agreement so tainted as to preclude its enforcement. Thus, the fact that a fire insurance policy is issued to cover a house in which an illegal activity is carried on will not defeat the insurance contract. The purpose of the insurance is to provide protection against damage to the house by fire and not to further the illegal activity carried on in the house. If, on the other hand, the insurance were obtained to protect against the possibility of illegal goods being destroyed, then the contract would be directly related to an illegal transaction and would be void. Thus, insurance protection for contraband whiskey or machine guns would be illegal and void, and in the event of loss, no recovery could be had under such a policy.

Severable Contracts Many contractual agreements involve a number of promises and stipulations. Where contracts contain some provisions that are legal and others that are illegal, a court may enforce the legal parts. Such action is taken at the discretion of the court and only in cases where the legal and illegal parts can be readily separated. If the illegal provisions are considered to have tainted the entire transaction, then the courts will void the agreement in its entirety and will not afford relief to either party. For example, a contract to deliver goods to a sporting goods store, which includes separate provisions for sale of camping equipment, bows and arrows, and high-powered rifles, will not be declared illegal and void if the rifles are subsequently declared illegal for sale. The court in such case would enforce the sale of camping equipment and arrows but would not afford a remedy for the sale of the guns.

Repenting of Illegal Acts It is the policy of the law to discourage the performance of illegal acts. In keeping with this policy, courts in some jurisdictions will permit a party to repudiate an illegal agreement prior to its completion and to obtain return of whatever consideration has been paid. Thus, in the case of a wager on a race, with two parties placing $100 each in the hands of a stakeholder, either of the parties may repudiate the agreement prior to running of the race and obtain return of the $100. A person electing to repent of an illegal act before it is consummated may recover whatever money or goods were transferred under the agreement. Once the agreement has been completely performed, then courts will not lend their assistance to the party who repents of a loss.

Illegality in Insurance Contracts

Insurance contracts must involve a legal subject matter. Courts will refuse to enforce any insurance contract that tends to injure the public welfare. It is against public policy to issue such contracts. Thus, an insurance policy that purports to pay for traffic violations is invalid, since it tends to encourage disregard for the law. Contracts that tend to increase crime or violations of the law are invalid.

Contraband Insurance coverage obtained on illegally owned or possessed goods is invalid. Such property as heroin, quantities of marijuana, and illegal weapons (machine guns, flamethrowers, or cannons owned by other than the military or police) may not be legally possessed, and insurance on such goods is void and unenforceable. Where it appears the insurance is simply incidental to an illegal purpose, then the contract will still be enforceable. A fire insurance policy on a building in which illegal gambling or prostitution is carried on will still be enforceable, notwithstanding the illegal activity in the building. Such coverage is considered only incidental to the illegal purpose. The primary purpose of the fire policy is to protect the building and not the activity carried on therein. The illegal business in the building will not so taint the fire insurance contract as to render it void. While there are no known cases, business interruption insurance on an illegal gambling activity or house of prostitution would be void and unenforceable.

Insurable Interest Public policy requires that a person have an insurable interest in the property or in the life of another in order to have enforceable insurance coverage on that property or life. If such insurable interest does not exist, the policy is considered illegal and void.

In property insurance, an insurable interest exists when a person has any right or interest in property so that its destruction will cause a direct monetary loss to the individual involved. In life insurance, everyone may obtain insurance on his or her own life. An insurable interest in the life of another exists if one can expect monetary gain from the continued life of the other person. Relationship by blood or close marriage is generally sufficient. The insurable interest in life insurance must exist at the time the insurance coverage is obtained. In property insurance the insurable interest must exist at the time the loss occurs. If these conditions are not met, then the policies will be declared illegal and void since they essentially involve gambling on the lives or property of others and increase the moral hazard that intentional harm or destruction will be done. The concept of insurable interest is discussed more fully in CPCU 1, Principles of Risk Management and Insurance.

No Profit from Wrong While the insurance contract may have been legal when obtained, the wrongful conduct of the insured may render the policy unenforceable against the insurer. In the case of a fire insurance policy where the insured either burns or obtains the destruction of insured property, no recovery may be had under the policy. Such illegal activity on the part of the insured precludes recovery by the insured. In such case the insured need not be convicted of arson in order for the policy to be unenforceable. The insurer, in order to avoid payment, needs only to establish by a preponderance of the evidence that the insured committed arson. Thus, the fact that the insured may have been acquitted of a charge of arson in a criminal court (where the case must be established beyond a reasonable doubt) would not preclude the assertion of arson in a civil action for recovery under an insurance policy. In the latter case, as noted, a mere preponderance of the evidence may show arson, and such showing would be sufficient to establish a defense against payment by the insurer.

Similar questions regarding illegal conduct by the beneficiary under a life insurance policy are frequently seen. When the beneficiary causes the death of the insured, courts in many states limit the conditions under which the beneficiary may recover the benefits of a life policy. Generally, if the killing was in any way willful on the part of the beneficiary, recovery is precluded. The beneficiary in such case will be considered to have predeceased the insured, and benefits will be paid to the estate of the insured deceased.

Under the law of most states, where the killing of the insured by the beneficiary is clearly accidental, such unintentional killing does not work a forfeiture of life insurance benefits. The same has been held where the beneficiary kills the insured while acting in self defense, or where the beneficiary was insane at the time of the killing.

Where it can be shown that a policy of life insurance was obtained by the beneficiary with the intent at the time to kill the insured to obtain the proceeds, then the insurer may avoid payment of the proceeds. Both the illegal intent of the beneficiary and fraudulent concealment would serve as a basis for avoidance of the contract. In this case, the policy would be considered entirely void, and no benefits would be payable to anyone.

Chapter Notes

1. Uniform Commercial Code, Section 2-403.
2. Restatement, Contracts 2nd, Section 75, American Law Institute Publishers, 1973.
3. Uniform Commercial Code, Section 2-209-1.
4. Uniform Commercial Code, Section 1-107.
5. Uniform Commercial Code, Section 2-209 (1).
6. Uniform Commercial Code, Section 2-205.
7. Uniform Commercial Code, Section 2-203.
8. Uniform Commercial Code, Section 2-107.
9. Freitag v. Boeing Airplane Co., 55 Wash. 2d 334, 347, P2d 1074.
10. Uniform Commercial Code, Section 2-201.
11. Uniform Commercial Code, Section 2-201 (2).
12. Uniform Commercial Code, Section 2-201 (3c).
13. Uniform Commercial Code, Section 2-201 (3a).
14. Uniform Commercial Code, Section 8-319.
15. Uniform Commercial Code, Section 9-203.
16. Uniform Commercial Code, Section 1-206.
17. Uniform Commercial Code, Section 2-202.
18. Uniform Commercial Code, Section 2-202-a.
19. Uniform Commercial Code, Section 2-202-b.
20. Uniform Commercial Code, Section 2-302.

CHAPTER 4

Genuine Assent

REQUIREMENT OF GENUINE ASSENT

General

One important requisite of an enforceable contract is that there be a genuine or real assent among the parties. A contract may appear to be valid but may still be unenforceable if the consent of either party was not genuinely given. An innocent party whose real assent was lacking may avoid the contract. Absence of genuine assent may be found where:

1. *Fraud* is involved.
2. Either or both parties were acting under *mistake*.
3. *Duress* was used.
4. *Undue influence* is shown.
5. *Innocent misrepresentations* have been made.

In such cases the courts will rescind the contract and, under some circumstances, will award monetary damages to the aggrieved party. In contracts, as in all other fields, the law will not permit one party to take wrongful advantage of another.

In Insurance Contracts

Of the several requirements for an enforceable contract, most insurance contract litigation has involved questions of genuineness of assent. The insurance contract is not only subject to the rules concerning fraud, mistake, duress, and undue influence, but also, being a personal contract that requires the utmost good faith between the

139

parties, must be free of concealment or misrepresentation by either party. It is in the field of insurance law that the concepts of concealment, misrepresentation, and warranty have received their fullest consideration. Before examining these concepts, we shall first discuss the basic contract requirements relating to fraud, mistake, duress, undue influence, and innocent misrepresentation, which are, of course, applicable to the insurance contract.

FRAUD

General

Where one party to a contract has been guilty of fraud, the contract is voidable at the election of the innocent party. Although the law protects against fraud, it does not protect against carelessness. The law therefore attempts to distinguish between fraud, and folly, and mere carelessness.

The infinite variety of ways used to deceive makes it difficult to define fraud precisely. Instead, the courts, when called upon to decide whether fraud was perpetrated, apply certain well-established elements of fraud to the case.

If all the elements of fraud are present, the defrauded party may choose one of two remedies. First, a suit may be brought to rescind the contract. If rescission is granted, the defrauded party has no further duties under the contract and is entitled to restitution of all that was paid or given under it, and must return what was received. The parties are put back where they were before the contract was made. Rescission is the remedy usually requested.

Alternatively, the defrauded party may choose to sue for damages. This is a tort action, usually called an action in *deceit*. In addition to the elements of fraud necessary for rescission, the plaintiff must also prove that damages were incurred.

In addition to responsibility for one's own fraud, a principal is responsible for the fraud of an agent committed within the scope of the agent's authority. Although an agent is not authorized to make a fraudulent statement, if the agent does so in connection with the principal's business both the principal and the agent are responsible for it in an action of *deceit*, and the defrauded party may bring an action for rescission of the resulting contract.

Elements of Fraud

Courts generally require the presence of the first four of the following five elements in order for a contract to be rescinded on the basis of fraud. The fifth element is added if damages are sought. The elements are:

1. *False representation*—of a past or existing fact.
2. *Intent to deceive*—party must have intended to deceive or have been recklessly indifferent to the truth or falsity of the statement made.
3. *Material fact*—the fact influenced or induced the other party to enter the contract.
4. *Reasonable reliance*—it must appear that the innocent party was justified in relying on the statement.
5. *Detriment*—in a suit for damages injury or loss must be shown.

False Representations False representations that relate to a past or existing fact clearly fall within the first element of fraud. False representations regarding the profit made by a business last year, or the identity of the artist who created a painting, are statements of fact.

Opinion. False statements of opinion, however, do not generally constitute fraud. If one knows that another is merely stating an opinion, one relies on that opinion at one's peril. To express a false opinion that one does not really hold, however, lays the basis for a possible fraud action. False opinions have been held to be fraudulent in cases in which the utterer knew the truth to be different. For instance, a statement by a seller of real estate that the tenant was "very desirable" when the seller knew that the tenant's rent had often been in arrears has been held to be a sufficient basis for rescission.

Statements made regarding one's *opinion* concerning the value of a particular property are not viewed as statements of fact, but as expressions of personal judgment or feelings. However, if one is or claims to be an expert with markedly superior experience and knowledge of the subject matter, misrepresentations by such an expert will be considered fraudulent if the other elements of fraud are present. Thus, the statement of a layperson concerning the value of a painting could not form the basis of fraud since it would have to be recognized as an opinion. A similar statement by an expert, falsely made and reasonably relied upon, could constitute fraud.

Law. Statements are frequently made by individuals concerning the law. A statement by a layperson concerning the law is considered to be a statement of opinion. A statement made by an attorney, however, who is presumed to be expert in the law, may be considered one that may be reasonably relied upon. If the statement was false and the other elements such as intent to deceive were present, fraud may be established.

In the final analysis, whether a statement is fact or opinion is a matter for the trier of fact, judge or jury, to resolve. The representation may be oral or written, may consist of conduct (e.g., merely shaking one's head), or in some instances may consist of silence. A misleading partial truth may form the basis of fraud just as though it were entirely false.

Misrepresentation by Silence. The general rule is that *silence* in the absence of a duty to speak does not constitute fraud. The law does not impose a duty to speak on parties who "deal at arm's length" in the marketplace. However, the law recognizes at least four situations in which there is a duty to speak the truth and failure to do so will constitute fraud. In each of these cases it would manifestly be unfair to permit one of the parties to remain silent.

The first exception is when the parties stand in a *fiduciary relationship.* Such relationships impose special duties of trust and confidence on the parties. The relationship between agent and principal, guardian and ward, director and corporation, or among partners, is so close that the parties do not deal at arm's length and have the duty to disclose all facts relating to the transactions. The partner who sells property to the partnership and fails to reveal material facts relating to the condition of that property may be guilty of fraud, just as though the facts had been stated falsely.

A second exception is where property contains *latent defects* that cannot be discovered by reasonable inspection. For reasons of equity and fairness, the seller of a house who knows that termites infest the dwelling must reveal that information to a prospective buyer. In each case it must appear that the defect was one that the buyer would not uncover by making a reasonable inspection, and that the seller in fact knew of the defect. Mere reason to know of the defect is not sufficient.

Where the parties had previous negotiations during which certain *representations were made but the facts changed* before the contract was actually entered into, there is a duty to disclose the change. A true representation was made but conditions later changed to make those representations false. Under such circumstances, a duty is generally imposed on the party who made the representation and knew of the changed condition to inform the other party. Failure to do so constitutes fraud.

A fourth situation in which a duty to speak is imposed by law is in contracts that require the *utmost good faith* between the parties. Their relationship must be such that one must rely upon information given by the other. The insurance contract represents the contract in which this exception is most frequently applied. As will be discussed in greater detail under the doctrine of concealment, the parties to the insurance agreement owe a duty to reveal all material facts relating to the contract. Failure to do so will normally afford a basis for avoiding the agreement.

The usual contract rule that we are "not our brother's keeper in the marketplace" prevails in most contract negotiations. Subject to the exceptions stated above, parties do not normally owe a duty to one another to reveal all facts that are known to them regarding the transaction.

Intent to Deceive In order for fraud to be found, the party making a false representation must either (1) intend to deceive, or (2) be recklessly indifferent to the truth or falsity of the representation. The deceiver must also intend the injured party to rely on the statement. Intent to deceive is often referred to by courts as *scienter*, which derives from the Latin word meaning "knowingly," and includes any representations calculated to mislead or deceive. The surrounding circumstances may be shown in each case in order to establish such intent. The mere fact that a person made a false statement, or made a statement without caring whether the statement was true or false, is itself some evidence of intent to deceive.

If the seller of an automobile has no idea of its mileage, and represents that it has been driven less than 20,000 miles, such a statement constitutes fraud if it is later shown that the true mileage materially exceeded that figure. It should be noted, however, that the wrongdoer will be guilty of fraud only to persons who were intended to be deceived. The fact that an injured party happened to overhear the false representation and relied upon it is not sufficient to satisfy the requirement of an intent to deceive. If, however, the wrongdoer makes a public announcement concerning the subject matter offered for sale, then any member of the public who reasonably relies on that announcement can maintain an action for fraud. Thus, an advertisement which falsely describes the goods that are offered for sale may form the basis for avoidance of the contract for fraud.

Material Fact and Reasonable Reliance Although these two requisites of fraud are often treated separately in discussions of fraud, they are really two sides of the same coin. A material fact is often defined as one that influenced or caused a party to enter a contract. One cannot reasonably rely on an immaterial fact, but if the fact is relied on by the party claiming fraud the chances are that the party will be found to have relied on it.

Clearly a misrepresentation will not constitute fraud if the party to whom it is made knows the truth to be different, or makes an investigation and learns the true facts.

The basic question is whether the false representation in fact influenced or induced the other party to enter the contract. If, in the judgment of the trier of fact, it did influence or induce the formation of the contract, the fact was material.

For example, S offers to sell a horse to B and tells B, falsely, that the horse was bred in C's stables. C is not an important horse-breeder, and C's horses do not bring premium prices. The misrepresented fact would not be material since it would not have influenced or induced a reasonable person to enter the contract. In each case the question is one of fact.

Suppose, however, that in the example given S had told B that C was an important horse-breeder, knowing that he was not and knowing that B was not knowledgeable and intending to deceive B. Should B be required to investigate? Should S be able to defend a suit for fraud on the ground that his victim should have investigated C's reputation? The classical view was that an investigation should be made if the injured party had a ready means of investigation and failed to do so. Judgments of that nature are so difficult to make, however, that modern courts and the Restatement of Contracts have adopted the view that actual reliance rather than reasonable reliance is sufficient.[1] Of course, the less reasonable the reliance the less the misrepresentation is likely to have induced formation of the contract.

The question of reliance often comes up when one of the parties fails to read the contract. Of course, if a party is induced to sign a document different from the one that was negotiated (as by some sleight of hand) a clear case of fraud exists. Suppose, however, that a party is induced not to read a contract because of reliance on misrepresentations concerning its contents. If the parties are in a relation of trust and confidence, failure to read will probably be found to be reasonable. In other situations the courts are split. The older view is that there is no excuse for failing to read a contract. More modern decisions hold that fraud is no less fraud even if the plaintiff was careless, because the very purpose of the misrepresentation was to induce carelessness.

Detriment As a practical matter some damage or injury can be shown in most cases involving fraud. Generally the value of the property received is less than the property was represented to be worth. Injury has resulted when the party is not in as good a position as he or she would have been had the statements been true. The injured party may request that the contract be rescinded, or a request may be made for an award of monetary damages.

In the event that a request is made for rescission of the contract, courts have not insisted on a showing of actual monetary damage. The presence of the other elements of fraud are generally sufficient to justify cancellation of the contract and restoration of the parties to their original positions.

If, instead of suing for rescission, a suit in tort for damages is brought, the plaintiff must prove a fifth element, the nature and extent of the damages. In computing damages, most states apply the benefit-of-the-bargain rule rather than the usual tort rule of out-of-pocket damages. For instance, suppose a plaintiff bought a watch for $100 that was fraudulently represented as capable of a certain accuracy. The watch sold to the plaintiff was actually worth $75, but had it been as accurate as was stated it would have been worth $150. Under the benefit-of-the-bargain rule the plaintiff would be entitled to $75, the difference between the value of the watch as represented and its actual value. Under the out-of-pocket rule the plaintiff would only be entitled to $25, the difference between the actual value of the watch and what was paid for it. The benefit-of-the-bargain rule is obviously a greater deterrent to fraud.

Beyond recovery for compensatory damages under either theory, it may also be possible to obtain an award of punitive damages. Because of the intentional nature of fraud, juries will sometimes award damages in excess of the actual loss as additional punishment against the wrongdoer. The subject of damages is discussed more fully in Chapter 5.

Fraud in Insurance Contracts

As with any contract, an insurance contract that has been induced by fraud may be avoided by the victim. A person who is fraudulently induced to make or sign an application for a policy may sue to cancel or rescind that policy. Where an insurance agent fraudulently misrepresents the nature of the document the applicant is signing, or the protection that is being purchased, the victim of the fraud may rescind and recover any premium paid.

As far as the right of the insurer to cancel an insurance policy for fraud, any fraudulent conduct in the procurement of the policy will permit the insurer to avoid the contract. Thus, where the insured in making application for a health policy misrepresents the material fact that x-ray treatments were then being received for a tumorous condition, such fraud will permit avoidance of the policy.

Fraudulent Impersonation of the Applicant The substitution of one person to take the medical examination for another in connection with life and accident and health policies is one of the more blatant types of fraud seen in insurance transactions. Since the fraud is usually not discovered until after the death of the insured, proof largely depends upon the recollection of the medical examiner who must recall the identity of the deceased through photographs. If the substitution can be shown, courts uniformly hold such contracts to be void rather than merely voidable. The contract is treated as though it never existed. Even the incontestable clause in life insurance policies will not prevent raising this type of fraud.

When fraudulent impersonation of the applicant is involved, it is not necessary that the insurer prove the misrepresentation was material (i.e., that the named applicant was uninsurable). The fact of the substitution itself justifies an inference of materiality. Neither is it necessary to prove that the named applicant was a participant in the fraud. A finding that the applicant's signature was forged, or that the applicant was induced to sign by a fraudulent misrepresentation as to the nature of the instrument being signed, so taints the transaction as to render the policy void from the beginning.

Collusion Between Agent and Third Person   A person who knowingly colludes with an agent to defraud the agent's principal cannot hold the principal to such a contract, and the knowledge of the agent will not be imputed to the principal. Thus, where the applicant for health insurance and the insurance agent agree that adverse information concerning the medical history of the applicant be withheld from the insurer, such fraudulent collusion will provide grounds for later avoidance of the policy by the insurer. Where, however, the applicant informs the agent of negative information which the agent fails to record, or assures the applicant a report is unnecessary, there is no collusion and the insured will be permitted to recover. Once the applicant steps over the ill-defined line that separates ignorant innocence from fraudulent collusion with the agent, the insurer may successfully defend.

Concealment   In the field of insurance, misrepresentation by silence is technically called "concealment" and is the subject of many cases. There are several reasons for the significance of the doctrine of concealment in insurance agreements. As noted in Chapter 1, the insurance contract is a personal contract which requires the utmost good faith between the parties. The insured in each case has superior knowledge concerning the loss exposure involved, and owes a duty to the insurer to reveal this information. The insurer must rely upon the applicant's full disclosure regarding that loss exposure in order to make a reasonably correct estimate of the characteristics of the loss exposures about to be undertaken. Thus, the parties to an insurance contract do not deal at arm's length, but on the basis of mutual confidence and good faith.

Another reason given for the importance of full disclosure in insurance contracts is that they are aleatory agreements. That is, for the promise of a relatively large sum of money to be paid upon the happening of some uncertain event the insured pays a much smaller sum, the premium. If one who knows that the event will occur obtains insurance without disclosing all material information, the transaction is like betting on the long-odds horse in a fixed race; it is nearly a sure thing. In the common understanding of most people, this is not dealing in good faith. For example, if a homeowner finds his or her home on fire at 2 P.M. and immediately calls an insurance agent to obtain fire coverage to be effective at noon that date, it is clear that a material fact has been concealed and no recovery can be obtained from the insurer.

The Marine Rule. The father of insurance law, Lord Mansfield, was the first to clearly define the doctrine of concealment. In 1776, in a case involving a marine insurance contract, a rule of disclosure now known as the "marine rule" was set forth by Lord Mansfield in a fashion that is still the law in marine insurance.[2] He held that an insured is required to voluntarily disclose all material facts relating to the property or item insured that are known to the insured. Lord Mansfield reasoned that (1) the insurance contract has a special contingent (i.e., aleatory) character; (2) the insured has a superior knowledge of the property or item to be insured; and (3) the insurer necessarily relies upon the applicant's full disclosure. This complete reliance makes any nondisclosure of a material fact, however innocent, a deception of the insurer and will justify avoidance of the contract.

Applicants for marine insurance are bound to disclose, voluntarily, all material facts known to the insured, whether the applicant regards known facts as material or not.

This strict interpretation has continued for marine insurance because frequently the subject matter of the insurance, be it ship or cargo, cannot be inspected by the underwriter who is considering the application for insurance, as the ship may be in a distant port, or on the high seas. An underwriter in such cases is entirely dependent upon full disclosure by the insured to properly evaluate the application. Even though modern communications systems have lessened the strength of this reason, the rule continues. It is stressed that in marine insurance even a good faith (i.e., innocent) failure to disclose any material fact constitutes concealment and precludes recovery. The courts have uniformly held that the duty to disclose is violated by the fact of concealment, even where there is no intention to deceive.

Lord Mansfield speaking in the Carter case stated:[3]

Although the suppression should happen through mistake without any fraudulent intention; yet still the underwriter is deceived and the policy void: because the *risk run is really different from the risk understood and intended to be run* at the time of the agreement. . . . The special facts, upon which the contingent chance is to be computed, lie most commonly in the knowledge of the insured only: the underwriter trusts to his representation, and proceeds upon confidence that he does not keep back any circumstance in his knowledge, to mislead the underwriter into a belief that the circumstance does not exist, and to induce him to estimate the risk, as if it did exist. (emphasis added)

The British Marine Insurance Act of 1906, in codifying the law of concealment, used much of Lord Mansfield's language. With the exception of one phrase, the following sections of the British Act also represent a correct statement of the American law of concealment in marine insurance coverages:

Section 17. A contract of marine insurance is a contract based upon the utmost good faith, and if the utmost good faith be not observed by either party, the contract may be avoided by the other party.

Section 18. (1) Subject to the provisions of this section, the assured must disclose to the insurer, before the contract is concluded, every material circumstance which is known to the assured and the assured is deemed to know every circumstance which, in the ordinary course of business, ought to be known by him. If the assured fails to make such disclosure, the insurer may avoid the contract. (2) Every circumstance is material which would influence the judgment of a prudent insurer in fixing the premium, or determining whether he will take the risk.[4]

Courts in the United States, unlike the English statute, do not impose a duty on an insured to reveal knowledge that could have been acquired through the exercise of reasonable diligence. In a leading U.S. case on this point, a shipowner did not go to the post office to pick up a letter that would have told him that his ship had been stranded.[5] The shipowner later obtained a marine insurance policy on a "lost or not lost" basis. Recovery was challenged on the grounds that the insured, by not going to the post office, did not exercise reasonable diligence, that the insured should have known the material fact that his ship had been stranded, and that concealment of this fact was a valid basis for avoidance of the contract. The court declined to apply the British rule and permitted recovery. There was no evidence that the insured expected or suspected any bad news, and he was not charged with knowledge of the stranding. The insured must reveal the facts he knows, but has no duty with respect to information that he ought to know.

The early rule of disclosure was at first applied to all types of insurance contracts. The rule was later modified in branches of insurance other than marine coverage to require that an *intentional* concealment of a material fact be shown.

Concealment in Nonmarine Insurance. Although the defense of concealment is much more limited in property and life insurance coverages than in marine insurance, it is still of great importance.

The general concealment rule in property and life insurance contracts may be stated as follows: intentional concealment of a material fact by an applicant for insurance is a good defense against a claim made under the policy. The requirements of the rule are (1) the fact concealed was *known* by the insured to be material (innocent concealment is not sufficient), and (2) the *fact was concealed with intent to defraud.*

The reason for easing the rule in nonmarine insurance is that the insurer can make its own investigation and is less dependent upon the insured for facts relating to the loss exposure.

In an early leading case that involved the application of concealment rules, the state supreme court explained why a fire insurance policy should be subject to a less rigid rule:

> The reason of the rule, and the policy in which it was founded in its application to marine risks, entirely fail when applied to fire policies. In the former [marine], the subject of insurance is generally beyond the reach and not open to the inspection of the underwriter, often in distant ports or upon the high seas, and the peculiar perils to which it may be exposed, too numerous to be anticipated or inquired about, known only to the owners and those in their employ; while in the latter [fire], it is or may be seen and inspected before the risk is assumed, and its construction, situation, and ordinary hazards, as well appreciated by the underwriter as the owner.[6]

In the Harmer case, the insured had failed to tell the insurance agent that the building to be insured had shortly before been on fire and that the insured suspected that the fire had been of incendiary origin. The court, in finding for the insured, held that the applicant was not bound to disclose the previous fire. Nondisclosure by the insured of any material fact is a bar to recovery only if the fact was fraudulently concealed.

In nonmarine insurance, if the insurer makes no inquiry, the insured's silence concerning a material fact is not a ground for avoidance of an insurance contract if there is no intent to defraud. The insured may assume that the insurer has satisfied itself as to the characteristics of the loss exposure.

Requisites of Concealment in Nonmarine Insurance

Material Facts. To constitute the defense of concealment, the fact concealed must have been material to the transaction. The test most frequently applied to determine materiality in insurance contracts is: *Would the disclosure of the fact have influenced the insurer's decision to accept the application?* If it would have influenced that decision, the fact was material. Materiality is primarily a question of fact. Whether the insured thinks a given fact is or is not material is not the determining factor, for only a judge or jury can make that decision.

Courts are agreed that any fact that is the subject of a specific inquiry is material. Thus, standard applications for life insurance ask questions regarding drug use, scuba diving, auto racing, parachute jumping, aviation, speed contests, body-contact sports, and similar activities. Since the questions are specific, facts relating to these activities are material, and failure to disclose them is strong evidence of concealment which may give the insurer adequate grounds for defending against claims made under the policy.

Suppose, however, that the question concerns a loss exposure not covered by the policy. Consider a life insurance application form that asks questions concerning participation in aviation, but the written policy contains a specific exclusion of death that results from aviation. If the peril or hazard in question is not in fact covered under the policy, may the insurer assert that the fact was nonetheless material? While courts are not in agreement on this point, the trend of the decisions is that facts that do not relate to coverages provided by the policy are not material. Thus, if an applicant for life insurance either fails to answer or incorrectly answers a question regarding participation in aviation, and death from aviation activities is specifically excluded, the concealment would not be material under the policy. Recovery would be permitted in most jurisdictions.

If, however, the misanswered question relates to drug use, then the relationship between the question and the event insured against (i.e., death) would clearly be material. If the drug usage question was incorrectly answered in the negative, the insurer could later avoid the contract even though the applicant died of a nondrug-related accident. The incontestable provision of life insurance policies under which defenses of concealment, fraud, etc., must be raised within a certain period (normally two years) will be considered later in this chapter.

When no question is asked but the insured is aware of an unusual hazard, the test of materiality is the same. Would the fact influence the insurer's decision to enter into the contract? In an application for a life or accident policy, the fact that the applicant is about to embark on a one-year mission to the Antarctic would likely be material. Even though no question was asked concerning expected travel plans, a trier of fact would very likely conclude that knowledge of this fact would have influenced the decision to accept the application in question. The loss

potential is clearly affected. Still, the second requirement of concealment must be established. This relates to the intention of the party
concealing the particular fact.

Intent to Defraud. The test generally applied to determine
whether there was an intent to defraud is: *Was the fact clearly and
obviously material,* and did the insured knowingly and in bad faith fail
to disclose it? If so, an intent to defraud will be found.

Intent to defraud generally will be found only where the facts are
clearly and obviously material. Some courts refer to the requirement
that the facts be "palpably material," such as that one's hobby was
skydiving, or that the applicant was about to embark on a hazardous
venture, if life or accident insurance was involved. The fact that one's
hobby involved making explosives in a home basement laboratory
would be material to many types of coverage. The concealment doctrine
is thus limited in nonmarine insurance lines by the requirement of an
intent to defraud, which is based on a test that the fact concealed be
clearly and obviously (palpably) material.

As previously noted, when a particular fact is the subject of a
specific inquiry, as when the insurer raises the question on the
application, then the fact is conclusively deemed material. The insured
must answer fully and accurately. Still, facts of general knowledge,
such as the fact that a war is going on, or facts relating to well-known
trade usages applicable to this loss exposure, need not be disclosed to
the insurer. An insurer is charged with knowledge of general facts, but
not with information peculiarly within the knowledge of the applicant.

Where no specific question is raised regarding a particular
transaction or activity that may affect the loss exposure, the question
of intention is, again, for the trier of fact. Would the fact that the
insured is about to undertake a hunting safari in Africa be a clearly and
obviously material fact that must be revealed to the insurer? The trier
of fact must attempt to determine in each case what the insured
honestly believed. The test is subjective; the insured's belief is the
crucial consideration. The jury will weigh the past experience, knowledge, etc., of the insured in reaching its decision regarding the
insured's knowledge that the fact was material.

In a recent case involving concealment in the purchase of credit life
insurance, it was found that the defendant's wife had died of cancer
sixty-eight days after he purchased a car in their joint names, financing
$5,000 of the price with a bank in a transaction secured by a credit life
policy on the wife. The court recognized the conflicting interests
involved. If the defense of concealment was not permitted, spouses of
terminally ill persons might make purchases and shift the cost thereof

to policyholders generally. Permitting the insurer to avoid such claims, however, ignores the fact that credit life policies are written without requiring medical examinations, or inquiries into health, on an aggregate loss exposure basis. The court held that there was a duty to disclose under the circumstances. The purchase of a credit life policy that any reasonable person knows would not be written if the facts were disclosed constitutes concealment of a material fact and provides a basis for avoiding the obligations of the policy.[7]

Failure to Reveal Prior Losses. As previously noted in the Harmer case, courts generally have not imposed a duty to reveal prior losses or claims in the absence of a specific question regarding loss history.[8] In another leading case, a woman lost her jewels on a West Indies cruise.[9] It was found that she had been in the habit of losing things, particularly those things she happened to have insured. The insurer rejected the claim on the ground that, in applying for the policy, she should have disclosed her history of similar losses as well as her history of financial difficulties. The jury was instructed by the judge that the insured "had a right to assume that the fact concealed was not material unless she knew, even though no inquiry was made, that the fact was material and with that knowledge she willfully concealed it with intent to cheat and defraud" the insurer. The jury held for the claimant and the appellate court pointed out that the more limited nonmarine rule was correctly reflected in the judge's charge to the jury. The jury had the discretion to find that no fraudulent intent to conceal information was involved. In the absence of an inquiry by the insurer prior to issuance of the policy, the insured properly assumed that concealment of the fact of prior losses of similar articles was not material. Under the rule in nonmarine insurance, the insured must know the fact was material and must conceal such fact with intent to defraud.

Concealment of Embarrassing Facts. Many cases have dealt with the question of whether applicants for insurance must reveal facts of an intimate and embarrassing nature. In the absence of a specific question, should a person be required to reveal a past venereal disease to an insurance agent when making application for a life or health policy? Must the applicant be required to volunteer such information?

Some courts have contended that an insured need not disclose facts that tend to disgrace or embarrass him or her, but most authorities recognize that such a rule might logically be applied to nearly all concealment cases and thereby end the doctrine of concealment. For that reason, most courts have held that cases involving self-disgracing or embarrassing facts are subject to the general rule for nonmarine insurance. If a highly embarrassing fact is *material,* fraudulent nondisclosure of it will avoid the policy.

ILLUSTRATIVE CASES NOT INVOLVING FRAUD. Courts have found no fraud and continued the policy in force although the insured failed to disclose excessive use of intoxicants in making an application for a life policy, failed to reveal a previous insanity commitment, failed to reveal pregnancy in making a life application, or failed to reveal that the insured was about to lose his job. In each of these cases, no specific reference was made to the fact in question and the court found that no fraud was involved in failing to volunteer the information.

ILLUSTRATIVE CASES INVOLVING FRAUD. Failure of an applicant for life insurance to reveal a previous history of syphilis has been found to be fraudulent. Another case found concealment and thereby voided the policy where the applicant concealed a prior conviction for conspiring with others to submit a false proof of claim under an insurance policy. Fraudulent concealment is generally a question of fact to be answered by a jury.

In one interesting and unusual case, the insured was found to have concealed a material fact even though he told the absolute truth. The facts were as follows: Joseph DeBellis applied for life insurance in the amount of $5,000. DeBellis was his correct name. Five months after the policy was issued, the insured's body was found, stabbed to death, under a railroad bridge. The death certificate named the deceased as Joseph DeLuca. This was the first notice to the insurer that the insured had been known by that alias. The insurance company denied the claim on the ground that the insured had concealed a material fact from the company by not revealing his correct identity. The insurer introduced evidence showing that "Joseph DeLuca" had an extensive criminal record. In finding for the company, the court held that it was not sufficient that the insured answer all the questions propounded to him. He was bound to tell the whole truth without waiting to be interrogated. The contract of insurance requires good faith, and the insured's concealment of his alias identity breached the obligation of good faith.[10]

In a somewhat similar case, an applicant for life insurance indicated his occupation as "plasterer" and that he had been so employed for fourteen years. In fact, for almost half that period, he had been in a penitentiary serving a sentence for robbery. A policy was issued to the insured and he later was killed in a gun battle. The court held the policy was voidable by the insurer because of the insured's intentional concealment of his past. Recovery was denied.[11]

Termination of Duty to Disclose Most courts agree that an applicant for insurance must be reasonably diligent in notifying an insurer of material facts that come to the applicant's knowledge after making the application and up to the time the contract is effective. The insured, however, owes no duty to disclose facts learned after the insurance contract has been entered into, even though actual delivery of the insurance policy may not occur until later. The questions considered in Chapter 2 regarding the effective date of the policy thus become crucial. Any material fact coming to the insured's attention prior to the time the policy actually goes into effect must be revealed to the insurer. Once a binding contract has been concluded and coverage is in force, however, the duty to disclose material facts ceases.

To illustrate, suppose X applies for health insurance and it is provided that the policy will not be effective until approved by the Home Office of Company Y. After the application has been submitted but before the Home Office has approved the correctly completed forms, X discovers that he suffers from an ulcer. Under these conditions, X would owe a duty to disclose the new condition; nondisclosure would constitute concealment of a material fact. In an Illinois case, a few hours after completing an application for automobile insurance the applicant had an accident in which the other driver who was uninsured was killed.[12] The effective date of the policy was to be 12:01 A.M. the date of the accident. Four days later the insurer mailed a policy conforming to the application to a local agent for delivery. However, the insurer learned of the accident in time to retrieve the policy from the agent, voided the entire transaction, and it never appeared on the company's books. The company's acceptance had not been made conditional on either delivery of the policy or prepayment of the premium. The issue naturally arose as to whether the applicant's uninsured motorist coverage was in force.

The court held in this case that the company was not liable under the policy. The court stated that the applicant for insurance has an obligation during pendency of the application to notify the insurer of any changed condition materially affecting the risk. Not having done so, the good faith requirement was not satisfied by the applicant. Hence, the uninsured motorist coverage was not in force.

Silence as Concealment   As has been seen, most courts impose a duty on the insured to reveal material facts to the insurer. The insured's silence or failure to advise the insurer of material facts may constitute concealment. Words or actions constituting concealment are not required. If the applicant knows the property is subject to some unusual hazard, such information must be revealed to the insurer and failure to do so may constitute concealment and permit avoidance of the policy. A duty to speak is imposed by law where the fact is clearly material.

MISTAKE

General

A *mistake* is a perception which is at variance with the facts. Many different kinds of mistakes are possible, and the law does not treat each one in the same way. Mistakes may be made regarding the facts of the transaction or the law affecting the agreement. Mistakes may involve errors in typing, in arithmetic, or in the value of the property in question. While some mistakes have no effect on the rights of the parties, others make the agreement voidable or unenforceable.

A common way of classifying mistakes is to determine whether one or both parties were mistaken. If only one party was mistaken, there was a unilateral mistake. If both parties were mistaken, the mistake was bilateral.

Unilateral Mistake

The general rule is that a mistake or error on the part of only one of the parties does not affect the contract. For example, an offer that is mistakenly transmitted may be accepted by the offeree as it is received. An important qualification to this rule is when the other party (the offeree) knew or had reason to know that the offer was mistakenly made. Thus, where a contract bid is so low that it is obvious a clerical or arithmetic mistake has occurred, the offeree may not take advantage of the error by accepting the offer. Courts will not permit one party knowingly to exploit the mistake of another. The law does not lend its support, however, if the carelessness or lack of diligence of one of the parties results in a mistake that is not known to the other party.

Some courts recognize still another exception to the rule that a contract may not be avoided because of a unilateral mistake of fact. Thus, where a contractor bids on a public works project and makes an error in the bidding process, such bid may be retracted if (1) the retraction is made promptly after discovery, and (2) the governmental agency involved did nothing more in reliance on the bid than to accept it. In such cases it must appear that the contractor's error was material in terms of costs. Thus, where a contractor overlooks certain substantial items in the bidding process, a timely withdrawal of the bid may be made immediately upon discovery of the mistake. As a matter of policy, it is felt not to be in the best public interest to enforce mistakenly made bids against contractors for public works projects.

Ordinarily, however, a mistake of fact by one party does not affect the rights of the parties. To illustrate, *A* contracts with *B* to buy an expensive ring from *B* on credit. *B* believes *A* to be a wealthy man of the same name. *A* does not know of *B*'s belief and acts in good faith. The unilateral mistake made by *B* is immaterial, and the contract is enforceable against *B*.

Bilateral Mistake

Bilateral or mutual mistakes occur when both parties to an agreement make the same mistake of fact. Agreements entered into under such conditions are generally voidable. Since both parties have acted upon factual assumptions that were false, no genuine assent to an agreement exists and no contract is created. The mutual mistake must relate to a material fact, about one of the matters that form the basis of the agreement. Mistakes regarding collateral considerations, which were not regarded by the parties as crucial to their agreement, will not provide grounds for avoidance.

Mistakes Concerning Value In many cases the parties have been mistaken as to the value of the subject matter. Recognizing that courts should not remake bad bargains, a distinction is made between mere mistakes as to value and mistakes as to *identity of the subject matter*. Mutual mistakes as to the value of the subject matter are not a basis for avoiding a contract. Thus, where the parties contract for the sale of a particular stone, with neither of them knowing the stone's true value or making value a condition of their agreement, the contract may not be avoided if the stone has a different value than either or both parties anticipated. However, if the mistake relates to the identity of the subject matter, then the parties may rescind the agreement.

For example, *A* and *B* entered into a contract for the sale of *A*'s summer cottage in the mountains. *B* had seen and inspected the cottage but immediately before the contract was signed the cottage burned to the ground, unknown to either party. Since both parties were mistaken concerning the existence of the subject matter, there was no genuine assent and the contract may be avoided.

It should be noted that in the first illustration the parties contracted knew the identity of the subject matter. If it is later shown that both parties incorrectly estimated the value of the subject matter, the courts will not remake the bargain. In the second illustration, however, the identity of the subject matter was incorrectly believed by both parties to be a cottage. This fact formed the basis of the agreement. A mutual mistake regarding the true identity of the subject matter would, in such case, permit avoidance of the contract for lack of genuine assent. As in the case of mistakes of value, mistakes of opinion or mistakes in judgment will not render a contract voidable. Only mutual mistakes of material fact will afford such a remedy.

Assuming Responsibility of Mistake Many contracts are made with full knowledge that all the facts are not known. When an insurance company issues a "lost or not lost" policy it takes the chance that the ship may already be lost, even though both parties think the ship is safe. In agreements to settle disputes, both parties give up their rights to sue even though facts may later be discovered that provide a basis for suit. The buyer of a used car does not know and the seller may not know the extent of wear on each and every part. Such assumptions do not constitute mistakes.

Mistakes in Insurance Contracts

Of the many thousands of insurance policies issued each year, a considerable number contain mistakes. The correction of mistakes over the protest of one party gives rise to difficult legal problems. The law does not correct mistakes in judgment or relieve a party of the consequences of an act simply because those consequences were unforeseen or undesired. While courts will not relieve parties from the consequences of their folly or misjudgments, courts will under some circumstances correct their errors in expression. Mistakenly worded insurance policies may be remedied by court interpretation or by reformation.

Court Interpretation In an action at law brought on an insurance policy, an ambiguity or incorrect description may require that the court interpret the policy to conform with the true intent of the parties. The ability of the court to interpret the policy is limited to some extent by the restrictions of the parol evidence rule. This rule requires the court to refuse to hear any evidence offered to show that the terms of the contract were different from those plainly embodied in a complete written policy. As noted in Chapter 3, however, there are several well established exceptions to the parol evidence rule. Thus, where an insurance policy mistakenly indicates the wrong address for an insured property, in the event a loss occurs the court will reject the incorrect street number and interpret the policy to cover the building intended by the parties. Similarly, where the beneficiary of a life insurance policy is designated "my brother-in-law, Charles Jones" and there are two brothers-in-law with that name, the court will permit the introduction of parol evidence to clarify the ambiguity.

Reformation The remedy of reformation is granted only upon proof of mutual mistake or of mistake on one side of which the other was aware. It will not be granted for unilateral mistake, an error of one party, unknown to the other. Although courts will not add to the coverage of a policy through interpretation, if clear and convincing evidence of the true intent of the parties is produced, a court of equity will reform the policy to conform with the intent of the parties. Thus, if it is clearly understood between the applicant for insurance and the insurance agent that coverage of a particular type is to be issued, and that coverage is not issued, the policy issued may be reformed by the court in keeping with the agreement. Reformation will be discussed more fully in Chapter 5.

Mistakes of Law It is often said that mistakes of law, whether unilateral or bilateral, do not affect the binding nature of a contract. This is true to the extent that the law is not clear, and that court decisions may change the law after the contract has been made. The doctrine that mistakes of law do not entitle either party to a remedy was generated in early nineteenth-century England, when several cases held that money paid because of a mistake of law could not be regained. However, the distinction between a mistake of law and a mistake of fact is often quite difficult to make. Consequently the courts have engrafted so many exceptions on the rule that the Restatement of Contracts does not recognize the distinction.[13]

As an illustration of an exception, suppose that both parties to an insurance contract erroneously believe that property insurance obtained in an individual partner's name will adequately protect the partnership's interest in the property. Upon the occurrence of a loss, the court may correct the policy to cover the firm's interest, even though it is a mistake of law.

DURESS

A party may seek to avoid or rescind a contract on the ground that wrongful force was used to obtain assent to the agreement. In order to establish sufficient duress to escape liability under a contract, it must be shown that the threat of violence or other harm actually restrained the free choice of the victim. In weighing this decision, the physical health, mentality, experience, education, and intelligence of the victim are considered. The question for the jury is whether this particular person was deprived of free will in entering the agreement. If so, the contract may be avoided.

Situations Involving Duress

Threats to do bodily harm to the victim or to close relatives of the victim clearly involve sufficient duress to justify avoidance of a contract. Similarly, a threat to burn down the home or to destroy other valuable property of the victim will constitute duress. A threat to prosecute a person for a crime will also constitute duress. Thus, where D confronts the father of an employee with the fact that the son-employee had embezzled funds, and threatens to prosecute the son unless the father agrees to assign stock in an amount equal to the amount of the missing funds, the father may later avoid the assignment on the ground of duress. Generally, the threat of economic loss is not sufficient to constitute duress. Even in this situation, however, duress may be found if it can be shown that the victim would suffer irreparable loss which could not adequately be compensated. A contract entered into under threat of eviction and action to adversely affect the credit standing of the individual may be sufficient to constitute duress. Again, the combined circumstances of each case must be considered. The crucial question will be whether the action of the wrongdoer caused sufficient fear to deprive the victim of free will or volition with respect to the transaction.

Facts Insufficient for Duress

As a general rule, the threat of economic loss or the threat to bring a civil action is not enough to deprive a reasonable person of free will. Thus, the threat to no longer do business with a person has been held not to constitute sufficient duress to permit avoidance of a contract. Likewise, a threat not to pay for work already done unless additional work is performed free of charge would not justify a finding of duress. A threat to bring a civil action on a promissory note that was due but not paid before the maker died will not constitute duress against an executor, even though settlement of the estate might be delayed by such action. In such cases, the fear of force imposed on the victim is not considered sufficient to permit avoidance of contract obligations.

UNDUE INFLUENCE

General Requisites

Undue influence, like duress, involves as an essential element the fact that a person making a contract did not exercise free will in so doing. In the case of undue influence, a confidential relationship must exist between the parties. One party must exercise some control and influence over the other. Thus, the relationships of parent and child, nurse and invalid, attorney and client, doctor and patient, guardian and ward, or agent and principal give one party a position of dominance over the other. An element of helplessness or dependence must be involved. In contracts between such individuals, the exercise of undue or wrongful influence will be remedied by the law. Undue influence is presumed whenever the dominated person receives inadequate benefit from a contract made with the dominating person.

A contract entered into between parties to a confidential relationship from which the dominated party obtains inadequate benefits must be proved by the dominating party to be free of undue influence. Although the difficulty of proving such a negative point is apparent, the rule is necessary to protect the integrity of such relationships as well as the interests of the weaker party. If undue influence is not disproved, then the contract will be avoided by the court.

Mere persuasion and argument are not of themselves undue influence. The nagging insistence of a spouse or friend is not normally considered undue influence. A confidential relationship involving clear elements of dependence must be involved. Undue influence is sometimes viewed as a catch-all defense for matters not embraced in other elements affecting genuineness of assent, such as fraud or duress.

Mental Infirmity

A weakened mind may also form the basis for a claim of undue influence. Even in absence of a fiduciary relationship, where a person is shown to have had a mental infirmity which seriously impaired judgment, though not sufficient to constitute lack of legal capacity, undue influence may be found. The mentally infirm person may have known the nature or subject matter of the contract, but the motive for entering into the contract may have been the product of seriously impaired judgment. Thus, courts will look carefully at contracts entered into by bereaved widows and widowers, for example, and others who suffer from mental disability even though temporary. Undue influence may thus involve a party taking advantage of the fiduciary relationship or mental infirmity. Most cases that involve undue influence concern gifts and wills by dominated persons.

INNOCENT MISREPRESENTATION

General

In general contract law misrepresentation involves situations in which the elements of fraud are present, except that the person making the misrepresentation honestly and reasonably believes the statement to be true. The materiality and reasonable reliance requirements of fraud, however, also apply to misrepresentation. If a party innocently misrepresents a fact and that fact is material and is relied upon by the other party, the transaction may later be avoided by the innocent and injured person. If the element of wrongful intent is involved, the transaction more properly involves fraud rather than misrepresentation, but the latter is easier to prove since intention to deceive need not be shown.

The victim of an innocent misrepresentation can always obtain rescission of the contract. The older and still majority view, however, is that a court will not award money damages for an innocent misrepresentation. The reason may be because in many instances an innocent misrepresentation is difficult to distinguish from a mutual mistake of fact. Suppose, for instance, that relying on a mistaken identification of a painting by an expert, S represents to B, a potential buyer that the work was painted by a certain famous artist. B, relying on the statement, makes the purchase. There is a mutual mistake, but there is also an innocent misrepresentation by S to B. Since, however, many cases of innocent misrepresentation cannot alternatively be treated as cases of mutual mistake, the reason for the dominant rule is probably the long-standing rule of case law that damages will be granted only for fraud.

The newer and minority rule that damages will be granted for an innocent misrepresentation has as its stimulus the fact that the injured party is equally injured whether the misrepresentation is innocent or willful. In addition, since intention to deceive is difficult to prove, the older rule may permit a skillful deceiver to escape damages. As in the case of fraud, the courts do not agree on how to measure damages; i.e., whether the benefit-of-the-bargain or the out-of-pocket rule should be used. Consequently some of the minority courts expressly provide for the out-of-pocket rule and merely permit abatement of the purchase price if the article purchased has a lower market value than it was represented to have by the seller.

Misrepresentation in Insurance

Definitions *Representations* are statements concerning the loss exposure made by an applicant for insurance and are intended to induce the insurer to make the insurance contract. They may be oral or written, and may be in papers not connected with the policy contract. Representations precede and accompany the execution of the contract which they are intended to induce. They are collateral to the contract, and are not matters about which the parties contract. Thus, an insured may represent that he or she has no history of traffic violations or accidents. The representation is an inducement to the insurer to issue a policy, but the representation is not the subject matter of the contract.

Misrepresentations involve misstatements of a past or present fact. While some facts, such as the kind of construction in a building, the make of a car, or the location of a piece of property, are easily verified, others are not, and some element of reliance is involved on the part of the insurer. Although it is clear that the rule permitting avoidance of an insurance contract because of misrepresentation had its origin in the concept of fraud, something less than fraud is sufficient to establish misrepresentation.

Statements of the applicant for an insurance policy are called declarations and are usually classified as either (1) *representations* or (2) *warranties*. They will be considered in that order.

A *false representation*, or *misrepresentation*, makes a contract of insurance voidable. The elements required to establish false representation are (1) misrepresentation of, (2) a material fact, (3) relied on by the insurer.

It should again be noted that these elements are the same as those of fraud with the exception that no intent need be shown. Detriment to the insurer is presumed from the fact that a policy was issued in reliance on false information. The fact that there was neither intent to deceive nor reckless disregard for the truth is the most crucial difference between fraud and misrepresentation. Even an innocent misrepresentation, if material and relied upon by the insurer, will make the contract voidable.

The rationale for the rule relating to misrepresentation rests solely on the fact that the loss that an insurer is being called upon to indemnify is a different likelihood of loss from that which was assumed. As Lord Mansfield stated, "The risk run in such case is different from the risk understood."

Misrepresentation of Opinion and Belief Misrepresentation is the making of any untrue or misleading statement, and most courts do not require that the false representation be intentional. Some cases involving expressions of *opinion* qualify this rule, and statutory language sometimes specifies that the misrepresentation must be willful or intentional.

Statements of opinion and belief involve matters of judgment, uncertainty, and personal viewpoint, rather than objective fact. Since an insurer should recognize this subjectivity, courts frequently require that fraudulent intent be shown before they will permit rescission or avoidance of the insurance policy on the ground of misrepresentation. However, if there is an innocent misrepresentation of fact, and not merely of opinion or belief, the policy may be avoided if the fact was material and the insurer relied on it, even in absence of fraudulent intention.

In insurance law, therefore, it is important to determine whether the misrepresentation was of fact or of opinion. If the latter, one must determine whether the opinion given was actually held. If not, the misrepresentation is grounds for avoidance of the policy. Although a willful misrepresentation of opinion is "fraudulent," many cases have merely invoked the term "misrepresentation," and this practice has resulted in considerable overlap in the use of these two terms. An innocent misrepresentation of a material fact, however, relied on by the insurer, is grounds for avoidance of the policy.

It is in the field of life insurance that most cases, and most of the confusion in the law regarding misrepresentation, have arisen. To illustrate the distinction that courts have attemped to draw between fact and opinion, consider the following.

In completing an application for life insurance the applicant is asked: (1) "Have you ever had any ailment or disease of the stomach?" and (2) "Have you had medical consultation within the last five years?" Assume that the insured answers both questions in the negative, although at the time of the application the insured had a spasm of the esophagus and had undergone treatment for the ailment by a physician within the last five years. It is shown that the insurer would not have issued the policy had it known these facts when the application was made, hence the representations were material.

In these circumstances, most courts would view the response to the question regarding "ailment or disease of the stomach" as opinion. A layperson could not be expected to know accurately whether an ailment of the esophagus was an ailment of the stomach. Hence, the applicant's statement regarding this point would be a mere expression of an opinion. If made in good faith there would be no ground for avoidance of the policy by the insurer. Note, however, that the statement regarding prior medical consultation was a representation of fact. The applicant either did or did not have medical consultation with a physician within the past five years. A statement indicating incorrectly that no consultation had been held would permit avoidance of the policy, even though no fraudulent intent was shown. Even innocent misrepresentations of material *facts* will permit an insurance policy to be avoided.[14]

Representations of opinion and belief are subjective because they reflect one's impressions only. Statements of opinion are false only if the person did not have that opinion at the time the statement was made. Thus, the actual intent of the insured is important, and the insurer defending on the ground of misrepresentation of opinion and belief must establish that the insured spoke fraudulently by showing that the insured did not entertain that opinion.

Certainly an insurer knows that an insured's opinion of his or her health, or of the value of his or her home, may be mistaken. Still, the fact that such opinion is honestly entertained by the insured may be valuable to the insurer's estimate of the loss exposure. If the opinion is not honestly held, but is misrepresented, then the insurer is induced to accept a loss exposure other than that agreed upon and will be permitted to avoid the contract.

To consider another example of the distinction between representations of opinion and representations of fact, suppose that a person owns a building with an actual value of $30,000, carrying a mortgage of $15,000. In applying for insurance on the building, the owner represents that the building is worth $45,000 and the outstanding mortgage is $9,000. The representation of the value of the building is an opinion and, although the amount estimated was far from accurate, that fact alone will not justify avoidance of the policy by the insurer. The insurer must show that the applicant actually did not hold this opinion, but fraudulently misrepresented its value. The question of intent is vital when the representation concerns opinion and belief. The representation regarding the amount of the mortgage would, by contrast, represent an external fact and not a question of opinion or judgment. The fact is material and would permit avoidance of the policy even though the misrepresentation was innocently made. The question of the intent of the insured is immaterial in the case of objective or descriptive representations.

Material Fact   A second essential element for the defense of misrepresentation is that the false statement relates to a material fact. As in the doctrine of concealment, the test of a material fact is whether the insurer was influenced or induced to enter into the contract in reliance on the representation. If so, the fact was material. It is generally held that mere silence on the part of the insured does not constitute a representation. A representation requires some active statement or conduct, even as little as shaking one's head. Mere silence, however, is sufficient to give rise to the defense of concealment. A duty to speak is imposed in many cases involving concealment, but there is no such duty in the law of misrepresentation. Concealment, of course, requires fraudulent intent to be proved.

In cases involving fire insurance, the fact that a house is represented to be "brick" when in fact the house is constructed of wood obviously involves a misrepresentation of a material fact. The insurer in such case assumes a much different loss exposure than is represented. Such a policy could be avoided, assuming that the insurer's reliance on the representation was reasonable. If, however, the house is represented to be white in color, when in fact it is blue, such a statement involves a false representation although it does not relate to a material fact. A policy could not be avoided for misrepresentation of such an immaterial fact.

An interesting U.S. Supreme Court case, decided some years ago, involved an application for a life insurance policy.[15] The applicant represented that he was single when in fact he was married. It was argued that this was an immaterial misrepresentation as far as the insurer was concerned, and even favored the insurer, since married men usually tend to have longer life expectancies on the average than single men. The Supreme Court held that asking a specific question regarding the marital status of the applicant made that fact material, notwithstanding the argument raised. When specific questions are raised and false answers are given, the policy may be avoided by the insurer, who is entitled to know the correct facts.

Time to Which Misrepresentation Refers Misrepresentations (as well as representations) refer only to the time the contract is made. Promises of conditions to exist subsequent to the completion of the contract may involve warranties or conditions, but not representations. Thus, conditions that are represented to exist must be so at the time the contract is made, but not necessarily later. Representations found to be untrue may be withdrawn at any time prior to the completion of the contract, but not afterwards.

Reliance by the Insurer To be a ground for avoiding an insurance policy, a misrepresentation must have been relied upon by the insurer. Even though a fact is falsely represented by the insured, avoidance of the policy will not be permitted if the insurer does not rely upon the representation.

An insurer's independent investigation of the facts reported by the insured will affect the insurer's right to avoid the policy because of misrepresentation. If, however, the insurer's investigation discloses the falsity of the representations, no reliance on them can be shown. If the investigation discloses facts that place upon the insurer the duty of further inquiry, then it is difficult for the insurer to show reasonable reliance upon the insured's representations.

For example, suppose M received notice that his driver's license had been revoked four days after he applied for an automobile policy. The insurer knew M had previously been insured with an insurance company which specialized in substandard automobile insurance business. M's application reported two tickets for traffic violations in an eight month period just prior to the application. An independent investigative agency was requested to check M's background, but no check was made or requested regarding the motor vehicle records. The application itself showed facts that placed a duty upon the insurer to investigate further than it did. The duty was not discharged and the insurer had no right to rely on the representations made. An insurer may not avoid a policy for misrepresentation, even where it did in fact rely, if reliance was not justified.

Statutory Qualifications   Because of the ease with which an insurance contract might be avoided for innocent misrepresentations, several statutory modifications have been adopted that limit that defense. The legislation may require that the misrepresentation be intentional or it may speak to the requirement of materiality.

Statutory Requirement of Intent.   The New York standard fire policy of 1943, which has been adopted as the standard fire policy in nearly every state, provides that:[16]

> This entire policy shall be void if, whether before or after a loss, the insured has *willfully* concealed or *misrepresented* any material fact or circumstance concerning this insurance or the subject thereof. . . .

Therefore the fire insurance policy, and policies which contain fire insurance coverage (such as the homeowners policy), cannot be avoided because of innocent misrepresentation.

Many states have similar provisions for life insurance. Of these, about half the states set forth alternative requirements. The misrepresentation must either (1) have been made with the "intent to deceive," or (2) have materially affected or increased the likelihood of loss.

Determination of Materiality.   It may be generally stated that a statement of fact is deemed material if there is reason to believe that it influenced the insurer's appraisal of the risk or influenced his estimate of the premium to be charged.

In automobile liability insurance, misrepresentations are generally considered to be material when they relate to previous driving record, moving violations, and prior cancellations.

For example, a recent case held that a failure to disclose previous cancellations was material to the acceptance of the risk. Additionally, there was also proof that the insurer would not have accepted the risk had it known of the cancellations.

However, another recent case held that nondisclosure of a traffic ticket for failure to yield right-of-way, which did not involve another vehicle, was not sufficient to avoid the policy where there was no evidence that the insurer would not have issued the policy had it known of the traffic ticket.

Although not readily apparent in these two cases, materiality is usually determined on two different bases. The first one is the *objective reasonable insurer's standard* which asks: What would a reasonable insurer have done with knowledge of the true facts? In the first example, the court could have reached the conclusion if, by applying the objective reasonable insurer standard, it found that the insurer, acting reasonably and naturally in accordance with the usual practices *of most insurers*, would not have accepted the risk. Whether this particular insurer would have accepted the risk is irrelevant to the court's determination.

The second test the court might apply is the *subjective individual insurer's standard* which asks: What should this particular insurer have done with knowledge of the facts misrepresented? In the first example, the court could have reached the conclusion by applying the subjective individual insurer's standard since there was evidence that *this insurer* would not have accepted the risk.

Statutory Modification of Materiality. Consistent with the general purpose of barring immaterial or technical defenses, many states have enacted statutes modifying the common-law defenses as to the effect of the insured's statements. These statutes fall basically into two groups with respect to evidence of materiality, requiring (1) proof of an increase of risk or (2) that the violation contribute to the loss.

INCREASE-OF-RISK STATUTES. The increase-of-risk type statutes are more common and may or may not express a choice as to an objective or subjective standard for determining materiality. The New York statute regarding misrepresentation expresses a choice for the subjective individual insurer standard, by providing in part:

> No misrepresentation shall be deemed material unless knowledge by the insurer of the facts misrepresented would have led to a refusal by the insurer to make such a contract. Determining the question of materiality, evidence of the practice of the insurer which made such a contract with respect to the acceptance or rejection of similar risks shall be admissible.

The Massachusetts increase-of-risk type statute provides in part that no misrepresentation shall be deemed material unless the misrepresentation *increased the risk of loss*. The Illinois statute uses the phrase "materially affected the risk," which appears to have been intended to convey the same meaning as increase of risk.

An example that would clearly fall within the scope of the above mentioned statutes is provided by a case where, contrary to the insured's representation, there was a driver under twenty-five years of age in the household. Since automobile insurers customarily charge higher premiums to younger insureds, probably no one would argue that the *risk of loss* was not increased, or *materially affected.*

CONTRIBUTE-TO-LOSS STATUTES.   Contribute-to-loss statutes modify the law much more radically and are not as common as increase-of-risk statutes.

The rule under most statutes of this type may be stated that *regardless of materiality* the breach of a provision does not avoid the contract where, from its very nature, it could not contribute to bring about the destruction of the property, i.e., in the case of fire insurance. On this theory, courts have held that a contribute-to-loss statute prevents avoidance of a fire insurance policy where the breach related to:

> (1) a representation that the insured had never been refused other insurance; (2) a provision requiring the insured to install mechanical fire extinguishers; (3) a requirement that the insured furnish a certificate of a magistrate or notary public as a part of the proof of loss; and (4) a provision against other, concurrent, or additional insurance.

Misrepresentation of Age.   One of the most common misrepresentations is that of age. Both men and women misrepresent their ages, and invariably they represent that they are younger. If the question of age is asked in the insurance application, it is a material fact. In the case of life insurance, the age of the applicant is crucially important to underwriting and rating.

To deal with age misrepresentation, most states' statutes require that all life and health insurance policies issued in the state contain a so-called "age-adjustment clause." A typical clause might be as follows:

Age and Sex
If the age or sex of the Insured has been misstated, any amount payable by the Company under this policy shall be such as the premium paid would have purchased on the basis of the correct age or sex.

Under this provision the amount payable upon the death of the insured is adjusted if it is shown that age was misrepresented. No cases are known concerning misrepresentation of sex. Insurers set different premium rates for different ages. The amount payable upon death is the amount of insurance the premium paid would have purchased for an applicant of the actual age and sex of the applicant at the time the insurance was taken out. Clearly, understatement of age is a material misrepresentation, and would be a ground for avoidance of the life insurance policy if there were no age-adjustment clause.

Construction of Representations   Misrepresentation of facts, ideas, and circumstances can assume myriad forms. The problem of when a representation becomes a "misrepresentation" sufficient to justify avoidance of an insurance policy is most difficult. Courts take the position that representations are to be construed liberally in favor of the insured; they are required only to be "substantially true" in the opinion of the triers of fact. Even though a representation is not literally true, it is not a misrepresentation if it is substantially true.

To illustrate, an application for an accident and health policy asked whether the insured had ever experienced a "serious injury." Only in a suit on the policy was it shown that the applicant had fallen forty feet from a tree when he was fourteen years of age. The court held that whether that injury was considered serious was for the jury to determine. The court recognized that if failure to mention all injuries sustained through an active life were made the basis for policy avoidance, few policies would stand.

Whether an objective fact that is inaccurate is substantially true depends upon its materiality to the agreement. The test of materiality, in turn, is whether the contract would have been made had the truth been told.

Representations made by insureds play an important role in the law of insurance. A second category of statements, or declarations, has also resulted in much litigation. These statements, contained in the policy, are referred to as "warranties," which will be considered later in this chapter.

Incontestable Clause

The incontestable clause, which is universally included in life, accident and health, and group life insurance policies, is unique in contract law. In no other field of business enterprise is it customary for the parties to agree that the validity of the contract will not be contested after a certain period.

This unique clause is contrary to one of the basic maxims in contract law—that fraud vitiates consent. Genuine assent cannot be based on fraud. In life and accident and health insurance, however, the maxim is revised to read: "Fraud vitiates consent, except in a life insurance contract after the contestable period has expired." Thus, material misrepresentation, concealment, or fraud in connection with life insurance applications may not be asserted by an insurer when the policy has been in force longer than the contestable period (usually two years) during the life of the insured. The insurer in effect agrees to waive these defenses after this time period.

The incontestable clause had its origin in the desire of life insurance companies to give the greatest possible assurance to policyholders that their beneficiaries would receive payment. Cases in which policies had been in force many years, only to be challenged by insurers on the death of the assured, created many difficult problems for beneficiaries and insurers. The beneficaries, on one hand, were denied the policy proceeds; and the insurance companies, on the other hand, found that people were reluctant to purchase policies if the policies might be found invalid after their deaths. The incontestable clause meets both problems by assuring that the insurer cannot dispute the policy as written after a stipulated period. The law of every state requires the clause to be inserted in all life policies.

The incontestable clause resembles a short statute of limitations, because it limits the period during which the insurer may avoid the contract because of misrepresentation, concealment, fraud, breach of condition, or otherwise. The theory is that the company should have a reasonable opportunity to investigate the statements made by the applicant, and that the stated time period is sufficient.

Application of the Incontestable Clause The incontestable clause does not extend coverage. If a policy excludes death resulting from flying an airplane, death resulting from that cause will not be covered by the policy even though two years have elapsed. Nor does the incontestable clause preclude showing that the person who took out the policy had no insurable interest in the life of the insured party. The strong public policy requiring insurable interest to exist when a life insurance policy is purchased (i.e., because such contracts involve wagering on human life) prevails over the public policy that favors the incontestable clause.

Although the incontestable clause applies to fraud, if the fraud is particularly vicious the court may find the policy was invalid at the outset (i.e., void *ab initio*) and may permit the fraud to be shown even after the contestable period has expired.

Thus, a life insurance policy taken out as part of a scheme to profit from the murder of the beneficiary, or the substitution of another person to take the insured's medical examination, are instances in which the incontestable clause will not prevent the insurer from defending an action brought on the policy. The public policy against such flagrant wrongs outweighs the reasons for the incontestable clause.

What Is a Contest? In order for an insurer not to be barred by the incontestable clause from raising a defense, the insurer must institute a "contest." Most courts agree that a "contest" means a formal court action, such as a suit in equity seeking cancellation of the policy. Mere denial of liability under the policy is generally considered not to be a contest. If a court contest is instituted, however, the requirement of the incontestable clause has been met and the insurer may contest liability in the action brought or in a later action.

Contestable Period   The date of issue of the policy or the date the coverage attached, whichever is earlier, controls the period within which the contest must be commenced. The usual incontestable clause requires that the policy must have been in effect for two years *during the lifetime* of the insured. Thus, the policy will not become incontestable if the insured dies during the two year contestable period. The policy will become incontestable only if the insured lives for two years after the incontestable period starts to run. If the insured dies within the two year period the incontestable clause becomes inoperative and the policy is contestable by the insurer.

WARRANTIES

Generally

In contract law, a warranty is a written or oral statement that a certain fact is true. A warranty, unlike fraud, does not require an intention to deceive. Both express and implied warranties usually accompany sales of real and personal property. Warranties may also be promissory. Warranties in sales transactions are discussed in Chapter 13.

In Insurance Contracts

In insurance law warranties are statements or promises contained in an insurance policy that if untrue would render the policy voidable, irrespective of their materiality.

Strict application of this common law definition too often resulted in insurers attempting to escape liability for reasons not material to the person or property involved. Because of the harshness of the warranty doctrine, the courts have whenever possible construed statements as representations rather than as warranties. Courts now agree that in order for a promise or stipulation to be a warranty it must be shown that (1) the parties clearly and unmistakably intended it to be a warranty, and (2) the statement forms a part of the contract itself. If both of these requirements are not met, the court will find the stated fact or promise to be a representation, rather than a warranty.

In the absence of a special statute, an insurer may require that the applicant for insurance agrees to a policy provision that statements of fact or promises in the application are to be construed as warranties. This is called "incorporation by reference," because the policy refers to another document as part of the policy itself. In that event, if the facts stated by the applicant are wrong in any respect, the policy may be avoided.

Classification of Warranties

Affirmative and Continuing (Promissory) Warranties An affirmative warranty states that specific facts exist *at the time the contract is made.* A continuing or promissory warranty states that certain things shall be done or that certain conditions shall continue to exist during the term of the policy. Because they relate only to conditions that existed at the time of the contract, affirmative warranties are less harsh than continuing warranties, and courts prefer to interpret warranties as affirmative. This approach accords with the general rule that where a policy of insurance has two interpretations, the interpretation favorable to the insured will be applied. If an insurer wants a continuing warranty, the language of the policy must clearly state that the warranty is to apply to future and continued use.

For example, a fire insurance application asks, "Who sleeps in the store?" The applicant writes, "Watchman on premises at night." This has been judicially construed to be an affirmative warranty of conditions at the time of the contract. If a watchman slept on the premises at the time the application was made, the warranty was not breached. The fact that at some later date a watchman was not on the premises at night would not constitute a breach of this affirmative warranty.

If the insurer wants a watchman on the premises at night during the term of the policy, the language must clearly say so. Language referring to the future, such as that a watchman *will be* on the premises at night, must be used.

Implied Warranties Implied warranties are very important in sales of goods transactions. Unless expressly excluded, they are applied by the courts and include such warranties as title, merchantability, and fitness. All warranties in insurance law, however, are expressed in the policy or incorporated in it by reference, except for marine insurance. An impliedly excepted cause, such as an insured's act that is designed to cause a loss under the policy, should not be confused with an implied warranty.

The traditional implied warranties in *marine insurance* policies are as follows:

1. *Seaworthiness*—the insured vessel is impliedly warranted to be reasonably fit in all ways (e.g., hull, engines, crew, etc.) to encounter the ordinary perils of its intended and insured voyage.

2. *No Deviation*—it is impliedly warranted that the goods and vessel are going to leave port with reasonable promptness and proceed along the course and at the speed contemplated by the policy. If the vessel deviates in time, destination, or course the policy may be avoided. Reasonable deviations, such as because of a storm or other hazard, are permitted.

3. *Legality*—with certain exceptions, such as evasion of revenue laws, it is impliedly warranted that the venture insured is a lawful one and will be carried out in a lawful manner.

Lessening the Effects of Warranty Doctrine

Insurers generally prefer that statements made by an insured be construed as warranties rather than as mere representations because for a representation to be grounds for avoidance of the policy, it must be proved to have been material. Insurers also prefer that warranties be construed as continuing, and therefore extend through the policy period. Courts and legislatures, however, are generally advocates of the insured and reverse that order of preference.

In life insurance law a discussion of warranties is at best academic and historical. The statutes of most states require that life insurance policies contain a provision that "all statements made" by the insured "in the application shall, in the absence of fraud, be deemed representations and not warranties." They are called "entire contract statutes" because no statement outside the policy and the attached application may be incorporated into the policy by reference.

Although the warranty doctrine continues in force in property and liability insurance, its harshness has been ameliorated. As previously noted, courts, whenever possible, construe statements as representations of fact and not as warranties, and also prefer to construe warranties as affirmative rather than as continuing.

When possible, courts will also construe a policy as severable, so that noncompliance with a warranty bearing on one type of covered property will not defeat coverage for another type of loss exposure under the policy to which the warranty does not relate.

The doctrine of substantial compliance has also been used to ease the insured's burden of compliance. This doctrine takes two forms:

1. Was the insured's compliance substantially as effective as the compliance required?
2. Did the insured do all that one reasonably could do to comply under the circumstances?

Not many courts expressly use this doctrine, and it is more likely that a court that does not want to harshly apply a continuing warranty will give the warranty an equitable rather than a literal interpretation.

The *temporary breach* of a continuing or promissory warranty has been a most troublesome problem for the courts. There are three judicial views on the effect of a temporary breach. If the breach has been cured a court using the oldest view would hold that the policy nevertheless was avoided by the breach. A generous court would hold that since the breach was stopped and the insured is now in compliance that the breach had no effect on coverage. A moderate court would agree with the latter view, unless the now-cured breach caused a continuing increase of likelihood of loss. Modern cases involving the temporary breach of a continuing warranty that has been cured generally involve safety precautions required to be maintained.

The modern fire insurance policy has reduced warranties to two— the "while the hazard is increased" clause, and the "while a building. . .is vacant or unoccupied" clause. It is clear from the wording of these clauses that curing the condition precludes the avoidance of the policy by the company. The use of the word "while" is clearly more favorable to the insured than the prior word, "if."

Under the doctrines of waiver and estoppel, discussed below, the insurer may be deemed to have waived the breach of warranty, or by its actions to be estopped from asserting the breach of warranty. In every case, courts strictly construe the language of a warranty against the insurer. At least partly because of these rules of construction, warranties are not usual in insurance policies.

Judicial Construction of Warranties   The basic rule is that the intention of the parties determines whether a statement or stipulation in the policy constitutes a warranty or representation. Such intention is to be determined by construing the policy as a whole, including the hazards insured, the language employed, and the situation of the parties. The use of the word "warranty" or "representation" is not conclusive. For instance, where stipulations declare statements of fact to be warranties, they will be disregarded where other provisions or circumstances do not indicate that this was the intention of the parties.

Another general rule followed by courts is that a statement is a representation rather than a warranty unless the language unequivocally evidences an intent that it should be construed as a warranty. Where any doubt exists the construction is against a warranty. This conforms to the oft-stated rule that provisions of a contract of insurance will be strictly construed against the insurer, and that forfeitures of rights will never be declared if, by any reasonable construction, such result can be avoided.

Particular applications of these rules stated in the preceding paragraphs demonstrate the ways in which courts avoid results which are unconscionable and/or inconsistent with the reasonable expectations of most policyholders. For example, the representation may be implied from the words used in the policy, as where, by the terms of the policy, the insured event was to begin from the loading, and the risk was at and from a named port. It was held by the court that the words were not a warranty to load at the designated port, but a representation. Here it was not clearly evident that the parties intended a warranty. Another instructive example is provided by an applicant for life insurance who stated that he did not have any disease or ailment of the stomach, when in fact the applicant had cancer of the stomach. The court stated that since the applicant did not have any medical knowledge, such question called only for an opinion to the best of the applicant's knowledge and not for a warranty, and since ambiguities are construed against the insurer who drafted them, the policy was not subject to a rescission because of the false statement.

Statutory Modification

Statutes Eliminating the Distinction Between Representation and Warranty. Whether a statement is to be regarded as a representation or as a warranty is sometimes decided by statute. Although warranties are legal they are often unfair and harsh. In an effort to guard against these unfair and harsh results, some states have adopted statutes which make a breach of warranty no more burdensome for the insured or beneficiary than a material false representation. The Massachusetts statute is typical and provides in part that no oral or written *misrepresentation or warranty* by the insured shall be deemed material or defeat or avoid the policy unless such misrepresentation or warranty is made with actual intent to deceive, or unless the matter misrepresented or made a warranty which *increased the risk of loss.*

The distinction that existed between representation and warranty has also been eliminated in some states employing a *contribute-to-loss* statute. This combination is the most favorable type statute for the insured.

Statutes Modifying Traditional Elements of Warranty. Some states have enacted statutes which modify particular elements of the warranty concept without completely eliminating the distinction between representation and warranty. For example, some statutes prevent the insurer from specifying that representations shall have the same effect as warranties. Other statutes relate to the strict compliance aspect of warranties and specify that only substantial compliance is necessary. Still other statutes relate to the time in which the breach of warranty existed and prevent avoidance of the policy unless it existed at the time of the loss.

It has been held by the courts and provided for by statutes that because of the remedial character of these legislative enactments, they are to be liberally construed by the courts against the insurer in order to effectuate the legislative intent.

Warranty Distinguished from Representation

The different legal requirements and consequences of warranties and representations make it important that they be clearly distinguished. (See Exhibits 4-1 and 4-2.) Distinctions are generally made on the following basis:

1. Warranties are part of the final contract of insurance. Representations are merely collateral inducements to the contract.
2. Warranties are presumed to be material and their breach makes the contract voidable. Representations must be material (i.e., the insurer must prove that the representation induced it to enter into the contract) for the misstatement to permit avoidance of the contract.
3. Warranties are either written in the policy, expressly or incorporated by reference. Representations may be oral, written in the policy, or written on a totally disconnected paper, and need not be expressly incorporated by reference.
4. Subject to the foregoing discussion of their lessening effects, warranties must be complied with strictly. Representations require substantial truth only.

WAIVER, ESTOPPEL, AND ELECTION

Significance of Doctrines

An insurer may deny liability for a claim for any of the reasons just discussed—fraud, concealment, mistake, misrepresentation, or breach of a condition of the policy by the insured. The insurer, however, may be unable to assert these defenses because the insurer has (1) waived the defense, (2) become estopped from asserting the defense, or (3) elected not to take advantage of the defense.

The legal doctrines of waiver, estoppel, and election have been used more frequently in insurance law than in any other field of the law. The terms are often confused, or used incorrectly as synonyms. The doctrines apply to almost every ground on which an insurer may deny liability. Whenever an insurer asserts a policy defense, such as

Exhibit 4-1
Statements of Insured Pertaining to Risk When Applying for Insurance

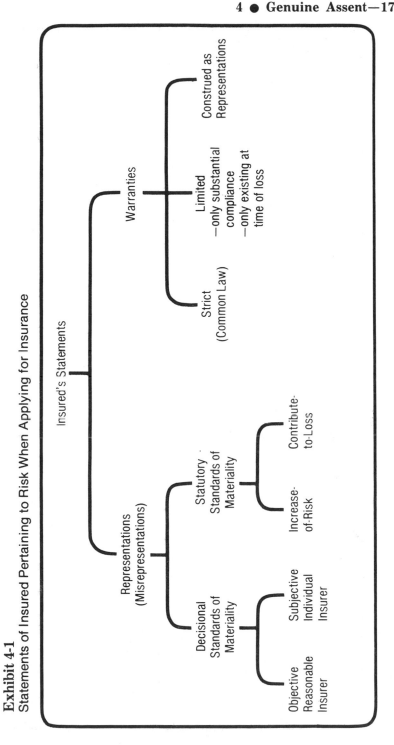

Exhibit 4-2
The Insurer's Defenses Arising Out of the Description of the Risk

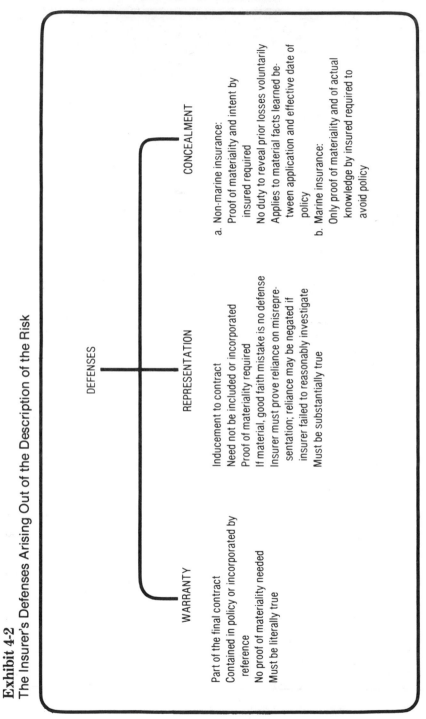

DEFENSES

WARRANTY

Part of the final contract
Contained in policy or incorporated by reference
No proof of materiality needed
Must be literally true

REPRESENTATION

Inducement to contract
Need not be included or incorporated
Proof of materiality required
If material, good faith mistake is no defense
Insurer must prove reliance on misrepresentation; reliance may be negated if insurer failed to reasonably investigate
Must be substantially true

CONCEALMENT

a. Non-marine insurance:
Proof of materiality and intent by insured required
No duty to reveal prior losses voluntarily
Applies to material facts learned between application and effective date of policy

b. Marine insurance:
Only proof of materiality and of actual knowledge by insured required to avoid policy

lack of notice, failure to sue within the prescribed time, fraud, concealment, or the like, the insured will usually respond by invoking either waiver, estoppel, or an election not to assert the defense.

Reasons for Doctrines

There are several reasons for the frequent use of these doctrines in insurance law. As has been seen, the doctrines are ways to avoid the harsh consequences of breach of warranty. Breach of warranty may permit the insurance company to rescind the policy whether or not the breach is material, but these doctrines counter that strictness. They also help the insured to temper the harshness of a contract drafted by the insurer for its own benefit and with little regard for the concerns of the insured.

The doctrines assist the usual insured who does not read the contract but who relies instead on the statements of the insurance agent. Application of the waiver doctrine is a recognition of the fact that insureds often place greater reliance on the oral statements of their insurance agents than on the actual terms of the written contracts.

The basic rationale of the rules is that it would be unconscionable to permit either party to an insurance contract to set up its own wrong as a defense to an obligation incurred under the policy.

Waiver

Waiver is defined as the intentional relinquishment of a known right. It requires both knowledge of the facts, and relinquishment of a right based on knowledge of those facts. Waiver involves conduct of an insurer or its representative that has the legal effect of relinquishing a defense based either on the insured's noncompliance with a condition or on the insured's misrepresentation. No payment or other consideration is required to support a waiver. It may be expressed or implied from the circumstances.

For example, a life insurance company issues a policy to an insured which provides that if the insured enters the military service the company may declare the policy void. The insured subsequently enters the service and is killed in battle. A representative of the company, learning of the death, writes the beneficiary (widow) stating that since the insured died in the service of his country, the company waives its defense that death occurred in military service. Thereafter, the company writes another letter stating it has changed its position and is declaring the policy void. Under these circumstances, a court would find that the first letter constituted an express waiver of a defense and of the power to declare the policy void. That letter would be binding even though it was not based on consideration and even though the beneficiary had not changed her position (as required for estoppel) in reliance on the letter. The company knew the facts and intentionally relinquished its rights when the first letter was written.

When the Doctrine of Waiver Is Inapplicable From the definition of a waiver as an intentional relinquishment of a known right it necessarily follows that there must be an existing policy. A statement made before the contract comes into existence is not a waiver of a known right; it is an attempted waiver of a future right. Suppose in the foregoing case of a clause in a life insurance policy that enabled the insurer to declare the policy void if the insured entered the military service, that the insured in applying for the policy expressed his intention to join up at some later date. Suppose further that the agent said that the company had no intention to enforce the clause. The attempted waiver would be ineffective. The technical reason is that evidence of the conversation would be excluded under the parol evidence rule since the policy represented the integrated contract of the parties.

In addition, the doctrine of waiver does not apply to a peril that is not covered or is excepted in the policy. A peril not covered is simply one that is not included in the policy. An excepted peril, however, is expressly excluded from coverage. It differs subtly but importantly from a condition. It is one thing to provide that the policy does not cover a given peril, and quite another to say that the company has the right to cancel the policy if certain conditions exist. The right to cancel may be waived by the insurer and the full policy remains in force except that the insurer has disabled itself from enforcing that right. A peril that has been excluded expressly, however, is scarcely a right of the insured; it is a duty that has not been assumed. A practical rationale for the same conclusion is that an insurer should not be required to pay a loss when no premium was paid for assuming the loss exposure. For example, suppose that an insurance agent orally represented that an automobile liability policy covered the insured while driving an employer's automobile. In fact, the policy contained a nonowned automobile clause that excluded coverage while driving an automobile furnished for the insured's regular use. Coverage would not be extended to this excluded situation, notwithstanding the agent's representation. The agent might personally be liable for the misrepresentation, but not the insurer.

What May Be Waived A party to an insurance contract may ordinarily waive any right or privilege under an existing contract. Thus, the insurer may waive the benefit of any provision of the policy, even though it is a standard form prescribed by statute. Even a provision in the policy that specifically prohibits waivers may be waived. Agents may waive provisions with respect to notice or proofs of loss, stipulations that the policy is not to take effect until the property has been inspected or a medical examination completed, provisions concerning suspension of the policy for nonpayment of premiums, provisions concerning occupancy and nature of the insured property, and the like.

What May Not Be Waived While virtually any provision inserted in an insurance policy for the benefit or protection of the insurer may be waived, either in whole or in part, a few matters cannot be waived. Thus, an insurer may not waive privileges that are in furtherance of public policy. The requirement that the insured must have an insurable interest in the property or life insured is one example of a rule of public policy. To permit an insurer to waive the lack of insurable interest would clearly be contrary to a basic public policy requirement, and therefore cannot be waived.

Also, although privileges may be waived, facts may not. An insurer does not have the power to change or waive facts as they actually exist. An agent of an insurer will remain the agent of the insurer, even though the insured may agree that the agent is the insured's. Facts are stubborn and may not be avoided. Attempts to have the agent considered the agent of the insured are invariably ineffective on this ground.

When Waivers Require Consideration The law of waivers in insurance law differs markedly from the general law. In general law, voluntary waivers are not binding. In insurance law, however, they are binding. In general law a binding waiver requires some form of consideration.

Some waivers are binding in insurance law without any consideration. An example is the waiver of a right to a proof of loss after the time for filing a proof of loss has lapsed. Other waivers, arguably, have consideration in the reliance by the insured on a promised waiver. An example is a promise not to enforce the occupancy clause of a fire insurance policy, followed by an extensive absence by the insured. This latter instance, however, may also be supported by the theory of estoppel, which will be discussed later. Some waivers, such as a promise to reinstate a forfeited policy upon the payment of the next premium, are clearly supported by consideration. There is no single or unitary theory that can explain waivers in insurance law.

It is clear, however, that the formation of a substitute contract requires consideration. Assume that an insured desires coverage for a specifically excepted peril. Any language by the insurer that purports to be a waiver will be ineffective to afford the coverage unless supported by consideration. An additional premium must be paid to make the attempted waiver enforceable.

To illustrate, the New York standard fire policy excludes loss resulting from theft. As an excepted peril under the policy, an attempt by an agent to cover theft under the policy could not be accomplished by waiver in the absence of additional consideration to support the new and substitute agreement. Only an agreement that the loss would be covered upon payment of an additional premium would make the waiver (now supported by consideration) effective. This is said to be a "contractual waiver," but is actually a new contract.

Another example of a "contractual waiver" is a waiver of premiums provided for in the policy during the period of the insured's total disability. The consideration for this waiver is that the peril is covered by part of the policy premium. It is therefore contractual. Although this is a standard analysis of the problem, from a conceptual point of view the waiver of disability premiums is functionally an additional coverage; the insurer assumes the contingent financial obligation of the insured's total disability to the extent of the premiums due during that time.

Requirement of Knowledge   An insurer must have knowledge of a breach of condition under the policy before it can be held to have waived that breach. Once having such knowledge, however, the insurer must immediately act to disclaim. Failure to act will be deemed to be a waiver of the breach. Whether a right has been waived depends upon the facts of each case. Thus, where the insurer requests information regarding a loss after the expiration of the twelve-month suit clause in the policy, such inquiry is not a waiver of the suit clause. But where an insurer denies liability and refuses to pay a claim, the refusal is a waiver of the policy requirement regarding filing a proof of loss. It is only pertinent knowledge that will qualify as a waiver. Where an agent knew that the insured was constructing a new addition to the insured plant, this knowledge did not indicate that the sprinkler system would be shut off. Failure to act was not a waiver of the automatic sprinkler clause. Once an insured has denied liability on one ground, most courts hold that it may not thereafter defend on a different ground; it is deemed to have waived the other grounds.

Where a liability insurer defends an action brought against an insured, with knowledge of facts that take the case outside the coverage of the policy (and without taking a reservation of right or nonwaiver agreement), the defense will preclude the insurer from denying liability because of noncoverage.

Policy Provisions Prohibiting Waiver   Most property insurance policies contain a provision that, "no permission affecting this insurance shall exist, or waiver of any provision be valid, unless granted herein or expressed in writing added hereto." Policy provisions requiring waivers to be expressed in writing in general are not as a practical matter enforced by the courts. When necessary, courts employ the doctrine of estoppel to circumvent the waiver provision. To hold otherwise, to permit the insurer to negate the defense of waiver by simply inserting a provision in the policy, would be to defeat the law of waivers entirely. Waiver is primarily based on contract theory, which includes the rule that valid and legal provisions of a contract should be enforced, and therefore a nonwaiver provision should be enforced. Even that view, however, has loopholes. Suppose an agent has the right to make certain changes in the policy in writing. Does it necessarily follow that the agent may not orally promise to do so? Ameliorating the contract view, in addition, is the theory of estoppel which is equitable in nature. Although waiver does not always require the reliance needed in estoppel, waivers given contrary to an express nonwaiver provision in the policy will be binding upon the company if all the requirements are met concerning the intentional relinquishment of a known right. In analyzing such problems courts tend to blur the distinction between waiver and estoppel.

For example, an insurance agent tenders X a life policy which contains the condition that the policy shall not take effect unless the first premium is paid in cash. The policy also provides that no waivers may be made unless in writing. X, who is out of funds, offers a ninety day note, which the agent agrees to accept. By the better view this is a waiver, even though it appears to be an agreement contradicting one of the terms of the contract. The condition requiring prepayment in cash may be orally waived by an agent who is otherwise authorized, and this is true even though the policy contains a nonwaiver provision.

How Waiver Is Effected Any words that express, or acts that clearly imply, an intention to give up the right to rescind the contract, or the privilege to assert a known defense, can constitute a waiver. The insurer must know of the breach before it can be waived. Acts which may show an intent to continue the contract in force and therefore constitute waivers include:

1. Receipt of a premium with knowledge of a breach of policy conditions.
2. A demand that appraisers be appointed or that a dispute be submitted to arbitration pursuant to policy provisions, or any other demand by the insurer that it is entitled to only if the policy is in force.
3. Waiver in open court during the course of judicial proceedings.

4. Request for proof of loss after knowledge of a breach without taking a reservation of rights or nonwaiver agreement.
5. Silence of the insurer where silence is for an unreasonable time. Thus, where a defect exists in the proof of loss, the insurer's silence concerning the defect for an unreasonable time will constitute a waiver.
6. Delivery of a policy to the insured with full knowledge of facts that would permit avoidance of the policy, such as knowledge of the falsity of representations made in the application, is a waiver of the right to avoid. Where the insurer knows at the time of delivery of the policy that the insured suffers from asthma, it cannot later claim the insured was not "in good health" at the time of delivery.

Estoppel

General Estoppel is a broad, general principle of law that is found in many areas: the law of agency, contracts, partnerships, corporations, and others. As a concept its outlines are familiar to everyone. Someone makes a statement to another person, the other person in some way relies on that statement, and the maker of the statement does not want to abide by it. This is the common social problem of the broken promise. In law, however, it has strict requisites. A promise that is broken and results in bad feelings is not necessarily one that is legally subject to the doctrine of estoppel in law.

In Insurance Law Estoppel in insurance law is a representation of fact by one party that is relied upon by the other in such a way that it would be unfair to allow the first party to refuse to be bound by the representation. The requisites of estoppel are (1) a false representation of a material fact, (2) reasonable reliance on the representation, and (3) harm or prejudice resulting if the representation is not binding. The elements of estoppel reflect a concept originally developed in the field of equity: the doctrine of equitable estoppel.

For example, a fire insurance policy is issued to an insured on a building located on leased land, a fact the insured disclosed when making the application. The agent delivered the policy to the insured with the statement, "Here is the policy and it fully covers your building." The policy expressly provides that it shall be void if the building insured is located on leased ground. The insured accepts the policy without reading it and puts it with other valuable papers. When the building later burns the insured learns of the policy provision, and the company denies the claim. All the elements of estoppel are present. The company, through its agent, made a false representation by stating that the policy covered the building. The insured reasonably relied on the representation by accepting the policy. The failure of the insured to read the policy does not negate reasonable reliance. For the insurer to assert the policy defense would be prejudicial to the insured, since insurance coverage would be lost. All the elements of estoppel being present, the insurer will be prevented or "estopped" from denying the fact that coverage existed. (Note that no waiver was involved, since there was no intention on the part of the insurer to give up any right under the policy.)

What Raises an Estoppel   Any words or acts of an insurer who is aware of the existence of a breach of condition or other defense under the policy that are reasonably interpreted by the insured as representations that the contract is valid will estop the insurer from setting up the defense.

Since the doctrine of estoppel is an equitable concept, the insured must not be guilty of fraud or bad faith. Equity requires that the insured come into court with "clean hands." The insured must show that his or her actions were in good faith, and in reasonable reliance on the insurer's representation.

It should be remembered that not every utterance is legally binding. The law usually allows people to change their minds, provided a legal obligation has not been assumed.

The rationale of the estoppel rule is not to punish fraud or falsehood but to adjust the loss equitably between two parties, one of whom must bear it, and it is considered that the one who caused the loss should bear the loss.

In the case of Clauson v. Prudential, Clauson was insured under a group life insurance policy issued to Chrysler automobile dealers.[17] The insured had said at the outset that he was not interested in the coverage unless he could obtain $50,000 in life insurance. He was advised by the manager of the Dodge division that he was eligible for only $30,000. However, after some negotiations it was agreed that a $50,000 policy would be issued and a certificate was issued in that amount. Clauson was then accidentally killed. The beneficiary (widow) submitted a claim, and it was found that Clauson had been eligible, under an established credit-point system, for only $30,000 life coverage. The company paid $30,000 and refunded the premium for coverage over that amount. The court held that all the elements of estoppel were present. There was a false representation of a material fact, a reasonable reliance, and harm resulted. The company was required to pay the additional $20,000.

Where an insurer's agent misinterprets questions or falsifies the answers in the application and misleads the insurer into thinking that the questions are answered truly, when in fact they are not, an estoppel will exist. Note that it is the *insurer's* agent who has made the misrepresentation; hence it is the insurer who is estopped to deny the truth of the statements.

For example, a man insures his son, who is captain of the high school football team and also works during vacations as a salesman. The agent describes the son on the life application as a salesperson. The son is later killed in a football game. The insurer attempts to avoid the policy obligation on the ground of the false representation of the nature of the loss exposure. It is proved that the premium charge would have been higher had it been known that the young man played football. In such case, the insurer is estopped to deny the truth of the application. Unless there is evidence of wrongful collusion between the insured and the agent, coverage will exist under the policy as issued.

Similarly, if an insurer's agent states that acts required by the policy of the insurer, such as including a certain policy endorsement, have been done when in fact they have not, the representation will give rise to an estoppel. Thus, where the agent states that an endorsement will be added to a policy to permit a building to be vacated for certain periods, and the policy is delivered without the endorsement, the insurer will be estopped to deny the validity of the intended endorsement. The fact that the insured failed to check the policy will not generally negate the element of reasonable reliance. Oral or parol evidence may be introduced to prove the facts.

Distinguishing Waiver and Estoppel

In the law of insurance the distinction between waiver and estoppel is often blurred. Although the legal effect of the two defenses is the same, they are in fact different and involve distinct elements. The more carefully reasoned cases note the following distinctions between the two concepts:

1. *Waiver* is contractual in nature and thus rests upon agreement. *Estoppel* is tortious in nature and rests upon a false representation.
2. *Waiver* gives effect to the intention of the party waiving. *Estoppel* is enforced to defeat the inequitable intent of the party estopped.
3. *Waiver* is subject to the parol evidence rule. The parol evidence rule has no application to *estoppel.*

Application of Parol Evidence Rule

As noted in Chapter 3, the parol evidence rule prohibits, among other things, the introduction into evidence of oral agreements made prior to or contemporaneous with the execution of a written contract. Waivers, which are agreements, are subject to the parol evidence rule. Thus, a waiver cannot be proved by oral evidence that preceded or accompanied the written contract or policy. Waiver agreements that are alleged to have arisen from words or acts prior to or contemporaneous with the inception of the policy are merged therein, and parol evidence to establish them is not admissable. Waiver agreements made *after* the inception of the policy, if properly authorized, are provable by parol testimony. In the case of waivers, then, an oral promise by an agent to waive future breaches before, or at the time of issuance of, the policy is ineffective as a waiver because of the parol evidence rule. Such promises may not be introduced in evidence.

Parol evidence has no application to estoppel, which is a remedial process of equitable origin, grounded upon inequitable conduct, and collateral to the contract. Any words or acts raising an equitable estoppel may be shown by parol testimony, and it is immaterial whether they occurred before or after the making of the formal contract.

Doctrine of Election

Election is the voluntary act of choosing between two alternative rights or privileges. If the insurer (or insured) chooses between two available rights, this may imply a relinquishment of the right not chosen.

Application of the doctrine of election, a cross between waiver and estoppel, limits a party's range of choices. The concept may be useful to the party asserting it since it softens (1) the waiver requirement of voluntary relinquishment of a known right, and (2) the estoppel requirement of detrimental reliance. Properly viewed, waiver, estoppel, and election are not interchangeable doctrines.

The thrust of the election doctrine is that an insurer (or insured) may not adopt a "heads I win; tails you lose" position. The insurer may not treat the contract as valid for the purpose of collecting premiums and invalid for the purpose of indemnity.

Examples of election may be seen wherever one of the parties has two or more alternatives and chooses one of them. Very frequently an insurer must decide between rejecting a tender of premium and affording coverage. If the insurer elects to accept the premium, it should be bound by that choice and not thereafter be permitted to reverse its position and to declare that no coverage exists.

Another example in which election is a more accurate term than waiver or estoppel involves a choice between alternative rights under the policy. The standard fire policy gives the insurer the option, in case of loss, to repair or rebuild instead of paying money compensation. When the insurer has by words or acts led the insured to believe that it will pay a loss in money, the insurer may be said to have elected that method of discharging its duty under the policy. The insurer had reserved the privilege of electing between two alternative duties and, having elected, it extinguished the privilege of choosing the second alternative. The insurer is not permitted to pursue the course most advantageous to itself in each instance. It is bound by its election once made even though no voluntary relinquishment of a known right was made (i.e., no waiver) and even though no detrimental reliance is established (i.e., no estoppel).

Election by Insured The doctrine of election also applies to choices made by the insured. In many instances the insured must make a choice between two inconsistent legal remedies. Having elected one course of action, the insured may not thereafter pursue the other.

For example, a life insurance company cancels a life insurance contract that includes provisions for the payment of disability benefits. The insured thereupon elects to bring an action against the company for fraudulent breach of the contract and is awarded damages. Later, the insured attempts to bring another action to recover disability benefits that would have accrued prior to the date of the previous suit, had it not been for cancellation of the contract by the company. In the first suit the insured alleged that the contract was breached and that the insured was entitled to damages. In the second suit the insured demands benefits that would have been payable if the contract had not been breached. The second cause of action is inconsistent with the first. Invocation of the first remedy is an election that, by the commencement of the action, will bar the insured's right to invoke the other remedy. The insured is bound by the first choice (the award of damages) and cannot proceed with the second action for the payment of disability benefits. The insured has elected to treat the contract as canceled, and that election has barred the right to pursue the second and inconsistent remedy.

Choosing Among Waiver, Estoppel, and Election

While the doctrines of waiver, estoppel, and election are in theory available to either party to the insurance contract, in the majority of cases these concepts have been invoked by insured claimants. Such

Exhibit 4-3
Major Doctrines Aiding Insured

	Waiver	Estoppel	Election
Defined	—voluntary and intentional relinquishment or abandonment of known right (by insurer)	—detrimental reliance (by insured) upon some representation (by insurer) express or implied in words or in conduct	—voluntary action or choice of inconsistent alternatives (by insurer); choice of one aiternative precludes subsequent selection of different alternative
Relative Advantages for Insured	—no proof that insured relied to his detriment is required	—no proof of voluntary relinquishment of known right	—softens the respective requirements of voluntary relinquishment and detrimental reliance
Relative Disadvantages for Insured	—requires proof of voluntary relinquishment of known right	—proof of detrimental reliance required	—difficulty of proof
Other Distinguishing Characteristics	—act or conduct of one of the parties (insurer) to the contract required	—proof of act or conduct of both parties to the contract required —insurer: representation of a fact —insured: reliance on the representation only to suffer disadvantage	—act or conduct of one of the parties (insurer) to the contract

claimants are usually well advised to rely on the doctrine of estoppel, as opposed to either waiver or election. The central element of estoppel, which makes it particularly effective, is that the claimant has changed his or her position and suffered detriment in reliance on the position taken by the opposition. Reliance and detriment are usually easier to establish than the insurer's intentional relinquishment of a known right (waiver) or choice between two remedies (election). (See Exhibit 4-3.)

Guarding Against Waiver, Estoppel, or Election

When there is a claim made against the insured the insurer has three main alternatives. The insurer may (1) refuse to defend the insured, (2) investigate and/or defend under a reservation-of-rights notice or nonwaiver agreement, or (3) investigate and/or defend without any reservation. (See Exhibit 4-4.)

Justified Refusal A justified refusal by the insurer, where the claim is outside the policy coverage, presents no problem. All cases agree that, where the insurer justifiably refuses to defend, the insurer is not guilty of a breach of contract and no liability attaches to its action. Thus it would have no obligation under the policy concerning any claim arising out of the noncovered loss.

Unjustified Refusal If the insurer wrongfully refuses to defend an action against the insured, i.e., the claim is determined to be within the policy coverage, the insurer is liable for breach of contract. This is the case even though the refusal is based on an honest mistake. In such a case, the insurer is liable for the amount of the judgment rendered against the insured or of a reasonable settlement made by the insured. In addition to a possible judgment which may be in excess of the policy limit, all reasonable expenses, such as court costs and attorney fees, are recoverable.

An obvious result of an insurer's refusal to defend is the release of the insured from the contractual obligation to leave the management of the suit to the insurer. In such case the insurer cannot subsequently complain about the conduct of the defense. Similarly, the insured is released from other affirmative policy provisions such as proof of loss, notice of suit, and provisions requiring cooperation, aid, and assistance. The insurer by his unjustified refusal waives any possible defense based on such noncompliance.

Defense in the Absence of an Effective Reservation of Rights Where the insurer with knowledge of a ground of forfeiture or noncoverage assumes and conducts the defense of an action brought against its insured without giving timely notice of its reservation of rights, it is precluded from asserting such ground of forfeiture or noncoverage.

Investigating and Defending Under a Reservation-of-Rights Notice or Nonwaiver Agreement Reservation-of-rights notices and nonwaiver agreements are instruments used by insurance companies to prevent claims by the insured for avoidance of certain defenses against liability that the insurance company may have under the terms of the policy. They are frequently used by claims personnel where the

Exhibit 4-4
Post-Loss Alternatives Available to Insurer Where Coverage is Questionable

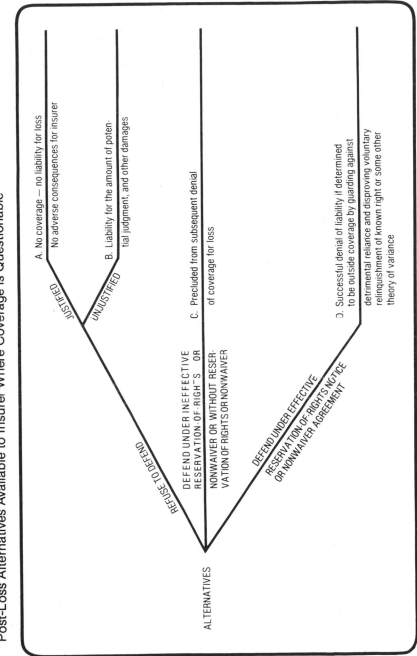

investigation of the loss reveals the possibility that for one reason or another coverage under the policy may be denied. Should the company proceed with further investigation of the loss after the possibility of such a policy defense comes to its attention, the insured, under certain circumstances, might claim the benefit of waiver, estoppel, election or some other theory by virtue of the company's proceeding with the handling of the loss on the merits, and thus he could establish rights for coverage at variance from or contrary to the terms of the policy contract.

This possibility poses a dilemma for the insurer: if it continues with investigating the loss on the merits without deciding whether or not it has a coverage defense, it may be found to have prejudiced the insured's rights and to have brought about a waiver or estoppel or some other variance with the policy provisions and thereby to have forfeited its policy defense; or, in order not to fall into the trap of such potential forfeiture of defense, it must stop all activity with respect to the loss itself and make a determination of whether or not the policy covers the situation. The latter course is occasionally a time-consuming procedure itself and could cause the danger of not being able to limit the magnitude of the loss by timely activity and thus incurring a potential increased liability should it decide later to grant coverage. Nonwaiver agreements and reservation-of-rights notices are designed to solve this dilemma. Their purpose is to allow the insurer to go on record of advising the insured that the company's activities in connection with the loss on the merits are not to be construed as the relinquishment of its rights to stand on policy provisions (which may establish its non-liability) and thus to prevent the arising of waiver, estoppel or other rights at variance with the policy. Having done so, the insurer is in the position to continue with its investigation and evaluation of the loss on its merits, an activity beneficial to the interests of both the insured and insurer. Simultaneously, the insurer can investigate and determine the question whether the policy terms have been violated by the insured and whether or not it will accept the liability under the contract.

Nonwaiver is simply a contractual agreement in which the insured and the insurance company agree in writing that neither party will waive any of its rights under the policy as a result of the investigation or defense of an action brought against the insured. It is bilateral, in that it is executed by both parties. A reservation-of-rights notice differs from this in that it is unilateral, usually taking the form of a letter from the insurer to the insured.

As a matter of claim practice, the insurer's representative will attempt to enter into a nonwaiver agreement with the insured as soon as the potential coverage question surfaces. The nonwaiver agreement, being contractual in nature, requires the signature of both parties, i.e., insurer and insured.

Occasionally some practical difficulties arise in the attempt to secure the insured's consent and signature:

1. If the claim representative clearly explains the significance of the nonwaiver agreement, the insured may nevertheless become alarmed and refuse to sign. This will at least delay the investigation of the loss which the agreement is supposed to expedite.

2. If the claim representative does not explain the importance of the agreement fully and fairly to the insured, the binding force of the nonwaiver agreement becomes questionable, even if signed by the insured. It may give rise to a later claim of lack of contractual intent, of misunderstanding, duress, distraction or other defenses which may conceivably jeopardize its validity on the theory of disallowing unconscionable advantage.

In the first case, the only way the company can protect itself against later claims of variance is to resort to the device of the reservation-of-rights notice. This is a unilateral declaration and notice to the insured to the effect that the insurer intends to safeguard its rights to dispute liability under the terms of the policy and that its conduct in investigating the loss should not be construed contradictory in this respect.

Both the reservation-of-rights notice and the nonwaiver agreement are designed to prevent subsequent claims of not only waiver, but also of estoppel, election, and other theories of rights at variance with policy provisions.

Certain elements must be present in order for a reservation-of-rights notice or nonwaiver agreement to be effective.

First, relevant to the reservation-of-rights notice, it must be communicated to the insured. This is usually accomplished by letter and when appropriate is supplemented by entry into the court record. In any event oral notice is seldom used because of difficulty of proof.

Another important consideration is that the notice must be timely. The reason that a reservation-of-rights or nonwaiver notice prevents estoppel is that it gives the insured an opportunity to hire his own counsel to take over the defense if the insured so desires. Since the notice must give reasonable time to assume the defense, the safest course for the insurer is to give notice as soon as it obtains knowledge of the policy defense.

Consistent with the purpose of the reservation-of-rights notice, it must be drafted so as to fairly inform the insured of the insurer's position. Basically, it should include the particular policy provisions relied on by the insurer, and the facts, which if proved, would result in a denial of liability.

Examples In a case where a liability insurer questioned coverage under an automobile policy, the insurer wrote six letters to the insured, informing him that it would defend an action against him, but with express reservations of its rights to contest the policy. The insured contended that it never received the letters sent to him and did not actually execute a nonwaiver agreement. The court held that the rule of estoppel was not applicable as against the insurer because the failure of the insured to execute a nonwaiver agreement did not affect the validity of the insurer's reservation of rights and that in view of the fact that the letters had been addressed to him at his residence and place of employment, a presumption arose that the letters were received by him.

While no precise rule can be stated, it appears that if the insurer acts in good faith and uses every reasonable method to contact the insured, the insurer will not be precluded from asserting its policy defense.

An example of the rule that an insurer must disclaim liability within a reasonable time is provided by the following case. The insured was involved in an automobile accident. The application and the policy provided that the use of the car would be for "pleasure and business." In accordance with the policy provisions the insurer undertook the investigation of the claim and seven months after the accident the insurer discovered that at the time of the accident the automobile was being used to carry passengers for hire, which was excluded from coverage. Upon learning this fact, the insurer disclaimed liability. The court, in holding that the insurer was *not* estopped from raising the policy defense in spite of the seven months elapsed between the accident and the date of the disclaimer, said that (1) the insurer could rely upon the insured's report of the accident which did not disclose that he was carrying passengers for hire at the time, (2) the insurer disclaimed liability as soon as it learned of the true facts, and (3) a year and a half elapsed before the case went to trial, so that the insured had ample time to prepare his own defense.

Illustrations of the two instruments follow:

Nonwaiver Agreement

It is hereby agreed by and between the (insurance company) and (insured or other party signing the agreement) that no action heretofore or hereafter taken by the (insurance company) shall be construed as a waiver of any of its rights and defenses under policy number issued to (insured) with respect to any claim or suit arising in connection with an accident or loss which occurred on or about (date) and at or near (place).

It is further understood and agreed that by the execution of this agreement (insured or party executing agreemeent) does not waive any rights which he may have under said policy.

Signed (Insured)

Signed (Insurance Company Representative)

Reservation-of-Rights Notice

To (insured or other person claiming protection under the policy)

Subject: Accident or loss on (date) at or near (place)

Your letter reporting the above accident was received on (date). In view of the delay in reporting this matter and for other reasons which may become evident as a result of our investigation, such investigation is being made with full and complete reservation of all rights afforded to the (insurance company) under policy number . . . . . issued to you.

Signed (Insurance Company Representative)

Chapter Notes

1. Restatement, Contracts, Sec. 471, Comment (i).
2. Carter v. Boehm, 3 Burr. 1905 (1776).
3. Carter v. Boehm, 3 Burr. 1905 (1776).
4. 6 Edward VII, Chap. 41, Sections 17 & 18.
5. Neptune Insurance Co. v. Robinson, 11 Gill & J (MD) 256 (1840).
6. Hartford Protection Insurance Co. v. Harmer, 2 Ohio State 452 (1853).
7. National Life Ins. Co. v. Harriott, 268 So. 2d 397 (FL App. 1972).
8. Hartford Protection Insurance Co. v. Harmer, *supra*.
9. Betty Blair v. National Security Ins. Co., 126 F.2d 955 (3rd Cir. NY).
10. DeBellis v. United Benefit Life Ins. Co., 372 (PA) 207 (1953).
11. DePee v. National Life & Accident Ins. Co., 62 P.2d 923 (KS 1936).
12. Carroll v. Preferred Risk, 215 N.E.2d 801 (IL 1966).
13. Restatement, Contracts, Sec. 502, Illustration 4.
14. Metropolitan Life Ins. Co. v. Madden, 117 F.2d 446 (FL 1941).
15. Jeffries v. Life Ins. Co., 89 U.S. 47 (1874).
16. New York Standard Fire Policy of 1943, lines 1-5.
17. Clauson v. Prudential, 195 F. Supp. 72 (MA 1961).

CHAPTER 5

Interpretation of Contracts

CONSTRUCTION AND INTERPRETATION

General

Many principles and maxims are applied by courts to determine the meaning of contract language. Just as it is necessary for courts to interpret legislative enactments and constitutions, they are also called upon to construe and interpret contracts. The basic purpose of construing or interpreting a contract is to determine the intention of the parties who drafted it. If the language is clear and unambiguous, construction or interpretation is easy; the intent expressed in the agreement will be followed. When the language of a contract is ambiguous or obscure, courts apply established maxims of construction in order to ascertain the supposed intent of the parties. These maxims are not used to make a new contract for the parties or to rewrite the old one. They are applied by courts merely to resolve doubts and ambiguities in the agreement.

It must be stated at the outset, and kept in mind throughout the discussion of interpretation of contracts, that the application of the maxims of interpretation is more of an art than a science. The maxims that will be considered do not point with unerring accuracy to one and only one interpretation. They are sometimes ambiguous in themselves, and sometimes conflict with one another. Therefore they cannot properly be called "rules" of construction. They are in essence the customary legal way of attempting to interpret contracts, and serve their best purpose in sharpening analysis and in bringing out possible alternative interpretations of the words and phrases used.

The general standard of interpretation is to use the meaning that the contract language would have to a reasonably intelligent person who is familiar with the circumstances in which the language is used. Thus, language is judged *objectively*, rather than subjectively. What one party may have thought was meant is immaterial, since words are given effect in accordance with their meaning to a reasonable person under the circumstances. In determining the intention of the parties, it is the expressed intention that controls, and this will be given effect unless it conflicts with some rule of law or public policy.

Words Given Normal Meaning

A basic maxim of contract interpretation is that words are to be understood in their plain and normal meaning. This rule is followed even though the consequences may not have been within the contemplation of the parties. The language is judged with reference to the contract's subject matter, nature, objects, and purposes. Although everyday language is given its ordinary meaning, technical words are given their technical meanings. Words with an established legal meaning are given their legal meanings. In interpreting the words and conduct of the parties to a contract, a court seeks to put itself in the position the parties occupied at the time the contract was made. The law of the place where the contract was made controls the formation of the contract. In every case the circumstances under which the contract was entered into may be shown, and this is true whether the contract was oral or in writing. The circumstances of the agreement, the subject matter, the relationship of the parties, and the object of the agreement will all be considered in determining the meaning of the agreement and in giving effect to the intent of the parties.

Although the plain meaning standard is usually appropriate when attempting to ascertain the intention of both parties to a contract, it may not be applicable when attempting to ascertain the intention of only one party. Consider the case of an applicant for life insurance who names as his beneficiary "my wife." At the time the policy was taken out the insured was living with a woman who was not his legal wife because he had gone through a ceremony of marriage with her without divorcing his first wife. The "plain meaning" of the term "my wife" clearly conflicted with the intention of the insured, and a court may well ignore the plain meaning in favor of the insured's intention.

Attempt to Effectuate Intent

A fundamental principle of contract construction is that courts apply the interpretation that best effectuates the intention of the parties. To ascertain that intention, the instrument is read as a whole.

If several writings relate to the transaction, all of them are considered together. Individual clauses and specific words are construed in relation to the main purpose of the contract. The intention expressed in the contract will control, and not the subjective intention of one of the parties. If the intention appears to be clear from the words used, there is no need for the courts to go further; the words govern. Courts do not attempt, under the pretext of interpretation, to make a new contract for the parties. Neither do they change a written contract to make it express an intention different from that expressed by the parties in the words of the agreement. People generally are taken to mean precisely what they say. Courts do not make the agreement for the parties; they ascertain what their agreement was, if not by its general purport, then by the literal meaning of its words.

Entire and Divisible Contracts

In an entire contract, the party first to perform must render full performance in order to be entitled to performance from the other party. For instance, unless otherwise provided, goods must be delivered before they need be paid for. In a divisible contract, however, the performance of a separate unit entitles the performing party to immediate payment. For instance, in a contract that provides for the delivery of goods in installments, the price to be paid for each installment when delivered is generally stated. Similarly, in most contracts of employment the courts permit recovery by the employee for the number of weeks or months of service rendered, on the theory that such contracts are divisible. A contract is said to be divisible if performance by each party is divided into two or more parts and it appears that the parties contemplated that each installment of the series of performances would be compensated for separately. Therefore, failure to perform one installment would not constitute failure to perform the entire agreement.

Parties seldom provide in their contracts that the contract is divisible or entire. The courts must determine whether so-called "agreed equivalents" were involved. If it is established that the parties intended that each would accept the part performance of the other in return for his or her own without regard to subsequent events, the contract is divisible. If, however, the division of the contract into parts was only for the purpose of providing periodic payments to be applied toward the amount due upon completion of the contract, it is an entire contract. Courts prefer to construe a contract as divisible, if reasonably possible, in order to avoid the hardships resulting from construing the contract as entire. If a contract is construed as requiring an entire performance, no duty to pay arises under the contract until full performance is completed.

Under the Code The Uniform Commercial Code (UCC) provides that a sales contract is entire unless the parties have agreed otherwise. Thus, all of the goods called for by the contract must be tendered in a single delivery, and payment in full is due upon such tender.[1] If the contract permits installment deliveries, the seller can demand a proportionate share of the price as each delivery is made, provided the price can be apportioned, as when goods are sold for a certain price per item. If there is a substantial default on an installment, as may occur if the goods tendered do not conform to the contract, the buyer may reject the installment.[2] When an installment breach is one that cannot be cured, or if the seller will not give adequate assurance that the breach will be cured, the buyer can rescind the entire contract. If the buyer accepts a nonconforming installment without giving notice of cancellation or without demanding that the seller deliver goods that conform, the breach may not be used as a basis for rescission.[3]

Clerical Errors and Omissions

Courts correct obvious clerical errors or mistakes in writing and grammar. Thus, words may be transposed, rejected, or supplied, if necessary, to make the meaning clear. In every case the court will attempt to read the contract as the parties intended, unless the error or omission makes it impossible to determine the intent of the parties.

Implied Terms

Certain contract terms, though unexpressed, are read into contracts by courts unless a contrary intention was expressed. The law presumes that the parties intended some provisions. Thus, courts generally presume that payment under the contract was to be made in legal tender, and not in foreign currency, or some substitute for money. In service contracts it is implied that the service will be rendered with reasonable care and skill. If time of performance is not specified, it is generally implied that performance will take place within a reasonable time. If in the trade it is customary to extend credit, such trade practices are normally read into the contract. Thus, every provision of a contract need not be set forth. Some are implied by the courts if it is reasonable to do so to effectuate the intent of the parties. The unexpressed or implied obligations in these instances are those that are believed to be inherent in the transaction. The parties are held not only to what they expressly intended, but also to intentions that the court presumes they would have had, had they thought about the matter at all. For an intention to be read into the contract, however, it must be a necessary legal implication. When a contract is made, it is presumed that the parties intended to embody all the legal consequences of their acts whether they knew them or not.

Under the Code In the formation of contracts for the sale of goods, the UCC restates and expands the rule that every provision need not be set forth in order that a contract be binding on the parties. The UCC provides that "even though one or more terms are left open a contract for sale does not fail for indefiniteness if the parties have intended to make a contract and there is a reasonably certain basis for giving an appropriate remedy.[4] Thus, in contracts for the sale of goods, if the parties fail to state a price for the goods, a reasonable price is implied.[5] If no time for performance is mentioned, performance will be implied to be within a reasonable time.[6] In both these cases a reasonably certain basis for affording a remedy exists. Where the parties have failed to specify the quantity of goods to be sold, the courts are reluctant to imply the amount intended by the parties. If no quantity was mentioned, a court will probably find that the contract fails for indefiniteness and will not imply the amount of goods intended to be sold. If one of the parties has agreed to purchase all requirements from the other party (a requirements contract), or to sell all output to the other party (an output contract), the UCC implies that these provisions mean "such actual output or requirements as may occur in good faith. . . ."[7] In those types of contracts, therefore, a court determines whether the output tendered or requirements demanded were in good faith or whether they were "unreasonably disproportionate to any stated estimate or . . . to any normal or . . . comparable prior output or requirements. . . ."[8] Strictly speaking, output and requirements contracts are not indefinite; they are indefinite as to quantity at the time they are entered into, but actual events make the quantities definite as output or requirements become known.

Contradictory Terms

If clauses in a contract are in conflict but an interpretation is possible to give effect to them, that interpretation will be adopted. A similar difficulty is often experienced when the parties have made typewritten or handwritten changes in a printed contract form. The courts have established a system of priorities: handwriting prevails over typewriting; typewriting prevails over printing. This is a common sense approach because handwritten changes are usually the last to be made. If there is a conflict between words and figures (as on a check drawn on a bank), the words will prevail over the figures. In construing such conflicting language, the courts give preference to acts that require greater attention to detail and effort. The result presumably reflects the true intent of the party most accurately.

Ambiguity

The term "ambiguity" has two meanings. First, it may mean that a provision of the contract can reasonably be interpreted in more than one way. Second, it may mean that after using all the tools of interpretation the court cannot determine the meaning of the language used.

If a provision can reasonably be interpreted in more than one way, the courts adopt the interpretation least favorable to the party who incorporated the provision into the contract and most favorable to the party who merely assented to it. It is well known that courts construe insurance policies against the insurer who designed the policy. Similarly, words in an offer are construed against the proposer, and words in an acceptance are construed against the acceptor. Words in a promissory note are construed against the maker. Words in a conveyance of property are construed against the grantor. The principle on which this rule is based is that persons are responsible for ambiguities in their own expressions. Having initiated the expression, and thereby having the power to phrase it as they please, they cannot expect a court to construe the ambiguity in their favor.

If a provision is so ambiguous that a court cannot determine what it means, using the usual tools of interpretation, evidence from outside the contract may be admitted. A court will, for instance, permit evidence of prior or contemporaneous agreements to shed light on the meaning of the ambiguous language. This evidence will not be excluded by the parol evidence rule because that rule prohibits only evidence that tends to contradict the express terms of the contract and does not prohibit evidence that tends to show the true meaning of the language used.

Interpretation Placed by Parties

The interpretation that the parties have placed on their contract, as shown by their conduct subsequent to its formation, has great weight with the courts in determining the meaning of doubtful terms. The parties know best what they meant by their words, and their actions under the agreement are some of the best indications of what they meant.

The UCC provides that if a contract for the sale of goods ". . .

involves repeated occasions for performance by either party with knowledge of the nature of the performance and opportunity for objection to it by the other, any course of performance accepted or acquiesced in without objection shall be relevant to determine the meaning of the agreement."[9] The UCC thus recognizes that the actions of the parties are strong evidence of their intentions.

If there is no ambiguity in the agreement and the meaning of its terms is clear, the fact that the parties have by their subsequent conduct placed an unreasonable and erroneous interpretation upon the agreement does not prevent a court from enforcing the contract in accordance with its terms. A court will not remake the agreement for the parties simply because they have acted contrary to its provisions.

Construed as Lawful and Fair

If two interpretations of a contract are possible, one lawful and the other unlawful, the courts assume that the lawful interpretation was intended by the parties. If there is a choice, a contract is construed as reasonable and fair rather than unreasonable and harsh to one of the parties. Under that approach interpretations that avoid a forfeiture of property are adopted when possible. If the terms of the contract itself leave its meaning in doubt, courts invariably ascribe to the parties an intention to enter into a fair agreement and adopt a construction that makes the contract equitable.

The "unconscionable contract or clause" section of the UCC brings out this approach clearly. That section, which applies to the sale of goods, provides that a court may find all or any part of a contract to be "unconscionable" and may either refuse to enforce it at all or may apply it in a way that avoids "any unconscionable result."[10] This approach transcends and ignores interpretation and means simply that a harsh and one-sided sale of goods agreement is not to be enforced. The intention of the parties is not material. This approach is slowly being incorporated into areas of law other than the sales of goods.

Trade Usage and Course of Dealings

In interpreting contracts, usual words are given their ordinary meanings, technical terms are given their technical meanings, and consideration is given to local, cultural, and trade usage meanings. In attempting to establish the intent of the parties, courts also consider their prior course of dealings and their manner of performance under the contract. The UCC recognizes that these considerations can create difficulties in interpretation. The UCC attempts to define and distinguish "trade usage," "course of dealings," and "course of performance," and establishes an order of priority between the three concepts to resolve conflicts among them.

Trade usage is defined by the UCC as ". . . any practice or method of dealing having such regularity of observance in a place, vocation or trade as to justify an expectation that it will be observed with respect to the transaction in question."[11] This is basically the standard used in mercantile law for centuries, and differs from common law "custom" applied in nonmercantile cases which generally required universal observance from the beginning.

A *course of dealings* relates to similar transactions between the parties prior to the contract in question. *Course of performance* involves the actual performance of the contract in question that has been rendered without objection.

The UCC has established priorities to be used when these four considerations are in conflict. The order of priority is (1) the express terms of the agreement, (2) course of performance, (3) course of dealings, and (4) trade usage.[12] If a court is seeking to determine the intent of the parties, and the express terms of the agreement do not indicate that intent, the prior course of dealings by the parties should be given preference over usage of the trade to establish the meaning of the agreement, and evidence on these questions is admitted by the courts.

Parol Evidence Rule and Rules of Interpretation

The parol evidence rule provides that once an agreement has been reduced to writing by the parties, no evidence may be introduced that tends to contradict its terms. The rule assumes that all the negotiations and agreements of the parties were integrated into the final agreement, which may consist of one or more writings. Any evidence, therefore, that tends to contradict or upset that integrated agreement will not be permitted in evidence over the timely objection of the other party. If the other party does not object, the right to exclude the evidence is waived.

So understood, the parol evidence rule has no application to the introduction of evidence to explain ambiguities. The purpose of such evidence is to make clear what the final agreement was intended to mean. The evidence is intended to explain, not to contradict. Therefore, evidence of the course of performance under the contract, or of the parties' prior course of dealings, or of the usages of trade, are all clearly admissible to assist the court in determining the meaning of the contract.

Public Regulation of Contract

Freedom of contract has had a checkered history in our law. The concept of a contract as we know it is scarcely four hundred years old. Medieval bargains were strictly controlled by law and custom, but with the advent of mercantilism political philosophers of the seventeenth and eighteenth centuries speculated about the natural rights of people, their rights to life, liberty, and property. Translated into law, the rights became those of property and contract, which are really two sides of the same coin.

After the Civil War, the virtual identity of the interests of government and business impelled the courts to carry freedom of contract to a new high. Based in part on interpretation of the due process clause of the Fourteenth Amendment to the U.S. Constitution, statutes enacted by the states to regulate contracts, particularly those that regulated the relations between employers and employees, were declared unconstitutional.

The twentieth century, however, has seen a change in the attitude of the courts. With increasing recognition of the fact that not all contracts are the result of free negotiations between parties of equal bargaining power, and with recognition of the fact that private contracts may have considerable impact on society as a whole, courts have not only permitted the legislatures to interfere in the making and enforcing of contracts, but have themselves created doctrines that control and affect the contract-making process.

Consequently, today we have statutes that give previously nonexisting rights to consumers, employees, minority groups, military veterans, corporate shareholders, and many others. The UCC in many of its provisions requires a standard of "good faith" that is not usually found in sales of goods contracts. "Good faith," as required of merchants by the UCC, is defined as ". . . honesty in fact and the observance of reasonable commercial standards of fair dealing in the trade."[13] That standard, therefore, is flexible and changes as commercial standards change.

In the field of insurance law, freedom to contract for insurance protection is circumscribed by legislation, government regulation, and court interpretation. The insurance policy is no longer viewed as a mere agreement between an insured and an insurer. Legislation in the various states prescribes standardized language and provisions to be included in many types of coverage. State insurance departments have the authority to approve policy forms, and can be quite exacting in their insistence on the inclusion or exclusion of certain policy language. Courts uniformly construe the insurance contract as affected with a public interest, and consider the social utility of insurance in addition to the immediate rights of the parties.

No longer can a contract be considered a strictly private arrangement in which social interests play no part and which is immune from governmental interference. The new theory of contract is that societal interests must be dominant if not paramount. Not only is this based on the fact of differing bargaining power among contracting parties, but also on the idea that contracts that do not foster societal interests, as perceived by those who pass the statutes and promulgate the rules, either should not be permitted to be formed, should be controlled in their performance, or one or both of the parties should be held to account either by the criminal or the civil law.

INTERPRETATION OF INSURANCE CONTRACTS

Contract of Adhesion

As discussed in Chapter 1, an important characteristic of the insurance contract is that it is a contract of adhesion. That is, it is generally drawn by the insurer, and its language may either be accepted (adhered to) or not accepted by the insured. The courts assume that the insurer had every opportunity to draft the language in a form favorable to itself, and conclude that any ambiguity or unclear meaning should be strictly construed against the insurer. The concept of strictly construing the language of a contract against the party who drew it is not unique to insurance law, but has received considerable emphasis in the field of insurance. Great effort and expense are employed by insurers in an attempt to structure insurance contracts, or policies, in language that has precise legal meaning. This effort tends to result in documents that are difficult to read, and adds to the tendency of courts to support such emerging concepts as the principle of reasonable expectations.

Principle of Reasonable Expectations

Not sufficiently applied by the courts to be called a doctrine, and yet sufficiently referred to so as not to be ignored, the principle of reasonable expectations has been supported as a reasonable supplement to the general rule of resolving ambiguities against the insurer. One eminent authority on insurance law maintains that it is "a principle that insurance law ought to embrace."[14]

The principle is discussed more fully in Chapter 8, and at this point will be described only briefly. In general, it is the principle that courts should interpret the insurance contract to provide the coverage that a reasonable buyer of insurance would expect to obtain under the circumstances. Thus, the objectively reasonable expectations of applicants for insurance and of intended beneficiaries regarding the terms of insurance contracts should be honored even though careful study of the policy provisions would not have supported such expectations. The policy language is to be construed as a layperson would understand it and not according to the interpretation of those skilled in the law of insurance. Under this principle the right of insurers to use qualifications and exceptions from coverage that are inconsistent with the reasonable expectations of a policyholder is called into question. Proponents contend that the policyholder's reasonable expectations should control, even though the policy is explicit and unambiguous, because insurers know that ordinary policyholders do not in fact read their policies. Although the principle of reasonable expectations may be viewed as a corollary to the principle of resolving ambiguities against the insurer, the principle appears to be gaining broader application in current court decisions.

What Is Included in the Insurance Contract

The insurance contract is generally entered into following a series of negotiations. The question has frequently been raised as to which papers and conversations form the ultimate agreement. In general, and in keeping with the dictates of the parol evidence rule, it may be said that once the policy contract has been reduced to writing, all prior negotiations or agreements, written or oral, are considered to have been merged into the writing. Every contractual term contained in the policy at the time of its delivery, and those written in afterwards (policy riders or endorsements) with the consent of both parties, are part of the written agreement.

It is generally required that conditions, endorsements, applications, and other papers must be referred to in the policy if they are to become part of the policy. Thus, unless forbidden by law or by a provision of the policy, all papers expressly designated and made part of the policy contract by the terms of the policy thereby become a part thereof.

Advertising materials and circulars issued by insurers are not generally found to be part of the contract, unless they are expressly made so by reference in the contract. If such materials contain false representations, an action for deceit or a suit for rescission may be maintained against the insurer. As a general rule, however, courts do not admit evidence of such materials to vary the terms of the policy agreement.

Policy Riders   In the insurance business, it is often necessary to add a new term to a policy or to modify or waive an existing term. Insurers issue policy riders for these purposes. When riders are properly delivered and accord with policy provisions, they are binding on the parties as though contained in the original policy. Indication that a rider has been properly communicated to the insured is uniformly required by the courts.

RIGHTS OF THIRD PARTIES

General

The general rule of contract law is that one has no rights under a contract unless he or she is a party. Contracts affect only the contracting parties. Although a third party may expect to benefit under another's contract, it ordinarily does not give the third party any rights. The law recognizes, however, two situations in which third parties have rights and permits them to enforce a contract made by others: (1) an *assignment* of a contract by which one party transfers rights arising under a contract to a third party, and (2) *third-party beneficiary* contracts, in which one party contracts with another party for the purpose of conferring a benefit upon a third party. In each of these situations, the contract may be enforced by the third party.

Assignments

Assignment of contracts is common. A credit transaction, which entitles one person to receive money from another, is often assigned by the creditor to a third party, such as a bank. *Assignments* involve transfers to other persons of rights of performance under a contract. The party to the contract who makes the assignment is the *assignor*, and the party to whom the contract is assigned is the *assignee*. In the event the assignment is not honored, the assignee may generally sue the party failing to perform just as though the assignee had been a party to the original contract.

Rights Assignable   Most contract rights are assignable. Thus, a seller can assign the right to receive payment for the sale of goods to a third person, the assignee. The party owing the obligation to pay for the goods, the *obligor*, then owes the duty of payment to the assignee. Ordinarily, any right to collect a debt may be assigned, the reason being that it is usually no more difficult for a debtor (obligor) to pay the assignee the amount owed than it would have been to pay the original creditor (assignor).

Rights Not Assignable   Notwithstanding the general rule that contract rights are assignable, certain contract rights may not be assigned without the obligor's consent. The most common situations in which contract rights are not assignable are as follows:

1. When the right of assignment is restricted by law. Specific legislation prohibits assignment of some contract rights. Prior assignment of veterans' disability benefits, assignment of government pensions, assignment of wages in some states, assignment by a prospective heir of an estate inheritance, and assignment of workers' compensation are often restricted by law. Attempted assignments of such rights are not enforceable by the assignee against the third party.
2. When the contract itself prohibits the right of assignment. The parties to an agreement may specify that rights under the contract shall not be assigned to others. Such agreements are valid and enforceable. Thus, the standard fire insurance policy prohibits its assignment to new owners of the property insured without the consent of the insurer. An attempt by the insured to assign the policy to a new owner and to impose an obligation on the insurer to make payment to the assignee in the event of loss would be ineffective.
3. When the contract is personal. Thus, when a doctor or lawyer contracts to provide services, such as a surgical procedure or representation in court, the personal duties may not be delegated to another. It is also held that personal rights are not assignable. In personal service contracts actual performance by the obligor is required, and attempts to shift that performance to a third party will not be permitted unless the original parties to the contract agree to the change.
4. When the assignment materially alters or varies the performance of the obligor. Thus, if B contracts to deliver oil to A's premises in the city where A and B are located, A may not assign the right to receive delivery of the oil to C, who lives in a distant location. The assignment would materially alter the performance required of B.
5. When personal satisfaction contracts are involved. Hence, when the contract provides that the goods or services are to be satisfactory to the purchaser, the agreement is subject only to the buyer's judgment and the buyer may not substitute the judgment of a third-person assignee.
6. When a personal injury is involved and a judgment has not been obtained. The general rule is that a claim against another for damages resulting from personal injury may not be assigned.

If, however, a suit has successfully been brought and a judgment obtained, the judgment may be assigned. If the damage is to property, the right to sue for damages is assignable. An insurer, for instance, who reimburses the property's owner may receive an assignment of the right to proceed against the wrongdoer to collect the amount paid. Such assignments involve the right of subrogation, which enables the insurer to "stand in the shoes" of the insured to obtain damages.

Delegation and Assignment Under the UCC The UCC provides that the duties of either party to a sale of goods contract may be delegated unless the parties have agreed otherwise or where the nondelegating party has a substantial interest in having the "original promisor perform or control the acts required by the contract."[15] Thus, a seller can usually delegate to someone else the duty to perform the seller's obligations under the contract.

The UCC also provides that rights cannot be assigned "where the assignment would materially change the duty of the other party, or increase materially the burden or risk imposed on him by his contract, or impair materially the chance of obtaining a return performance."[16] Under the UCC, "unless the circumstances indicate the contrary," a provision prohibiting assignment only restricts the delegation of duties and does not prohibit the assignment of rights."[17]

Form of Assignment Neither formality nor writing is needed for an assignment to be effective. Any words or conduct that indicate an intention on the part of the assignor to transfer contractual rights effect a valid assignment. Assignments are transfers and need not be contracts. Therefore assignments made as gifts are nevertheless enforceable against the obligor.

It should be noted, however, that if an assignment involves subject matter covered by the Statute of Frauds, as when rights under a contract for land are assigned, the assignment must be in writing to be enforceable. Statutes of frauds in every state require all transfers of interests in land to be evidenced by a written document.

Requirement of Consideration Although an assignment is a transfer and not a contract, a promise to make an assignment must be a valid contract to be enforceable. Therefore, if A promises to make an assignment of a contract right to B, all of the requirements of a valid contract, including consideration, must be present. If, however, A makes the assignment as a gift, the assignee is entitled to enforce the assigned contract right against the obligor even though the assignee has given no consideration to the assignor for the assignment. This result is in accordance with the general law of gifts. A promise to give a gift is not enforceable, but once the gift is delivered the gift is legally effective and irreversible.

The gift of an assignment of a contract right, however, has one important difference: an assignor who has not received consideration for the gift has the right to rescind the assignment at any time before the contract has been performed by the obligor, without liability to the assignee.

Rights of Assignee   As a general rule the rights of the assignee do not exceed those of the assignor. The legal maxim is that "the rights of the assignee can rise no higher than those of the assignor." If the other party (obligor) has a defense to the original contract, the defense may be asserted against the assignee. Thus, if the original contract was obtained by the assignor through fraud or duress, the defense may be asserted against the assignee.

Consumer sales contracts often provide that if the seller assigns the contract, usually to a finance company or bank, the buyer agrees not to assert against the assignee any defenses that may be had against the seller-assignor. This clause is an attempt to equate the contract with a negotiable instrument, which affords special protection against defenses by persons taking the instrument under certain conditions. Adding such provisions to a sales contract makes the sales contract very marketable, since it places the assignee in a favored position. Recent legislation and case law at both federal and state levels have done much to abrogate the effectiveness of such provisions. For the most part, persons who receive assignments of sales contracts today take such assignments subject to any defenses good against the assignor.

Duties of Assignee   Although the assignee normally obtains rights under an assignment, duties may also be imposed by the assignment. The assignor who undertook performance is not, however, relieved of those duties simply by delegating them to the assignee. A primary obligation to perform usually remains with the assignor. In the event the assignee fails to perform in keeping with the terms of the original contract and the assignor is called upon to perform, the assignor will have a right of action against the assignee for failure to perform. Whether the assignee is also liable to the third party for the faulty performance is a question that can be determined only by careful examination of the entire transaction.

In general, if rights are assigned and obligations are delegated (the entire contract) to the assignee, the courts will permit enforcement by the third party against either the assignee or assignor, but not against both of them. For example, in the case of construction contracts the prime contractor normally delegates performance of all or a portion of the construction to subcontractors. These delegated duties are usually routine and it is contemplated by the parties that subcontractors will be involved. If a subcontractor fails to perform properly, the assignee (subcontractor) may be sued by either the assignor or the third party (obligee). If, however, the duty that was attempted to be assigned (as in personal service contracts, for instance) was not properly delegable, then the assignor alone remains liable for its faulty or improper performance, unless the other party has agreed to accept the assignee's performance.

Under the UCC, an assignment that is general in its terms, such as "all my rights under the contract," is considered both an assignment of rights and a delegation of obligations under the agreement. The assignee is assumed, unless the contrary is indicated, to have promised to perform the contract obligations, and the promise may be enforced either by the assignor or by the third party.[18]

Notice of Assignment A valid assignment takes effect immediately, even though the assignor has not advised the obligor of the assignment. The assignee should, however, immediately notify the obligor of the assignment. In the absence of notice, the obligor may pay the assignor without knowing of the assignee. The assignee's right to demand payment or performance from the obligor would thus be defeated.

Notice of assignment also protects third parties, who may take a later assignment from the assignor. The assignor would not have the right to make the second assignment, but would have the power or ability to do so. Thus, the original obligor might make payment to the second assignee.

Which of the two assignees has superior rights against the obligor is a question that has received different answers. The common-law view was that once the assignor had assigned the rights, a second assignment was impossible since the assignor had nothing left to assign. The second assignee merely had rights against the assignor. Another view, simple in operation, is that the first assignee to notify the obligor of the assignment has superior rights, and the tardy assignee merely has rights against the assignor. The third view is that the first assignee has superior rights regardless of notice, unless the second assignee receives payment from or a judgment against the obligor and has no knowledge or notice of the prior assignment.

If, of course, the obligor has received notice from both assignees or notice from one assignee and a demand for payment from the other, the obligor should file a bill of interpleader, thereby joining both assignees as defendants, pay the money into court, and have the court determine which assignee is entitled to payment. If the obligor pays one or the other, there is still the possibility that the wrong party is being paid.

Third-Party Beneficiary Contracts

Contracts may be made for the express purpose of benefiting some third party. These contracts, called *third-party beneficiary contracts*, are of two types: *donee-beneficiary* and *creditor-beneficiary*. Beneficiaries of both types have rights against the original promisor. A third category of beneficiary, the so-called *incidental beneficiary*, obtains no enforceable rights.

Creditor Beneficiary If the purpose of a contract is to discharge an obligation owed by one of the parties, the person to be paid is a creditor beneficiary. For example, *A* owes *C* $500. *A* sells his car to *B* for $500 in return for *B*'s promise to pay the $500 to *C* in discharge of *A*'s debt to *C*. *C* is a creditor beneficiary and has an enforceable claim against *B*. Unless *C* otherwise agrees, *C* still has a cause of action against *A* until the original debt is paid. *C* thus has two possible remedies: (1) to proceed against *B* as a creditor beneficiary, or (2) to proceed against *A* under the original $500 debt. If the intent of the promisee *A* in obtaining the promise from the promisor *B* was to discharge some obligation to a third party, *C*, either due or supposed to be due from the promisee to third party, the third party is a creditor beneficiary. It is the *intent* of the promisee (the party obtaining the promise) that is all important in these situations, not the intent of the promisor or of the third-party beneficiary.

Donee Beneficiary If the intent of the promisee in obtaining the promise was to make a gift to a third party, to confer a gratuity on that third party, the third party is then a donee beneficiary. To illustrate, *A* wishes to make a gift to *C* of $500. *A* sells his car to *B* for $500 and obtains *B*'s promise to pay *C* the $500 price for the car. *C* is a donee beneficiary of *B*'s promise for $500, and *C* has an enforceable claim against *B* for $500.

Characteristics of Beneficiary Contracts The relationship between the parties to a beneficiary contract may be portrayed as in Exhibit 5-1.

The elements of a third-party beneficiary contract are as follows:

1. There must be a binding contract between the promisor and promisee.
2. The parties to the contract must intend that the third party be benefited by and acquire rights under the contract.

Exhibit 5-1
Relationship Between Parties to a Beneficiary Contract

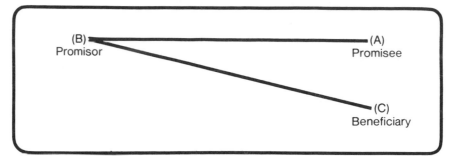

- If the intent is to discharge an existing obligation, the contract is a creditor beneficiary contract.
- If the intent of the promisee is to make a gift to a third party, the contract is a donee beneficiary contract. Some cases hold that the promisee's intention must merely be to benefit the third party.

3. Care must be exercised in each case to note to whom the performance in question is due. If the performance is owed to a third party, then there is a third-party beneficiary contract (either creditor or donee) and the third party can sue to enforce it; if, however, performance is to be made to the promisee only, then only the promisee can sue and no rights accrue to the third party against the promisor.

4. The beneficiary is always subject to defenses that the promisor may have against the promisee. Thus, the beneficiaries' rights are subject to the usual defenses in contract actions, such as lack of consideration, illegality, fraud, and so on.

Legal Trends in Beneficiary Contracts The long-held distinction between creditor and donee beneficiary contracts is becoming less important in the law. The Restatement of Contracts, Second, treats creditor and donee beneficiaries as one class, that of "intended beneficiaries."[19]

Suppose, for instance, that C enters into a valid and legal contract to purchase land from B, breaches the contract, and forfeits the deposit to B. Then suppose that A expresses an interest in the land, but finds out that C, whom he does not know personally, has forfeited a deposit. Believing that if B obtains the same purchase price from himself (A), and that this would not be fair to C, A agrees to purchase the land only if B will promise to repay C's deposit. B agrees, and a contract is drawn between A and B incorporating those terms. On the theory that

A intended to benefit *C* by obtaining *B*'s promise, and regardless of *A*'s motive in obtaining that promise, *C* would have a right to obtain the forfeited deposit from *B* under some modern cases.

Beneficiaries' Rights Under the Contract In general, beneficiaries under contracts, whether creditor, donee, or intended, may enforce the contract. Suppose, however, that the original parties, the promisor and the promisee, agree to annul or change the contract and to eliminate or reduce the rights of the beneficiary.

The contract between the original parties may, of course, provide either that they retain or do not retain the right to eliminate or modify the promisor's duty to the beneficiary. If nothing is said, the older view is that a donee beneficiary's rights may not be cut off without his or her consent, but that a creditor beneficiary's rights may be cut off by the original parties. The modern and growing trend, however, is to permit the original parties in all cases to cut off the beneficiary's rights unless: (1) the beneficiary can prove that his or her position has been changed materially in reasonable reliance on the contract, or (2) that he or she has already commenced suit on the contract.

Incidental Beneficiaries An incidental beneficiary has no rights under the contract. For example, the City of X contracts with Y Water Company to maintain sufficient water pressure at the hydrants for fire protection. A citizen of City X has a house that burns down due to insufficient water pressure. The citizen is an incidental beneficiary and has no enforceable rights under the contract. No performance is due the citizen under the contract. The duty to the citizen is at best indirect.

When a person claims beneficiary status, the court must decide whether the contracting parties intended to confer a benefit upon that person. Unless the person making the claim can convincingly show a direct interest in the performance of the contract, known to the contracting parties, the third party will be considered an incidental beneficiary only.

ASSIGNMENT OF INSURANCE POLICIES

General

There are two kinds of ownership rights in our legal system: *choses in possession* and *choses in action*. The word "chose" (pronounced "shows") derives from French and means "thing." A *chose in possession* is a tangible, physical object. It is called a chose in possession because one can see and feel it. If it is destroyed there is nothing left to own.

A *chose in action* is a right to sue. It is not tangible and cannot be destroyed by any physical means. It may or may not be evidenced by a writing. A written contract is evidence of a *chose in action*, but the destruction of the writing will not destroy the contract right. Destruction of the writing may make the contract more difficult to prove or, if evidence of the contract must be in writing to be enforceable under the Statute of Frauds, may make it impossible to prove.

The term "assignment" refers to transfers of *choses in action*. Policies of insurance are *choses in action* that are assignable under the same general rules that govern assignment of other rights to sue.

Two important considerations affect the validity of an assignment of an insurance policy, a *chose in action*:

1. Whether the assignment is made before or after loss.

   • An insured loss creates a mere money claim, which is identical to other claims and can readily be assigned.

   • Assignments attempted before a loss occurs raise special problems because of the special nature of the insurance contract. Since the insurance contract is a personal contract that requires the utmost good faith between the parties, consideration must be given to the next point.

2. The type of insurance policy involved. Does the policy involve life, fire, property, accident and health, or other types of coverage? The nature of the coverage will determine its assignability.

Assignments After Loss

As a general rule, after a loss occurs the policy represents a claim for money and may freely be assigned. The moral hazard has distinctly been reduced since the loss has already occurred, although there is the possibility that the assignee may collude with a corrupt contractor and submit a fraudulent claim. The insured's right to be paid for the loss is assignable without the consent of the insurer. Thus, if an insured's property is damaged by fire to the extent of $5,000, the right to collect that amount from the insurer under a fire policy may be assigned to a third party, even though the original policy could not have been assigned without the consent of the insurer. After the loss the insured has a mere claim for money that may be freely assigned. When, however, an attempt is made to assign an insurance policy prior to loss, the type of policy involved will control whether assignment is possible.

Loss-Payable Clauses An insured may provide in the policy for a future assignment of a claim for a loss. Such an arrangement is called an "anticipatory assignment," and is accomplished by including a loss-payable clause in the policy. A loss-payable clause is only an assignment of the loss claim, if any, and is not an assignment of the policy. Hence, it is valid even if made payable to a person who has no insurable interest in the property insured. The insurer still promises to indemnify the insured, and compliance by the insured with the conditions of the policy is still required. The insured, not the assignee, is the proper person to file proof of loss. The provision in most policies requiring that the insurer consent to an assignment does not apply to anticipatory assignments under loss-payable clauses. Even the addition of the words "as interest may appear" to the clause does not mean that the payee must have an insurable interest in the property.

Property Versus Life Insurance Policies

In analyzing the provisions of property insurance policies, the dual usage of the term "insured" in property insurance contracts must be kept in mind:

1. Broad sense. This means the person whose economic interest is protected by the contract, most often the owner of certain property but also includes creditors of the latter, such as mortgagees, *provided* certain inportant contractual formalities and provisions are fully complied with. The most important such provision is the mortgage clause in the standard fire policy and other policies covering real property.
2. Narrow sense. This means only the person or persons named as "insureds" in the policy. There is an interesting contrast as to the rights of such "named insured" between property and liability insurance policies. In the former, it is possible that persons other than the named insured, such as designated mortgagees, have rights *superior* to the named insured, whereas in liability insurance policies the "named insured" is always the one most favored among all classes that may claim protection under the contract.

For assignment purposes the law distinguishes between policies of property insurance on one hand and policies of life or accident insurance on the other. Property insurance policies, such as fire and inland marine, are highly personal contracts. These policies invariably expressly prohibit assignment without the consent of the insurer. The character, credit, activities, and conduct of the insured materially affect the insurer's decision to underwrite the applicant. Property insurance does not attach to the property that is the subject of the insurance, nor does it pass to a transferee with the property; it does not "run with the land." The fire policy may be transferred or assigned to the new owner only with the consent of the insurer.

A property insurance contract cannot be assigned before loss without the insurer's consent. The insurer must have the opportunity to examine the characteristics of the assignee (new insured) and to decide whether to accept the assignment. If consent is given, a new contract is formed between the insurer and the assignee.

Assignment of Fire Insurance Policies Assignments of fire policies can occur either before or after loss. Assignments made after loss represent mere claims for the amount of damage and may be freely made. In assignments of fire policies made before loss, three fact situations should be distinguished.

Assignments to the Vendee of the Insured's Interest in the Property. These assignments are ineffective without the consent of the insurer. After transfer to the vendee, the insured no longer has an insurable interest in that property. The insurer cannot be required to accept a loss exposure that could well present factors not acceptable under the underwriting standards of the insurer. (Perhaps the transferee engages in different, more hazardous activities.) If the insurer consents to accept the new insured, however, the assignment constitutes a _novation_, that is, an entirely new contract between the insurer and the assignee of the policy, even though a physically new contract is not issued. Because the approved assignment is a new contract with the assignee, the assignee takes the contract free of any defenses or defects that may have been raised against the old contract when owned by the assignor (original insured). Also, since the assignor is now a stranger to the contract, its validity cannot be affected by the assignor's subsequent acts or omissions. It should be carefully noted, therefore, that novation differs from a true assignment because the new insured takes the policy free of any defenses that existed between the original parties. The insured has a new policy. In the usual case of assignment, the rights of the assignee rise no higher than those of the assignor. The assignee has only the old contract, with all its attributes and defects. (This topic is covered further under the heading "Vendor's and Vendee's Interests.")

Assignments Made to Mortgagees or Other Lien Holders. A valid assignment of a fire policy can be made to one who has a mortgage or other lien on the insured property. Here the assent of the insurer does not constitute a novation. The assignor-insured retains an interest in the insured property and in the policy that is, in effect, pledged to secure the debt or mortgage. In case of loss, the insured-mortgagor is entitled to any surplus insurance money remaining after payment of the mortgage debt, and the insured remains in possession and control of the insured property. Consent to the assignment by the insurer does not make the assignee-mortgagee a party to the contract, but it is a recognition by the insurer that the mortagee is to receive whatever money may become payable under the policy. Thus, in the absence of a special clause creating an independent agreement between the insurer and the mortgagee, the assignee-mortgagee's interest is subject to being defeated by the insured's default or breach of policy condition.

Under the provisions of the *Standard* or *Union Mortgage Clause*, however, default on the part of the mortgagor does not invalidate the rights of the mortgagee under the policy. Under the *Standard Mortgage Clause*, appended to most fire and homeowners policies, the rights of the mortgagee (assignee) can rise above those of the assignor. For instance, under that clause, the fact that the insured-assignor's own neglect resulted in the loss occurring will not prevent the mortgagee from collecting under the policy to the extent of the mortgagee's interest in the property.

The mortgagor's fire policy is, in effect, collateral pledged to secure the debt. Therefore, the mortgagee may normally reassign the fire policy, along with the underlying debt, to still another mortgagee without the necessity of obtaining the original insurer's consent.

Assignment to a Stranger as Collateral Security for a Debt. An issued fire policy may be deposited as collateral security with a creditor who has no interest in the property insured. A pledge of a policy is perfectly valid, even without the consent of the insurer, as an *equitable assignment* of any sum that may become payable under the policy. Because the assignee has rights only after a loss, such assignments do not come within policy provisions prohibiting assignments without the insurer's consent. The pledgee cannot, of course, claim greater rights than the insured, and is subject to all defenses available against the insured.

The methods whereby persons and interests claiming protection under a property insurance policy may be designated can be tabulated in the manner shown in Exhibit 5-2.

Assignment of Marine Policies Marine policies are a well-established exception to the rule that property insurance policies may not be assigned. The reason for assignability is that sales of goods to be shipped by marine transportation are usually CIF contracts. That means that the seller's price includes the cost of the goods, the cost of insurance, and the cost of freight. It is entirely possible that the buyer will resell the goods while in transit, and therefore it is essential that the insurance placed on the goods by the original seller be transferable to the new buyer.[20] This practice accommodates the difficulty of insuring goods at different points in transit and is a practical necessity.

Exhibit 5-2
Types of Interest Designations in Property Insurance Policies

Additional Insureds— all listed as such— "As their interests may appear" proportionately in the damaged property	"Loss Payee" or "Assignee of the Chose in Action" by "Loss-Payable Clause" —entitled to policy proceeds though has no interest in insured property	Assignee of the Policy or person designated in "Mortgage Clause" (mortgagee) —substituted as insured with independent interest in the property insured
	—has no better rights than named "Insured" (mortgagor) and may be defeated by latter's policy violation	—has rights independent from original named "insured" (mortgagor) and not defeasible by latter's policy violation
	—may be created without insurer's consent	—may be created only with insurer's consent

The marine policy normally runs "for the account of whom it may concern." The marine policy does not, however, "run with the goods." The vendee of the goods has no rights under the insurance policy unless the vendor-insured in fact assigns the policy. If an assignment is made, the vendee-assignee may later sue under the policy in his own name. As with most assignments, the assignee of a marine policy takes only the assignor's rights and is subject to any defenses the insurer may have against the assignor.

Assignment of Life Insurance Policies In contrast to property insurance assignments, the assignment of life insurance contracts is affected by different considerations that cause different consequences. The property insurance contract is pure protection and has no investment features. The life insurance contract, however, is not only protection for the beneficiaries, but it can also be a very valuable asset of the insured owner. In addition, the property insurance contract is written after taking into account the moral hazard, but the moral hazard is slight in life insurance. Third, in life insurance the law of assignments must take into account the interests of the beneficiary, but in property insurance the "beneficiary" is the insured.

To the extent that life insurance is an asset and an investment, public policy requires that assets, including life insurance contracts, be alienable, that is, capable of being sold or given away. "Unreasonable" restraints on alienation are, and have been, void.

Therefore, both practical and legal considerations lead to the result that the owner of a life insurance policy may not only assign proceeds on death of the insured, or the policy when it is paid up, but may also assign the policy while it is a contingent right. This right of assignment applies to term life insurance, industrial life insurance, as well as to group life contracts. While language in some master group life contracts continues to limit assignment of certificate holder interests under the contract, the trend is clearly away from permitting such restriction. Rulings of the U.S. Supreme Court, U.S. Treasury Department, and specifically enacted laws in many states have recognized and expanded the right of assignment of group life insurance interests. The principle supported is that people have the right to deal freely with all types of property interests, including interests in life insurance policies, unless there is a law expressly limiting such right.

Assignment of Life Policies for Benefit of Creditors   Almost all life policy assignments are to creditors to secure debts. This use of the assignment clearly takes advantage of the investment quality of life insurance. The creditor may contract for the protection of the cash value during the debtor's life, and in any event is entitled to payment from the proceeds should the debtor die during the pendency of the loan.

Assignment of Life Policies as Gifts   Just as the owner of an asset should have the right to use it as security for a debt, so the owner should have the right to give it as a gift. Generally this is an intrafamily arrangement, accompanied by designating the donee as the beneficiary if this was not already true. The new owner is a "volunteer," that is, has given no consideration for the assignment. The new "volunteer" owner has all rights under the policy that the original owner had.

Assignments to Purchasers for Value   Although an owner of an asset should be able to sell it, assignments to persons who are neither creditors nor natural objects of affection may serve as cloaks for illegal wagering transactions. For example, if the assignee induced the insured to apply for life insurance, promised to pay the first and all subsequent pemiums and perhaps a cash consideration in addition, the intention to wager on human life would clear. The pretended assignee would be the real purchaser, using assignment as a subterfuge to procure an illegal contract of insurance. Some courts would hold the entire transaction void; others, reluctant to permit insurers to escape policy liability altogether when premiums have been paid over a period of time, would void only the assignment. The beneficiary or the personal representatives of the assignor (insured) would be entitled to the proceeds, after the gambler-assignee recovered the premiums and consideration paid.

Suppose, however, that the insured under a life policy finds it impossible to pay the premiums. Unless a sale to a third person can be made, the value of the policy may be substantially or completely lost. Under those circumstances a sale to a third party that is not found to be a wagering contract generally will be valid. This may be true even though the assignee has no insurable interest in the insured's life, because the investment and asset characteristics of life insurance, which require free alienability to be meaningful, outweigh the insurable interest doctrine.

Rights of Beneficiaries Versus Assignees The beneficiary's interest may be irrevocable or revocable. The former is rare today, but if irrevocable an assignment may not infringe upon that person's rights under the policy without that person's consent. If revocable, however, most courts hold that an assignee's rights are superior to those of the revocable beneficiary; the assignment changes the beneficiary to the extent of the assignee's interest. If the assignee is a creditor, for instance, he or she is entitled to repayment of the debt, the interest, and any expenses incurred to keep the policy in force. The revocable beneficiary is entitled only to the excess, if any. The same is true if the estate of the insured is named beneficiary.

Form of Assignment of Life Policies The normal practice is to deliver the policy to the assignee or agent accompanied by a written assignment. Policies usually provide that a copy of the written assignment be filed with the insurer.

A few states require (1) a contract to assign life insurance in the future, and (2) a present assignment, to be in writing under their statutes of frauds. There is a paucity of authority on the question, but it appears that the requirement that the assignment be in writing can be bypassed by independent proof of the assignment, such as proof of delivery of the policy to, and payment of the premiums by, the assignee. This accords with the spirit of the Statute of Frauds rule as applied to sales of goods, that proof of part performance is sufficient to prove an oral contract up to the extent of the actual part performance.[21] The part performance rationale does not seem to apply to a contract to assign a life policy in the future.

INSURANCE AS
THIRD-PARTY BENEFICIARY CONTRACT

General

Insurance contracts provide many examples of third-party beneficiary agreements. The life insurance policy is one of the best known examples. The contract between the insured and the insurer is for the benefit of a third person, the beneficiary, who seldom gives consideration for this benefit and is usually a donee beneficiary. The rights of beneficiaries under life insurance policies usually may be altered or eliminated during the life of the insured if the policy provisions permit. In addition, consider a few of the other areas in which third-party interests frequently become important in insurance contracts.

Third-Party Interests in Liability Insurance   Liability insurance protects an insured against loss caused by that person's tort liability to a third person. Although the policy is obtained by a named insured, the protection may extend to others, such as additional drivers of the insured's car. The victims of the insured's negligence also benefit from that liability coverage. In recent years some states have adopted "direct-action statutes," which permit injured persons to sue the defendant's insurance company directly, or to at least join the insurer in an action brought against the insured. In most jurisdictions, however, the theory continues that the purpose of liability insurance is to indemnify the insured who is required to pay a loss caused by the insured's negligence. Under this view, the third party has no standing to sue under the insurance policy until the claim has been reduced to judgment against the insured. Only after a favorable judgment, and after the insurer has declined payment of benefits may the third party pursue the insurer.

Vendor's and Vendee's Interests   Though frequently unaware of it, purchasers (vendees) of real estate are exposed to loss. For reasons shrouded in the mists of an early seventeenth century English statute, a vendee of real estate obtains an equitable interest in it at the moment the agreement of sale is signed by both parties. The real estate is the vendee's, subject to the payment of the purchase price. This is called the doctrine of *Equitable Conversion.*

One consequence of this equitable ownership is that the vendee bears the chance of loss. If the property is destroyed by casualty before the legal conveyance has been made and title transferred, the vendee must nevertheless pay the full purchase price. The doctrine runs counter to common understanding, but is so imbedded in the law that only a few states have changed this consequence.

The vendee may eliminate the problem by having the contract provide that the burden of any loss shall be on the seller (vendor) until the title to the property is actually transferred. After that time, of course, the loss exposure lies with the new owner and the old policy of the vendor terminates.

If the loss exposure is on the vendee, there are three fact situations to consider: (1) only the vendor has insurance coverage on the property sold, (2) both the vendor and vendee have separate coverage, and (3) the vendor and the vendee purchase a policy of insurance together.

The first arrangement, that the vendor alone has insurance, is by far the most common in sales of residences. If the property is damaged or destroyed by fire, the sale will nevertheless go through. Because of the principle of indemnity, the vendor is not permitted to recover on the policy and obtain the full purchase price. In accordance with lay expectations, under the majority view courts credit the amount of insurance proceeds received by the vendor to the purchase price. The theory is that the vendor holds the proceeds as a constructive trustee for the vendee. (To avoid the harsher result of violating the principle of indemnity, the courts must violate the principle that insurance is personal and does not run with the land.) To the extent the insurance coverage is inadequate, of course, the vendee suffers the excess loss.

The second arrangement, that the vendor has and the vendee purchases insurance on the property to protect their respective interests, is usual in commercial transactions and in some sales of residences. This is a good arrangement for the vendee who then controls coverage in amount, type, and carrier. The general rule is that both will recover to the extent of their respective losses. If the loss is complete, both recover completely. The vendor has an insurable interest in the entire property because the vendor holds legal title until it is transferred. The vendee has an insurable interest in the entire property because the vendee holds equitable title and a loss exposure. Another approach applied in a recent case is to prorate the loss between the two carriers, and still another is to treat the vendor's insurance as primary and the vendee's insurance as excess coverage. Both these latter views accord with the general philosophy that one loss should give rise to only one recovery.

The third arrangement is the most sophisticated. If the vendor and vendee together have obtained fire insurance on the property covering their respective interests "as they may appear,"any insurance proceeds will be distributed to make each party whole. The vendor collects policy proceeds to the extent of the unpaid purchase price, and the vendee collects to the extent of the deposit.

Sellers and Purchasers of Goods The doctrine of equitable conversion applies only to real estate, and not to sales of goods. Even after full payment of the purchase price, a seller of goods who keeps possession of them until the buyer comes to get the goods assumes the chance of loss until the buyer either receives the goods or refuses to accept them.[22] The seller, having control of the goods, must take care of them and, to protect against possible casualty or theft loss, should insure them.

Mortgagor's and Mortgagee's Interests   Both the mortgagor and mortgagee have insurable interests in the mortgaged property. These interests are separate and distinct. Although it is customary for the parties to stipulate, in the mortgage, who will have the responsibility for obtaining insurance on the property, the provision is sometimes omitted. If no provision for insurance is made, one of three situations may exist:

1. The mortgagor may obtain separate insurance on the property. If so, the policy is only for the benefit of the mortgagor. Proceeds will be free of any lien or other claim by the mortgagee.
2. The mortgagee may obtain separate insurance on the property. If so, money paid by the insurer in the event of loss will not accrue to the benefit of the mortgagor. To the extent of the amount paid, however, the mortgagee may not retain any claim against the mortgagor, since it passes by subrogation to the insurer. Neither may the mortgagee collect more than the amount of the outstanding mortgage debt, which is the measure of the mortgagee's insurable interest in the property. A greater recovery would violate the principle of indemnity.
3. The mortgagor may obtain insurance for the benefit of the mortgagee. The mortgagee may be made an assignee of the policy, or the policy may contain a standard mortgage clause making the policy payable to the mortgagee "as his interest may appear." The latter is customary. Under either arrangement any money paid under the policy must be applied to the payment of the mortgage debt. The mortgagee is the beneficial payee of the policy.

Leases, Life Estates, and Other Limited Interests in Realty
The courts are divided with respect to the rights of the lessor and lessee to recover under insurance policies covering the insured property. One group, upholding the principle of indemnity, subscribes to the theory that the total insurance payment cannot exceed the loss, while the other does permit a profit from an insured loss. The operation of the two rules is illustrated by the cases of Ramsdell v. Insurance Company of North America [23] and Citizens Insurance Company v. Foxbilt, Inc.[24] respectively.

Until relatively recently fire insurers of the lessor have not been making subrogation claims against the lessee for the latter's liability in causing fire damage to the insured property. Since the 1950s, however, such activity has definitely existed. Protection against it may take the following forms:

1. An endorsement of the lessor's fire policy by which the insurer waives its subrogation rights against the lessee.
2. Inclusion of a provision in the lease placing "all-risks" loss on the lessor.
3. Making the lessee an additional insured on the policy of the lessor.
4. Purchase of an insurance policy by the lessee protecting him or her against liability for causing damage to the lessor's property.
5. Purchase of a separate fire policy by the lessee, covering the leased premises.

Life Tenant and Remainderman The general rule is that if a building has been insured before and is destroyed after the creation of a life tenancy, the destruction converts the interests in the property to personal property, and the life tenant is entitled only to a life estate in the proceeds of the insurance contract. This is not a satisfactory arrangement from the standpoint of either the life tenant or the remainderman, both of whom would be better off if specific arrangements were made in advance for insurance coverage to apply toward repairs.

A life tenant, holding a policy in his or her own name without designating the remainderman as additional insured, may recover the entire value of the property in case of a loss, even if it would exceed the cash value of his or her life estate. However, insurers often choose to overlook this deviation from the principle of indemnity. The reason for this is that by doing so they would be asserting a position inconsistent with having collected the premium corresponding to the full value of the property. Furthermore, the amount saved by resisting the life tenant's claim might not be worth the cost of defense in expense and loss of goodwill. Also, the life tenant could be considered an "insured," possessing a representative insurable interest in part on behalf of the remainderman. If so, however, some of the proceeds should be held for the benefit of the latter.

Generally, in the absence of specific provisions to the contrary, the life tenant is not bound to keep the premises insured for the remainderman's benefit or to repair accidental damage to the property not due to his or her fault.

Other Interests in Property Many other dual interests in property exist under the law: conditional sellers and purchasers, heirs and the estate of the insured, and bailor and bailee interests. All give rise to interests that may be insured individually, for the benefit of both, or for the benefit of the other party to the transaction. With slight variations, the rules are very much as stated above. A party may insure his or her own interest in property, and thereafter recover for any loss up to the extent of that interest. Recovery beyond that amount is held in trust for and accrues to the benefit of the other party. The best way to avoid disputes is to state, in the appropriate documents, whose responsibility it shall be to obtain insurance, to make premium payments, and to whom the benefits will be paid in the event of loss.

DISCHARGE OF CONTRACTS

General

When contract obligations come to an end, it is said that the contract is "discharged." The duties of the parties under the contract are terminated. There are many methods by which a person's contractual obligations may be discharged. The usual and intended method of discharge is complete *performance* by both parties of their obligations under the agreement. Also, both parties may agree that their previous contract shall be discharged, as by substituting a new agreement, by waiver, novation, accord and satisfaction, or other *agreements*. Discharge also arises from *impossibility* of performance. Thus, the destruction of the subject matter of the contract may result in discharge through impossibility. A contract may also be discharged by *operation of law*, as by bankruptcy or a change in the law that makes performance illegal.

Discharge by Performance

Most contracts are discharged by performance. When each party fulfills all promises that have been made, no problems exist and the agreement is terminated. The contract ceases to exist. There are a number of ways by which performance may be accomplished under a contract.

Payment If a money debt is owed, payment discharges the contract. If a person owes several separate debts to another and makes a part payment, which debt is discharged? As a general rule the debtor has the right to specify the debt to be discharged, and the creditor is required to apply the payment as directed. If, however, the debtor does not indicate the specific debt, the payment may be applied as the creditor sees fit. The creditor may even apply the payment to a debt that has been barred by the Statute of Limitations, or to payment of an unsecured, rather than a secured debt.

Tender of Performance A *tender* is an offer to perform one's duties under a contract. Tenders may be either: (1) offers to perform a promise to do something; or (2) offers to perform a promise to pay something. Depending on whether an act or a payment is being tendered, a rejection will have different results. Rejection of a tender to do something discharges that obligation; rejection of a tender of payment of a debt does not discharge the debt.

Thus, in a contract for the sale of goods, if the seller attempts to deliver the goods contracted for, and the other party refuses to accept delivery, the seller is discharged from performance. Refusal to accept permits the tendering party to sue for breach of contract and to defend a later action for breach of contract. If, however, the performance due is the payment of money, an offer to pay the money and a refusal to accept will not discharge the debt. A valid tender, however, stops the running of interest on the obligation and the most the creditor can collect is what was owed on the date of the tender. For the tender to be valid, the entire amount of the debt must be tendered, not merely a part.

Substantial Performance Many contractual obligations are most difficult to perform entirely. A major construction contract, for example, will likely result in some deviation of performance as the building progresses. Rather than permit the promisee to completely escape liability on the ground of nonperformance, courts consider whether the performance actually given was substantial and was made in good faith. If so, recovery will be permitted notwithstanding a minor deviation from contract specifications. Courts carefully compare the nature of the performance expected with the performance given, and determine whether the deviation was willful. Failure to substantially perform, or intentional deviations in performance, will likely result in a finding that the contractual obligations have not been discharged. If substantial performance is found, the party receiving performance is required to pay the contract price, with possible allowance for variance in the value of the performance. The important result is that the party substantially performing is entitled to receive the contract price minus damages for nonperformance, rather than to receive nothing at all for failure to perform.

Personal Satisfaction Contracts If a contract provides that the promisee must be "personally satisfied," or that "satisfaction is guaranteed," the taste or personal judgment of the promisee must be satisfied and the good faith decision of that person controls. After all, that was the agreement of the parties. In absence of a clear showing of bad faith on the part of the party making the decision, performance is not adequate in the absence of personal, subjective, satisfaction. Thus, if a portrait of an individual is to be painted "to the satisfaction of" the promisee-subject, then a good faith rejection of the completed portrait precludes recovery by the promisor. Courts, however, impose an objective standard when personal satisfaction relates to utility, fitness, or value. Thus, if the promise is that a vehicle is to be "fit" for operation, fitness is determined in accordance with the expectations of a reasonably prudent person under the circumstances. If a reasonable person would be satisfied, then the performance is adequate.

Performance by an Agreed Time Many contracts fail to provide the time of performance. In general, each party has a reasonable time to perform. Whether performance takes place within a reasonable time is a question of fact for the trier of fact. More problems arise when the parties specify a time for performance, but fail to perform by that date. Assume that a contract requires delivery by November 1, but delivery is made on November 5. Must the promisee accept the late delivery? Does the date set establish a *condition precedent* to obligations under the contract?

If it is clear that late delivery results in little or no benefit to the recipient, the stated time is a condition precedent and the promisee need not take delivery. If the contract expressly provides that time is of the essence of the agreement, that provision is enforced and delivery on the due date is a condition precedent to recovery unless enforcement of the provision constitutes an undue hardship or penalty on the promisor. If time is not of the essence of the contract, either in actuality or according to the contract terms, the promisor must complete performance within a reasonable time after the time stated.

In general, failure to deliver within the required time, either exact or reasonable, is a breach of contract. The UCC has special provisions covering delayed delivery which will be covered under the heading, *"Code Provisions—Commercial Impracticability."*

Discharge by Agreement

The parties to a contract may agree in advance that if a certain event occurs, their obligations to one another will be discharged. For example, *A* agrees to paint *B*'s house unless *B* sells the house by June 1. If *B* sells before June 1, *A*'s obligation is discharged. The occurrence of that contractual condition (sale of the house) relieved the parties of performance. Parties may thus provide in their contracts that on the occurrence of an event their contractual obligations will be discharged.

Agreements to Rescind Just as the parties may agree to enter into a contract, so may they agree to rescind a contract. Unless the contract requires any subsequent modification or rescission to be in writing, the rescission may be oral. An attempted oral rescission in the face of a contract requirement that a rescission must be in writing may nevertheless constitute a waiver. A waiver, however, in the sale of goods, may be retracted by giving the other party reasonable notice that strict performance will be required of the performance previously waived, unless the other party has materially changed position in reliance on the waiver.[25]

Rescission of a contract for the sale of land, however, must generally be in writing. This is because the original agreement of sale effected a transfer of the equitable title of the land to the purchaser, and to retransfer that equitable interest in the land to the seller, a new writing is required under the Statute of Frauds.

In all cases a rescission must contain all the elements of a valid contract including mutual promises to surrender future rights under the contract in consideration for mutual discharge from future duties.

If the contract has been breached, giving the other party a right to sue for damages, the general rule is that the contract cannot be rescinded. It has been discharged by breach. Only executory rights and duties can be rescinded. The party entitled to sue, however, may waive or renounce that right. In general, a legally binding waiver or renunciation requires consideration or its substitute, in some states, a seal. In transactions covered by the UCC, however, "Any claim or right arising out of an alleged breach can be discharged in whole or in part without consideration by a written waiver or renunciation signed and delivered by the aggrieved party."[26]

Substituted Agreements Just as the parties may agree to rescind a contract, so they may agree to substitute a new contract for a prior agreement. The decision to replace an old contract with a new one is subject to the same rules that applied to rescission of agreements. In addition, the UCC provides that in sales of goods a modification of a written contract must be in writing if the original contract so requires.[27]

Novation A *novation* is an agreement that replaces an original party to a contract with a new party. To be effective, the substitution must be agreed to by all the parties. The remaining party must agree to accept the new party and must release the withdrawing party. The latter must consent to withdraw and to permit the new party to be substituted. If these essentials are present, the withdrawing party is discharged from the agreement. To illustrate, *B* contracts to perform certain services for *A*. Later, *A* and *B* agree that *C* will perform *B*'s obligations, and *A* expressly releases *B* from the original contract. When *C* agrees, *B* is discharged from the contract. If *A* does not expressly release *B* there would be no novation. *B* would merely have delegated performance to *C* and would remain liable under the contract.

Accord and Satisfaction   An accord is an agreement between contracting parties that one of them is to substitute a different performance for that required by the contract. This accord is satisfied when the substituted performance is completed. The accord is the agreement to accept a different performance, and carrying out that agreement is the satisfaction. For example, if *A* owes *B* $200 and they agree that *A* will paint *B*'s home in satisfaction of the debt, an accord exists. When the home is painted the obligation is discharged, since the accord and satisfaction are complete.

An accord and satisfaction may be useful to obtain the discharge of an agreed debt. If *A* owes *B* $500, in general an agreement by *B* to accept less than $500 in full payment is not binding because *B* receives no consideration for the promise to discharge *A*. However, if *B* agrees to discharge the debt for a lesser sum in return for payment before the due date, or in return for a lesser sum plus an item of value, whether or not the value of the additional item equals the amount of the unpaid debt, there is an accord and satisfaction. Performance other than that required under the contract has been agreed to and has been made. Problems may arise when a creditor accepts early part payment without agreeing that the early payment is consideration for the discharge of the entire debt. Therefore in order to avoid a possible assertion that an accord and satisfaction has occurred, acceptance of an amount less than the amount owed should be avoided under most circumstances.

Discharge by Impossibility

A promisor's duty to perform will be discharged if, after the contract is made, performance becomes objectively impossible. If the objectively impossible performance was the major undertaking of the contract, both parties will be discharged from all duties under the contract.

Objective Versus Subjective Impossibility   "Objective impossibility" means that the performance cannot conceivably be done. "Subjective impossibility" means that the performance cannot be done by the promisor, although performance is conceivable. The great majority of courts hold that only objective impossibility excuses the promisor's performance. Subjective impossibility does not discharge the obligation, because the promisor is held to assume the chance of personal inability to perform. For example, *B* contracts to build a house for *P* for $20,000. The price of the house is to be paid upon completion. The house is not insured and is destroyed by fire, through the fault of neither party, just prior to its completion. *B* is now insolvent and cannot personally rebuild the house. Such subjective impossibility does not excuse *B*'s nonperformance. *B* is still liable to rebuild. *B* may be sued under the contract for failure to build, and may not collect anything until the performance has been completed.

Change in Law Making Contract Illegal   If performance of a contract becomes illegal after the time of contracting due to a change in the law, or through some act of government, the promisor's performance is excused. Thus, changes in zoning ordinances or building codes may discharge a contractor's duty to build because the specifications would now be illegal. Similarly, governmental embargoes on certain exports discharge contracts for exporting such goods. The mere fact that governmental action makes an agreement more burdensome than was anticipated is not a basis for relief.

Death or Incapacity of Contracting Party   The death or incapacitating illness of a specific person necessary to perform a promise will discharge the duty to perform. The service must be "personal." Thus, where *A* promises to paint *B*'s picture, *A*'s death or illness discharges the contract. Conversely, *B*'s death or illness has the same effect. It should be noted carefully that ordinary contracts of production and sale of property are not personal and are unaffected by the death or illness of one or both parties. In the event of death, it is normally assumed that the contract is binding on, and must be carried out by the personal representatives of the deceased.

Destruction of Subject Matter   If the specific subject matter of the contract is destroyed or becomes nonexistent after the contract is entered into, without the fault of the promisor, the promisor's duty is discharged by impossibility of performance. Thus, a contract to furnish oil or gas from a specified well is discharged if the well becomes exhausted. Similarly, a contract to use an auditorium for entertainment purposes is discharged by the destruction of the auditorium. In contracts for the sale of goods, discharge by impossibility occurs only if specific and identified goods are the subject matter of the agreement. Thus, a contract to sell so many bushels of wheat to be grown on specified land is discharged by failure of the crop on that land. But, if no specific land or specific wheat is identified, the promisor's duty to supply wheat is not discharged even though the promisor intended to fill the contract from the crop that failed. Thus, destruction of goods that have been ascertained or identified to a contract will excuse performance. In the absence of specific identification, the obligation of the promisor to obtain and deliver identical goods from some other source continues.

Act of Other Party   If the other party's act prevents the performance, performance will be excused by reason of impossibility. Thus, if a contract requires the promisor to perform certain services on the promisee's land, and the latter prevents entry on the land, the promisor cannot perform and the contract is discharged.

Whether the party who is temporarily disabled from performance can demand the right to perform after the disability is removed depends on whether the late performance "materially" affected the other party. If late performance is "material," the contract is discharged.

Temporary Impossibility   Temporary rather than permanent impossibility merely suspends, rather than discharges, the promisor's duty while the impossibility continues. After the impossibility has come to an end, the duty to perform reattaches. Thus, where the promisor's illness or entry into the armed services prevents performance of a service contract, such obligation of performance may be reimposed upon removal of the disability.

Partial Impossibility   If the promisor's performance is only partially impossible, the duty to perform is excused only to that extent and the balance of the duty must be performed regardless of added expense or difficulty. For example, if *B* contracts to build a house and to use a certain type pipe for the plumbing, the fact that such pipe is no longer manufactured will discharge only the use of that pipe and not the entire contract. *B* remains under a duty to erect the house and to use substitute pipe of like quality.

Recovery for Part Performance   Impossibility of performance often becomes apparent only after partial performance. If a party has performed in part, such as by putting one of two coats of paint on a house before it is destroyed by fire, the reasonable value of the service may be recovered. If completion of a contract becomes impossible, the recipient of the work must pay the reasonable value of all work and material up to the date of impossibility. One must, however, differentiate between legal impossibility and a mere additional burden. The destruction of a partially completed building, for example, does not make performance impossible. By starting construction anew, performance is possible, although the cost will be greater than was anticipated and the additional cost must be borne by the contractor.

Frustration of Purpose Doctrine   In some cases the bargained-for performance is still possible, but the purpose or value of the contract has been totally destroyed by some supervening event.

Frustration of the purpose of the contract may discharge the contract. To illustrate, *A* owns a house along a street that a parade route is to pass. *A* rents a room to *T* for the day of the parade so that *T* may view the parade from the room. The parade route is changed so that it does not pass *A*'s house. The frustration of the purpose of the contract will excuse *T*'s performance.

The Restatement of Contracts appears to adopt this view in a section that states that, "Where the assumed possibility of a desired object or effect is or surely will be frustrated, a promisor who is without fault in causing the frustration, and who is harmed thereby, is discharged from the duty of performing his promise *unless a contrary intention appears.*"[28] (Emphasis added.) It is not clear whether the "contrary intention" must appear in the contract. It may appear from factors outside the contract terms, such as the customs of a trade or business, or may consist of a presumed assumption of the possibility of the frustration. In addition, some cases which are based on commercial frustration can be explained in terms of orthodox impossibility, as for example, a performance which has become illegal because of governmental action. At this time the only sure statement is that a doctrine of commercial frustration exists, but that its elements and definition are unsettled.

Code Provisions—Commercial Impracticability

As was noted previously, the UCC has several provisions for sale of goods contracts that become "impracticable." Two observations are important. First, "commercial impracticability" is more than commercial "frustration," and second, "impracticability" differs from "impossibility." "Frustration" means that one party will not obtain the "desired object or effect." The contract can be performed, but the prospective parade-watcher will not see a parade. If the identified subject matter of a contract is destroyed, however, the contract is "impossible" to perform.

Under the UCC, both delay in delivery and failure to deliver goods are excused ". . . if performance as agreed has been made impracticable by the occurrence of a contingency, the nonoccurrence of which was a basic assumption on which the contract was made, or by compliance in good faith with any applicable foreign or domestic governmental regulation or order whether or not it later proves to be invalid."[29] However, the seller must allocate production and delivery of available quantities among his customers and must give the buyer reasonable notice of the problem and how much, if any, of the goods can be delivered.[30]

The standards for "impracticability" are commercial as contrasted to actual impossibility. For instance, impossibility to perform a contract due to a wartime lack of shipping was held to be a hazard assumed by the shipper because the contract was made on the eve of a war at a time when a shipping shortage was foreseeable.[31] The question of impracticability, therefore, is one of fact to be decided in each case.

The UCC expressly provides, in a comment, that increased cost does not generally constitute commercial impracticability, but that commercial impracticability may exist because of "a severe shortage of raw materials or of supplies due to a contingency such as war, embargo, local crop failure, unforeseen shutdown of major sources of supply or the like, which either causes a marked increase in cost or altogether prevents the seller from securing supplies necessary to his performance."[32] Even in such cases, however, the seller must take commercially reasonable precautions to see that the source of supply is not shut off.

In order to refute an old rule, applied by some courts, that shipment must be made from the place and by the mode of transportation stated in the contract, the UCC provides for the substitution of the place of shipment or the mode of transportation if the contract terms become commercially impracticable and if a "commercially reasonable substitute is available."[33]

Statutes of Limitations Statutes of limitations prescribe time limits within which suits must be started after a cause of action arises. Failure to commence an action within the prescribed time is a complete defense to the suit. The times within which actions must be started vary among states and among types of agreements. In some states, claimants may be given two years to file suits on oral contracts and six years if the contract is in writing. Another state may prescribe periods of four years for oral contracts and fifteen years for written agreements. In any event, failure to commence an action within the prescribed period gives the defendant the right to plead the statute of limitations as a defense. If the defense is not pleaded, it is waived. The obligation is not extinguished (as it is by a discharge in bankruptcy), but an airtight defense is created.

Fraudulent Alteration Any material alteration of a contract made intentionally by one of the parties discharges the contract. The right to enforce the contract is destroyed by operation of law. Thus, where one party fraudulently alters the amount payable on a check, the material alteration will discharge the liability of the maker of the instrument as to the person who alters it.

Conditions in Contracts

Although all promises made in a contract are conditions, not all conditions are promises. If a promise in a contract is not fulfilled, the other party has a legal remedy. If a condition is not fulfilled, however, obligations under the contract are altered, limited, or discharged. The breach of a promise may be treated by the other party as a mere nonfulfillment of a condition and thereby waived. If goods are not delivered on the specific day required by the contract, for instance, the buyer may under some circumstances treat the nondelivery as a breach of the promise to deliver and sue for damages. The buyer may choose, however, to treat the nondelivery as a breach of condition that extends the duty to pay to a later date, and waive the breach of contract.

There are three main types of conditions: *conditions precedent, conditions concurrent,* and *conditions subsequent.*

Condition Precedent A condition precedent is an event that must occur before a duty of performance arises. Nonfulfillment of a condition precedent may act as a dischage of the contractual obligation. For example, filing a notice of loss under an insurance policy is generally a condition precedent to payment of a claim. This condition is not a promise, but until the condition precedent is met, the duty of the insurer to perform its obligation under the contract does not arise.

Condition Concurrent A condition concurrent is one which must exist as a fact when both parties to a contract are to perform at the same time. Thus, if a contract expressly provides, or if it can be inferred, that the performances of the parties are to be made at the same time, the conditions are concurrent. To illustrate, goods are sold under the condition that cash will be paid upon delivery. When the goods are delivered the vendee is insolvent and cannot pay. The conditions of delivery and payment are concurrent, and the seller may regain the goods since the buyer is unable to perform as the agreement requires. This condition is a promise, and the seller may sue for breach of contract.

Condition Subsequent A condition subsequent is a future event which may or may not occur after the contract becomes legally enforceable. In either case it terminates rights under the contract. Assume two provisions in a lease of a store in a shopping center—the lease provides that the lessor is to receive a certain set rent plus a percentage of the store's gross sales. If sales drop below a set dollar amount per month the lease will terminate at the lessor's option; and if the sales do not reach a set dollar amount per month within a year, the lease will terminate at the lessor's option. If the first condition subsequent occurs, the lessor may terminate all rights and duties under the lease, and if the second event does not occur the lessor may terminate all rights and obligations under the lease. In neither condition is there a promise.

Multiple Conditions Many contracts contain a number of conditions that may crucially affect the rights of the parties. To determine the legal consequences of the conditions, it is important to ascertain whether they were intended as conditions precedent, concurrent, or subsequent to the obligations of the parties. The insurance contract is a classic example of an agreement containing multiple conditions. It is not always easy to determine whether a condition was intended to be precedent or subsequent to liability under the agreement. Thus, the payment of the premium is generally considered a condition precedent to liability under the policy. Also, the actual occurrence of a loss is a condition precedent to the maturing of the insurer's liability under the contract. A condition that a suit on the policy must be commenced within one year from the date of the loss is viewed as a condition subsequent. The requirement that a notice of loss be submitted within sixty days may be viewed as either a condition precedent to liability under the policy, or, depending on the wording of the condition (e.g., "The insurer's obligation will be discharged if no notice of loss is given within sixty days"), as a condition subsequent. In every case, careful scrutiny is required in order to determine the intent and consequent legal effect of a condition.

BREACH OF CONTRACT

General

A breach of contract is an unjustifiable failure to perform all or some part of a contractual duty. A breach may be total or partial, and occur by failure to perform acts promised, by hindering or preventing performance, or by other conduct indicating an intention to repudiate the agreement. Breach of contract gives rise to certain remedies for the nonbreaching party that will be considered later in this chapter.

Repudiation A repudiation of a contract must be positive and unequivocal in order to constitute a breach. A mere statement of prospective inability to perform is not a repudiation. Thus, it is not repudiation of a contract between *A* and *B* that is to be performed on November 1 if, on October 15, *A* says to *B*, "I doubt that I'll be able to perform the contract, and the way prices are going up I don't think I want to anyway." A positive retraction must be by words as well as by conduct. *B* may not treat the statement as an anticipatory repudiation of the agreement and, thereby, sue for breach of contract. No action will lie until the time for performance has arrived and *A* has then failed to perform.

Anticipatory Breach In some cases courts will not require the nonbreaching party to wait until the actual date of performance to determine whether the contract will be breached. Thus, if there is (1) a clear expression of intention by a promisor not to perform, and (2) an executory, bilateral contract that entails mutual and dependent conditions, the aggrieved party may treat the repudiation as a present total breach and may sue immediately. This is an "anticipatory breach." For example, *A* promises to sell and *B* promises to buy Whiteacre for $10,000 on December 1. On November 15, *B* says to *A*, "I cannot and will not go through with our contract." The positive statement by *B* that he will not or cannot substantially perform the contract is a breach of contract by anticipatory repudiation. *A* need not wait until December 1, but may sue immediately for damages for breach of contract.

It should be noted carefully that the anticipatory breach doctrine applies only if there is a clear statement of intention to repudiate a binding promise. It does not apply to a unilateral contract, because in a unilateral contract the promisee has not made a promise but has the option to perform an act and thereby to become entitled to the agreed compensation. If the promisee does not perform the requested act, the promisor has no right to sue.

The doctrine of anticipatory breach was developed in order to avoid "enforced idleness" on the part of the aggrieved party, and to avoid making it necessary for that party to tender performance at the time stated in the contract in order to prove that the other party has breached the contract.

Material Versus Minor Breach Many courts draw a distinction between material (major) breaches and those that are minor. The materiality of the breach is a question of fact to be determined by the trier of fact. Several circumstances affect the materiality of a breach— the extent to which the breaching party has performed, whether the breach was willful, the extent to which the nonbreaching party has obtained benefits, and the extent to which the nonbreaching party can adequately be compensated.

A material breach excuses performance by the other party, and immediately gives rise to remedies for breach of contract. A minor breach causes only slight delay in performance or a slight deviation in quantity or quality. Minor breaches (1) temporarily suspend any duty of performance by the nonbreaching party that would have arisen on proper performance, and (2) give the aggrieved party a cause of action for damages caused by the breach, usually an offset to the agreed price, but not to remedies for breach of the entire contract.

Remedies for Breach of Contract

If a contract is breached, the injured party has one of three remedies: (1) to bring an action to collect money *damages* (in a contract for the sale of goods, an action for the price); (2) to request *specific performance* of the contract; or (3) to request an *injunction.*

Damages The remedy most frequently pursued for breach of contract is an action at law for money damages arising from the breach. Damages are intended to compensate for the breach, and are therefore called *compensatory damages.* The general theory is that the injured party should be placed in the same position as if the contract had been properly performed. Thus, an effort is made to give the injured party the "benefit of the bargain." Compensatory damages are the difference between the value of the promised performance and the plaintiff's cost of obtaining that performance elsewhere. It includes losses caused and gains prevented by the defendant's breach. In the case of contracts for the sale of goods, the UCC provides that, in general, measures of damages is the difference between the contract price and the market price at the time of breach.[34] The objective is not to punish the party breaching, but rather to put the injured party in as a good a position as he or she would have been if full performance had been made.

In addition to the standard measure of contract damages, a breaching party is also liable for any *consequential* or *special damages.* Recoverable loss thus normally extends to any loss resulting from the breach that the defendant, as a reasonable person, should have foreseen at the time the contract was entered into. Although it is often stated that the damages must have been reasonably in the "contemplation of the parties" at the time of making the agreement, consequential damages are recoverable only when the defendant was made aware of the probable occurrence thereof.

To illustrate, a manufacturer orders a supply of raw materials to be delivered on a certain date. The seller does not deliver until after the date set. The manufacturer then demands as part of the damages the loss incurred because of the shutdown of the plant due to lack of raw materials which were unavailable from any other source. Although that loss flowed directly from the breach, the manufacturer would not have a claim for them. This is because manufacturers normally order raw materials to be delivered in advance of actual need, and raw materials are usually available from substitute sources. The seller, therefore, has no reason to believe that a delay in shipment will cause a shutdown. If the manufacturer, however, informs the seller of the critical need and the seller, with that knowledge, promises to perform on a given day, delay in delivery makes the seller liable for the foreseeable loss arising from the shutdown.

Punitive or *exemplary* damages are awarded, regardless of the amount of actual damages, to punish a defendant if the act was malicious. They are not uncommon in tort actions, such as for an unprovoked and malicious assault and battery. The purpose is to deter such conduct.

Modern cases and legal thinking do not consider exemplary damages appropriate in most contract cases. They are not believed to be in keeping with the contract objective of damages—to afford the plaintiff the benefits of the bargain. If a seller of personal property is guilty of fraud or misrepresentation, however, punitive damages may be awarded, but such award is based on the fraud rather than the breach of contract.

Another important exception is in the field of insurance. If an insurer unreasonably delays payment, or contests a claim without reasonable grounds, the insurer may be liable to pay the insured's attorney's fees in suing for the claim and may be required to pay a penalty in addition. This type of remedy is generally created by statute.[35]

Another development affecting insurance involves the awarding of damages for breach of contract by the insurer that go beyond simply making good the loss of the benefit of the bargain. A few but influential courts have held that, in addition to damages based on the terms of the insurance contract (such as benefits payable directly to the insured under life, health, accident, property, medical payments, or uninsured motorist coverages), or those payable to third parties under liability coverages, a breach of the policy contract by the insurer may render the latter liable to its insured for additional damages. The theories under which such "extra-contractual" damages are assessed are (1) breach of duty of good faith and fair dealing said by these courts to be implied in every contract of insurance, and (2) intentional infliction of emotional distress on the insured by extreme and outrageous conduct on the part of the insurer, its agents, and its employees. Where one or both of these is found to have taken place, the insured may be awarded (1) consequential and (2) punitive damages. Such consequential damages may include compensation for physical and mental suffering and distress, loss of assets, and attorneys' fees. In most cases where they were awarded, the "extra-contractual" damages have far exceeded the contract damages involved in the breach.

The nonbreaching party to a contract owes a duty to *mitigate the damages*. Upon learning of a contract breach, the injured party is required to do what reasonably can be done to minimize the extent of the loss. Thus, when the buyer has breached a contract for the sale of goods, the seller must dispose of the goods at the best price possible. If the seller delivers a defective product and the buyer knows that the product is dangerous and may injure those who use it, the buyer must not permit it to be used. Similarly, if an employer fires an employee who has a term contract, such as for one year, without cause, the employee must make a good faith effort to seek a similar position and thereby mitigate the employer's damages. The improperly dismissed employee may not go on a vacation and expect the full remaining salary to be paid. If, of course, a position is found at a lower salary, the difference is the employee's damages.

Although damages must be mitigated, if actual mitigation does not take place the plaintiff is treated as though it had. If the employee does not try to get another position, for instance, a suit for damages for breach of contract will fail because damages cannot be proved. Suppose, however, that the employee locates a position for a lower salary, and then decides that it would be better to take a vacation. The maximum recovery for breach would be the difference between the salary for the job found and the salary under the breached contract. Or suppose a contract for the sale and delivery of goods is breached by the seller. If the purchaser does not purchase the goods elsewhere, damages would still be obtainable for the difference between what they could have been purchased for and the price under the breached contract.

The parties may agree in the contract for the amount of damages to be paid for breach. These are called *liquidated damages*. A *liquidated* amount is an agreed amount. If damages are not agreed on in advance, they are *unliquidated*.

Liquidated damage provisions are not always enforced. If they are found to be a *penalty* they will be disregarded and the injured party will have to prove actual damages. In order to be a valid liquidated damage clause the sum specified by the parties must be a good faith effort to estimate the actual damage that would probably ensue from a breach of contract. The courts consider in each case whether the contract involved subject matter that would make damages difficult to ascertain, and whether the amount agreed upon represented a reasonable estimate of the damages that might actually be incurred.

Action for the Price In a contract for the sale of goods, the seller has two remedies for breach. One remedy, damages, is available if the seller properly resells the goods and receives less than the contract price. The difference is the damages. If the seller receives more than the agreed price the excess need not be turned over to the buyer. It belongs to the seller.

The seller, however, may sometimes sue for the agreed price. This may be done only in the following circumstances: (1) when the buyer has received and kept the goods; (2) when the goods are destroyed or damaged after the buyer assumes the chance of loss; and (3) when the buyer wrongfully rejects delivery, and the goods cannot be sold after reasonable effort at a reasonable price.[36]

In general, the burden of loss passes to the buyer when the goods are accepted; when a carrier tenders the goods to the buyer if the contract requires the seller to ship the goods to the buyer; when the goods are delivered by the seller to the carrier if the contract provides only for delivery to the carrier and not to the destination; or, if the goods are held by a third party for delivery without being moved, when the buyer receives some document indicating the buyer's right to the goods or the third party acknowledges the buyer's right to possession.[37]

Specific Performance Sometimes the legal remedy of dollar damages is not an adequate remedy for an injured party. The only adequate remedy may be to require the breaching party to perform the contract by doing what was promised. A suit in equity for specific performance will not be admissible if money damages are adequate. To determine whether money damages are adequate, courts consider (1) the difficulty of valuing the subject matter of the contract, (2) the existence of sentimental and aesthetic qualities of the subject matter that make it unique, and (3) the difficulty or impossibility of obtaining a duplicate or substantial equivalent of the subject matter.

Actions requesting specific performance of a contract occur most frequently in contracts for the sale of real estate. Real estate is considered unique, and courts will order the seller to perform the contract and to transfer title to the injured party.

Specific performance of a contract to sell personally is ordered only if the item sold is considered in some way unique (e.g., antiques, paintings, or other one-of-a-kind items). Courts will not direct specific performance of personal service contracts; to do so would, in effect, require the courts to supervise the performance to assure that performance is adequate. In general, courts do not order specific performance of contracts that require supervision, such as building contracts, contracts to wash windows, and the like. It has also been argued that specific performance of personal service contracts, such as a contract of an artistic performer, would constitute involuntary servitude.

Injunctions Although specific performance of a personal service contract will not be ordered, if the personal services are truly unique a court may enjoin the promisor from performing elsewhere during the term of the contract. An injunction against performing elsewhere will probably not be granted against a singer in an opera chorus who breaks the contract, but certainly will be ordered against an important soloist.

Commercial contracts that contain negative covenants are enforceable by injunction. Assume that a business is sold and that the seller promises not to compete with the buyer in a given area for a given time and that the restriction is legal. If the seller breaches the provision and starts to compete, the buyer may request a court of equity for an order enjoining the seller from competing.

In both of these cases the legal remedy of money damages is inadequate. There is no way to assess the money value of the soloist's performance, and a series of lawsuits for damages from the illegal competition would be too burdensome on the buyer. Therefore the equitable remedy of an injunction is appropriate.

Reformation of Contracts Another contract remedy, but not necessarily involving breach of contract, is a request for reformation of a contract. Reformation is generally requested when a mistake was made in reducing the oral agreement of the parties to writing, or in contract cases in which one party made a mistake that was induced by the other party. The court in such instances is requested to "reform" or change the contract to conform to the true intention of the parties. Courts require that the evidence of the mistake be clear and convincing before reformation will be ordered. The basic theory is that the formal contract is being corrected to reflect accurately the actual agreement between the parties. Thus, if an insurance policy is issued that does not contain the coverage orally agreed upon, an action for reformation may be maintained to have the contract changed to conform to the true intent of the parties.

Chapter Notes

1. UCC, Section 2-307
2. UCC, Section 2-612(2)
3. UCC, Section 2-612(2)(3)
4. UCC, Section 2-204(3)
5. UCC, Section 2-305(1)
6. UCC, Section 2-309(1)
7. UCC, Section 2-306(1)
8. Ibid.
9. UCC, Section 2-208
10. UCC, Section 2-302
11. UCC, Section 1-205(2)
12. UCC, Section 1-205(4) and 2-208(2)
13. UCC, Section 2-103(1)(b)
14. Robert Keeton, *Basic Text on Insurance Law* (St. Paul: West Publishing Company, 1971), p. 351.
15. UCC, Section 2-210(1)
16. UCC, Section 2-210(2)
17. UCC, Section 2-210(3)
18. UCC, Section 2-210(4)
19. Restatement of Contracts, Second, Sec. 142
20. See UCC, Section 2-320, and comment 8. Added insurance needed to cover an increased price on the resale must be purchased by the new, second, buyer.
21. UCC, Section 2-201(3)(c). See, Keeton, n. 14, at p. 252
22. UCC, Section 2-509(3), and comment 3.
23. 197 Wis. 136, 221 N.W. 654 (1928)
24. 226 F. 2d 641 (8th Cir. 1955), 53 A.L.R. 2d 1376 (1957)
25. UCC, Section 2-209(5)
26. UCC, Section 1-107
27. UCC, Section 2-209(2)
28. Section 298
29. UCC, Section 2-615(1)
30. UCC, Section 2-615(2)(3)
31. Madeirence Do Brasil, S.A. v. Stulman-Emrick Lumber Co., 147 F.2d 399 (2d Cir., 1945), cited in UCC, Section 615, comment 8.
32. UCC, Section 2-615, comment 4
33. UCC, Section 2-614(1)
34. UCC, Section 2-708 and 2-713
35. Keeton, n. 14, at pp. 455-458
36. UCC, Section 2-207
37. UCC, Section 2-509. See also UCC, Section 2-510

CHAPTER 6

Agency—Creation and Authority

NATURE OF AGENCY

General

The term *agency* is used to describe the relationship that exists when one person acts on behalf of another. It is an essential fact of modern economic life that individuals and corporations must utilize the services of others to accomplish work that must be done. The rights and liabilities that arise among parties when one person represents another in dealings with third parties is the subject matter of the law of agency.

Agency is a fiduciary relationship in which one person (the principal) authorizes another (the agent) to act on his or her behalf in business dealings with third parties. Both the principal and the agent must agree or consent to the relationship, otherwise it will not arise. The relationship is called *fiduciary* because of the high degree of trust and confidence involved. In this and in other fiduciary relationships, such as those involving trustees, executors, guardians, and so on, the law imposes a higher standard of conduct than in the usual course of business. The agent owes a duty to act primarily for the benefit of the principal and to deal fairly with the principal in every way.

Purpose of Agency

The agency relation may be created only for a legal purpose. Attempts to create an agency for purposes that are illegal or contrary to public policy are ineffective. Thus, if an agent is employed to sell contraband, the agency agreement and all transactions that flow from that agreement will be unenforceable in the courts. That which a person cannot do directly cannot be done indirectly through an agent.

The law also recognizes that certain acts are so personal that they cannot be performed through an agent. The requirements of jury duty, voting, swearing to the truth of documents, and executing a will are but a few situations in which a person must act in his or her own right. Attempts to delegate these duties to others are ineffective, and may result in criminal or other sanctions against parties who attempt the illegal actions.

Types of Agency

There are two types of tasks that one person may perform for another. First, one may perform a physical task, such as painting a house or driving a truck. Second, one may perform a task that affects another's legal relationships, such as entering into or terminating a contract with third persons.

A person who performs a physical task for another may be either (1) an employee, or (2) an independent contractor. An employee is, subject to the law of labor relations, obliged to follow the instructions of the employer not only in the goal to be achieved but also in the manner of performance. A truck driver who is to deliver cargo to a distant city not only has that charge, but the employer also has the right to set the route to be followed. An independent contractor, however, is engaged only to achieve a goal, and is not subject to control on the manner of achieving it, except as may be provided in the original contract. An independent contractor who is engaged to deliver a cargo to a distant city may choose any route, as long as the cargo is delivered in accordance with the original contract of carriage.

The importance of the distinction lies in the fact that one is responsible for what one has a right to control. Therefore, one who employs a truck driver on an hourly wage and retains the right to set the route may be responsible for accidents that involve that truck driver. However, if one hires an independent contractor to perform that task, only the independent contractor is responsible for negligent driving. The distinction is also important because employees, under state and federal law, are entitled to certain privileges such as unemployment insurance, workers' compensation, and minimum wage scales in many instances. In addition, the employer must withhold income taxes, withhold social security taxes, and provide safe working conditions for the employee.

A person who affects the legal relationships of another is an agent. If an agent negotiates a contract on behalf of the principal with a third party, the principal will be bound to the contract just as though it had been negotiated by the principal. A given individual, of course, may have some agency duties and some physical duties. The principal of such a person, therefore, will be bound to the authorized contracts such person may enter on the principal's behalf and may be liable for injuries caused by that person in the performance of authorized physical tasks.

Control by Principal

The right to control the agent or employee results in the principal's or employer's responsibility to third persons. The fact that a given principal does not exercise control is immaterial. If an employee, for instance, is given maximum discretion and is not supervised, that fact will not relieve the employer of responsibility for the employee's actions.

Classes of Principals

Most principals are *disclosed*. The third party knows that the agent is working for a principal, and knows the identity of that principal. Sometimes, however, the principal may be *undisclosed* because the third party not only does not know who the principal is, but does not even know that he or she is dealing with an agent. This can happen when the principal does not want to reveal his or her existence, or when the agent fails to reveal the relationship.

A principal can also be *partially disclosed*. The third party knows of the *existence* of a principal, but does not know the principal's *identity*.

In the usual disclosed principal situation, an agent who enters a contract on behalf of the principal is not liable on that contract. If, however, the principal is partially disclosed or is undisclosed, the agent has certain liabilities that will be discussed in Chapter 7.

Classes of Agents

In general usage, anyone who represents another in any type of transaction is called an agent. Corporations, not being natural persons, can deal only through agents. In the insurance industry, adjusters, underwriters, salespersons, managers, attorneys, and doctors are often referred to as agents within their own areas of authority.

In legal usage, however, an agent is one who affects contractual relationships of the principal and third parties. Underwriters and doctors normally do not affect contractual relationships—they are employed to perform physical tasks. In the course of their employment, however, they may make mistakes or commit frauds that have legal consequences for their companies.

It is important to keep in mind that the general classes of agents described below do not necessarily apply to the insurance industry, and that in the insurance industry different practices result in different usages between life insurance on the one hand and fire, marine, and liability insurance on the other.

General Agency Classifications An agent who is authorized to conduct a series of transactions over a period of time is a *general agent*. The manager of a store who is authorized to transact all the affairs of the store on a continuing basis is one example. A *special agent* is authorized to conduct only a single transaction or a series of specific transactions. The authority terminates upon completion of the specific task or tasks assigned. New or fresh authority for future transactions is then needed.

A *broker* has limited authority to find a customer. The broker cannot close the deal, and the client must sign the final contract. A real estate broker thus has authority to find a buyer for the client's property, but the real estate remains under the control of the owner.

A *factor* is one who has possession and control of another's property with authority to sell the property. The factor normally has a property interest in the goods and may sell them in his or her own name.

General Insurance Agency Classifications Agency classifications in insurance are complex, and often depend on the specific practices of companies. Consequently, only some general ideas are set forth at this point.

Life Insurance Agents. In the life insurance industry very little authority is delegated to those outside the home office. *General agents* or *branch managers* generally solicit applications through their *soliciting agents*. The local office has some authority to issue a temporary, written, binding receipt.

This does not mean, of course, that the company is not responsible for their activities. As employees of the company they may engage in practices that result in liability for their companies, but this is done in their legal capacity of employees, not legal agents with authority to form binding contracts.

In life insurance the term *broker* generally refers to a person who is a *soliciting agent* for two or more companies.

Fire, Marine, and Liability Agents. In the fire, marine, and liability insurance fields, a *general agent* is one with authority to write insurance contracts and bind the company even though the company may be unaware of the contract. This is the usage of general agency law as well. A *soliciting* or *special* agent, however, takes applications and cannot bind the company. Notice that in this case the term *special agent* does not have the meaning it has in general agency law. In addition, sometimes a *soliciting* or *special* agent may have authority to bind the company under particular circumstances.

An insurance *broker,* again, is one who is not employed by the company but works as an individual or firm. A broker represents the insured for most purposes, although the broker gets a commission from the company and is the company's agent for a few purposes, such as collecting the premiums. Sometimes, however, the term "broker" is applied to persons who are employed by an insurance company, although this is neither the usual nor the generally accepted practice.

Subagents A subagent is a person appointed by an agent to perform functions undertaken by the agent for the principal. The appointing agent is responsible to the principal for the conduct of the subagent. The subagent is the agent of both the principal and the appointing agent. When the subagent performs acts which the appointing agent has authorized, such acts affect the legal relations of the principal to third persons just as if the appointing agent had performed them. Further, the subagent is also the agent of the appointing agent, with power to subject the appointing agent to liability to the principal for defaults in the performance of the principal's business. Similarly, the appointing agent has the same rights and duties to the subagent as any other principal has to an agent.

The term "subagent" is properly applied only if the appointed person is both the agent of the principal and an agent of the appointing agent. For subagency to exist, some duty of performance must be owed by the appointed subagent to the appointing primary agent. If the appointing agent's function is merely to appoint a person to act for the principal, the person appointed is an agent and not a subagent. In the latter situation, the appointing agent is liable only if negligent in making the appointment.

To illustrate: *P,* a liability insurance company, appoints *A* as its general agent for state *X.* It is agreed that *A* will open offices selected by him and will receive a specified commission for the business done in such offices. *A* is authorized to appoint subagents. The subagents owe duties of performance to both *P* and *A.* The subagents are able to enter into contracts that affect the legal relations of *P* with third persons. *A* is responsible to *P* for any defaults in performance by the subagents.

Capacity of Parties

A person may do through an agent anything that he or she can legally do. The contract of a person who lacks legal capacity to contract may be void or voidable. Therefore, a contract by an agent for a principal who lacks legal capacity is void or voidable as a contract made by the principal would be. Thus, a contract made by the agent of a minor is voidable to the same extent as if made by the minor.

Although a principal must be legally competent in order for an agent's contracts to be binding on the principal, the legal capacity of the agent is immaterial. A principal may employ a minor or otherwise legally incompetent person as an agent, and the principal is bound by the actions of that agent. The courts generally require some mental capacity on the part of the agent, however, and an insane person or a very young child does not have capacity to bind a principal. However, in all but the most unusual cases, it is the capacity of the principal and not of the agent that controls the validity of the agreement. The law recognizes that the contract is entered into by the principal, not by the agent. If the principal *assumes the risk* of representation by an incompetent agent, the principal rather than the third party stands the loss.

Notice to Agent as Notice to Principal

An agent is the *alter ego,* or other self, of the principal. The agent acts in the place of the principal and, within the scope of the authority granted, just as though the principal acted. Because of this legal identity, any notice to or knowledge acquired by an agent while acting within the scope of the agent's authority binds the principal. Since the agent is the principal's other self, what the agent knows the principal is also deemed to know.

Although all courts do not agree on the point, the majority hold that even notice acquired by the agent *prior* to creation of the agency relationship is binding on the principal. It is assumed that the agent will communicate the information to the principal and proceed to act in the best interests of the principal. If it appears the agent acted adversely to the interests of the principal, or in his or her own behalf, and the third party knew these facts, it will not be presumed that notice or knowledge was communicated to the principal. If there is collusion or fraud between the agent and the third party, notice to the agent is not binding on the principal.

Dual Agency

An agent may not act adversely to the principal's interests. This duty of loyalty includes the obligation not to represent another party in any transaction within the scope of the agency. The agent may,

however, act for adverse parties to a transaction if both parties are
fully informed of all the pertinent facts and that the agent represents
both. There is nothing illegal about a dual agency if there is full
disclosure. If one principal, however, is ignorant of the fact the agent is
also acting for the other principal, that principal has a legal right to
rescind the transaction. A principal may also recover any fee or
commission paid an agent who does not reveal a dual representation
and obtain that principal's consent.

Agency and Other Legal Relations

Partnership The law of agency and the law of partnership have
much in common. A partnership is an association of two or more
persons to carry on as co-owners of a business for profit. Partners are
agents of the partnership. Since each partner is both an agent and one
of the principals, the usual rules of agency law apply to all of their
dealings. Only the modes of creation and dissolution, which are
governed by statute, differ from agency law.

Bailments In a bailment one person, the bailor, delivers personal property to another, the bailee, who agrees to return the property to
the bailor or to a third party. No agency relation is created since the
bailee generally has no authority to make contracts on behalf of the
bailor or to have dealings with third parties as the bailor's representative. Wrongdoing of the bailee is not imputed to the bailor. If, however,
the bailee is also an agent of the bailor-principal, the rules of law
applicable to both agency and bailment apply.

Fiduciaries

One must distinguish between fiduciaries and those who only have
fiduciary duties. In many ways attorneys, agents, brokers, and even
those in a confidential relationship may have fiduciary duties. A
fiduciary, however, is a natural person or a corporation who is not only
in possession and control of property but who, in a fiduciary capacity,
owns it.

The term fiduciary includes trustees, executors, guardians of the
estate of a minor or an incompetent, and receivers in bankruptcy.
Sometimes they are appointed by a court, but individuals can appoint
fiduciaries, such as trustees, by deed or will, and executors are always
appointed by a will. All of them, however, are responsible to a court for
the faithful performance of duties and are not under the direct control
(are not agents) of the parties for whose benefit they act.

Fiduciaries, therefore, are principals, not agents. They act for themselves, but are subject to various duties. Some duties are created by the document that made them fiduciaries, such as a will or deed of trust. Other duties are imposed by statutes and by principles of law. They enter into contracts in their capacities as fiduciaries and the estates they control are normally bound by their contracts. In the absence of collusion or wrongdoing by those who have an interest in the estate (the beneficiaries), their negligence or other wrongdoing is not usually imputed to the beneficiaries.

CREATION OF AGENCY

Formality Required

Ordinarily, no formalities are required to create an agency. The relationship is consensual, not necessarily contractual. Therefore no consideration is required. One may consent to be an agent without compensation. The consent of the parties may be written or oral, expressed or implied.

Sometimes an agency must be evidenced by a writing. Under the Statute of Frauds either party may disavow an agency contract that is to last for more than one year from its making unless they have signed a writing that states otherwise. Some states require that a contract of a real estate broker to obtain a purchaser must be in writing to be enforceable. There is also the principle of "equal dignity," sometimes put into statutory form, that requires agency contracts to be in writing if the agency is for the purpose of negotiating a contract that must itself be evidenced by a writing under the Statute of Frauds. An agency contract, under that principle, to actually convey a deed to someone's real estate, must itself be in writing.

An agency may be formed unwittingly. Although consent of the parties is necessary, intent to form an agency is not necessary. Consent is objective, what is actually said and done, and not subjective, what is intended. Therefore, if a person requests another to return goods to a store and get credit for the return, an agency relationship is formed even though neither party may have been thinking in those terms.

Agency by Appointment

The usual method of creating an agency is by express authorization. That is, a person is appointed to act for or on behalf of another. No special language or particular form is generally needed. It is sufficient that one person indicates that another is to represent him or her, and that the second person assents to the appointment.

Consent by Agent The agent must consent to the agency relationship. A person may want to give another the right to be an agent, but the other person is free to accept or reject the offer. This is not surprising, since one need not accept even a gift. Since agency requires the agent to assume fiduciary duties, the right of free choice is even more important.

As in contracts, the proposal of the principal may make a communicated acceptance unnecessary. Thus, if the principal requests another to act and indicates that no further communication is needed, and the other person acts, the relation of principal and agent exists. For example, *P* writes *A*, a real estate broker, and requests *A* to purchase a particular property for *P* in *A*'s name. *A* makes the purchase in her own name and refuses to convey it to *P*. Under the circumstances an agency will be inferred. *A* made the purchase on *P*'s account and must therefore convey the property to *P*.

Power of Attorney Just as an agent cannot be appointed to perform some acts, such as getting married or being a witness at a trial, so some legal documents have to be signed in person or by an agent who acts under a power of attorney. A power of attorney is a written document, signed by a principal, that gives the agent (sometimes called an "attorney-in-fact" as distinguished from an "attorney-at-law") the power to sign personal documents. These documents include deeds to lands, stock certificates, titles to automobiles in title states, checks drawn on banks, and assignments of insurance policies. If an agent with authority contracts to sell the principal's real estate, for instance, although the contract to sell binds the principal, the actual deed must be signed by the principal, and the agent's signature on a deed has no effect unless the agent has been issued a power of attorney. Similarly, a bank need not honor an agent's signature on a check unless a proper power of attorney is on file with the bank.

A power of attorney may be very specific, such as a power to sell and convey a particular parcel of real estate. It may also be very general (such as those signed by persons in the Armed Forces who go overseas) and give the agent power over all the principal's property.

Powers of attorney are normally given only for transactions that require the principal's signature. Such powers are strictly construed, and unwritten powers are not inferred from the usual course of business as they are in usual cases of agency. Therefore anyone dealing with an attorney-in-fact under a power of attorney must scrutinize the document to see if the power exercised was actually given in writing, if the document to be signed is one that normally requires the personal signature of the principal. The usual form of signing the final document is "Richard Roe [principal], by John Doe, Attorney-in-fact."

Agency by Estoppel

In some cases the law imposes an agency relation even though there was no actual consent between the principal and agent. If the words or conduct of the principal causes a third person reasonably to believe that an agency exists, and the third person reasonably relies on that representation in dealing with the supposed agent, the principal will be estopped (prevented) from denying the agency. The reason underlying this rule is that one should be bound by one's words and conduct if another person materially relies on them.

Since there is no actual authorization of the agent, an agency by estoppel, sometimes called apparent or ostensible agency, is not a genuine agency. The practical legal effects, however, are the same to the third party as if the principal in fact appointed the agent. The principal will be bound by the acts of the apparent agent.

To create an agency by estoppel the appearances of agency must be created by the principal, not by the agent. Suppose that Z skillfully creates an appearance of agency for P by printing false stationery and business cards. As long as P neither knows nor should know of this activity, P may deny the agency. Anyone relying on the false stationery and cards would be relying on appearances created by Z, not by P.

A person, however, who knowingly permits another to represent that an agency exists may be estopped to deny the relationship. For instance, P owns a jewelry store and permits A to run a personal business in that store and to display merchandise to A's own customers, the profit to P to come from A's purchases of merchandise from P. Their businesses are separate, but the public is not aware of that fact. Although they are not principal and agent between themselves, any member of the public who deals with A believing A to be P's agent can hold P as a principal if it is found that the reliance was reasonable.

Estoppel by Silence Suppose Z falsely represents that P is Z's principal. Must P disavow the relationship? Can an estoppel be created by silence? The question cannot be answered with certainty, because the general rule is that P must do what a "reasonable person" would do to disavow the relationship. Clearly, if P comes face to face with a person who P knows believes that Z is P's agent, P must disavow. Suppose, however, that Z falsely represents the purported agency in advertisements in newspapers in a distant city in which P does no business? Although the legal question is what a reasonable person would do (which is a question for the jury, if there is one), it is doubtful that a court would submit the question to a jury in the absence of most unusual circumstances. A person does not create appearances if disavowing a misrepresentation would be an unreasonable burden. The prudent course of action for *P*, of course, is to do somewhat more than *P* thinks legally should be done to refute the misrepresentation.

Agency by Ratification

If a person acts as agent without the actual consent or authority of the purported principal, the latter has the option to (1) refuse to approve the unauthorized acts of the purported agent, or (2) ratify or confirm the transaction. The purported principal has the right to either accept or reject the transaction, if the conditions of ratification are met.

Ratification is an express or implied affirmance, with knowledge of all material facts of a contract performed on one's behalf without authority by another who at that time purported to act as agent. If the principal elects to ratify the transaction, the defect of lack of authority is cured and a contract is formed between the principal and the third party.

Any unauthorized act can be ratified if it could originally have been authorized. This rule assists when there are minor defects in an agent's authority and helps to prevent unnecessary law suits. Conversely, unauthorized acts which the principal could not have authorized originally may not be ratified. Thus, in a state where gambling is illegal, a principal may not ratify an unauthorized promissory note given in his or her name by an agent to pay a gambling debt.

Ratification Requirements Four conditions must be met to effect a ratification. First, the agent must have purported to act for the principal. If the agent failed to disclose the existence of a principal, the undisclosed principal may not ratify the agreement. The purported agent need not identify the principal, but must purport to act for someone. Thus, a partially disclosed principal (i.e., existence known but name not revealed) may ratify a contract, but a totally undisclosed principal may not ratify.

A second requirement for ratification is that the principal must ratify the entire transaction. The principal may not elect to ratify only those portions of the agreement that are favorable. To be ratified, the agreement must be approved in its entirety. The principal must take "the thorns with the roses."

Third, ratification must be made before the third party elects to withdraw from the agreement. If the third party withdraws, dies, or becomes incompetent to contract before the principal has made the election to ratify, the ratification will be ineffective. Ratification does not require actual notice to the third party, only some objective manifestation of ratification.

Finally, the principal must have available all material facts before the ratification will be binding. If the agent and the third party contract for sale of the principal's property, which had special value unknown to the principal, this lack of knowledge precludes effective ratification.

Mechanics of Ratification and Ratification by Silence

Ratification may be either express or implied. Express ratification provides the clearest evidence. Sometimes express ratification is required. If a formality such as a writing is required to create a particular agency, ratification must be in writing. Thus, if an agent purports to bind the principal to sell real estate, ratification of the transaction must be in writing since the agent's original authority should have been evidenced by a writing.

Implied consent is found when the principal simply elects to take the benefits of the agreement. Thus, if the principal accepts title to property purchased by an unauthorized agent, the act of acceptance is a ratification.

Effective Date of Ratification

Ratification dates back to the original transaction, and makes the transaction effective as of the prior date. If rights of innocent third parties have intervened in the interim, those rights will not be defeated by the ratification.

An unauthorized contract may be made on behalf of a purported principal by (1) a person who has no agency relationship whatsoever, or (2) an agent who is exceeding all of his or her authority. The general rule is that if there is no preexisting agency relationship, ratification requires some positive words or conduct. Silence is not a ratification. If, however, the agent had authority which was totally exceeded, the principal must actively disavow the contract on learning of it or will be held to have ratified the contract. Silence is a ratification in that instance.

Ratification can come about unwittingly. Suppose that an existing agent makes an authorized contract to sell the principal's goods to a third person, and also gives that third person a totally unauthorized credit against the price because of a complaint about the adequacy of a prior shipment. The principal learns of both the sale and the credit and, believing that the unauthorized credit is not binding, ships the goods. The act of shipping is an effective implied ratification of both parts of the transaction.

Circumstances Not Affecting Ratification

Ratification is unilateral on the part of the principal. The third party need do nothing. Also, a principal may first indicate repudiation of the unauthorized agreement and later ratify, unless the third party withdraws before the ratification or in some way (such as by selling unique goods that were the subject of the unauthorized contract) changes his or her position in reliance on the first repudiation. In addition, both the third party and the purported agent can be fully aware that the original contract was not authorized, or totally unaware that it was not authorized.

Agency by Estoppel Distinguished from Ratification The doctrine of estoppel is for the benefit of third persons who deal with a person who appears to be but is not an agent. An estoppel does not create an agency relationship; it only prevents the third person from suffering a loss that would result if the agency were successfully denied. Ratification, by contrast, establishes the agency relationship. In both cases, agency by estoppel and agency by ratification, the legal effect to the third party is the same. The third party has an enforceable contract with the principal.

Agency by Operation of Law

Public policy sometimes requires an agency by operation of law. Courts imply such agency relations because of necessity and in order to do justice between parties.

Husband-Wife Agency A husband must, under law, provide necessaries for his wife. Necessaries are generally defined as goods and services befitting a person's "station in life." If a husband refuses to provide such support, the wife may purchase and charge the necessaries to the account of the husband. She is, by law, acting for her husband in making the purchases. The agency relation is imposed by operation of law to further the welfare of the neglected wife. To illustrate, a wife has implied authority to act as agent for her husband, who is absent or refuses, in providing clothing for herself or their minor children.

Parent-Child Agency An unemancipated minor child is entitled to support from parents. The necessities of life, those goods and services essential to the health and welfare of a child in his or her station in life, may be purchased by the child on the credit of the parent. The parent must have refused to provide the necessity, and the goods or services must in fact be necessary. An agency by operation of law is then imposed, and the transaction is made on behalf of the parent.

CREATION OF INSURANCE AGENCY

Types of Insurance Agents

Although virtually all insurance company employees are sometimes called agents, in general conversation we think of an insurance "agent" as someone engaged in selling insurance. Recognizing that many types of agents are involved in the conduct of the insurance business, the classification and scope of authority of those agents actually engaged in selling the insurance product must be carefully considered. It is through their efforts that the insurance contract is entered into. The authority granted them to bind the contract and to modify the agreements they contain has crucial legal implications for all parties.

Sales forces of insurance concerns differ greatly. So-called "direct writing" companies employ their own agents. Many other companies rely upon independent insurance agents to represent them. Although many of the usual terms, such as general and special agent, are used in the insurance field, the terms often have quite different meanings than in traditional agency relations. Thus, an insurer may refer to its selling agents as "special agents," (usually called "soliciting agents") and yet give them very general power to enter into insurance contracts. It is necessary in each case to examine the actual authority given, and to consider the type of insurance coverage involved, in order to establish the nature and extent of the agent's authority. (The different types of insurance marketing systems are discussed in CPCU 5, Chapters 2 and 3.)

General Agents   Most types of property and liability insurance are regularly sold through general insurance agents. Such agents normally have authority within specified limits to make and modify contracts of insurance. Regardless of what he or she is called, an agent authorized to pass upon and accept applicants, to agree upon the terms of the insurance, and to execute and deliver policies, is considered a general agent. Such agents may normally waive conditions of the policy, extend time for payment of premiums, waive proofs of loss, and exercise other customary powers. The general agent thus has broad powers to represent the insurance company in a given area and with respect to specific lines of business.

Soliciting Agents   The authority of soliciting agents, sometimes called "special agents" in the property and liability fields, is normally much more limited than that of the general agent. Their power is ordinarily confined to soliciting applications from prospective insureds. The power of such agents is much more ministerial than contractual. Their customary function is to persuade third parties to make applications for insurance. In the field of life insurance, the function of the agent is generally that of a soliciting agent, even though the life agent may be called a "general agent." This is true because the life insurance agent is primarily soliciting applications and has no authority to complete the insurance contract. The life insurance contract is not intended to be binding until it is approved by the insurer's home or regional office, is delivered to the insured, and the first premium is paid.

Many states have statutes that cover the licensing and authority of "solicitors" of insurance. The solicitor is frequently understood to be an agent of the insurance agent, with authority only to solicit applications for insurance that the agent may transmit to the insurance company. The solicitor thus is a subagent. Statutes in many states also state clearly that the solicitor is the representative of the insurer and not of the insured in the event of a dispute between the parties.

The circumstances surrounding the appointment of the agent control what authority was granted. Authority is interpreted more narrowly for solicitors than for general agents. Solicitors normally have no authority to extend time for payment of premiums, to collect premiums other than in cash, or otherwise to modify or waive any terms of the insurance contract as general agents might be empowered to do.

Brokers   Most states have a category of insurance agents called insurance brokers. Even in those states that do not license "brokers," an agent who represents a number of insurers may still be referred to as a broker. In narrower terms a broker procures insurance for persons who apply for that service. The broker is therefore the agent of the insured. The question of whether the broker is the agent of the insurance company or of the insured can greatly affect the legal rights and liabilities of the parties for reasons discussed more fully below. In a given case, the broker may represent the insured for some purposes in the transaction, and the insurer for others. Thus, the broker may act for the insured in procuring the insurance, and therefore any concealment or misrepresentation by the broker binds the insured. The broker may also represent the insurer in the same transaction in collecting the premium and delivering the policy, thereby binding the insurer if these matters are mishandled.

Adjusters   An adjuster is a special agent who investigates and negotiates settlements of claims under insurance contracts. As a practical matter, the adjuster generally works with fire, liability, property, and marine insurance contracts. Health and life insurance coverages are normally reviewed by claims examiners since they seldom involve adjustment of unliquidated amounts as do settlements in the property and casualty field. Adjusters may work for either an insurer or an insured. Most adjusters are employees of insurers. Independent adjusters work for insurers in the adjustment of losses, and so-called "public adjusters" serve insurance claimants in reaching settlement with insurers where special technical skills may be required, such as settling a large fire insurance loss. Insurance brokers and insurance sales agents may also adjust claims. An increasing number of states require licensing of insurance adjusters under testing systems similar to those required of sales agents and brokers.

Capacity of Insurance Agents

Whether an insurance agent is called a general agent, special agent, solicitor, or broker, the laws of each state provide for testing and licensing before the agent may represent an insurer or insured. Engaging in the insurance business without first complying with the licensing requirements makes the noncomplying parties subject to possible fine and prosecution. Each state has its own legal qualifications and testing standards for insurance agents. The tests are administered by the state insurance department, which issues the appropriate license to the agent upon satisfaction of its requirements. State regulations also specify the circumstances under which an agent's license may be revoked. Termination by an insurance company of the right of an agent to write business for that company does not result in cancellation of the agent's right to be licensed with other companies. Engaging in the insurance business thus involves the two-fold process of being licensed by the state and being granted the privilege to represent a particular insurer.

Insurance Agency by Estoppel

The vast majority of insurance agency relations are created by proper licensing of the agent and by the appointment of that agent to represent a particular company. Notwithstanding the licensing requirement, an insurance agency may be created by estoppel. If an insurance company's conduct toward the agent or third party is such that a reasonable person is justified in assuming an agency exists, the company may be estopped from denying the agency. To illustrate, before a prospective agent is properly licensed by the state, X, an insurance company, provides the proposed agent with a window sign and application forms implying that the agent represents X. A third party who does not know that the agent is not yet authorized to write business may still hold X liable upon a contract of insurance. A reasonable person could be justified in assuming that the agent was, in fact, authorized to represent X. Reliance on the company's representations, which results in detriment to the third party, produces an agency by estoppel. Similarly, liability may follow if upon termination of the insurance agency the insurance company fails to require the terminated agent to return the advertising signs and application forms. Retention of these items may raise an agency by estoppel, and permit the third party to hold the insurance company liable. The company may, in turn, have a right to bring suit against the former agent for misrepresentation, and to recover for any loss to the company that results from the misrepresentation.

Insurance Agency by Ratification

It is also possible to create an insurance agency by ratification. If an insurance broker, for instance, represents to a client that the insurance applied for will be placed with insurance company Y, Y may later ratify the transaction by agreeing to accept the risk. The usual ratification requirements must be met: (1) the agent must purport to act for the principal-insurer at the time of the original transaction; (2) the company must ratify the entire transaction, which will be presumed from the execution and delivery of the policy; (3) the company must ratify before the third party elects to withdraw; (4) the company must have full knowledge of all the facts; and (5) the contract must be legal. If all these elements are present, the company ratifying the act of the agent is bound by the contract and the effective date of the agreement dates back to the time of the original contract. Although the licensing requirements of the state may affect the legal relations between the insurance company and the purported agent, as far as the third party is concerned, the ratified insurance contract is binding on the insurer.

Ratification by Insured Ratification of the insurance contract usually involves ratification by the insurer. The insured, however, may also ratify. Thus, if a licensed insurance broker pays a large life insurance premium during the grace period in order to keep the policy from lapsing, the insured may later ratify the transaction if all the elements of ratification are present. If, under these circumstances, the insured later retains the policy with knowledge that the payment was made, the insured will have ratified the transaction and may not later dispute the agent's authority to pay the premium.

Choice of Insurers by Agent

It is possible for an applicant for insurance to have a contract with a company the applicant never heard of. If an insurance agent represents a number of insurers, and the applicant leaves the selection of the insurer to the discretion of the agent, the agent's selection prior to a loss will bind that insurer. It must appear that the agent in some way—by notation, dictation, or some other external method—designated this insurer as the one that will provide the coverage. Merely having a particular insurer in mind is not sufficient to place that insurer on the loss exposure. In the absence of some showing of a designation prior to the loss, the great weight of authority excuses all the insurers represented by the agent and holds the agent alone responsible to the applicant either under the theory that the agent was negligent in failing to procure the insurance or breached a contract to obtain insurance. To illustrate, if the agent represents a number of insurers and obtains an application for fire insurance without making some notation, however brief, of the company with which the application is to be placed, the agent may be liable for a fire loss that occurs prior to placement of the insurance. If the agent makes a note or transcription placing the application with a particular insurer, that insurer would be bound on any loss—provided the agent was authorized to write the coverage for the company.

Agency in Group Insurance

A group insurance contract is a three-party relationship. The frequent question is whether the group policyholder is the agent of the insurance company or of the individual certificate holders. The policyholder, be it an employer, labor union, or school, is the primary party to the group contract. The contract is entered into for the benefit of third persons, the certificate holders, who are the employees or members of the group. The policyholder generally assumes certain administrative responsibilities such as enrolling members, making payroll deductions, reporting changes in the insured group, and other acts that serve to minimize the administrative costs of the insurance and to keep the insurance in force for the certificate holders.

The majority view is that the group policyholder is the agent of the certificate holder if, indeed, it is the agent of anyone. The employer-policyholder acts as agent of the employees, and not as agent of the insurance company, in performing duties in connection with the policy. The important result is that the insurance company is not liable or accountable for the mistakes of the employer-administrator; nor is the knowledge of the administrator imputed to the insurer.

Under the majority view, the result might benefit or hurt the certificate holder. Thus, if an employee tenders a premium to the employer-policyholder, and the employer refuses it, the tender is not a tender to the insurance company. Hence, the insurer is not liable to the employee if the insurance is terminated for nonpayment of premium. If, however, the certificate holder requests the employer to cancel the group life insurance coverage, but the request is not relayed to the insurance company, the insurance continues in force since this is not notice to the insurer of the request for cancellation. These rules are applicable in most jurisdictions in the absence of a specific group contract provision to the contrary.

AUTHORITY OF AGENTS

General

For a principal to be liable for transactions entered into by an agent, an agency must exist either by appointment, estoppel, ratification, or operation of law. Second, it must be established that the transaction was *authorized.* It thus is important to consider the source, scope, and limitations of the agent's claimed authority.

The *scope* of an agent's authority may be (1) actual (either express or implied, or authority to act in an emergency); or (2) apparent (authority by estoppel).

Actual Authority

Express Authority Express authority is anything the principal specifically instructs the agent to do. This authority includes acts incidental to carrying out the specified instructions. The extent of express authority is determined by the meaning of the words used in granting the authority. Thus, if authority is conferred "to collect" an account owed the principal, the agent has express authority not only to press the debtor for payment, but also to institute suit, enforce any judgment obtained, and incur reasonable expenses and costs (including attorney's fees) to that end. Note, however, that the mere authority "to collect" probably would not authorize compromising or settling the account for less than is due.

Specific Authority. To determine the scope of the express authority the specific goals must be examined in light of all surrounding circumstances (i.e., nature of the business, trade usage, and so on). To illustrate, the power "to sell" generally is authority to sell for cash, not credit, and to make customary warranties. If a "sales agent" is not given possession or some indication of ownership, there is no authority to collect the purchase price. The agent only has authority to solicit orders in most trading situations or to produce a buyer with whom the principal may deal.

Implied Authority Actual authority may also be impliedly conferred by custom, usage, or conduct of the principal indicating an intention to confer such authority. To illustrate, for many years P delivered goods to A, a dealer in such goods, and A sold them for the best price available. Upon P's current delivery of such goods, and in the absence of contrary instructions, A has implied authority to sell and deliver the goods at the best price.

In defining the scope of implied authority, courts sometimes draw a distinction between general and special agents. A general agent may bind the principal to third parties by all acts that are usual and customary in such businesses and transactions. The implied authority of special agents, however, is restricted to acts that are "essential" to the performance of the specific tasks assigned.

Custom is the most common source of implied authority. An agent may reasonably infer that his or her actions may accord with prevailing custom, unless the principal gives the agent different instructions. Without special direction, an agent's authority extends to (and is limited to) what a person in this agent's position usually does. Thus, managers and general agents are not, because of their positions, authorized to make unusual contracts.

Authority to Act in an Emergency An unforeseen emergency occurs when an agent cannot contact the principal to obtain additional authority necessary to protect or preserve the property or rights of the principal. If an agent reasonably believes an emergency exists, the agent has authority to do acts beyond or even contrary to the instructions of the principal to protect the principal's interests. Emergency authority generally includes the right to delegate authority to others. If the agent can communicate with the principal by reasonable means, such communication should be made. If contact cannot be made the agent has the authority to do what is necessary. To illustrate, while on business for P, A negligently injures a third person. Immediate communication with P is not possible, and A obtains the services of T, a physician, to treat the injured party. T may later collect from P for the value of the services. Although A's authority normally does not include employment of a physician, emergency authority to hire T exists under these circumstances.

Emergency authority is limited by what a reasonable person believes the principal would wish to be done. It is based on the theory that the principal would want the agent, in an unforeseen emergency, "to act for me as a reasonably prudent person would act in any emergency." Emergencies often require quick action on humanitarian grounds, in addition to the need to protect the interests of the principal.

If an agent acts reasonably in an emergency, authority to act exists even though he or she is mistaken as to the necessity of the action and even though the agent is at fault in creating the emergency. The agent, however, may be liable to the principal for expenses caused by the agent's wrongful conduct. To illustrate, A has been ordered not to sell goods to T on credit. During P's absence, and while P cannot be reached, A sells to T on credit. A then learns that T obtained the goods by fraud and intends to leave the state with the goods. A employs an attorney and commences an action to recover the goods. A has emergency authority, but is liable to P for the expenses incurred. The attorney employed by A may collect directly from P for the legal services.

Apparent Authority

The three types of authority discussed above, expressed, implied, and authority to act in an emergency, are given to the agent by the principal and are therefore called *actual* authority. Apparent authority is authority that is not given to the agent by the principal, but is based on the third party's reasonable belief, based on appearances created by the principal, that the agent has authority. It is often called *authority by estoppel* on the theory that if a principal creates the appearance of authority in an agent, and a third person reasonably relies on those appearances, the principal should be estopped to deny that authority. The term "apparent authority" stresses the reasonable belief of the third party, and the term "authority by estoppel" stresses the words, acts, or conduct of the principal that creates the impression of authority. The concept is the same as used in the creation of an agency by estoppel, previously discussed, but here an agency relationship already exists and the question is to what extent, if any, the agent has more authority than the principal actually granted.

Apparent authority is based on appearances created by the principal. It can never be based on appearances created by the agent. Apparent authority includes all the authority that a reasonably prudent person, acquainted with the customs and nature of the business, would be justified in assuming that the agent had. Apparent authority generally arises in one of two overlapping circumstances: (1) a principal grants less actual authority to the agent than the usual agent in such a position in that business is granted, or (2) the method of operation of the principal's business differs from the method of operation of other businesses of the same kind in the principal's area.

For example, P, a principal, instructs A, the agent, not to sell goods on credit if the total credit to a customer is over $200. The usual agent in that business is not subject to that restriction. A sells goods on credit to T for over $200. The agent has violated the instruction and has no actual authority to make that credit transaction. T, however, neither knew nor had reason to know of the restriction. A's authority, therefore, was created by P putting A in a position as agent where the third party could reasonably believe A had the authority. The authority was apparent, and P is estopped to deny the authority. The secret limitation is not effective.

Or, suppose that an agent is put in charge of a store and is instructed not to stock or sell a certain product. All other stores of a similar nature in that area, however, stock and sell that product. The agent, contrary to instructions, contracts to purchase a stock of the forbidden product. The agent has apparent authority to do so as long as the seller is unaware of the restriction on the agent's authority. Again, the secret limitation is not effective.

Analyzing Types of Authority For the purpose of analyzing a problem of an agent's authority, one should first look for actual authority. Only if no actual authority exists should one see if the requisites of apparent authority or authority by estoppel are present. To illustrate, P writes to A, a dealer in rare books, requesting A to sell P's library and sends a copy of the letter to T who is a prospective purchaser. A has actual authority to sell the library. Even though T reasonably believes that A has authority, there is no reason to speak in terms of apparent authority. In addition to the power to bind the principal, A has the right to do so. In cases of apparent authority, however, although A has the power to bind the principal to the third party, A has no right to do so. An agent who acts under apparent authority, and therefore outside the actual authority granted, is subject not only to discipline, but is also liable to the principal for any loss caused by the unauthorized act.

Evidence of Ownership Apparent ownership is created by giving a person evidence of ownership, thereby making it appear that the person is the owner.

When one has *apparent ownership* of property one's powers over that property are those of an owner. Thus, if a principal gives an agent evidence of personal ownership that leads a third person reasonably to believe that the agent, in fact, owns the goods in his or her own right, the agent may deal with and dispose of the property as if the agent were the true owner. If an owner of goods delivers a bill of sale or deed to property and gives possession of the property to another, the other person may sell the goods to a third party who has no knowledge of the agency, and the principal will not be permitted to assert the invalidity of the sale, even if the sale was not authorized.

A person who has apparent ownership of property and deals with the property in an unauthorized manner is liable to the principal for any loss caused by his or her acts. The liability is caused by the apparent owner's breach of the relationship, just as an agent who acts solely under apparent authority or authority by estoppel is liable to the principal for any loss caused by going beyond or contrary to the granted authority. Both persons have the *power* to bind the principal, but do not have the *right* to do so.

Duty to Ascertain Scope of Authority

The representations of the principal to a third party determine the existence and the scope of apparent authority. A third person is not entitled to rely on the statements of the *agent* concerning the scope of the agent's authority. Only the actual authority given by the principal, or the apparent authority manifested by the principal to the third party, control the extent of the agent's authority. If an agent acts in a manner adverse to the best interests of the principal, the third party is placed on notice that the agent may be exceeding his or her authority. The third party must then ascertain the scope of the agent's authority by a direct inquiry to the principal. The only sure way the third party can be protected, and can ultimately bind the principal, is by such direct contact.

This is not to suggest that a third party must always ask a principal to confirm the scope of an agent's authority. The principal's conduct may have given the agent a broad range of authority. Only when the agent makes a representation concerning the extent of his or her authority that would appear to a reasonable person to be excessive must the third person be careful to check the true extent of the agent's authority. If the third party fails to inquire and the agent is not in fact authorized, then the principal is not bound by the transaction in question.

Limitations on Powers of Insurance Agents

It is, of course, proper for an insurer to place limitations on the authority and power of an insurance agent. As a general rule, any limitations imposed by the insurer upon the authority of the agent are binding upon third parties, provided such limitations are (1) properly communicated to the third party, and (2) legally reasonable and not opposed to public policy.

Communication of Limitations Restrictions on an agent's authority may be communicated in a number of ways. First, the limitation may be a term of the insurance policy. These limitations are effective and bind the insured after the policy is delivered. They are not, however, effective before the agent delivers the policy, since the insured does not know of the policy limitation until the policy is actually delivered.

A second method of communicating limitations on the agent's

authority is by the language of the application for insurance. Limitations contained in the application bind the insured if the application is signed. This is true even though the limitations are not actually read by the insured. Persons are expected to read and understand documents they sign.

Still a third method of communicating limitations is orally or by a writing not immediately connected with the insurance contract. When proven, these limitations bind third parties in all transactions subsequent to the communication.

Improper Limitations If a limitation on an agent's authority is opposed to public policy, it is not binding on the parties. Thus, policy provisions frequently specify that agents of the company are not authorized to waive or alter any condition of the policy except in a specified manner. The courts agree that such limitations do not bind general agents. General agents are authorized and empowered to fix the terms of policy contracts, and attempts of insurers to take away from this authority are seldom supported by courts. Such limitations are not in keeping with customary practice. Similarly, attempts to provide that an agent shall be considered the agent of the insured, rather than of the insurer, are viewed as unreasonable limitations. They are considered to be contrary to fact and to law and are not given effect. Any attempt to impose a limitation that is contrary to well-established rules of law will not be enforced. It is a well-established rule of agency law that knowledge of the agent is imputed to the principal. Therefore, a provision that the insurer shall not be charged with knowledge acquired by the agent in the course of the employment is held invalid by most courts. That attempted limitation is against public policy.

Delegation of Authority

Since agency is a consensual relationship, the general rule is that an agent cannot delegate the authority granted by the principal to another person. The agent is selected because of certain personal qualifications, and to permit performance of the agency by someone appointed by the agent is unfair to the principal. Thus, authority given to conduct a transaction does not include authority to delegate to another the performance of that task. The rule is that a delegate may not delegate. As with most rules, there are some qualifications.

Ministerial Duties Agents often perform routine or mechanical tasks. In general, the greater the authority of the agent, the larger the number of such tasks. If the performance of certain tasks does not require any real element of judgment or discretion an agent may delegate their performance to another. Most clerical functions, such as typing or sealing envelopes, are ministerial duties that involve little discretion. If an agent's duties include such tasks, the agent is authorized to employ another, sometimes called a subagent, to perform routine functions.

Customary Appointments If normal custom and usage of a particular business involves the delegation of authority, the agent may delegate. To illustrate, trading in many types of property customarily involves the services of specialized brokers. An agent authorized to dispose of the principal's stock, real estate, or cotton crop, is authorized to employ a broker who deals in such transactions. The actions of the person appointed by the agent bind the principal in the same manner as if performed by the original agent.

Emergency Appointments In an emergency that reasonably requires the appointment of another in order to protect the interests of the principal, the agent may make an emergency appointment. Thus, where an agent has the responsibility of guarding the principal's property, or taking tickets at the principal's place of business, upon the sudden illness of the agent, the agent may appoint another to assume duties necessary to complete the task.

It should be noted that whenever an agent has authority to appoint another to accomplish the purposes of the agency, the appointment was within the reasonable contemplation of both the principal and the agent at the time the agency was created. The surrounding circumstances in each exception reasonably require that the agent have authority to delegate performance to another.

TERMINATION OF AGENCY

General

As in many human dealings, it is often more difficult to terminate an agency relationship than it is to enter into it. The agency, as well as the authority of the agent, may be ended in several ways: through lapse of time; through accomplishment of the purpose of the agency; through revocation or renunciation by either or both of the parties; through death or loss of capacity of one of the parties; or through impossibility.

Power Versus Right to Terminate It may be helpful to distinguish at the outset between the power and the right of the parties to terminate the relationship. If the agency is "at will," either the principal or the agent have *both* the power *and* the right to terminate the agency at any time without legal liability. If, however, the agency is to continue for a certain time or until a specific purpose is accomplished, then both the principal and the agent have the power, but not the right, to revoke.

Agency is a very personal relationship, and because it is impossible for a court to supervise performance, and because of its fiduciary nature, courts do not order specific performance of an agency contract. Courts do, however, grant damages that can be proved by the innocent party. Therefore, although either party has the power to terminate an agency contract, if that power is not exercised rightfully, the termination is a breach of contract and the terminating party is subject to possible suit if the early revocation violates their agreement.

Termination Through Lapse of Time

An agent's authority granted for a specified time will terminate at the expiration of that period. If no time is specified a reasonable time is implied and the authority will terminate at the end of a reasonable period. What is a reasonable period depends upon the circumstances, such as the purpose of the agency, the likelihood of a change in purpose, and so on. Thus, if P authorizes A to sell certain personal property for P, and five years go by without any communication between P and A, the agency probably terminated through lapse of time. A no longer has authority to sell the property. If, however, A had made occasional reports to P on prospective buyers, and P had given no indication that the authority was terminated, A would continue to have authority to sell.

Termination by Accomplishment of Purpose

If the agent's authority is to perform a specified act or to accomplish a specific result, authority terminates upon its accomplishment. This is true even though the performance is by another agent or the principal. To illustrate, P gives authority to two separate agents, A and B, to lease or sell P's house. B leases the house to T, as A knows. A's authority to lease or sell the house is thereby terminated. After the lease neither A nor B is authorized to sell P's house, and neither may rescind the transaction with T and make a new lease to T.

Unless otherwise agreed, courts generally hold that an agent's authority continues until the agent has received notice that the purpose of the agency has been accomplished. Thus, P authorizes A to buy a car and, without notice to A, a car is purchased by P before A acts. A's authority does not terminate until A receives notice of the purchase. A's contract to purchase a car on P's behalf will bind P unless notice was received before the purchase. "Notice" is received when the agent gains knowledge, has reason to know, or should know of the accomplishment of the purpose of the agency.

Termination Through Revocation or Renunciation

Revocation by Principal The principal may revoke the agency by any word or act indicating that the agent is no longer to exercise authority. The agent must receive notice of the principal's intention. A contract provision that authority shall be revoked only in a specified manner does not prevent termination of the agency through other means. As previously noted, the principal always has the power to terminate the agency, although improper termination in violation of a contract between the agent and principal may result in a suit for damages by the agent.

The principal's appointment of another agent to accomplish the authorized act revokes the authority of the original agent if the new appointment is inconsistent with the first. Thus, if a client obtains a new attorney to try a case, and the original attorney-agent has knowledge of the appointment, the latter's agency is terminated. The two appointments are inconsistent. However, the mere fact that a second agent is given authority to sell the same property as the first agent is not of itself sufficient to terminate the original agency. Unless an agent is given an exclusive right to sell particular property, the principal reserves the right to sell or to authorize another agent to sell. The appointments are not inconsistent and the first agent who sells gets the benefit.

Renunciation by Agent Termination of the relation by the agent is called a "renunciation of authority." The fact that the agent is contractually bound to perform, and that the renunciation is a breach of contract and exposes the agent to liability in damages, does not prevent the renunciation from being effective. For example, *P* hires *A* to represent *P* for two years. After one year, *A* resigns. Although *A* may be liable to *P* for the cost of finding a replacement, the resignation effectively terminates the authority and ends the agency relationship.

Termination Through Death or Loss of Capacity

The death of either the principal or agent terminates the agency relationship since the agent can no longer act after his or her own death and an agent cannot act for a nonexistent (i.e., dead) principal.

Notice to Agent Cancellation of the agency occurs upon death of the principal even though the agent or third party has no actual notice of death. The reason for this rule, which has its basis in early common law, is that death is a matter of public record, and everyone is on notice of the fact. The lone widespread qualification to this rule is in the payment or collection of negotiable instruments. In order to encourage commerce by assuring the acceptability of negotiable instruments, it is uniformly held that until a bank receives notice of a depositor's death the bank has authority to pay checks drawn on the account. Similarly, when the holder of a check deposits it for collection by a bank, the bank may proceed with the collection even after the death of the depositor until notice is received by the bank. The necessities of modern banking and commerce require a relaxation of the general rule that death terminates the agency relationship immediately.

Loss of Capacity   Courts generally treat the loss of capacity by the principal in the same way as if the principal had died. This is true even though the transaction might still be conducted in the principal's name, since the principal is alive. It is uniformly held, however, that since the agent acts in the place of the principal, and the principal is incapable of acting, the authority is discontinued during the period of incapacity. Thus, incapacity will terminate the authority of the agent when the principal is declared legally incompetent by a court, or when the principal is shown to be so insane as to not understand the consequences of what is being done or that a contract is being made. The general rules relating to capacity to contract discussed in Chapter 3 are applicable to the question of capacity to be represented by an agent. It should be noted that if the principal's incapacity is merely temporary, the agency is terminated only during the period of incapacity.

Slightly different rules are applied to the incapacity of agents. Certainly if the agent loses the right to act as an agent because of some licensing restriction, such as disbarment of an attorney or revocation of a real estate broker's license, the agent's authority will be terminated because of lack of legal capacity to carry out the authorized acts. When, however, the loss of capacity relates only to the mental capacity of the agent, it does not follow that the agency is terminated. An agent does not need contractual capacity. The capacity of the principal controls, and not that of the agent. A principal may well be represented by an insane agent and, unless this fact is known by the third party with whom the agent deals, the principal will be bound by the contract of the agent. The principal has a right to terminate the agency upon learning that the agent has become insane, but in absence of termination an agent may represent the principal even though the agent is, or has become, insane or otherwise incompetent. Thus, if P authorizes A to sell P's property and A enters into a contract to sell to T while A, unknown to T, is severely affected by the use of drugs, the contract binds P.

The legal maxim that "as between two innocent parties he who caused the loss shall be made to bear it" is said to apply. The principal who permits an insane agent to represent him or her will be bound by the contract of such agent.

An exception to the rule that incapacity of an agent does not terminate an agency is when the agent is declared incompetent by a court. Since the court record is a public record, all persons within the jurisdiction of that court, at least, are bound by that public notice.

Termination Through Impossibility and Changed Circumstances

An agent has no power and hence no authority to accomplish results which are impossible to achieve. Thus, when the subject matter of the agency is destroyed, the agent's authority is terminated. Partial destruction of the subject matter also terminates the agency if further actions by the agent would not be in the best interests of the principal. To illustrate, P authorizes A to sell P's automobile. Prior to the sale, the vehicle is completely destroyed in an accident. Having no notice of this, A purports to sell the automobile to T. A has no power to contract for the sale of the vehicle.

If from a substantial change in circumstances the agent should reasonably infer that the principal would not wish the agency to continue, authority to act is terminated. Thus, if P authorizes A to sell land, and oil is discovered under the land prior to the sale, A's authority to sell for the amount authorized prior to the discovery is terminated. An agent may exercise authority only when the agent has reason to believe the principal wishes it to be exercised. In unforeseen circumstances, the principal's knowledge and actions are most important. If the principal and agent are in close contact, and the principal is aware of the change of events, the agent can reasonably construe the authority as continuing in absence of new instructions from the principal.

Bankruptcy The bankruptcy of the principal will normally terminate the authority of the agent as to all assets that come under the control of the bankruptcy court. As in the case of death, the termination occurs by operation of law. In bankruptcy, the assets of the principal pass for the most part to a trustee in bankruptcy. The power to deal with those assets also passes to the trustee even though no notice is given the agent. The record of the bankruptcy proceedings necessarily is a matter of public notice.

Ordinarily, the mere insolvency of the principal (i.e., the inability to meet bills as they fall due) is not sufficient to terminate the authority of the agent. In cases of reasonable doubt, the agent should communicate directly with the principal.

If the bankruptcy of an agent affects the ability of the agent to perform the purposes of the agency, or if the agent's bankruptcy affects the principal's business standing, then the agency is deemed to terminate upon the agent's bankruptcy. In the absence of either of these conditions, however, the agent's personal financial difficulty or bankruptcy does not necessarily terminate the agency relationship. The capacity of the agent, financial or otherwise, is not crucial to the relationship.

Change of Law When an agent is authorized to perform a specific act which is subsequently made illegal by a change in, or new interpretation of, the law, the authority to perform that act terminates. Thus, suppose P authorizes A to sell certain goods. Later a law is enacted in the jurisdiction where the sale is to occur that makes the sale of the goods illegal. That law terminates the authority of A to sell the goods.

Disloyalty of Agent The disloyalty of the agent also terminates the agency. As will be noted in greater detail in Chapter 7, an agent owes a duty to the principal to be loyal, to act in the best interests of the principal. When an agent enters a transaction for the agent's own purposes, and in disregard of the principal's interests, there is no authority to act and the agency terminates. Thus, an agent who receives a bribe in connection with the principal's business has no authority to complete the transaction on behalf of the principal. Similarly, an agent who embezzles money from the principal's business has no further authority to act for the principal. Notice of such a termination must be given to third parties in accordance with the usual rules.

Agency Coupled with an Interest

If an agency is "coupled with an interest," the important legal result is that the principal cannot terminate the agency, nor is the agency terminated by the death of either the principal or the agent. An agency is coupled with an interest when the agent has a vested interest in the subject matter of the agency. A mere agreement that the agency shall be irrevocable does not create an agency coupled with an interest. The agency must be created for the benefit of the agent or a third person, rather than for the principal. Two illustrations may demonstrate the type of interest that is required in order to create an agency coupled with an interest.

Interest in the Authority   An agency is coupled with an interest in the authority granted when the agent has given consideration for the right to exercise the authority. Thus, *P* owns a number of apartments. In return for a loan from *A*, *P* gives *A* the right to collect rents from the property on *P*'s behalf in discharge of the debt. *A* is *P*'s agent to collect the rents, but because the agency is coupled with an interest, the right or authority to collect the rents may not be revoked by *P* until the debt is paid. Neither *P*'s nor *A*'s death will revoke the agency, since the personal representatives of the estates of each will be authorized to fulfill the purposes of the agency.

Interest in the Subject Matter   An agency may also be coupled with an interest in the subject matter of the agency. Assume *P* owes *A* money. *P* authorizes *A* to sell *P*'s car and to use part of the proceeds to discharge the debt. *A* has an interest in the subject matter of the agency that may not be revoked by *P*, and that will not be revoked by *P*'s death or incapacity. The authority to sell the car may not be revoked until the loan is repaid.

It should be noted that an agency coupled with an interest differs from the usual agency in a very important way: it is not created primarily for the benefit of the principal. The primary intention is to enable the agent to achieve an objective, rather than to enable the principal to benefit. Therefore any attempt by the principal to revoke the authority is ineffective. The agent is entitled to obtain specific enforcement in equity of the principal's grant of authority because it is not a personal service contract and because contract duties, not fiduciary duties, control. The agent is acting in his or her own interest and not in the interest of the principal. An agency coupled with an interest, sometimes called an agency given as security, may be terminated only by a surrender of authority by the beneficiary of the authority (the agent), or by full performance of the contract.

The agency coupled with an interest is an important exception to the general rule that both parties have the power to terminate the agency relationship.

Effect of Termination

Termination of the actual authority of the agent does not necessarily terminate the apparent authority of that agent. In order to terminate the apparent authority of an agent, notice must be given to third parties of such termination.

Termination of Apparent Authority   Just as the principal's conduct as to third persons is the basis for apparent authority, so, too, is it necessary that the principal give notice to third persons of the termination of authority. In absence of notice, the agent may have apparent authority to bind the principal. The principal must give individual notice of termination of the agency to all persons who had dealings with the agent on behalf of the principal. To all others as to whom the agent may have appeared to have apparent authority, the notice may be by advertisements in newspapers of general circulation in the area in which the terminated agent conducted business. If the principal leaves evidence of agency representation in the possession of the terminated agent, it may lay the basis for apparent authority, and result in the principal being bound as to innocent third parties. Thus, the principal should remove contract forms, applications, or other indications of authority that might mislead a third person. If the principal gave written authority, such as a power of attorney, to the agent, the principal must reclaim the writing or notify those persons with whom the agent dealt in order to effectively revoke the authority.

The actual authority of the agent is effectively terminated by notice given by the principal to the agent, and the possibility of apparent authority is eliminated by notice to interested third parties. These two notices end all legal power by the agent to bind the principal to any transaction.

Termination of Subagents

The rules for terminating the authority of subagents are the same as those for terminating the primary agency relation. Since a subagent obtains authority through an agent, termination of the original agent's authority terminates the subagent's authority. Thus, if the original agent dies or becomes bankrupt in such a way as to reflect unfavorably upon the credit of the principal, both the agent's and subagent's authority and power are terminated. Also, a revocation of authority received by the subagent from either the original principal or from the agent terminates the subagent's authority. Notice to the original agent of revocation of part of that agent's authority to transact business is not binding upon the subagent until the latter has been notified of the change. In order to avoid apparent authority in the subagent, the need for notice to third parties follows the same rules as are applicable for the agent.

DUTIES OF PRINCIPAL AND AGENT

Duties of Agent to Principal

In an agency relationship the parties have certain powers and authority. At the same time, the parties have duties and liabilities. Agency normally results from a contract between the parties. The agency contract imposes certain duties of performance on the parties. In addition to these contractual duties, other duties are implied by the law as the result of the fiduciary nature of the relationship. The special fiduciary duties imposed on the agent by virtue of the unique nature of the relationship include the duties of (1) loyalty, (2) obedience, (3) reasonable care, (4) accounting, and (5) giving information.

Violation of any of these duties subject the agent to discharge and to liability for damage that may result to the principal. Failure to discharge these implied duties is a breach of the agency relationship, even though they are not mentioned in the contract. In absence of a specific agreement to the contrary, these duties are essential to the fiduciary and confidential nature of the agency relationship.

Duty of Loyalty One of the agent's most important duties is loyalty to the interests of the principal. This loyalty must be undivided.

Generally, the agent must not undertake any business venture that competes with or interferes in any manner with the business of the principal. An agent may not secretly represent the agent's own interests or the interests of a third person in a transaction for the principal. Thus, a sales agent may not buy the principal's property for the agent's own use, unless the principal specifically consents. Any transaction that violates this rule may be avoided by the principal. This is true even though the agent was entirely fair to the principal. The rule is absolute and unqualified in order to remove all questions of an agent's motive or incentive when self-dealing.

Any secret profits realized by the agent in dealing with the principal's property may be claimed by the principal. Thus, where the agent receives a gift from a third party in the course of transacting the principal's business, or where a bonus or commission is received by the agent from someone other than the principal, such rewards belong to the principal. This is true even though the entire transaction was beneficial to the principal, the objective again being to discourage any possibility of abusing the relationship.

Trade Secrets. The duty of loyalty also prohibits the agent from using or revealing trade secrets gained during the course of agency. An agent who learns of a secret process of the principal or who obtains possession of customer lists may not use such information for the agent's own purposes either during or after the termination of the agency. The principal may sue to enjoin the use of such information and may obtain from the agent any profits the agent makes from selling the information to others.

Mere knowledge and skill obtained through experience are not in themselves trade secrets. Agents may use the fruits of their experience in later employment or in working for themselves.

The duty of loyalty extends beyond the period of the agency itself. Many difficult problems can arise in applying this rule. To illustrate, *A* is the driver of a milk route truck for *P*. As *A* prepares to leave the employ of *P*, *A* instructs the new driver concerning the route and leaves the only written list of customers with the new driver. *A* then accepts employment with another milk company, and, relying only on memory, attempts to solicit his old customers for the new milk company. Should a court enjoin *A* from using the information concerning customers that *A* carries in his mind? Although there is a property right in trade secrets and confidences that the law protects, most courts hold that the use of memory regarding customer lists is not an interest that should be protected against in modern commercial enterprise.

Although the duty of loyalty may not prevent an agent from contacting previous customers of the principal, the agency agreement itself may contain restrictions upon the agent's right to compete with the principal upon termination of the agency. In order that such a limitation not be unenforceable as an unreasonable restraint on trade, the limitation must be necessary to the protection of the principal's interests and must be reasonable. Thus, considering the type of business involved and other circumstances surrounding the agreement, an agreement by an agent not to compete with the principal or not to become employed by a competitor will be upheld *if* the agreement restricts the agent for a reasonable period and within a reasonable distance from the former principal's business. If such a contract exists, one may not compete even if one only relies on memory to recall prior customers.

Dishonesty of Principal. The duty of loyalty does not obligate the agent to shield a principal who is acting illegally or dishonestly. To illustrate, *A* learns that his principal, *P*, cheated a third person, *T*, on various contracts that *A* arranged between *P* and *T*. *A* may disclose *P*'s actions to *T*. If *T* obtains a judgment against *P* for *P*'s improper dealings, *P* may not recover from *A* for breach of the duty of loyalty. *A*'s duty does not extend to concealing *P*'s dishonest acts from persons affected by them.

Duty of Obedience An agent owes a duty to obey the lawful instructions of the principal. If the agent disobeys a reasonable order, the principal may bring an action for any damages that result and may also terminate the relationship. Generally, the agent may not challenge the instruction, unless it calls for illegal or immoral acts. The fact that the instructions seem impractical or are distasteful to the agent does not affect the agent's duty to obey the principal's lawful directions.

The obligation of an agent to follow the principal's orders applies to an agent who performs without compensation, as well as to the agent who receives compensation. Agents who undertake to perform the functions of an agent must follow the instructions given. The agent owes a duty to perform in accordance with the directions of the principal. The test of whether instructions are followed is what a reasonable person would do under the same or similar circumstances. If potential harm to the agent is possible, or if an emergency arises, the agent may be justified in disobeying the principal's instructions. If ambiguous instructions have been given, the agent owes the duty to exercise his or her best judgment in interpreting them.

Duty of Reasonable Care   An agent is required to exercise the degree of care and skill that a reasonably prudent person would exercise under the same or similar circumstances. An agent with special skills or training is held to the standard of care of a reasonable person possessing those skills. Thus, a real estate broker employed to sell property is required to exercise the care of a reasonably prudent real estate broker in dealing with the property. It is not an adequate defense for the broker to show that the care of a reasonably prudent person was exercised. Having special skills, the broker is held to a higher standard.

The duty of exercising reasonable care does not make the agent an insurer of the success of the undertaking. To be liable the agent must be negligent in some way. That is, the agent must fail to exercise the degree of care required under the circumstances.

An agent's failure to act, when action is reasonably required, also constitutes a breach of this duty. The agency contract implies that the agent will carry out the duties of the agency with reasonable care in order to avoid injury to the principal. To illustrate, *P* requests *A*, an insurance broker, to obtain a casualty and liability policy for *P*'s automobile. *A* obtains a policy and delivers it to *P*, but liability insurance is not included within the coverages provided. *P* suffers an accident and finds that no liability coverage is in force. *P* may sue *A* for breach of the duty of reasonable care. If an insurance agent or broker undertakes to procure a policy of insurance for another, affording protection against a designated loss exposure, the law imposes a duty to exercise reasonable care. *A* is liable to *P* for loss resulting from failure to perform that duty. *P* may sue *A* either in tort for negligence or for breach of the agency contract requiring the exercise of reasonable care.

Care of Gratuitous Agent   It makes no difference whether the agent is paid or not paid for the services. The duty to exercise reasonable care under the circumstances is owed by all agents to their principals. Liability is generally imposed on gratuitous agents under the theory of tort rather than contract. Gratuitous agents cannot be compelled to perform the duties of the agency, but once they commence performance they are held to the standard of reasonable care under the circumstances. For example, real estate broker A gratuitously promises to act as P's agent in the sale of P's real estate. P would have no cause of action against A for A's failure to make efforts to sell the property. But, if A procured T as a buyer of P's property and failed to have T sign a binding sales agreement, and T later changed his mind and declined to proceed with the sale, P would have a cause of action for negligence against A for A's failure to exercise the degree of care reasonably.

Limiting Agent's Liability. The agent and principal may enter into an agreement that the agent is not to be liable to the principal for ordinary negligence. Such agreements are generally binding between the parties since it is recognized that an agent may limit as well as expand his or her liability to the principal.

An agent, however, may not be insulated from liability for gross negligence or from exercising reasonable care when performing a public duty. If an agent is grossly negligent or engages in willful misconduct, it is against public policy to limit the agent's liability for that wrongful conduct. Similarly, when in the performance of a public duty, such as the operation of public transportation, an agreement that the agent's liability for negligence shall be limited is generally found to be against public policy.

Duty of Accounting An agent owes a duty to account to the principal for all property and money of the principal that comes into possession of the agent. As part of this duty, the agent must keep the property and money of the principal separate and apart from that of the agent. If the agent commingles the property it is assumed they all belong to the principal unless the agent clearly proves otherwise. Money held by the agent should be deposited in a bank in a separate account in the name of the principal. If the agent deposits it in the agent's own name and the bank then fails, the agent is liable for any loss sustained by the principal. The agent should account promptly for any money of the principal that the agent holds. Failure to do so will make the agent liable for interest payments to the principal.

If the agent makes improper use of funds the principal may trace the funds and have a constructive trust imposed upon them or on items purchased with those funds. If the funds are obtained by a third party who is innocent of any knowledge of the agent's wrongdoing, the principal's rights are only against the agent. If proceeds in the agent's possession increase in value, a trust may be imposed on the agent's estate to the extent of the increased value. A constructive trust is a procedure by which one who wrongfully acquires property of another is made to hold that property and the proceeds from it in trust for the benefit of the person who was wronged.

In accounting to the principal, the agent is entitled to set off any amounts that the principal may owe the agent in the conduct of the agency. The agent may not, however, set off amounts due the agent from outside, nonagency transactions between the principal and agent.

The agent's accounting may be informal, and need not involve keeping books. Cash registers are used for the accounting of sales persons in stores. The time of accounting may be specified by the parties or upon a reasonable demand by the principal. During the course of the agency and at the termination of the agency, the agent must make full accounting of all property and money of the principal. The principal has a right to make reasonable inspection of the agent's books of account, including the original entries.

If the agent fails to account properly, the principal may bring an action for breach of the agency contract, may sue for money had and received, or may bring a bill in equity for an accounting.

Duty to Give Information   An agent owes a duty to keep the principal informed of all facts relating to the agency. The principal is entitled to all information that materially affects his or her interests. Thus, when the agent is authorized to sell the principal's property for a specified amount, and the agent thereafter learns that the value of the property has changed materially, the agent owes a duty to give the principal that information.

Since the knowledge of the agent obtained during the course of performing the principal's business is imputed to the principal, the law imposes on the agent the duty of giving the information to the principal. Most courts do not impose a duty to communicate information that the agent obtains outside the scope of the agent's employment. Also, if an agent acts adversely to the interests of the principal, as when an agent colludes with a third party to defraud the principal, that knowledge will not be imputed to the principal.

Notwithstanding those exceptional situations in which the agent's duty to provide information may be qualified, the general rule remains that the agent owes a duty to make reasonable efforts to provide the principal with information that is relevant to the affairs entrusted to the agent. Failure to perform this duty makes the agent liable to the principal for loss(es) resulting to the principal.

Duties Owed by Subagents

The subagent owes the same duties to the principal as the original agent owes. In addition, an original agent is responsible to the principal for any violation of duty by a subagent, even though the agent exercised good faith in selecting the subagent. Further, a subagent owes the agent who did the hiring substantially the same duties. A subagent is liable to the agent for any loss sustained because of the subagent's improper performance.

Where a subagent is employed without authority from the principal, there is no agency relationship between the principal and the subagent. The principal is not liable to third persons for acts of the unauthorized subagent. At the same time, the unauthorized subagent owes no duties to the principal. The agent, of course, is liable for performance of the assigned duties and is liable for any loss sustained by the principal because of the conduct of the subagent.

Duties of Insurance Agents

Agents of insurance companies owe the same duties to their principals as agents in other businesses. The duty of loyalty owed by the insurance-sales agent raises some special considerations. Normally, a person who is employed by two others to conduct a transaction between them (all the facts being known to both parties) is the agent of both and owes a duty to each to deal with them fairly. The basic question is whether the insurance agent owes primary allegiance to the general employer (the insurer) or to the insured. In the case of the insurance broker, who represents the insured in obtaining insurance, duties may be owed to both the insured and the insurer depending upon the particular act. Thus, the broker may be the agent of the insured in securing a policy, and if required by specific statute, may also be the agent of the insurer in receiving the premiums. The problems of dual agency and of allegiance to two masters in insurance transactions come from the fact that a person may be an agent for one principal for part of a transaction, and an agent for the other for the remainder.

In the usual insurance company sales-agent relationship, courts tend to draw the inference that the fiduciary duties of the agent are owed to the insurer. Statutes in many states stipulate that insurance agents, or insurance solicitors, are agents of the company and not of the insured. Thus, notice given the agent, or payment made to the agent, is binding upon the insurance company. Attempts by insurers to include policy provisions that stipulate that the agent is the agent of the insured have not been given effect by the courts.

Insurance agents thus owe a duty to be loyal to the interests of the insurer-principal, to provide all material information concerning transactions, and to account to the principal for any funds obtained in pursuance of the principal's business. Also, the standard of care to which the agent is held is that of a reasonably prudent insurance agent holding himself or herself out to the public as having the skills that agents dealing in insurance services normally possess.

Specialists If the agent holds himself or herself out as being a specialist in a particular line of coverage, a higher standard of care is expected. The normal performance of agents with special skills in this area is considered in determining, as a question of fact decided by the trier of fact, whether reasonable care was exercised.

Agent Wrongdoing An infrequent but troublesome example of a breach of a number of fiduciary duties by insurance agents is when a sales agent fails to promptly forward an application and insurance premiums to the insurer. The agent may compound the difficulty by commingling the premiums with the agent's own funds, and may even attempt to settle claims from these funds when a loss occurs during this period. These combinations of oversights or wrongdoings can result in serious consequences for the agent, the insurer, and the insured. Clearly, the agent breaches the fiduciary duties of loyalty, reasonable care, and duty to account to the principal. The insurer has a right of action against the agent for the loss that results. The right of the applicant for insurance against the agent or the insurance company will be considered in the next chapter.

The statutes of each state provide criminal penalties that include loss of license, fine, or imprisonment if an insurance agent is found guilty of certain misconduct. Legislation often prescribes that life insurance agents who knowingly misrepresent the terms of a policy, or who make improper comparisons between policies to induce a person to change life insurance companies, is liable to criminal penalties. These statutes are often referred to as "anti-twisting" laws.

Remedies of Principal

The principal has a number of possible remedies for the default or wrongdoing of an agent. The selection of the appropriate legal remedy has important implications. Thus, when an agent makes improper use of the principal's property, the principal has the option to (1) bring an action for breach of the agency contract, (2) sue in tort for the harm done, (3) sue for the value of the benefit received by the agent, or (4) sue to require the agent to transfer to the principal the property improperly held.

If the agent is insolvent, the principal's best remedy is a suit to obtain return of the property. If the agent has obtained a personal gain from the transaction, then an action to obtain the benefit of what the agent received represents the best alternative. In other cases, a suit for breach of contract may be preferable to an action in tort for the wrongdoing of the agent, because the statute of limitations for contract actions (i.e., the period of time within which the action must be brought) is generally longer for contract than for tort cases. In still other cases, the principal may sue in equity to obtain an injunction prohibiting the agent from revealing trade secrets obtained during the course of employment, or from competing with the principal after termination of the employment in violation of an agreement not to compete.

Duties of Principal to Agent

Just as the agent owes various duties to the principal, so the principal owes duties to the agent. The principal is, of course, subject to the duty to perform the contract made with the agent. The principal owes a contractual obligation to continue the employment in accordance with the terms of the agreement.

Period of Employment A contract of employment may normally be terminated at the will of either party unless the agreement specifies a fixed period of employment. An agreement to pay a salary by the month or year does not necessarily indicate that employment is assured for the stated period. The promise of an agent to serve, or a principal to employ, for a specified period makes the parties liable for breach of their agreement within that period. Since the agency relation is consensual, the parties may still refuse to continue the relationship during the period of the contract, but are then subject to damages for breach of the agreement. Promises of permanent or lifetime employment are not usually enforced by the courts. These promises are generally interpreted as an intention on the part of the employer to retain the employee for a reasonable period. When the employment contract provides for a specified period of employment and the principal's business is terminated during the period, it is generally held, as an implied term of the contract, that it shall terminate if the principal goes out of business because of changed conditions and not merely to avoid contractual duties.

Opportunity to Work A duty is inferred from the agency contract that the principal will afford the agent the opportunity to work. If the principal employs an agent to work at a specified salary, and thereafter refuses to permit the agent to work, but pays the salary, the refusal constitutes material breach of the contract of employment. Similarly, if a salesperson is employed to sell the principal's goods, the salesperson can expect that a fair proportion of the goods of the principal will be made available for sale. The salesperson, however, cannot ordinarily expect the principal to enlarge the manufacturing capacity simply because the salesperson is capable of selling an exceptionally large quantity of goods. The principal is required only to make reasonable efforts to enable the agent to continue performing as contemplated by the terms of the contract of employment.

If the principal gives the agent the exclusive right to represent the principal in a particular area, the principal may not grant to another a right to sell in that area. Granting an exclusive right to sell also precludes the principal from selling in competition with the agent.

If a principal breaches the agency contract, the agent normally has the option to (1) sue the principal for the reasonable value of the agent's services up to the date of the breach or discharge from services; (2) treat the contract as continuing to exist and sue for damages sustained, which include what the agent would have earned had the contract been completed according to the agreement; or (3) sue at the expiration of the contract period for damages that flowed from breach of the contract, if the agent makes an effort to mitigate damages by seeking other employment or by performing in the best way possible after the breach.

In addition to the obligations imposed by the agency contract, the law generally recognizes three important duties that the principal owes the agent: (1) compensation, (2) reimbursement, and (3) indemnity.

Duty of Compensation The principal has a duty to pay the agent the agreed compensation for the services performed by the agent. If no compensation agreement exists, the agent is entitled to the reasonable value of the services rendered. Obviously, a gratuitous agent expects no compensation. However, if one appoints an agent who would normally be paid for services, compensation is required for the reasonable value of the service even if payment is not mentioned. An agent may, of course, agree to work on a contingent salary basis or for no income at all. An agent who breaches the duties of the agency is not entitled to compensation.

In absence of a contrary agreement, a sales agent is entitled to recover when the sale is made, even though the sale is not actually carried through or performed. Thus, when a real estate agent obtains a firm offer from a responsible buyer, the owner-principal cannot deprive the agent of a commission by refusing to deal with the prospective purchaser. The commission is also earned when the owner contracts with the purchaser, even though the buyer does not go through with the agreement. The owner is generally held to *assume the risk* of performance upon executing the contract with the buyer that has been presented by the agent-broker. Contract language between the parties may provide otherwise, and in such case the contract provisions are binding.

A principal is not responsible for the compensation of a subagent when no authority to hire subagents was given. Even if authority to hire was given, the principal is not liable unless the authority contemplated the hiring of additional personnel. If the agent is merely allowed to delegate authority to another, and uses subagents to perform the agent's duties, the subagent must normally look to the agent for compensation.

Note, also, that there is no duty to compensate for services that are rendered officiously and without request, even though the "principal" benefits. Thus, if a real estate broker without previous communication with the principal obtains a buyer for the principal's property having represented to the buyer that he or she is the principal's agent, there is no obligation to compensate the broker unless the principal actually ratifies and accepts the bargain. Compensation must then be made for the reasonable value of the services, on a so-called *quantum meruit* (i.e., as much as reasonably deserved) basis.

Duty of Reimbursement The principal is under a duty to reimburse or repay the agent for any disbursements and expenses necessarily incurred for the proper discharge of agency duties. The agent may not, however, recover disbursements made for illegal purposes nor for expenses incurred through the agent's own negligence or fault. The principal is required to reimburse the agent for any advances made on behalf of the principal by the agent. If, for example, in order to accomplish the purposes of the agency, the agent is required to incur travel and advertising expenses, these expenses must be reimbursed by the principal. It must appear that the money was reasonably spent, and that the expenditure was not the result of carelessness on the part of the agent. Thus, if the agent's negligent conduct results in unnecessary expense, that expense is borne by the agent rather than by the principal. If the agent negligently damages the agent's own automobile while on the principal's business, the agent is required to assume the cost of the damage.

Duty of Indemnity The principal owes a duty to indemnify the agent for any losses or damages suffered without the agent's fault, but arising on account of the agency. If the agency at the direction of the principal commits a wrong against a third party, and the agent did not know the act was wrongful, the agent is entitled to be indemnified for the amount the agent is required to pay. To illustrate, a principal directs the agent to cut down and sell trees on land that the principal incorrectly believes is owned by the principal. An agent who enters on the land at the direction of the principal, not knowing of the mistake, is entitled to be indemnified by the principal in the event the agent is required to pay for the damage caused to the third party's land. Similarly, if an innocent agent is liable to the true owner of personal property, having disposed of the property through sale, the principal must indemnify the agent.

Any expenses that the agent incurs in defending actions by third persons brought because of the agent's authorized conduct, the agent again being innocent of intentional wrongdoing, must be indemnified by the principal. In many states, corporate directors are entitled to be indemnified for the expenses of successfully defending stockholders' derivative actions against them for negligent conduct of the corporation's business. In most instances, however, the agent is not entitled to indemnification if the agent's own intentional or negligent conduct was responsible for the expense incurred. An agent who knowingly commits an illegal act ordinarily has no right to indemnity from the principal, even though the principal has directed that the act be committed. The agent is barred from indemnity by the illegality of the transaction. To illustrate, P agrees with A, a traveling salesman for P, that P will reimburse A for money paid out by A in giving gratuities to purchasing agents of the firms to which goods are sold. A is not entitled to indemnification from P for money illegally paid out.

Indemnity of Subagents An agent who makes payments or becomes subject to liability to third persons because of the authorized conduct of a subagent has the same right to indemnity as if the conduct were the agent's. The agent who is required to indemnify a subagent as the result of expenses and damages suffered by the subagent in performance of the principal's business is entitled to full indemnity from the principal. Since a subagent is an agent of both the immediate employer (the agent) and the agent's employer (the principal), the subagent is entitled to indemnity against either of them.

Remedies of the Agent

An agent may maintain actions at law for compensation, indemnity, or reimbursement, and may also obtain a decree in equity requiring an accounting from the principal. Also, in an action brought by the principal, the agent may maintain a set-off or counterclaim, for the value of the agent's services and expenses. The agent may use self-help by refusing to perform further services if the principal breaches their agreement.

An agent who has been discharged by the principal during a specified period of employment may maintain an action for compensation for the remainder of the period. In absence of special legislation affecting the rights of labor, the agent may not successfully maintain an action for specific performance requiring the principal to continue the employment. The principal always retains the power, if not the contractual right, to terminate the relationship.

Agent's Lien   Agents may also exercise a lien, or right to retain possession of the principal's goods, until the principal has compensated the agent for amounts due from transaction between them. Some agents, such as attorneys, bankers, factors, and stockbrokers are entitled, in the view of most courts, to enforce a so-called *general lien* against the principal. These latter specialized agents are given the right to hold the principal's goods and papers until the entire balance of all accounts between the principal and agent are settled. The general lien is not limited to the immediate transaction between the parties. Most agents are entitled to assert only a *special lien,* which permits retention of the principal's property until the account between the principal and agent for the immediate transaction is settled.

CHAPTER 7

Agency—Liability to Third Parties

CONTRACT LIABILITY

General

The agency relation contemplates activities between an agent and a third person that will bind the principal as though the principal dealt personally with the third person. The agent may enter a contract or commit a tort. The extent to which the actions of an agent will impose contractual or tort liability on the principal, as well as the rights and liabilities of the agent and third party, are the subject of this chapter.

In contract cases the existence of the agency, the extent of the agent's authority, and whether the principal was disclosed are essential factors affecting the liability of the parties. When torts are alleged to have been committed, it is necessary to determine whether an employment relation existed and whether the act committed was within the scope of that employment.

The rights of third persons against the principal in contract, the rights of principals against third persons, and the rights of agents and third persons against one another will be examined first. This will be followed by a consideration of the law relating to employment under which the torts of the employee are held to impose vicarious liability on the employer.

Liability of Principal to Third Party

Three Types of Principals The general rule is that a principal is liable to third parties for the properly authorized and executed contracts of an agent. This rule is subject to some qualification, depending on whether the principal was disclosed, undisclosed, or partially disclosed. As previously noted, a principal is *disclosed* when the third party knows of both the principal's *existence* and *identity*. The principal is *partially disclosed* when the third party knows of the principal's *existence* but is unaware of the principal's identity. The principal is *undisclosed* when the third party does not know the principal exists.

In contract dealings the law relating to partially disclosed principals is much the same as that relating to undisclosed principals. The agreements are entered into largely on the strength of the agent's credit, and the agent is liable upon such agreements until such time as the third party elects to hold the principal. The third party, on learning of the principal's existence or identity, may elect to enforce the contract against the principal rather than against the agent. The undisclosed principal is responsible for all contracts entered into by the agent within the scope of the agent's actual authority, and the principal may be sued when his or her existence becomes known. Being unknown, the principal could not have created any apparent authority; thus liability is limited to actual authority—that which is expressly given or which may be implied as incidental thereto.

Effect of Settlement with Agent   The right to sue an undisclosed principal on a simple contract is subject to two exceptions. The first of these relates to *settlement* with the agent. Thus, the third party cannot sue the principal if the principal has made a good faith settlement of the account with the agent regarding the contract. Where an undisclosed principal has supplied the agent with money to purchase goods but the agent purchases the goods on credit and retains the money, a settlement will be deemed to have occurred, and the principal will not thereafter be liable to the third party for a second payment. The undisclosed principal may settle with the agent either before or after the contract is made, provided the payment of money by the undisclosed principal occurs before disclosure of the principal's existence or identity to the third person. Any good-faith settlement between the principal and agent before disclosure releases the principal. A payment will not have this effect when it is made after the third party learns of the existence of the principal, and the principal is aware that his or her identity is known. The settlement doctrine is based on equitable rules. It is fair to the third party in that it provides that person with all the protection he or she bargained for in any event, and it is fair to the principal in that it affords protection against a second demand for payment.

Election by Third Party   A second limitation on the third party's right to sue the principal is when the third party has *elected* to hold the agent and not the principal. When the third party has learned of the existence and identity of the principal, an expression of intention to hold the agent liable on the agreement will normally be binding on the third party. To constitute an election, the third party must have knowledge of the identity of the principal and thereafter elect to take judgment against the agent. Thus, although the third person normally has a right against either the undisclosed principal or the agent, satisfaction may be obtained from only one of them. When the third party sues and obtains a judgment against the agent prior to obtaining knowledge of the principal's identity, the third party may later sue the principal when the latter's identity is learned. Although procedural rules in many jurisdictions permit an action to be brought against both the principal and the agent, the third party is required to elect prior to judgment which party (principal or agent) will be held liable. Selection of one party has the effect of discharging the other. In the event action is commenced against both the principal and the agent, and neither defendant objects to the joinder, a judgment may be obtained against both. The third party will still be limited to a single recovery on the judgment.

The rule of election does not apply if the principal is partially disclosed. In such case the right of the third party is regarded as a concurrent right, rather than an alternative one, against both principal and agent. The third party may thus obtain a judgment against either the agent or partially disclosed principal without discharging the right against the other.

The doctrine of election has been criticized on the ground that the third party may obtain a judgment against the wrong person and thereafter be unable to obtain relief. To avoid inequity, some courts provide that the third party is entitled to levy upon whatever right of indemnification the agent may have against the undisclosed principal. Under that rule, the principal may still be required to discharge the debt that he has authorized.

Indication of Agency

An agent who enters into a written contract should, of course, name the principal and sign as "agent for *P.*" If the agent does not indicate the identity of the principal on the writing, or if the indication is unclear, the agent may be liable personally on the contract. However, oral evidence may be introduced to prove that the third party knew the identity of the principal and that the principal, therefore, was disclosed.

Negotiable instruments are subject to a different rule. The Uniform Commercial Code provides that only those persons named or described in a negotiable instrument may be held liable on it.[1] Therefore a person who signs, or who signs "as agent," is personally liable if the name of the principal does not appear on the instrument. Parol evidence may not be introduced to prove that the signer signed as an agent for another person, but may be used to clear up an ambiguity.

The rule for negotiable instruments, however, does not mean that the principal will not be liable at all. Every negotiable instrument is given in connection with an underlying transaction, and the principal may be liable on that basis. For instance, an agent does not indicate the principal's name on a promissory note and gives it to a seller for goods purchased on behalf of the principal. The goods are delivered to and accepted by the principal. The principal is liable on the underlying contract even though the principal may not be sued on the note. Of course, the principal may have defenses on the underlying contract that would not be available against a holder in due course of a note.

If an instrument is required to be under seal by state law, and if an agent signs the instrument and affixes a seal without indicating the name of the principal, only the agent has rights or duties under the document. If the seal is unnecessary for any reason, even though affixed, parol evidence may be introduced to prove that the third party knew the identity of the principal unless the document is a negotiable instrument.

Improper Purpose of Agent

An agent who acts with an improper motive in representing the principal will nevertheless bind the principal to the transaction, unless the third party had notice of the agent's improper motive. Thus, if P authorizes A to borrow money from a bank, and A borrows the money with the intention of stealing it, P is liable for repayment of the loan unless the bank knew of A's wrongful intent. The agent had authority to borrow the money, and what is done with it is the principal's responsibility. The principal had the opportunity to investigate the agent before appointment, and the risk of the agent's dishonesty is therefore on the principal.

Improper Purpose of Undisclosed Principal's Agent This rule does not apply to undisclosed principals. Undisclosed principals are treated in the same manner as assignees, and have their rights because their agents intended to benefit them, just as an assignor assigns a contract to an assignee with the intention of benefiting the latter. Thus, if an agent of an undisclosed principal makes a purchase with the secret intention of retaining the goods, the agent does not intend to benefit the principal nor intend that the principal have any interest in the goods. The third party has the liability of the person with whom he or she dealt, and there is no reason to give the third party the advantage of the principal's liability.

Third Party's Knowledge of Improper Purpose   The test of knowledge of the agent's improper purpose is what a reasonable person, knowing what the third party knew, would have believed under the circumstances. It is a question of fact. Thus, if an agent is authorized to issue checks for a principal, and uses a check to pay a personal obligation owed to a third party, the creditor is probably on notice that the agent is acting improperly. Under the circumstances, the instrument could not be enforced by that third party against the principal. A later innocent holder in due course of the check, however, might still enforce it against the principal.

Revealing Principal's Identity

An agent who disobeys the principal's instruction not to reveal the existence or identity of the principal to the third party nevertheless binds the principal to an otherwise authorized contract. If the agent successfully carries out the business purpose of the principal in concluding a particular transaction, it is ordinarily immaterial that the orders of the principal with respect to nondisclosure of the principal's identity were not followed.

Liability of Third Party to Principal

Right of Principal to Enforce Contract   As a general rule, if the principal is bound by a contract to the third party, then the third party will also be bound to the principal. As between the principal and agent, the principal is entitled to all benefits of the contract and the agent acquires no beneficial interest therein. It is generally immaterial that the third person thought the contract was with the agent alone, and knew nothing of the principal's existence. Thus, in transactions between agents of disclosed and partially disclosed principals and third parties, the third party is subject to liability to the principal to the same extent as if the principal had conducted the transaction. When undisclosed principals are involved, the liability of third persons to such principals may be subject to qualification.

Fraudulent Concealment of Principal's Identity   When an agent fraudulently represents to a third party that the contract is made on behalf of the agent alone, or that the agent is representing someone other than the real principal, the third party is given the right to rescind the agreement. If the agent or principal knows or should know that the other party is unwilling to deal with the principal, the personality of the principal becomes a material fact. Representations that there is no principal, or that the principal is someone else, constitute fraud and the transaction is voidable by the third party. If the agent does not actively misrepresent the existence of the principal but knows the other party would not enter into the contract if the facts were known, most courts hold that a duty of disclosure exists. Failure to disclose the identity of the principal under such circumstances constitutes fraud. Thus, (1) if the agent knows or has reason to know the third person would not deal with the principal, and (2) either misrepresents or fails to reveal the material fact of the principal's true identity, then the third party has the right to rescind the agreement. Mere knowledge on the part of the agent that disclosure of the principal's identity might prejudice the bargain by forcing the price higher is not sufficient to impose a duty to disclose the principal's identity. This qualification to the rule of third-party liability is imposed only when there is knowledge or reason to know the third party would not deal with *this* principal.

Greater Burden Imposed An undisclosed principal is also denied the right to enforce a contract against the third party if enforcement would impose a substantial additional burden on the third party. To illustrate, *A* contracts to purchase from *T* "all of the oil which *A* shall require." If *T* did not know that *A* was in fact representing *P*, whose oil requirements are substantially greater, *P* cannot enforce the contract against *T*.

Personal Performance Contracts An undisclosed principal cannot substitute personal performance by the principal for performance by the agent required by the contract. If a contract calls for personal performance by the promisor-agent, the agent's performance may be required by the third party and may not be delegated or assigned to the principal to perform. Thus, if *A* contracts to paint a portrait of *T*, the painting must be done by *A*. If *A* completes the painting, it may be tendered or delivered by *P*, who may then enforce the original agreement against *T*. Similarly, in *credit contracts* the third party is entitled to insist upon enforcing the agreement against the person to whom the credit was extended. Thus, if sale of property is agreed upon between *T* and *A*, with the provision that payment of the balance of the purchase price will be secured by *A*'s promissory note, *T* can refuse to accept a promissory note tendered by *P*.

If the contract is for the skill, confidence, or credit of the agent, and would not have been entered into but for such considerations, an undisclosed principal may not demand performance. The contract is not assignable because personal rights and duties are not transferable without consent.

Other Defenses Available to Third Party In transactions conducted by an agent for a disclosed or partially disclosed principal, the third party may assert any defense that would have been available had the principal made the contract in person. Thus, if the principal had committed fraud or if the other party has a counterclaim against the principal, the fraud or offset may be asserted by the third party in any action brought by the principal. Claims that the third party may have against the agent may *not* be set off in an action by the principal. In the absence of some special business custom, the contract is that of the principal and not of the agent. Thus, the agent's liability to the third party either through this or other transactions is immaterial in an action between the principal and third person.

If an undisclosed principal instructs the agent not to reveal the existence of the principal, the third party will be permitted to set off any claim of the third party against the agent. The third party has the right to assume that the agent is acting on the agent's own behalf, and is, therefore, entitled to assert any claims that may exist against the agent in an action brought by the principal.

Effect of Judgment Between Third Party and Agent When an action is brought by the third person against the agent on an agreement entered into by the latter on behalf of an undisclosed principal, a judgment against the agent destroys the right of the principal against the third party. Because the actions of the agent could have destroyed the contract prior to the principal's becoming known, it follows that a judgment obtained against the agent under the contract should be equally effective to defeat the rights of the principal. However, a judgment obtained by the third party after the identity of the principal becomes known, either for or against the agent, does not necessarily bar or diminish the rights of a principal who took no part in the litigation. In most states, under the doctrine of election the third party loses any rights against the principal by electing to proceed against the agent of a disclosed principal. As previously noted, the rule of election does not apply where the principal is either partially disclosed or undisclosed. That is the choice of the third party, however, and not that of the principal. The unilateral decision on the part of the third party should not be a bar to later action by the principal.

Liability of Agent to Third Person

An agent is not generally liable on contracts entered into on behalf of a disclosed principal. The liability is solely that of the principal. It is recognized that the agent acts only on behalf of the principal, and is not intended by the parties to assume personal liability under the contract.

This rule of non-liability of the agent on authorized contracts entered into on behalf of a disclosed principal is subject to a number of exceptions.

Breach of Warranty of Authority An agent may attempt to act for a principal even though the agent has no actual authority to do so. Whenever an agent purports to act on behalf of a principal, the agent is said to *impliedly warrant* that he or she had actual authority to represent the principal. If the agent was not in fact authorized, or if the agent exceeded the authority granted, the implied warranty of authority is breached and the agent will be liable for such breach. In such case, the agent's liability is not under the contract itself but rests on the ground of breach of warranty of authority. No liability may be imposed on the principal in such cases in absence of ratification of the agreement by the principal or of apparent authority. The fact that the agent may not have been aware of the lack of authority is immaterial. If authority was not granted, or if the authority granted was exceeded, the agent is liable to the third person for any damages resulting from the failure to bind the principal.

If the agent intentionally misrepresents the existence or extent of authority, the agent may also be liable in a tort action for fraud. If sued for fraud, punitive as well as actual damages may be granted.

If the third party knows the agent lacks authority or is mistaken concerning the extent of that authority, the agent is not liable for breach of warranty. Similarly, if the agent has told the third person of uncertainty as to the existence or extent of the authority granted by the principal, the warranty of authority is not breached. The agent may avoid liability for damages arising from lack of authority by making a full disclosure to the third party of all facts relating to the agent's authority. If all the facts are available, the third party is as capable of judging the limits of the agent's powers as is the agent.

Effect of Ratification by Principal If the principal ratifies the transaction, the agent's liability for breach of warranty terminates. Ratification creates authority as of the time of the contract. Ratification must occur before the third party withdraws from the transaction. Thus, if the third party notifies the agent of cancellation of the agreement because of the agent's lack of authority, or if the third party institutes suit against the agent for breach of warranty of authority, the principal's later attempt to ratify the agreement is ineffective to discharge the agent from liability to the third party.

Incompetent Principal Part of the agent's implied warranty of authority is that the principal is capable of being bound under the contract. Thus, if an agent acts on behalf of a minor or a mentally incompetent person, the agent is personally liable for breach of warranty of authority if the third party was not aware of such incapacity.

A vexing problem is created if an agent makes a contract with a third party for a principal who, unknown to the agent or the third party, died a short time earlier. Two basic principles of law, one of agency and the other of contract, collide. Under agency law one cannot be an agent of a dead person, and therefore there is a breach of warranty of authority. Under contract law the existence of the principal was a material fact, and therefore because both parties were mistaken as to that material fact, there is no contract. Case authority is sparse, and both views have been taken.

Undisclosed and Partially Disclosed Principals An agent must disclose both the principal's identity and existence in order not to be held personally liable on a contract entered into with a third party. This liability is on the contract, and not for breach of warranty. The third party intended to contract with the agent, and the agent purported to act personally and not for the principal.

To avoid liability as a contracting party, the agent must disclose the identity of the principal to the third party. It is not sufficient that the third party knows facts that would, if pursued, disclose the principal's identity. Actual disclosure is required.

Personal Liability of Agent The third party may always request the agent to agree to personally guarantee the contract. The personal credit standing of the agent may be a crucial consideration of the third person. An agent who voluntarily assumes responsibility for performing the agreement is liable for nonperformance by the principal. The principal is liable on the contract, and the agent is liable on the guaranty.

Sometimes the third party may not want to deal with the principal, and wants a contract with the agent only. If the agent agrees, the agent and the third party alone have rights and duties under the contract, even though it is made for an existing and fully disclosed principal. This is called the *exclusive credit* doctrine. The doctrine does not apply if credit is granted to the agent of an undisclosed principal, because, in granting credit, the third party had no choice to make.

Agent's Liability to Account As noted in the previous chapter, an agent owes a duty to the principal to account for any money or property received during the course of the agency. No fiduciary relation exists between the agent and the third party; therefore, the agent owes no duty to account to the other party. If an agent is authorized to receive money from a third party, and does not turn it over to the principal, it may be recovered in an action by the principal against the agent.

If, in contrast, money is paid to an agent who has no authority to collect it, and who does not turn it over to the principal, the third party may bring an action against the agent for the money. Thus, if a salesman collects a payment on an open account, without authority, the third party may bring an action against the agent to recover the payment if the agent fails to deliver the money to the principal. Similarly, payments made to an agent due to the agent's mistake or misconduct may be recovered from the agent even though the agent has turned the funds over to the principal—culpability may not be avoided by subsequently paying the wrongfully collected funds to the principal. Generally, any overpayment may be recovered from the agent of an undisclosed principal, because the third party was unaware of the principal's existence.

Agent's Liability for Torts and Crimes   An agent is liable for harm caused a third party by the agent's fraudulent or malicious acts. The fact that the agent was acting in good faith under the direction of the principal or was following instructions is not a defense against personal tort or criminal liability. Thus, if an agent wrongfully injures a third party or is guilty of the crime of theft, the agent will be personally liable without regard to the fact the agent was acting as an agent.

Defenses Available to Agent   In an action brought against an agent on a contract entered into on behalf of the principal, the agent may set up personal defenses as though the agent were the sole contracting party. These include the right to assert that the contract was performed by the principal or agent, that the third party failed to perform, or that the statutes of frauds or limitations were complied with. Any counterclaim that the agent may have against the third party may also be alleged. With the consent of a disclosed or partially disclosed principal, the agent may assert defenses or counterclaims that the principal has against the third party. The other party should not be in a better position by bringing an action against the agent than by bringing it against the principal. Defenses that are purely personal to the principal are not available to the agent. Thus, defenses of the personal incapacity or immunity of the principal, as when the principal is a minor or is bankrupt, are not available to the agent.

Liability of Third Party to Agent

Normally, the third party is not liable to the agent for breach of a contract that the agent has made with the third person on behalf of a disclosed principal. The fact that the agent has a right to compensation does not give the agent an interest in the performance of the contract.

However, just as an agent may be liable to the third party, the third party may be liable to the agent.

Agent Intended to Be Bound If the third party knows the agent is acting as an agent but the parties provide that the agent is obligated on the agreement, the agent may sue the third party for breach of contract. Thus, if the credit standing of the principal is not acceptable to the third party, the agent may assent to be a party to the agreement. This assent results in possible liability of the agent and, at the same time, affords the agent the right to sue the third party for breach of the agreement. If the agent agrees to be merely a guarantor of the principal's performance, however, the agent is liable to the third party on the guaranty and may raise defenses against the third party but has no contractual rights against the third party.

Principal Undisclosed or Partially Disclosed If the contract is entered into without the third person's knowledge of the existence and identity of the principal, the agent may sue the third party for breach of the contract. The fact that the action may be brought by the agent will not prevent suit by the principal. Indeed, the right of the principal to sue the third party is superior to the right of the agent. The contract was, after all, entered into on behalf of the principal.

Auctioneers and Commission Merchants Long-standing custom gives auctioneers, and commission merchants (also called "factors"), who are entrusted with possession of their principal's goods, special rights against third-party purchasers. These two types of agents have the right to sue in their own names to collect the purchase price of goods sold.

All other agents must be specially authorized to bring suit on contracts. The procedure for doing so and the manner in which an agent may sue on behalf of a principal differ among the several states.

Defenses Available to Third Party In an action brought by an agent in the name of the agent, but for the benefit of the principal, the third party may raise any substantive defense that could have been raised had the action been brought by the principal. The principal cannot deprive the third party to the contract of defense simply by authorizing the agent to bring the action. Thus, the third party may raise the defense of nonperformance or misrepresentation whether the action is maintained by the principal or agent. The third party is also entitled to all set offs and counterclaims that would have been available if the action had been brought by the principal.

Torts of Third Party It is a fundamental principle of common law that each individual is responsible for his or her own wrongs. A third party may, of course, commit a direct tort against the agent. The third party may slander the agent in a statement to the principal and cause the principal to discharge the agent. The third party would then be liable in damages to the agent. Obviously, if the third party commits a tort against the agent's person or property the third party is liable to the agent.

The agent also has rights against the third party if the third party commits a tort against the principal's goods while they are in the agent's possession. The agent is a bailee of those goods, and has the rights of a bailee, which include a right to bring an action against anyone who interferes with the bailee's possession. Any proceeds of the suit, of course, must be held for the benefit of the owner.

If goods entrusted to the agent are taken without permission, or not returned in accordance with an agreement, the agent has a right to bring an action against the third party for possession of those goods. This principle is also based on the fact that the agent in such a case is a bailee.

The agent has no action against the third party, however, for a tort that directly injures the principal or the principal's goods and only indirectly affects the agent. Thus, an agent may not maintain an action against a third party who negligently or willfully destroys the principal's place of business, or who kills the principal. These actions may damage the agent, but the damage is indirect.

Agent Acting Without Authority An agent who falsely represents that he or she is authorized to act on behalf of a principal, and who, therefore, fails to bind the principal to the contract, cannot later maintain an action on the contract. The action cannot be maintained, since the agent is unable to prove the existence of the contract that was purported to be made. To illustrate, A represents to T that he has authority to contract on behalf of P to sell certain of P's goods to T. The contract is entered into indicating that A is acting for P. On the date of delivery of the goods, A admits that he had no authority from P and that P has not ratified the transaction. Although A tenders delivery of the goods referred to in the agreement, T may refuse to accept. A may not maintain an action against T for such refusal. The misrepresentation of A concerning his authority will serve as a defense to T.

Liability of Insurance Agents and Brokers

Insurance agents and brokers owe the same duties to their principals as do agents in other businesses. Although the law is gradually putting agents and brokers in a learned professional status, the standard of care imposed on the agent and broker remains that of a reasonably competent professional in the field. The standard is applied by the trier of fact, either jury or judge, generally without requiring the testimony of other professionals in the field concerning whether the agent's conduct was reasonable under the circumstances.

Although the obligation to exercise reasonable care is the duty most likely to be breached by an insurance agent or broker, the duties to be loyal to the principal, to obey instructions, to give information, and to account to the principal each form the basis for possible agent liability. Violation of any of these duties subjects the agent to liability for damages to the principal.

Depending on the nature of the agency, the principal to whom the agent's duties are owed may be either an insured or an insurer. In some circumstances, insurance agents and brokers are in a *dual agency* relationship, in that they may be considered agents for both the insured and the insurer in the same transaction. Thus, an insurance broker may be agent of the insured for the purpose of obtaining the insurance, and agent of the insurance company for the purpose of collecting the premium.

Agent-Broker Distinction A broker is one who is engaged in the business of procuring insurance for persons applying for that service. For most purposes, the broker is the agent of the insured. An insurance agent, on the other hand, maintains a fixed relation with one or more insurer-principals that the agent represents on a continuing basis. Such agents are, for most purposes, deemed agents of the insurers they represent.

The obligations of dual agency are imposed in many cases, whether the intermediary is a broker or an insurance agent. As previously noted, dual agency is permitted if the representation is with the full knowledge and consent of all parties. In determining the liability of the agent or broker it is important to determine (1) whether the intermediary represented the insurer or the insured; (2) what duty was alleged to have been breached; and (3) which party, insured or insurer, had the primary obligation to perform the duty owed. Each of these inquiries involves questions of fact and the question of whether there was a breach of duty by the agent or broker in the case under consideration.

Liability to Insured An insurance agent or broker who undertakes to obtain coverage is obligated to exercise the care that would be exercised by a reasonably prudent and competent professional agent or broker. If failure to exercise such care results in loss to the principal-insured, the agent or broker is liable for the loss. The insured's action against the agent or broker may be brought in tort for breach of a duty to exercise care in obtaining the insurance coverage requested. If there was an agreement that the agent or broker would provide the coverage requested, an action may be brought for breach of contract. Whether reliance is on tort or contract theory, all monetary loss that can be shown to have resulted from the agent's actions may be recovered.

Virtually every service an agent or broker performs for an insured may subject the agent or broker to liability if the service is not performed with reasonable care. Thus, if an agent fails to give the insured timely notice that the insurer has rejected the application, thereby depriving the insured of the opportunity to seek insurance elsewhere, the agent will be liable to the insured for any loss caused by the lack of notice.

Where an agent and insured agree that the agent will obtain a certain kind of coverage, and the agent fails to obtain such coverage, and fails to advise the insured of such failure, the agent will be liable for any uninsured losses that result. Liability may be imposed in this situation for failure to procure insurance, as well as for failure to obtain adequate coverage. In all cases it must be shown that the agent or broker failed to exercise the degree of care of a reasonably prudent insurance agent or broker under the same or similar circumstances.

An agent is required to exercise good judgment in obtaining suitable coverage for the insured. This requires the agent to inform the insurer of any special facts relating to the exposure so that the policy that is issued will actually cover the insured's insurance needs. Failure to exercise reasonable care in selecting coverages that the agent has reason to know are needed by the insured can subject the agent to liability. Thus, an agent who knows an insured has a large quantity of valuable jewelry, and who obtains a policy of insurance that fails to provide coverage for loss of such jewelry, may be subject to liability for negligent failure to obtain proper protection. The knowledge of the agent and the discussions between the parties of the need for, and assurances of, protection of the insurable interest involved are relevant to the question of whether the agent exercised reasonable care under the circumstances.

When an agent or broker explains to the insured the coverages provided by the policy, the explanation must be accurate. If incorrect statements are relied upon by the insured, the agent may be liable for damages to the insured that result. The insured's failure to read the policy is not a defense for the agent or broker. The law recognizes that insureds do not read their policies, and holds that insureds are entitled to rely on the representations of their agents concerning the coverage afforded by the policy.

Insurance agents who talk the insured into excessive coverage that the insured cannot afford and that is of little benefit for the insured invite liability. For example, an insurance agent purports to devise a financial security program for the insured that considers the insured's tax bracket and numerous other personal factors. In fact, these considerations are not weighed in the program sold. The insured may recover any loss that results from dropping and converting previously held policies. Thus, it is possible that liability may be imposed for selling unneeded insurance. The duty of reasonable care includes the obligation to protect the insured with the best needed coverage available at the best rate obtainable.

Liability to Insurer   As with all agents, the insurance agent is liable to the principal-insurer for any improper action that results in loss to the principal. Thus, an agent who misrepresents facts about an insured, causing the insurer to cover an exposure it would not have accepted had the truth been known, is liable to the insurer for any loss it must pay as the result of the misrepresentation. Similarly, if an agent acts outside the scope of actual authority, the agent is liable to the insurer for any resulting loss. Thus, an agent who is instructed not to write automobile coverage for drivers with special risk characteristics, and who nonetheless purports to bind such a driver on behalf of the insurer, may be liable to the insurer for a loss sustained.

When an agent, during the term of a policy, learns of conditions that would suspend the coverage, failure to notify the insurer of the condition may result in a duty to indemnify the insurer in the event of loss. Thus, under a fire insurance policy, if an agent learns of the existence of a condition that materially increases the hazard involved, and then neglects to take action so that the company is later found to have waived the condition, the agent may be liable to the insurer for the loss it is required to pay.

An agent who fails to adequately investigate the nature and degree of an exposure submitted may be liable in damages to the insurer. It is the agent's duty to make a reasonable inquiry concerning the exposure and to give the insurer the information necessary to evaluate the loss potential. Thus, if an agent has reason to know that an applicant for automobile insurance is considered a poor exposure but nonetheless binds the coverage for the insurer and fails to investigate or provide the insurer with information necessary to determine whether the applicant is acceptable, the agent may be liable to the insurer for any resulting loss.

Liability to Third Persons   As a general rule an agent is not personally liable to a third party. Exceptions already discussed are when an agent agrees personally to be bound to the third party, exceeds his or her authority, or commits a direct tort against the third party.

Another possible exception is when the third party is a third-party beneficiary of the contract. Suppose, for instance, that an agent or broker misrepresents the protection afforded by an insured's annuity policy that has a named beneficiary. That beneficiary may bring an action against the agent or broker who may be required to pay the amount that was represented to be payable.

Suppose, however, that the injured party is a member of the public not specifically named in the policy? As an illustration, an agent agrees to procure automobile liability insurance for an applicant and does not do so for an unreasonable length of time. Does the third party who is injured in an accident with the applicant have an action against the agent?

If the failure to place the insurance coverage was a result of negligence, the agent breached the duty of care to the principal-applicant. If a loss is suffered, the applicant has an action against the agent. The injured third party, however, is not named in the policy.

A recent 1974 New Jersey case held that the third party has an action against the agent under those circumstances.[2] The theory of the case was that the injured person was a third-party beneficiary of the agreement between the principal and the agent that the agent shall procure insurance. The basis for applying that theory was public policy. The court stated that not only was it public policy in New Jersey that drivers be insured to protect their own assets, but also that there be a fund from which the damage claims of others may be satisfied. The court noted that New Jersey required drivers to be covered by automobile liability insurance and also had an unsatisfied claim and judgment fund. Alternatively, the court was also willing to base the holding on a breach of a tort duty owed to the third party by the agent, stating that ". . . the potential lack of recompense to a potential injured party is a natural and foreseeable result of an agent's or broker's actions if he negligently fails to obtain proper coverage in accordance with his instructions."[3]

As of now, this view is found only in the court decisions of New Jersey and, perhaps, Illinois.[4] So far it applies even in those states only to failure to procure automobile liability insurance.[5] Whether and to what extent this view will be adopted by other jurisdictions is, of course, in the realm of conjecture.

Defenses Available to Agent or Broker   Whether the action is brought by the insured, the insurer, or a third person, a number of defenses are available to the agent or broker. The defense that reasonable care was, in fact, exercised by the agent or broker is asserted in nearly every case alleging agent liability. Attempts are made to establish that all necessary actions were pursued by the agent with reasonable promptness, that the agent made a reasonable effort to obtain and transmit the necessary information to the insurer, and that the insured was informed of coverage and noncoverage problems along the way. Questions in these areas are factual and must ultimately be decided by the trier of fact, be that judge or jury.

In any action for negligence it must be established that there was not only a breach of some duty owed the plaintiff, but also that the breach was the *proximate cause* of the injury sustained by the plaintiff. Thus, the agent or broker may assert by way of defense that the acts of the agent were not the proximate cause of the loss sustained, or that even though the agent was in some way neglectful in obtaining insurance, the insurance coverage would not have been issued in any event. If the defense can be established, the agent may escape liability, unless the agent's delay resulted in the insured's being unable to obtain the needed coverage elsewhere.

The contributory negligence of the insured is still another defense available to the agent or broker when sued for failure to exercise reasonable care. Thus, if an insurance policy lapses because of the failure of the insured to pay premiums, this is a defense in an action alleging the agent's liability. Similarly, a mistake by the insured in valuing property that results in lack of coverage for a portion of that property may be shown as contributory negligence on the part of the insured.

In an action against the agent or broker based on breach of contract to obtain insurance, the defense of contributory negligence is not available. Some courts refer to *contributory fault* in such contract actions, which is a defense that raises many of the same arguments as are raised in defense of tort actions for negligence. An agent may also defend breach of contract actions by showing that the promise to perform a certain action was unsupported by consideration and, thus, is not enforceable. If the promise of the agent was entirely gratuitous, the defense of lack of consideration may be successful. Thus, if a finance concern requests an agent to add its name to the loss payable clause of a policy issued to an insured, the agent's failure to do so may not give rise to a breach of contract action, because of the lack of consideration passing from the finance company to the agent or insurer, unless the requirements of promissory estoppel are met.

Ratification by the insurer of the agent's or broker's unauthorized actions is a defense by the agent or broker in a subsequent action by the insured. Thus, even though the agent violates the instructions of the insurer in obtaining coverage for a risk, when the insurer ratifies the transaction by accepting the risk with full knowledge of the facts, the ratification is an acceptance of the agent's conduct and frees the agent from further liability to the insured.

The principal's ratification of an agent's unauthorized acts will also, in general, free the agent from any liability to the principal. Section 416 of the Restatement of Agency, Second, however, lists two exceptions to the general rule. These are, first, if the principal "is obliged to affirm the act in order to protect his interests" and, second, if the principal "is caused to ratify by the misrepresentation or duress of the agent."

For legal purposes, truth is not what is stated in the courtroom: it is what the court believes. Therefore, findings on what the agent agreed to do, what information was requested of and given by the insured, and what information the insurer knew or had reason to know, are vital to the question of liability. When the insured's loss is substantial, the sympathy of the judge or jury may not be with the agent or the insurer. Still, if the facts are made clear and the testimony is credible, the nonliability of the agent or broker may be established under any of the foregoing defenses.

EMPLOYMENT

Generally

A most important type of agency involves the relation of *employer* and *employee*. In this species of agency, referred to in some cases as the *master-servant relationship*, the employer (master) is held vicariously liable to third parties for physical harm or other wrongdoing by the employee (servant), committed while the employee was acting within the scope of the employment. Liability is imposed without regard to fault on the part of the employer.

In the usual principal-agent relationship, the principal is not liable for the physical harm caused by the agent. It is only where the principal has retained the *right to control the physical conduct* of the agent in the performance of the duties of the agency that the employment relationship will be found to exist. If such right of control was present, then liability for wrongs (torts) of the agent, acting within the scope of the employment, will be the responsibility of the employer as well as of the employee.

The theory that the employer should be held liable for the torts of the employee committed in the course of employment is referred to as the doctrine of *respondeat superior*.

Doctrine of *Respondeat Superior*

Respondeat superior (let the master respond) is the phrase used by the courts to describe an employer's liability of the torts of employees that are connected with the employment. Any third person injured by the employee's tortious act can proceed against *both* the employee and the employer. The employee is liable for his or her wrongful act since all persons are responsible for their own wrongdoings. The employer's liability is vicarious.

Various theories have been devised on the historical origins of the doctrine of *respondeat superior*. Some say it derives from the slave owner's liability for the acts of the slave. Others say that it is a corollary of the proposition that the master had absolute control over the servant's acts, and therefore was responsible for them. The "deep pockets" theory maintains the employer's liability exists because the employer, generally, has greater financial resources than the employee.

Each of these contains a measure of truth. The slave owner was liable for the acts of the slave because the slave was property, and a slave's acts against others were as much the responsibility of the master as if the master's bull gored a neighbor. The control theory has truth, because at one time an employer was not liable for an employee's act unless it was expressly and specifically ordered to be done. The "deep pockets" theory contains historical truth, because at one time the employer was not liable to the third party unless and until the employee could not pay the judgment.

None of these theories, however, is relevant today. The doctrine of *respondeat superior* is based on business and public policy. The business policy theory, sometimes called the "entrepreneur theory," is that injuries to persons and property are inevitable in business, and is a cost that the business should bear rather than the innocent victim of the tort, or the public as a whole. It is in the public interest that persons harmed be able to obtain adequate redress for their injuries. The employer who placed the employee in the position that resulted in the harm should provide payment for the loss. The employer may shift the burden to consumers through a price structure that includes premiums for liability insurance.

Although *respondeat superior* is a rule of strict liability for the employer, that is, liability without violation of any duty by the employer personally, the employer is liable only when the employee's conduct is tortious. Some actionable wrong must be done by the employee. The rule tends to foster safety measures because the employer, aware of potential liability, is more likely to be careful in the selection and supervision of employees.

Requirements for Vicarious Liability of Employer

For an employer to be vicariously liable for the torts of an employee, three factors must generally be present: (1) the employee must commit a wrong for which the employee can be held liable; (2) the employer must retain the right to control the physical conduct of the employee; and (3) the wrong must be committed within the scope of the employment.

Other Bases of Liability The employer may also be held liable for the torts of an employee when (1) the employer has been negligent in the selection or supervision of an employee, or (2) the employer has attempted to delegate a "nondelegable duty" to an employee. Each of these requirements and bases of liability will be discussed.

Creation of Relationship

The employer-employee relationship, like that of principal and agent, is consensual, and exists only if there is an agreement manifesting assent by each of the parties to the creation of the relationship. The contract may be oral, but must be written under a Statute of Frauds provision if the employment contract cannot be performed within one year of the date of the contract. As in the creation of the principal-agent relationship, any person having the capacity to contract may employ another. Persons who lack contractual capacity ordinarily can appoint neither employees nor agents to act on their behalf. No special capacity is required to be an employee. An adult employer can be held vicariously liable for the negligent acts of employees who are minors.

Because the employer-employee relationship is consensual, the employee cannot foist his or her services on the employer without the employer's consent. But the mere fact that one party has not requested the other to render services does not prevent the employer-employee relationship from arising if the employer knows that services are being rendered and accepts the benefits. Thus, where *S*, a mere passerby, undertakes to help load a truck in front of *M*'s place of business, and *M* observes the act and accepts the benefits of *S*'s work, an employer-employee relationship may be held to exist if *S*'s actions result in injury to another.

Employee Defined

It is important to distinguish between an employee and an agent who is not an employee. The principal is not ordinarily liable for the wrongful acts of the latter. It should be noted that while the word "servant" has retained much of its earlier significance in the law, the word "employee" is gradually replacing the earlier term. In general, the word employee is synonymous with servant.

An *employee* is a person who is employed with or without pay to perform personal services for another, and who, in respect to the physical movements in the performance of such service, is subject to the employer's right or power of control. A person who renders service for another but retains control over the manner of rendering such service may be either a nonemployee agent or an independent contractor. As noted, the doctrine of *respondeat superior* is generally not applicable to the latter relationship.

One who is employed to make contracts may be an employee. Thus, a traveling salesperson or a shop clerk may be employees who could cause the employer to become liable for their negligence while driving an automobile on the employer's business or while dealing with customers in a store. The important distinction is between (1) service in which the actor's physical activity and time are surrendered to the control of the employer, and (2) service under an agreement to accomplish results. Those rendering service but retaining control over the manner of doing it are not employees. They may be agents, who owe duties to the principal to exercise due care in the performance of their tasks; or they may be persons employed to accomplish physical results, as where an independent contractor is paid to build a house. Where the employer has the right to control the physical performance of the employee, the employer will be vicariously liable for the conduct of the employee. Where the agent or independent contractor retains the right of control over the physical performance of their jobs, vicarious liability will be imposed on the principal only in exceptional situations.

Tests for Employment Relationship The question of whether the employee's conduct was subject to the right of control by the employer is determined by the trier of fact. Among the factors considered are (1) the extent of control provided for by the agreement between the parties, (2) whether the one employed is engaged in a distinct occupation, (3) the skill required in the occupation, (4) whether the employer or the worker supplies the instrumentalities, tools, and the place of work for the person doing the work, (5) the length of time for which the person is employed, (6) the method of payment, whether by the time or by the job, and (7) whether the work is part of the regular business of the employer.[6]

The term "employee" is by no means restricted to routine or manual labor. The president of a company, whose actions are subject to the right of control by others (i.e., directors), in the manner of performing various duties may be considered an employee. "Employee" indicates the closeness of the relation between the one giving and the one receiving the service, rather than the nature of the service or the status of the one giving it. The right to control the physical conduct of the employee is the crucial consideration.

Apparent Employees Although it is true that the employment relationship is founded on the agreement of the parties if (1) a person intentionally or negligently creates an appearance that another is employed and (2) a third party relies on the appearance of employment, the employer may be prevented (estopped) from denying the existence of the employment relationship. To illustrate, a store advertises that it employs a doctor to pierce ears in preparation for earrings. Relying on the advertisement, *T* has her ears pierced in the store by the doctor. If *T* is injured through the doctor's negligence, the store may be estopped from denying that the doctor was its employee (but was an independent contractor) in performing this service. The store created the appearance of employment by its representations; that appearance was reasonably relied upon by a third party; and therefore the employer-store is vicariously liable for *T*'s injuries. The same result follows if a person falsely represents an employer-employee relationship and the purported employer knows of the representation and has the opportunity to disavow it without undue hardship, but fails to do so.

Independent Contractors

The independent contractor is one with whom the employer has contracted for an end result that is to be brought about by the independent contractor. The independent contractor is not an agent, since there is no responsibility to make contracts with third persons for the employer. Neither is the contractor an employee, because the employer usually has no control over the details of the physical performance by the contractor.

The general rule is that the employer of an independent contractor is not liable for physical harm caused to a third person by the negligent act of the independent contractor in the performance of the contract, because the employer has no legal right to control the details of the physical performance of the contract. To illustrate: *A* contracts to build a fence for *P* at a cost of $500 and according to certain specifications. In such case it is clear that *A* is an independent contractor, with the completed fence to be the result. If, however, *P* had engaged *A* by the day to assist *P* in building the fence under *P*'s supervision and direction, an employer-employee relationship would have resulted.

Employees Versus Independent Contractors The legal distinction between an employee and an independent contractor is easy to state but more difficult to apply in practice. Frequently, the extent of control by the employer is disputed or unclear. The chief criterion remains whether the employer has the right to control the party's conduct in the performance of the services. Among examples of persons generally found to be independent contractors are the following.

Building Contractors. A general contractor who erects a building is generally an independent contractor, as is the subcontractor who contracts to furnish materials and services for a particular part of the job. Each usually has its own organization and employees, and the property owner usually has no right of direct control over the manner used to accomplish the job.

Physicians and Attorneys. Most courts hold that highly skilled persons such as doctors or lawyers are independent contractors even though they may be employed on a retainer basis. Such professions involve considerable skill and learning, and it is generally felt to be incompatible with the profession to hold that a doctor is subject to the complete control of another. Some exceptions to this rule are found in cases where a doctor is in the employ of a hospital where he or she is a resident. A right to control will be more readily found in such situations.

Insurance Agents Most insurance agents are considered independent contractors—nonemployee agents. The companies they represent seldom retain the right to control the physical conduct of the agent in the performance of agency duties. Thus, the typical insurance agent using his or her own car in carrying out the business of selling insurance does not impose vicarious liability on the insurance company for negligence in driving the vehicle. Although this rule applies to most insurance agents, an employer-employee relation may be found by applying the tests previously given. For example, if an insurance agent is in the employ of one insurer, is using the insurer's car in the performance of sales duties, and is closely supervised with respect to the schedule and conduct of daily business—the trier of fact could find that the insurance agent was in fact an employee. The primary function of the insurance agent is to obtain contracts of insurance for the insurance company. Thus, either as employee-agents or independent contractors, insurance agents daily subject their principals to contractual liability, and to tort liability, such as for fraud or deceit, connected with the contracts. Before liability for physical torts may be imposed vicariously on the principal-insurer, however, the right of the insurer to control the agent's physical conduct in the performance of the agency must be shown. The facts do not often support such a finding.

Employer Liability for Independent Contractor Several well-established exceptions have developed to the general rule that an employer is not liable for the torts of an independent contractor. Some authorities group the exceptions under the heading of *nondelegable* duties. Liability is imposed most frequently in the following categories.

Highly Dangerous Activities.   Persons who employ others to carry out ultrahazardous activities are generally held liable for ensuing harm, whether the one employed to do the act is an employee or an independent contractor. Thus, when an independent contractor is hired to perform blasting operations in connection with construction work, the independent contractor is liable for any harm resulting just as an employer is liable. Strict liability is imposed as a matter of public policy on both the employer and the independent contractor.

Work Close to Public Ways.   An employer is liable for the negligent act of an independent contractor when the very nature of the act is likely to cause harm to others if due care is not used. Thus, when an independent contractor is employed to work on a street repair or sidewalk construction project, and negligently forgets to leave a light or obstruction warning the public of the danger, liability may be imposed vicariously on the employer. The risk of harm is so apparent that the duty of care owed by the employer is considered nondelegable.

Action Is Illegal Unless Licensed.   When a license is required to perform certain acts, a licensed person who delegates performance of acts to an unlicensed person is liable for the negligence of the other. Thus, if a licensed interstate trucking firm permits an independent contractor to do the work, it is liable for the negligence of the contractor. A public utility may not discharge its liability by employing an independent contractor.

Negligent Selection of Independent Contractor.   When the employer is negligent in the selection of the independent contractor, the employer may be liable to third persons in negligence for the improper selection or retention of the independent contractor.

An employer is not, then, permitted to become insulated from liability when he or she has nondelegable duties. The responsibility for exercising reasonable care for the protection of others in these special situations is sufficiently important to preclude delegation of ultimate responsibility for harm that results. The shared responsibility tends to foster the exercise of greater care by the employer in supervising the activities of the contractor. That is the intent of the law.

Scope of Employment

Assuming that an employer-employee relationship existed, it must also be shown that the wrong was committed by the employee within the *scope of the employment.* Basically, this means that the employee must be engaged in work for the employer of the type that he or she is employed to perform. The employer is not liable when the employee steps aside from the employment to commit a tort or does the wrongful act in furtherance of the employee's own interests. If the tort is committed in furtherance of the employer's interests, even though against the employer's directions, vicarious liability is imposed.

There is no simple test to determine whether a tort is committed within the scope of employment. This is because the question is usually submitted to a jury. Jury verdicts often are based on nonlegal factors as well as on the judge's charge. In addition, jury verdicts do not create binding precedents. Therefore, one reading the cases finds inconsistencies not only among jurisdictions, but also in the same jurisdiction and sometimes in the same court. A court has some control over a jury, and occasionally will direct a verdict for the plaintiff or the defendant, and can set aside a jury verdict in an appropriate case and order a new trial if the judge thinks the verdict of the jury was totally unsuitable. Generally, however, jury verdicts stand.

A number of important factors are considered: (1) Was the act authorized, or incidental to an authorized act, by the employer? (2) Was the act one commonly done by such employees? (3) What was the time, place, and purpose of the act? (4) To what extent were the employer's interests intended to be advanced by the act? (5) To what extent were the interests of the employee intended to be advanced? (6) Was the instrumentality by which the harm was done furnished by the cmployer? (7) What was the extent of departure from the normal method of accomplishing an authorized result? (8) Did the act involve the commission of a serious crime?[7]

Authorization by Employer Very few employers knowingly authorize torts. It is not necessary to show that the employer authorized or permitted the act that caused the injury, as long as the act occurred in the scope of the employee's regular duties and employment. To illustrate, M employs S to make deliveries of goods, using M's truck. S uses his own vehicle to make a delivery for M and injures T in the process while driving negligently. Since the injury occurred within the scope of duties assigned to S (delivery of goods), M is liable even though S used a personal car.

Forbidden Acts The employer may be liable for the actions of the employee even though the wrong committed was specifically forbidden by the employer. To illustrate, M instructs S that S should never permit customers to enter a certain area of M's premises. S violates the instructions by taking T into the forbidden area, and T is injured through S's negligence while in that area. M is liable for S's actions, notwithstanding the violation of instructions.

Negligent Torts For the purpose of analysis the subject of an employer's liability may be divided into negligent torts, intentional torts, and crimes.

If the tort committed by the employee is purely negligent, and neither intentional nor a crime, the employer's responsibility depends on whether the act was within the scope of employment. The apparent simplicity of that statement masks many subtleties.

The first requisite is that the employee be an employee of the employer not only in general but also at the time and place of the specific act. In general, for instance, a person is not acting as an employee while going to or coming from one's place of employment. However, an employee who is on the street most of the time may be within the scope of employment while going directly from home to the place of business of a customer without going to the place of employment, if that is the usual procedure.

An employee who is instructed to go from point A to point B may, for personal reasons, detour via point C. The detour (or "frolic of his own" as the older cases described it) may be slight or may be major. If slight, the employee may be found not to have left the scope of employment; if major, a contrary finding may be made. The underlying question here is if and at what point the employee was serving personal concerns and, if that happened, at what point did the employee reenter the scope of employment and serve the employer's interests.

A second general requisite is that the act be something the employee was hired to do. Suppose that a gasoline station attendant smokes a cigarette while filling T's automobile's gasoline tank thus causing an explosion. Is smoking a cigarette within the scope of employment? Although older cases held that smoking was a personal matter, modern cases indicate that smoking that creates a hazard is merely an unauthorized way of doing an authorized act, and is therefore within the scope of employment.

In general, the concept of scope of employment in negligence cases has expanded in recent years. This may partly be a product of the fact that many cases have involved insurance coverage purchased by employers to cover accidents that occur within the scope of employment of their employees. Although the insurance company is usually not a party to the action, it is in essence the unnamed and unseen defendant. Many cases can most easily be explained on the basis that if the concept of scope of employment was limited, the plaintiff would, as a practical matter, not have been compensated for the injury. The same trend can be observed in workers' compensation insurance.

Intentional Torts Liability under the doctrine of *respondeat superior* extends to an employee's intentional torts, provided they occur within the scope of employment. If the intentional tort is within the apparent scope of the employee's or agent's employment or agency, the employer is liable to the third party in a civil suit whether or not the employee or agent intended to benefit the employer. For example, suppose an authorized agent of an insurance company falsely represents to an applicant that certain insurance has been placed and is therefore given and keeps the premium. Although this is a crime, and is not intended to benefit the company, the insurer is responsible for the agent's acts in a civil suit for damages. The third party had no reason to believe that the statements of the agent were not true, and the agent was within the apparent scope of the agency.

If the employee's acts are not within the apparent scope of employment, the question of the employee's intention becomes material. A large number of cases involve assaults by employees on customers of the employer. By no stretch of the imagination are assaults within the scope of an employee's employment. The employer is, of course, liable if the assault was ordered. If not ordered, the employer is nonetheless liable if the employee commits the intentional tort for the purpose, however misguided, of benefiting the employer. If, however, the employee's purpose is to vent his or her own spleen, the employer is not liable. Determining the category that applies to the incident is no easy task, and is usually a matter left to the jury.

Three examples illustrate these difficulties. First, suppose that a truck driven by E, and an automobile driven by T, collide. T and E alight from their vehicles, an argument ensues, and E assaults T. Second, suppose that E, the manager of a department in a store, accuses T, a customer, of shoplifting, detains and searches T, and learns that the accusation was, although innocent, false. Third, suppose that A is employed to collect for goods sold by P to third persons, and is specifically instructed not to attempt repossession of the goods, even peaceably, and is only to request payment. A nevertheless uses force in attempting to repossess T's goods, T resists the repossession, and A injures T.

Each of the employees' acts was intentional. Each would not have committed the acts in question except for the employment. Two policies of the law must be considered. The first is that the employer should be liable when the employee's tort is within the scope of employment. The second is that the employer should not be liable if the tort was committed by the employee solely for personal reasons of the employee.

The case of the truck driver seems clear. The truck driver was not employed to get into fights, but to drive the truck. The argument with the motorist seems to have been personal. Therefore, both the scope of employment test and the intention test point in the direction of the employer's nonliability. There are, however, cases that impose liability.

In the second case, of false imprisonment or false arrest, both the scope of employment test and the intention test appear to point in the direction of the employer's liability to *T*. The department manager has, as one responsibility, protecting the employer's property from theft. In addition, the employee thought the detention was in the employer's best interests, although it turned out otherwise. Case law agrees with that result.

In the case of the repossession, however, the two approaches appear to conflict. The act of repossessing was not within the employee's *actual* scope of employment, and, unless it was within the apparent scope of employment of *A*, that test appears to indicate the employer's nonliability. In attempting to repossess the goods, however, the employee apparently was attempting to forward the employer's interests, even though unwisely and contrary to instructions. The case, therefore, might go either way.

Two variants of the last illustration may be helpful. Suppose the employee was authorized to repossess, but instructed not to use force and to desist if *T* objected to the repossession. Because the possibility of force and injury was clearly contemplated by the employer, the employee's disregard of instructions is immaterial, and *P* is liable to *T*. Suppose, however, that in the original illustration *A* did not attempt to repossess the goods, but merely got into an argument with *T* that so enraged *A* that *A* lashed out and struck *T*. Not only was the striking outside the scope of *A*'s employment, but it was also a matter of personal grievance not intended to benefit the employer. In the latter illustration both tests, scope of employment and intention to benefit the employer, point to the employer's nonliability.

Employers' Liability for Agents' Crimes   Some crimes require intention, and others do not. If a statute provides a criminal penalty for doing an act, regardless of intention, the person who does the act is criminally responsible.

Automatic criminal responsibility is often applied to "business crimes." Short-weight, food and drug regulations, violations of the monopoly prohibitions of the Sherman Antitrust Act, sales of alcoholic beverages to minors or intoxicated persons, and stream pollution are common examples. An employee or agent who commits the forbidden act is criminally responsible. The statutes usually impose liability on the employer as well for an act done in violation of such statutes by an agent or employee who is acting within the scope of his or her employment or agency.

Other crimes require intention. Intention does not mean that one knowingly wants to commit a crime; it means intention to do the act that constitutes the crime. A person may, for instance, be ignorant of a statute that makes a certain act a crime but may intentionally commit the forbidden act. That is a crime.

The general principle is that no one is responsible for another person's crime. There is no vicarious criminal responsibility. The purpose of tort law is to reimburse victims of torts, and the liability of the employer is usually the best guarantee of payment. The purposes of the criminal law are not so clear-cut. In general, the criminal law exists to punish one who is guilty of violating fundamental rules of society, to inhibit antisocial conduct by all citizens affected, to make examples of convicted criminals so that others do not follow in their footsteps, or merely to wreak society's vengeance on malefactors. It follows that if an employer has nothing to do with an employee's crime, the principal is not criminally responsible. The employer may be civilly responsible to the injured third person in accordance with the foregoing discussion, but that is all.

If the employer orders the employee to commit a crime, it is clear that both are guilty. The employee cannot defend on the basis that the employer ordered the act, and the employer cannot defend on the basis that someone else actually committed the act.

If the principal does not order the agent to commit the crime, the principal can nonetheless be held criminally responsible. One basis, criticized in theory but applied in many cases, is that the principal is liable if the crime is committed within the scope of the agent's agency or the employee's scope of employment. It is possible for a court to find that a given crime was within the scope of the agency or employment even though the principal expressly forbade the act in question.

One basis for such a finding is that the principal adopted or ratified the illegal act. Adoption and ratification can, of course, be express. They can also be implied. If a given course of action has been long-standing, a court may find that the principal was aware of the activities and ratified or adopted them impliedly by doing nothing.

Another basis for criminal responsibility is that the employer should have been aware of a pervasive or long-standing criminal activity. On this theory, compliance with the law is the employer's responsibility, and the employer cannot evade that responsibility by delegating the duty of compliance to subordinate personnel. The duty to comply is not delegable.

Suppose, for instance, that an agent, with authority to bind the principal contractually, writes a letter to a prospect that contains fraudulent statements. Relying on the fraudulent statements the third party enters into a contract with the principal. The crime is using the mails to defraud. If the crime is committed only once, the principal normally will not be criminally responsible. The principal, of course, has civil liability to the third party and is subject to an action for damages or for rescission.

Suppose, however, that the agent makes a practice of writing fraudulent letters, and has done so for a considerable time. A court may find that the principal either knew or should have known of this pervasive activity, and find the principal criminally responsible. Supervision is a serious duty.

Therefore crimes such as conspiracy to fix prices, to force customers into tie-in agreements, and to defraud customers by various means have, when the activities have gone on for a period of time, resulted in the criminal responsibility of the employers. Generally corporations have been the defendants in those cases, but only because the corporate form of doing business is so general. There is no reason in principle why partners or an individual entrepreneur may not be subject to the same standards.

Agency in Family Relations

As a general rule, a parent is not liable for the torts of a child and a husband is not liable for the torts of his wife and vice versa. The law does not impose an agency or employer-employee relation by virtue of the family relationship. It can be shown, however, that the child or spouse was, in fact, acting as an agent for the parent or spouse in any given case. The same tests used in any proof of agency or employment are applied. Some states have qualified the foregoing rules of nonliability for torts of children and spouses. The most frequent exception concerns family automobiles.

Family Purpose Doctrine   The family purpose doctrine is that the owner of an automobile purchased and maintained for the pleasure of his or her family is liable for injuries inflicted by the vehicle while it is being used by members of the family for their own pleasure. Liability is imposed on the head of the household because of the dangerous character of the vehicle. The theory is that it is in the public interest to designate a dependable person who can pay for damages caused by the family's drivers. Some states accomplish the objective of the family purpose doctrine by statutes that impose vicarious liability for the negligence of youthful drivers on the parent who signs the youth's application for a driver's license. A small number of jurisdictions have legislation that imposes vicarious liability on any bailor for the negligent use of vehicles by a bailee; they are often called "permissive use" statutes. The theory again is that owners should be liable for the negligent use of their vehicles, and that this responsibility will spur owners to exercise care in permitting the use of their vehicles.

In absence of the family purpose rule or statutory liability on bailors of vehicles, the head of a household may be liable for negligence in the use of his or her automobile if, in fact, the driver was acting as an employee (servant) on a purely household errand. In absence of such a showing, vicarious liability is not imposed on the owner of an automobile.

Immunity of Agent

An agent may be immune from civil liability for a wrong committed in the course of employment, but the principal may not take advantage of that immunity. Thus, when an employee negligently injures his own wife or child while on the employer's business, the employee would be immune from suit in those jurisdictions where a wife or child may not sue a husband or parent for negligently caused injury. The purpose of the family immunity rule is to preserve the harmony of the family unit. The reason for the rule does not extend, however, to an employer. An employer is not relieved from liability to a person injured by an employee who, because of a personal relation between the two, is immune from liability. Thus, a wife or child injured as the result of an employee's negligent driving of the employer's vehicle on the business of the employer could still sue the employer for the negligence of the employee, provided, of course, it occurs in the latter's course of employment.

During the last few years, however, many states have abolished immunity based on a marital or parental relationship mainly because of the availability of liability insurance.

Automobile Liability Policies Most automobile liability policies provide coverage for the named insured and for persons using the insured vehicle with the permission of the named insured. Any person using the vehicle with permission enjoys the protection of the policy, even though no agency or employment relation exists. Suit is directly against the person who used the vehicle with permission. No action may be brought against the owner on the ground of vicarious liability, unless an employer-employee relation can be shown or unless a permissive use statute is in effect in the jurisdiction where the accident occurred.

Loaned Servant Doctrine

An employer may lend an employee to another, either for compensation or gratuitously. The loaned employee normally remains in the employ of the first employer insofar as statutory benefits under social security, unemployment, and workers' compensation are concerned. A more serious problem is which employer is liable for the torts of the employee during the period the employee is on loan.

To impose liability on the employer to whom the transfer was made, it must be shown that the employee was under a primary duty of obedience to the second employer when the tort was committed. As a general rule, when a person performs physical tasks for more than one employer, he or she is the employee of the one with the legal right to control the details of the physical work. To illustrate, an employer who leases equipment and its operator is presumed to retain the right of control over the way the operator performs. Thus, the lessor-employer is liable for the operator's torts. If, however, the primary right to control the activities of the employee is given to the second employer, particularly where the borrowing is for an indefinite or considerable period of time, the borrowing employer is liable for the torts of the employee.

The issue of which employer has the right to control the physical conduct of the employee at the time of the tort is a question of fact rather than one of law. The jury or judge considers the duration of the transfer, whether the employee was an unskilled laborer paid on an hourly basis, whether the first or second employer supplied the instrumentalities needed to carry out the employment, and whether the borrowing employer had the right to discharge the employee. The normal inference is that the employee's duty of obedience is to the first employer, who is liable for the employee's torts, unless the contrary is shown.

In some cases there may be a division of control over the employee. Thus, if the first employer lends an employee to the second employer, and the employee then makes deliveries in a negligent fashion on behalf of both employers, they will be jointly liable for the tort.

Fellow-Servant Rule

One well-recognized exception to the doctrine of *respondeat superior* is the "fellow-servant rule." Under this rule, an employer is not liable for the injuries inflicted by one employee on a fellow employee when the parties are engaged in the same general enterprise. A fellow servant is any other employee who serves and is controlled by the same employer in the same enterprise or household. The employees must be so related in their labor, because of proximity or otherwise, that there is a special risk of harm to one if the other is negligent. The rationale for the rule is that each employee assumes certain risks of injury from the acts of another employee, and each employee is as able as the employer to know of and protect against such risk.

Workers' compensation statutes, enacted by all the states, require most employers to pay employees for all employment-related accidents. Employees covered by workers' compensation insurance are not subject to the fellow-servant rule. Nevertheless, for employees not subject to workers' compensation the fellow-servant doctrine remains.

Courts generally recognize several exceptions to the fellow-servant rule. Thus, if the employer is negligent in the selection of the employee who caused the injury, an injured fellow employee may recover from the employer.

For example, M hires S to drive a truck, knowing that S has a long record of careless driving. If S injures a fellow employee while driving on the business of M, the fellow employee may bring an action against M in the absence of a workers' compensation statute prohibiting the action. The courts also decline to apply the fellow-servant rule if the employee injured was too young to appreciate the risks involved in the employment, if the employee was deceived into serving, if the employee was compelled to give service (i.e., inmates of institutions, etc.), or if the injured employee was employed in violation of statute. In these exceptional cases, the public policy of the fellow-servant rule that favors the employer is counterbalanced by other policies. Thus, if a statute forbids employment of persons under eighteen to engage in certain hazardous occupations, an employer who hires an underage person to work in such a job does not enjoy the protection of the fellow-servant rule. The young injured employee may sue the employer for the negligence of a fellow employee.

Workers' Compensation Laws Workers' compensation laws are designed to protect employees and their families from the risks of accidental injury, disease, or death arising out of and in the course of employment. Prior to enactment of these statutes, there were many obstacles to an employee's collecting from an employer for injury on the job. First, the employees were reluctant to bring suit against an employer because of expense, uncertainty, lack of knowledge, and fear of dismissal. Even when suit was brought, the employer could claim the common-law defenses of contributory negligence, assumption of risk, or actions of a fellow-servant. The fellow-servant doctrine has been explained. The defense of assumption of risk as applied to employees meant that if a certain job or task was inherently hazardous, the employee who accepted employment had no complaint against the employer for injuries sustained as a result of those inherent hazards. Injuries to employees occurring on the job often went uncompensated.

Today, every state has enacted a workers' compensation law. The laws vary on occupations covered and benefits to be paid. All the laws, however, provide that the employee need not establish the employer's negligence or that the employee was free from negligence. The only requirement is that the injury occur on the job during the course of employment. If so, the employer is liable without regard to fault. Some statutes give the employer the option of electing to be sued by employees. In those states, the employee must show employer negligence but is free from the common-law defenses of contributory negligence and assumption of risk.

Under workers' compensation acts employees obtain cash payments for loss of income, as well as reimbursement for medical expenses. Some laws provide for the establishment of state workers' compensation funds, and others require private insurance coverage to be obtained by the employer. Under some state laws, employers may be "self-insured" if they meet certain qualifying financial standards.

Workers' compensation laws have been criticized because of the number of occupations left uncovered, as well as for poor administration of the programs. Because the statutes were designed to remedy recognized defects in the common law, the courts tend to construe the statutes liberally. Whether deciding coverage or the scope of employment, courts tend to find in favor of injured employees. Reform of the workers' compensation system to include all occupations and greater benefits has been proposed. Enactment of a federal workers' compensation act may be the ultimate result.

Subemployees

To create an employer-employee relation it is not necessary that the employer hire the employee. The status is created if an authorized agent hires an employee for the principal. The new employee is then in a direct service relation to the employer, and the employer will be vicariously liable for the torts of the subemployee.

If the agent-employee who hires the subemployee also has the right to control the activities of the subemployee, then both the employer and the hiring-employee will be vicariously liable for the torts of the subemployee. Thus, if the owner of a building hires a janitor, who, in turn, hires an assistant, the assistant is a subemployee. Responsibility for the torts of the assistant may be imposed vicariously on either, or both, the building owner (employer) and the janitor (employee).

Unauthorized Hiring If an employee-agent has no authority, express, implied, apparent, or by ratification, to employ a subemployee, and nonetheless does so, vicarious liability is not imposed on the original employer. The employee-agent stands the chance of being liable under the doctrine of *respondeat superior*. If, however, the services of the subemployee require no particular skill, and are done within the scope of employment, courts tend to hold the original employer vicariously liable on the ground that the performance was tantamount to performance by the original employee. Thus, it must generally appear that the identity of the person performing the services was important to the employer, and that the hiring was not authorized, before the employer can escape liability for the acts of the subemployee.

Responsibility of Employers for Crimes of Subemployees
Suppose that *P* is president and chief executive officer of a corporation with authority to appoint and dismiss subemployees. Suppose that a subemployee commits a crime under circumstances that make the corporation criminally responsible. What, if any, is the criminal responsibility of the employee who appointed the subemployee?

Until 1975 one could confidently have stated that the employee had no criminal responsibility. However, a U.S. Supreme Court decision in that year changed the rules significantly.[8] A statute imposing automatic liability on corporations for committing certain forbidden acts was violated. The corporation did not contest its criminal responsibility. However, the company's president was also indicted. He defended on the ground that the act was committed by a subordinate, and that he, the president, when notified by the government of a violation, ordered the subordinate on two occasions to clear up the violation but the subordinate failed to do so. The president admitted to being the chief executive officer responsible for all the operations of the corporation.

The U.S. Supreme Court held that if the president was negligent in supervising the activities of the subordinate, the president was criminally responsible under federal law. Inadequate supervision, therefore, is a basis for criminal liability at least when intention is unnecessary. The statute in that case concerned impure foodstuffs.

Right of Employer with Respect to Injury to Employee

When a servant was viewed as the property of the master, the master could recover from a third party who negligently injured the servant. Under the modern view of employment, that the relationship is consensual, the employer has no property interest in and may not recover for negligent injury to the employee. Note, however, that because an intentional interference with contractual relations is an actionable tort, many courts hold that a third person who intentionally injures an employee may be liable to the employer for loss of the employee's services. The theory is intentional interference with contract, not intentional wrong to the employee.

Liability of Employer for Personal Breach of Duty

Apart from the vicarious liability under the doctrine of *respondeat superior*, an employer's liability for acts of an employee may be based on direct acts of the employer.

Act Directed by Employer When an employer specifically directs an employee to perform a tort, the employer is liable for harm resulting to third persons just as though the employer had committed the act. The act is considered that of the employer done through the employee. For example, the employer directs the employee forcibly to eject any persons entering the employer's premises. The employee forcibly ejects and thereby harms a third person who rightfully attempts to enter the employer's premises. The employer is liable for the injury without regard to the employment relationship. Persons are held to intend the reasonable consequences of their directions, and liability is imposed for harm that flows therefrom.

Negligent Hiring An employer owes a duty to exercise reasonable care in hiring employees if the employer knows, or should know, that failure to exercise that care may create an unreasonable risk of harm to others. For example, *M* hires *S* as a bill collector and does not trouble to learn that *S* has a long record of assault upon other persons. Negligent hiring of an employee who will deal with others under these conditions subjects the employer to direct action by a third party injured by an assault by the employee. The basis of the suit—the negligence of *M* in hiring *S*—is not based on the doctrine of *respondeat superior*. Although an employer is not generally liable for torts committed by an employee outside the scope of the employment, the employer's negligence in hiring is the basis for an action if the employer should have known the employee was likely to commit such wrongs.

Ratification by Employer Just as a principal may ratify the contracts of an agent who purports to act on the principal's behalf, so too may an employer ratify the actions of an employee. The tort of an employee may also be ratified so as to make the employer liable for the employee's actions. As in every case of ratification, it must be shown that the employee purported to act for the employer and that the employer ratified the entire transaction with knowledge or notice of all material facts. To illustrate, in the absence of *P*, the owner and manager of a small newspaper, his friend, *A*, takes charge without authorization and publishes several issues. In the course of these, *A* libels *T*. On *P*'s return, *P* affirms the publication. *P* is subject to liability to *T* for the tort of libel.[9] Note that the failure of the employer to fire the employee after learning of the wrongful act will not, of itself, constitute ratification. Some courts consider it "slight" evidence of ratification, however. Most cases dealing with ratification are concerned with the fraudulent misrepresentation of the employee or agent. The mere failure of the employer to inquire into all the representations by the employee does not constitute ratification. It must be shown that the employer knew or had reason to know of the misrepresentation before the employer is held directly responsible for the fraud of the employee. No affirmative duty to investigate is generally imposed on the employer.

Liability for Misrepresentations of Employees

An employer or principal is subject to tort liability for any loss sustained by third persons as a result of misrepresentations made by an employee or agent within the scope of the employment or agency. This does not mean that the employee or agent is authorized to make a misrepresentation. If it is within the scope of authority to make a truthful representation, it follows that although a misrepresentation is unauthorized, it may be within the scope of the employee or agent's employment or agency. Just as an employer is liable for the negligent and sometimes for the willful tort of the driver of a vehicle, which is doubtless not usually ordered or authorized, so the employer or principal is liable for the tort of fraud.

The tort of misrepresentation requires that a false statement be made concerning a material fact, with an intent to deceive, and that the statement be reasonably relied upon to the detriment of the person harmed. If these elements are present, and if the employee or agent is authorized to make representation, then the employer is vicariously liable for the harm resulting. It makes no difference that the agent or employee was acting from purely personal motives, or that the employer did not authorize the false statements to be made. It is sufficient that the employer has placed the employee in the position of making the representations, and that misrepresentations were, in fact, made—for whatever reasons.

A person who is induced by a fraudulent material misrepresentation by an agent or employee to enter into a contract may rescind the contract, even though the agent indicated he or she had no authority to make the representation. Thus, P authorizes A to sell P's real estate, but does not authorize A to make any representations concerning the property. A tells T that the land is good "growing land" and that the water is clear and pure. A then adds, "But of course, I have no authority to say these things." T buys the land, relying on A's statements, only to learn that the soil is poor and the water impure. T sues P to rescind the sale. P's defense is that A was not authorized to make the representations. *P,* however, benefited from the statement. Even though *A* indicated he had no authority to make the statements, they were, in fact, made and were relied upon by *T.* The statements constituted misrepresentations, and *T* is permitted to rescind the agreement.

Exculpatory Clauses To guard against misrepresentation by agents, employees, and independent contractors, contracts sometimes contain a provision that no representations have been made that are not in the final document. In most states, these exculpatory clauses have not been successful as a defense if fraudulent misrepresentation is shown. Whenever a transaction has been tainted by fraud, the law generally permits the defrauded party to prove the fraud.

Procedure in Tort Actions

Unlike contract actions that must be brought against the principal in his or her own name, the procedural law of most states permits the employer and employee to be sued either jointly or separately for the torts of the employee. The injured party is limited to one recovery for one cause of action (i.e., the tort), but the employer and employee are held jointly and severally liable. The third party may collect the judgment for money damages from either or both the employer or employee until the judgment is satisfied in full. If the employee is sued first, and a judgment is obtained that is not satisfied, that action will not bar a later suit against the employer. The amount of the judgment obtained against the employee will, in most jurisdictions, fix the limit of liability in the subsequent action against the employer.

If the employee is found not liable either in an action against the employee or in an action against both the employer and the employee, the suit against the employer on the basis of *respondeat superior* may not be sustained. The employer's liability is based on the liability of the employee, and if the employee is found to be free of fault the employer will have no vicarious liability.

Termination of Employment

The contract of employment may be terminated in the same manner as other contracts. As in the agency relationship, the employer has the *power* to terminate the employment, although contractual or legislative limitations may restrict the *right* to terminate. Thus, if a written contract provides for employment for three years, the employer and employee both have the power to terminate the relation at any time, but the breaching party may be liable in damages. The employment relation being consensual, the law does not force the parties to continue their relationship against their wills.

Most employment relations are terminable at the will of the parties. The employer may, therefore, terminate at any time either with or without reason. If employment is not terminable at will, but is for a term, the employer must establish nonperformance of duties, breach of instructions, disloyalty, or dishonesty in order to justify the discharge. Under modern statutes care must be taken in both hiring and firing to avoid discrimination because of race, sex, or age. Labor union contracts and statutory law at both the federal and state level are used with increasing frequency to define the rights of the parties in all employment matters.

Chapter Notes

1. UCC 3-401.
2. Eschle v. Eastern Freight Ways, Inc., et al., 128 N.J. Super 299, 319 A.2d 786 (1974).
3. 319 A.2d at 788.
4. In Gothberg v. Nemerovski, 58 Ill.App.2d 372, 208 N.E.2d 12 (App. Ct. 1965), a judgment creditor of a public liability policy applicant was held to have had sufficient interest in the undertaking of a broker to procure coverage for the debtor to enable the judgment creditor to bring suit directly against the broker.
5. In Schell v. Knickelbein, et al., 77 Wis.2d 344, 252 N.W.2d 921 (1977), a savings and loan association took and held payments in escrow to carry a homeowner's policy on the mortgaged premises. The savings and loan took out the initial policy but, even though they had the money in escrow, neglected to renew it. The plaintiff's husband died as the result of an attack by the mortgagor's dog. The plaintiff attempted to sue the savings and loan association on the basis of their neglect to renew the homeowner's policy which would have covered this risk. Held: the plaintiff had no cause of action against the savings and loan association. The court stated that there was "not enough of a contract" to show that the savings association and the owners entered into an agreement for the benefit of the plaintiff or others of her class. The court distinguished the Eschle case, footnote 2 above, on the ground that in applying for automobile insurance the car owners contemplated possible injury to third persons and the insurance coverage was for the direct benefit of third persons.
6. Restatement, Second, Agency, Sec. 220.
7. Restatement, Second, Agency, Sec. 229.
8. United States v. Park, 421 U.S. 658 (1975).
9. Restatement, Second, Agency, Sec. 84.

CHAPTER 8

Extra-Contractual
Rights and Obligations

INTRODUCTION

What Are Extra-Contractual Rights?

The rights and obligations of the parties to any contract, including an insurance contract, are governed by the provisions of that contract as expressed therein. However, language can be imprecise and in many cases the parties to a contract may have differing concepts of the rights and obligations they are assuming. As a result, it frequently becomes necessary for the courts to interpret the contract for the parties involved. Over the centuries these interpretations have developed into rules which are also applicable to the insurance contract.

Similarly, the legislatures of the various states have adopted over the years certain laws affecting contracts in order to protect certain of the parties (in the case of insurance, usually the insured). An example of a statute of this type is Section 150 of the New York Insurance Law which provides that no breach of warranty shall avoid an insurance policy unless such breach materially increased the risk of loss. This is an important change because at common law a breach of a warranty in a policy of insurance was fatal to the contract, irrespective of the materiality of the warranty or the breach, whereas a breach of a condition voided the contract only if both the condition and the breach were material. In effect, these statutes convert warranties in policies to representations.

Legislative or judicial changes and rules of this type have been referred to as rights at variance with the policy provisions. However, as the following discussion demonstrates, many of these so-called rights are not at variance with the contract but actually in support of it.

329

Sources of Extra-Contractual Rights and Obligations

Statutes It might be argued that any changes in a contract brought about by statutory enactment are not truly "extra-contractual" because the general rule of contract law holds that the contracting parties are presumed to contract in reference to existing statutory and case law. The complete statement of the rule is, "All existing applicable or relevant and valid statutes, ordinances, regulations and settled law of the land at the time a contract is made become a part of it and must be read into it just as if an express provision to that effect were inserted therein." (17 Am. Jur. 2d Contracts, Sec. 257, pp. 654-656)

Since both statutory and case law are found outside the contract, and neither is usually set forth therein, it is proper to refer to rights they create as extra-contractual, even though for interpretative purposes they are both treated as part of the contract.

Two fundamental problems arise in applying a statute. The first is the effect of a new statute on an existing policy. Parties frequently provide for existing or future laws in insurance policies by the use of a "Conformity with Statute" provision. However, in the absence of such agreement, the general rule is that a subsequent change of law cannot affect rights acquired under an existing insurance policy because of the constitutional prohibition (U.S. Constitution, Art.I, sec. 10) that no state shall pass any "Law Impairing the Obligation of Contracts." However, even this is not an absolute prohibition. The Supreme Court has upheld statutes abrogating certain contractual rights where there has been an emergency situation.

The second problem arises when the insurer and the insured are in different states and the laws of the two states differ. The problem is further complicated if the insurance contract was consummated in a third state. The majority rule at the present time is that the construction of an insurance contract is governed by the law of the state where the contract is made; that is, the state in which delivery takes place, if delivery is the last act legally necessary to bring the contract into force. However, several states have recently adopted a more flexible rule. It provides that the law of the state which has the most significant contacts with and interest in both the occurrence and the parties shall control. The matter of which state law applies can have a significant bearing on the contractual rights of the parties.

Court Decisions Any principles of law which have been enunciated by the appellate courts of the state control the validity and interpretation of the contract. An example is a judgment by the supreme court of one state that the "inception of the loss" under the standard fire insurance policy suit clause means the date on which the insurance company denies coverage. (Fireman's Fund Ins. Co. v. Sand Lake Lodge).[1] According to the supreme courts of other states, however, "inception of the loss" means the date of the destruction or casualty. (General State Authority v. Planet Insurance Co.)[2] Each of these conflicting decisions becomes incorporated into and applicable to contracts within its particular jurisdiction.

Court decisions, unlike statutes, affect all existing contracts as well as the contract of the parties. But frequently when a supreme court announces a decision changing a long-existing basic principle, such as a decision abrogating the right of charitable immunity from negligence suits, it will establish a date on and after which the revised principle will be applied.

Insurance Industry Practices Another source of extra-contractual rights is the practices of the insurance business itself. Frequently these practices affect the policyholder, but sometimes they affect only the contract rights of the insurers as between themselves.

Guiding Principles. An insured frequently has coverage for a given loss under two or more policies. The insured may have two or more policies of the same type, e.g., two fire policies or two liability policies; or the insured may have two different kinds of policies with overlapping coverage in some area, such as a dwelling fire contents policy and a personal articles floater policy, or a fire policy and a boiler policy. Disputes may arise in the adjustment or apportionment of losses or claims because of this overlapping coverage.

Frequently in such cases neither company would reimburse the insured until their separate liabilities had been resolved. This has led to adverse public relations because the insured was being penalized for having more than adequate coverage. To resolve this problem, the major stock insurance company trade associations recommended to their subscribing companies the adoption of a set of principles known as the "Guiding Principles for Overlapping Insurance Coverage," last amended in 1963. These Guiding Principles are now followed in large part by most of the insurance industry.

In cases involving overlapping coverage, the Principles were intended to provide for the equitable distribution of available insurance and to assist insurance companies in deciding among themselves where primary liability for loss falls. To that end, the agreement provides that as to themselves, (the insurers), the "other insurance" clauses which are contained in the policies, whether pro rata or excess type, will be set aside and be inoperative to the extent they are in conflict with the Principles. In addition, the Principles will not reduce recovery to the insured below what would have been obtained under any one of the applicable policies covering the risk.

Currently the Principles apply to two situations: (1) insurance covering the same property and interests, and (2) insurance covering the same property but different interests. No effort will be made here to go into the details of the Principles. However, a simple example will illustrate how they operate extra-contractually to change the obligation of the affected insurers.

Assume that there is a $100 fire loss to a neon sign. The insured has an inland marine neon sign policy in the amount of $100 and a fire policy in the amount of $25,000. The loss would normally be apportioned on a 100/25,100 basis for the inland marine policy and 25,000/25,100 for the fire policy. However, under the Guiding Principles, and in the absence of any deductible or coinsurance problems, the inland marine policy would pay the entire loss.

Liberalization Clause. Created voluntarily by the insurance industry, the so-called liberalization clause is contained in most property insurance contracts. While the clause itself is contained in the contract, it incorporates by reference changes which are outside the contract. The liberalization clause of the HO-76 reads as follows:

> *LIBERALIZATION CLAUSE:* If we adopt any version which would broaden the coverage under this policy without additional premium within sixty days prior to or during the policy period, the broadened coverage will immediately apply to this policy.

The above clause is a simplified version. More complex versions are used in commercial fire and multiple peril policies. Before this clause came into use, when there were form revisions which broadened coverage without an additional premium charge, agents would cancel and rewrite policies using the new broader form, causing unnecessary expense. The liberalization clause therefore automatically amends the policy as of the effective date of the new coverage to incorporate by reference the broadened features into the existing contract. (It does not apply to restrictions in coverage.) As a result of this clause, an insured may be the recipient of an extra-contractual right which was not contemplated when the policy was written.

Liberalization clauses were seldom used in liability policies until the advent of the simplified business auto and personal auto policies in the late 1970s. These policies now contain a provision in the changes condition reading:

> If we revise this policy form to provide more coverage without additional premium charge, your policy will automatically provide the additional coverage as of the day the revision is effective in your state.

Conformity with Statute. Many policies contain a so-called "conformity with statute" clause. A typical provision might read:

The terms of this policy which are in conflict with the statutes of the state wherein this policy is issued are hereby amended to conform to such statutes.

This clause enables a countrywide form to be used despite conflicting state statutes. Frequently a law will be passed affecting a relatively minor part of the contract and printing a special policy for that state would be an expense eventually paid by the policyholder. Although state statutes control insurance policies, the presence of this clause reassures some regulatory agencies, and if they agree that the "conformity with statute" provision will automatically amend the policy, everyone profits.

The clause also has been interpreted to amend automatically certain contract provisions to comply with existing state law. Thus, a state may have a statute of limitations of four years for bringing suit on a written contract while most insurance contracts require that suit must be brought within one year. In a few cases, it has been held that the "conformity with statute" provision amended the insurance contract to incorporate the four years provision in place of the one year provision. (C. F. Wulf v. Farm Bureau Insurance Co.)[3]

Further, this clause resolves the problem of whether a statute can be given retroactive effect. It will be recalled that the parties may by contract agree to incorporate future legislation. In effect, that is exactly what the "conformity with statute" provision does. (Norton v. Home Insurance Co.)[4]

Industry Interpretation. From time to time the insurance industry has, on its own (through its trade associations or rating bureaus), created extra-contractual rights for insureds either on a temporary or semi-permanent basis.

An early example is a recommendation by the casualty rating bureaus in the late 1960s that their affiliated companies voluntarily restrict their right to cancel private passenger automobile policies. Later this recommendation was incorporated into the policies.

Another example is the voluntary agreement to interpret existing policies according to a new law or regulation even though not legally required.

A third example is illustrated by package policies which at first used the standard fire policy as a model and had a noon inception time. Many casualty policies have a 12:01 A.M. inception and expiration time. If a package was written at the expiration of the liability policy, there could be a twelve-hour gap in coverage. The major bureaus agreed to request their companies to pick up this gap in coverage voluntarily, and this was done in several cases.

Still another example involved a voluntary industry agreement that animal collision under an auto policy would be treated as comprehensive coverage rather than collision, thus avoiding the deductible.

To Whom Are Rights Available?

Insureds Most extra-contractual rights apply to the insured and generally have been developed in an effort to balance what courts and legislatures perceive to be an unequal bargaining power between the "big" insurer and the "little" insured.

Insurers Extra-contractual rights may operate to the advantage of the insurer in some cases. This is even true of the extra-contractual rights created by the principle of Reasonable Expectation, a rule of contract interpretation originally designed to give the insured the protection it was reasonable for the insured to expect. Many courts use these doctrines not to punish an insurer or to counterbalance the scales but to produce what they believe to be fair and equitable results.

Affected Third Parties In certain instances persons who are not actual parties to the insurance contract may nevertheless have an interest in the contract and benefit from extra-contractual rights.

One of the most common instances is the so-called third-party beneficiary. A third-party beneficiary, as the term implies, is one who is not a party to the contract but who benefits from it and may enforce it independently of the parties. A detailed discussion of the law respecting third-party beneficiaries is set forth in Chapter 5 and will not be repeated here.

Following are several examples of how third parties are affected by extra-contractual rights and obligations.

In one case, the federal government supplied free medical service to a veteran for injuries arising out of an automobile accident. The government was held to be a third-party beneficiary of the medical payments provision of the veteran's automobile policy and was permitted to recover such medical payments from the insurer. (U.S.A. v. Automobile Club Insurance Co.)[5]

In another case, a domestic servant was injured in her employer's house. In an action brought by the insured against the insurer, the court held that under the doctrine of reasonable expectations, even though the homeowners policy which was sued upon had an exclusion of workers' compensation losses, the injured party would be permitted to recover. (Gerhardt v. Continental Insurance Co.)[6]

Another example is guest statutes. Under the ordinary automobile policy, there is no exclusion of liability with respect to passengers in the automobile. However, in many states by statute or by court interpretation, a so-called "guest" rule applies which requires a "guest" to prove that the driver was "grossly negligent" and has the effect of eliminating coverage for most guest passengers. Although the "guest" rule reflects a belief that such suits can be collusive, some such statutes have now been repealed and in a few cases have been found to be unconstitutional.

Another not uncommon case is where a mortgagor agrees to maintain insurance for the benefit of the mortgagee but actually obtains a policy written only in the mortgagor's name. In such cases it is held that the policy will inure to the benefit of the mortgagee as a third-party beneficiary even though not named therein. (Kintzel v. Wheatland Mutual Ins. Co.)[7]

Still another area is that involving joint tortfeasors. The general rule is that when two or more persons are jointly and severally liable in tort for the same injury to a person or property (joint tortfeasors), there is no right of contribution between them; if one pays the entire amount of the judgment, he or she cannot recover pro rata from the others. This of course affects the rights of their respective insurers in that the insurer of the one who pays the full amount in such a case may not recover from the insurers of the other joint tortfeasor. Under modern concepts, the equity of this position has been questioned and many states have now adopted the so-called Uniform Contribution Among Joint Tortfeasors Act which creates a right of contribution in such cases. This is treated in detail in Chapter 12.

PRINCIPAL RIGHTS
AVAILABLE TO BOTH PARTIES

General

Some extra-contractual rights and obligations are available to both parties to the contract and to third parties. Some are primarily in favor of the insurer and others are primarily in favor of the insured. In the following analysis of specific rights and obligations, an attempt is made to classify them under one of these three headings with the caveat that, under given circumstances, an extra-contractual right inuring generally to an insurer may very well benefit an insured and vice versa. This section will deal with rights and obligations that may be used generally by either party.

Mutual Mistake

It is fundamental contract law created by judicial fiat that when there is no genuine mutual assent there is no agreement and the contract may be rescinded. A material mutual mistake of fact in connection with the subject matter of a contract indicates that there was no such assent and prevents a binding contract from coming into legal existence. In such a case, the contract may be rescinded by either party by demonstrating that a mutual mistake of fact did occur. The effect of the rescission is to void the contract *ab initio* (from the beginning).

A simple illustration of a mutual material mistake of fact is a situation where an insured ordered fire insurance on Warehouse A and the person taking the order, in good faith, placed the insurance on Warehouse D. In this case, it was held that "there was no contractual relationship between the parties—their minds never met." Plaintiff's mind was in Warehouse A and defendant's in Warehouse D. (Stricker v. Umbdenstock)[8]

A similar situation arose where the insured, in good faith, represented that a certain building was protected by an automatic sprinkler system. This representation was accepted in good faith by the insurer and a policy was issued. Following a fire it was found that the building was not sprinklered. In holding the policy void the court said:

> This created a situation in which a mistake was made by one party and accepted by the other, both in good faith, with the result that the ensuing conduct of both parties was based upon a mutual mistake of fact which operated to prevent the execution of a valid contract. (Allstate Ins. Co. v. National Tea Co.)[9]

The parties to a contract should act with reasonable diligence to ascertain the facts. However, where there is no reason to believe the facts are other than as represented, the parties are entitled to rely upon honest representations.

Collateral Estoppel

The doctrine of collateral estoppel is an application of the estoppel concept to prior litigation. Simply stated, collateral estoppel means that the determination of an issue by litigation between two parties is binding in a subsequent suit involving essentially the same parties. As a New Jersey court phrased it, "Collateral estoppel is the doctrine that renders conclusive in a subsequent action on a different claim, the determination of issues actually litigated in a prior action." (Huck et al. v. Gabriel Realty Co.)[10]

Application of the doctrine requires three elements:

1. There must be an identity of issues in the successive cases.

2. There must have been a determination of these issues by a valid final judgment.
3. The parties must be identical, or in privity, or the party estopped must have refused an opportunity to participate.

The doctrine is based upon the theory that parties should not be permitted to litigate the same issue more than once, provided there has been a full and complete determination of the issue.

With respect to identity of issue required, the guidelines are as follows:

1. The issue previously considered must be identical.
2. It must have been material and relevant to disposition of the prior action.
3. The determination of the issue in the prior case must have been necessary and essential to the judgment therein.

The application of the doctrine is illustrated by the following example. *B*, while operating a portable conveyor, sustained a severe electrical shock. He sued the manufacturer, *C*, and the installer, *R*. The court found *C* not liable but held *R* liable. When judgment against *R* was returned unsatisfied, *B* sued *G* who was *R*'s liability insurer. *G* denied liability on the grounds that the injury came within the "completed operations" exclusion of the liability policy. *B* took the position that *G* was "collaterally estopped" to raise this defense because the judgment in the first case determined that there was an "incompleted operation." Applying the rules set forth above, the court held that the issue of "completed operations" has not been directly raised in the first case; it was not relevant to the decision in that case and therefore the insured could not avail himself of the extra-contractual right of "collateral estoppel" to prove his case. In this case, an insured tried to use the doctrine to prove his case. In many instances the doctrine has been invoked by an insurer to defeat a suit by additional plaintiffs after the first suit had been settled.

Collateral estoppel can also favor the insured. For instance, a mortgagee sued the insurer on a policy and the court found that the insurer had notice of destruction of a building. In a subsequent suit by the insured on the same policy, the court, under the doctrine of collateral estoppel, held that the insurer could not again litigate the question of notice. (Garcy Corp. v. Home Insurance Co.)[11]

Many jurisdictions now hold that a prior criminal conviction, such as for felonious assault, may be introduced in a suit on a liability policy involving the same accident under the doctrine of collateral estoppel. (Travelers Indemnity Co. v. Walburn)[12]

Insureds Under the Policy

The general rule is that only a party named in the contract can maintain an action on it in his or her own name. However, in the field of insurance law there are certain extra-contractual rights which make other persons insureds under the policy even though they may not specifically be named.

Third-Party Beneficiaries Third party beneficiaries may benefit from contracts including insurance policies, even though not named. (See the discussion of this subject in Chapter 5.) In order to be a third-party beneficiary, it is usually required that the parties must have so intended at the time the contract was made. An uninterested or incidental beneficiary has no right as a stranger to the contract to enforce its provisions or collect damages for its breach. The classic example is the life insurance beneficiary. However, the party need not actually be named in the contract to be a third-party beneficiary. (Honey v. G. Hyman Const. Co.)[13] One for whom a contract is made may maintain an action thereon in his or her own name. Where V and W purchased property, and G, who was V's husband, took out a fire policy on the property in his own name and did not mention V or W, it was held that V and W could sue as third-party beneficiaries. (Aetna Insurance Co. v. Solomon)[14]

In most other respects, the law distinguishes between property and liability policies and each will be treated separately.

Property Coverages. The property insurance contract being a so-called first-party coverage usually confines coverage to the named insured and in some cases, members of his or her immediate family. However, even in first-party contracts, there are some unnamed persons who benefit from the contract. The benefits may be initiated by the contract proper but their extent is governed in large measure by extra-contractual considerations.

One of these provisions is the "trust and commissions" clause. Practically every insured at one time or another has possession of the property of other persons. As far back as the 1860s, the fire policies included a "trust and commissions" clause which insured property of others "held in trust or on commission." The principal purpose of this clause was to cover the incidental, gratuitous bailee situation, but because of the phraseology it could not be confined to the incidental situation. Efforts were made to limit its application and the wording was altered to apply to property "for which the insured is liable" or "for which the insured is legally liable." In some cases the courts held this change to create a liability-type coverage and if the named insured had no legal liability to the third person for the property there was no coverage. A majority of the courts, however, still hold that this language merely delineates the kind or type of property covered and does not require the owner to establish legal liability on the part of the insured. That being the case, the owner can sue the insurer directly as a third-party beneficiary rather than first having to sue the insured to establish legal liability.

Even in the absence of a trust and commissions clause or a policy provision restricting coverage only to the property of the named insured, the courts have found coverage for third parties. For example, an insured had both his own equipment and leased equipment in his possession. The insured had agreed to purchase insurance on the leased property but no trust and commissions clause was included in the policy. The court held that the obligation to insure created an insurable interest in the insured (lessor) and that there was coverage under the item of "equipment" in the policy.

Similar results can be expected under contracts such as the homeowners policy which merely provides coverage for property "owned by others."

Liability Coverage. In the area of liability coverage, where there is no requirement of insurable interest and where the relationship of the parties can arise in an almost infinite number of ways, coverage is extended to many persons not specifically named in the contract.

In general, liability insurance contracts provide insurance protection not only for the named insured, but also for many other unenumerated persons. The other covered insureds may range from a small group, such as the spouse or immediate family, to much larger groups including employees and unrelated third persons, and to the all-inclusive group coming within the omnibus clause of the personal auto policy:

2. Any person using **your covered auto.**

Vicarious Liability In addition to the foregoing broad group of unnamed insureds it is possible to have other unnamed persons insured under the policy. An example of this is persons for whom the named insured may be "vicariously" liable either by statute or common law. Vicarious liability means liability which is imputed to a person who is not the wrongdoer, but who bears such a relationship to the wrongdoer that the wrongdoer's negligence will be imputed to the innocent person. Thus statutes in many states provide that the owner of an automobile is liable for injuries caused by that automobile regardless of the driver's identity or lack of permission to drive the vehicle. Similarly, a statute may provide that putting a dangerous instrument, such as a gun, in the hands of a minor will make the party vicariously liable for any injury caused by the minor. Neither of these parties is an insured under the terms of the contract, but the insured is protected if found vicariously liable. Vicarious liability is discussed in Chapter 12.

Date of Loss The date of loss is important for two reasons.

1. To bring the loss or occurrence within the inception and the expiration date for coverage purposes.
2. To establish the beginning and end of the time period during which the insured must commence suit against the insurer or from which an applicable statute of limitations begins to run.

Generally an insurance policy will pay for a covered loss only if it occurred during the policy period. However, judge-made qualifications on the general rule can result in coverage, or the extension of other time limits in the policy, well beyond the stated date.

Property Insurance. Loss must occur during policy period. Certain policies such as the standard fire policy do not expressly state that the loss *must* occur during the policy period. Duration of coverage is governed by the insuring clause which states that the insured is covered for the time specified, beginning at a certain time and date and expiring at a certain time and date. Many multiple peril policies contain a statement reading:

> *Policy Period:* This policy applies only to loss under Section I or bodily injury or property damage under Section II, which occurs during the policy period.

The burden is on the insured to prove that the loss occurred during the policy period. Where an insured claimed that the loss occurred on the same day the policy went into effect, but the policy was not written until late in the day, the court held that the insured had to prove that the loss occurred after the effective time of the policy. (White v. Allstate Insurance Co.)[15]

NO DUTY TO RENEW OR NOTIFY OF EXPIRATION. Most policies carry a definite expiration date and time, but frequently insureds with later losses invoke the aid of the courts either to extend the coverage past that time or to hold either the insurer or the agent liable for not notifying the insured of the impending expiration.

Especially with respect to personal coverages, these matters are now governed largely by statute, and this is discussed subsequently. Following are the general rules that apply in the absence of a statutory change.

As to the insurer, under the general rule, a loss that occurs after the policy period is not covered and failure to give notice of expiration, in the absence of past practice between the insured and the insurer involved, does not constitute a breach. (Waynesville Security Bank v.

Stuyvesant Insurance Co.)[16] As the court said in Norkin v. U.S. Fire Insurance Co.:[17]

> Plaintiff cites no authority, and we know of none, which required that an insurance company, a private business, must continue to contract with an insured after the original policy has by its terms expired. There being no such obligation, the insurance company was under no duty to disclose its intentions (not to renew) to plaintiff, assuming they existed.

As for an agent, where an agent has serviced a particular insured on several occasions and where the insured entrusted the agent with all its insurance business and can show reliance on the agent for review and renewal, the agent may be liable in damages to the insured for not renewing, although the insurer still would be off the risk by virtue of the expiration of its policy. (Security Insurance Agency v. Cox)[18] (See also Cancellation and Nonrenewal in this chapter.)

Although it is somewhat commonly held, the concept that there is an extra-contractual right of the insured to be informed of the expiration of the policy is incorrect. Failure, however, to give such notice is a possible source of litigation.

TIME PERMITTED FOR BRINGING SUIT. The second reason the date of loss is important is that it starts the running of the time within which suit must be brought under the policy. The usual property policy provides:

> No suit or action on this policy for the recovery of any claim shall be sustainable . . . unless commenced within twelve months next after inception of the loss.

Most courts hold that the inception of the loss means the actual date when the loss occurred. (Fletcher v. Pacific Indemnity Co.)[19] However, it is not essential that the insurer deny liability during this period and further discussion with the insured after the expiration of the twelve-month period or even a formal denial after the twelve months has run does not waive the period. (Cardente v. Travelers Insurance Co.)[20]

A very few courts treat the suit clause in the nature of "statutes of limitations" which commence to run on the date the cause of action arises. Thus it has been held that the "inception of the loss" means the date the insurer denied liability, and that date is when the cause of action arose (Fireman's Fund Insurance Co. v. Sand Lake Lodge, *supra*). Under that view, if the insurer did not formally deny liability the claim would be open for an indefinite period.

The better reasoned and generally accepted view seems to be the statement by the Pennsylvania Supreme Court in Lardas v. Underwriters Ins. Co.:[21]

> This is not a statute of limitations imposed by law, it is a contractual undertaking between the parties and the limitation on the time for bringing suit is imposed by the parties to the contract. Inception of the loss deals with an objective fact: the loss occurs and has its inception, regardless of whether or not the insured knew of it.

An intermediate view is that if the denial is received too near the end of the period the insurer will be estopped to assert the clause. It has been held that denial less than thirty days from the end of the period will not allow the insured a reasonable time within which to commence suit. (Friedberg v. INA)[22] But in another case a denial fifty-five days before the end of the period was held sufficient. (Vestevich v. Liberty Mut. Ins. Co.)[23]

A statute may of course extend the minimum period for bringing suit. In one case, a state had a specific statute that permitted a one-year suit clause only for property and marine insurance contracts but not less than two years for all other contracts, including theft. A theft loss occurred that was covered by a homeowners policy which contained a single one-year suit clause applicable to the entire contract. The Arizona Court of Appeals held that the twelve-month suit clause was not applicable to the theft loss because of the two-year minimum set by the statute. (Kearney v. Mid-Century Ins. Co.)[24]

Liability Policies. The usual liability policy by its terms takes effect at 12:01 A.M. on the date shown and expires at 12:01 A.M. on the stated termination date. Ordinarily there is no problem when the insured event occurs well into the time period, but if it occurs on the inception date, the insured must prove that the event occurred after the inception time of the policy.

The time of the happening of the insured event is more important under the liability policy than it is under the property policy. It not only shows that the loss occurred during the policy period but it starts the running of two essential time periods: (1) the time within which notice must be given the insurer, and (2) the beginning of the running of the applicable statute of limitations for suit by third parties.

Liability policies refer to the insured event in three different ways. The first is to provide that, "this insurance applies only to accidents which occur during the policy period." In this form, the initial question raised is the meaning of the term "accident." For example, a contractor negligently constructs a fireplace and after the liability policy has expired, the building burns down because of the contractor's negligence. Is the "accident" the faulty construction or the actual fire? The majority rule is that the accident is the event causing the injury, that is, the fire, and not the cause of that event, the negligent construction. Therefore, the fire loss was not covered under the contractor's policy. (Tiedeman v. Nationwide Mutual Fire Insurance Co.)[25]

The second way is more complex. A schedule in the policy limits liability for each "occurrence." "Occurrence" is defined as "an accident, including continuous or repeated exposure to conditions, which results in bodily injury or property damage." The latter are events "which occur during the policy period." The policy covers "occurrences" which happen during the policy period and therefore is commonly known as an "occurrence" policy.

Under this type of policy the bodily injury or property damage must occur during the policy period but the claim may be made at any time, even several years after the policy has expired. The advantage to the insured is having coverage for any occurrence during the policy period no matter when the claim is made. The date of the occurrence is usually readily ascertainable and thus can easily be assigned to the policy in force on that date. The principal disadvantage to the insurer is the possibility of being presented with a claim many years after a policy has expired, a so-called "tail" on the coverage. For example, in the case of malpractice insurance it is possible that a sponge may be left in the incision of a three-year-old child and not discovered for ten years and the child ordinarily would not have to sue until after reaching majority.

In an effort to remove this disadvantage, some policies are on a "discovery" or "claims-made" basis; only claims made during the policy year are covered regardless of when the act or injury occurred. This is most advantageous because it permits an insurer to assess loss experience each year and not be subject to a "surprise" loss for an event that occurred ten years ago under an expired policy. It may be disadvantageous to the insured who may go out of business and discontinue insurance coverage and if a claim is then made may be without coverage. Most insurers try to provide for extended discovery periods under special circumstances.

Some insureds have maintained that this type of clause is unconscionable, but the New Jersey court in Ratwein v. General Accident Group held that the clause is not per se impermissible.[26]

This clause has its own interpretation problem involving the meaning of the word "discovered." The best definition probably was set forth by the U.S. Supreme Court in American Surety Co. v. Pauley, which although old is still good:[27]

> Discovery means that time when the insured gains sufficient factual knowledge, not mere suspicion, which would justify a careful and prudent man in charging another with dishonesty.

Any other type of event can be substituted for dishonesty in the quote.

NO DUTY TO RENEW OR NOTIFY OF EXPIRATION. As is the case with renewal of property policies, the general rule is that "term insurance . . . carries no obligation on the part of the agent to renew the policy." (Walters v. Edwards)[28]Since the insured should know the stated expiration time neither the insurer nor its agent has any legal duty to give notice of expiration or to renew a policy automatically. (Burns v. Ramsey)[29]

TIME PERMITTED FOR GIVING NOTICE OF CLAIM. The typical policy provision for giving notice to the insurer of a possible claim reads:

> In the event of an accident or occurrence written notice . . . shall be given . . . to the company . . . as soon as practicable.

This means that notice must be given within a reasonable time under the circumstances. (Bernard v. National Guaranty Ins. Co.)[30]

The personal auto policy contains an example of the modernized simplified language reading:

> We must be notified promptly of how, when and where the accident or loss happened.

It is not believed this will have much effect on court interpretations as the cases hold that various types of phraseology, such as "immediately," "at once," "forthwith," or, "as soon as possible," make little or no difference and none requires instantaneous notice. Notice is necessary when there has been an occurrence that would lead a reasonable and prudent person to believe it might give rise to a claim for damages. Notice is not required where the accident is trivial or results in no apparent harm and gives no ground for the insured, as a reasonable and prudent person, to believe a claim is forthcoming. However, the burden of proving a legally acceptable excuse for a failure to give a required notice rests with the insured. A delay in sending notice, or a decision by a legally competent person that there is no liability, is at his or her own risk. The insurer is entitled under the contract to receive the required notice so that it may make an independent investigation. Whether a delay in giving notice is unreasonable depends upon the prejudice caused to the insurer as well as the length of, and reasons for, the delay. (Lumbermens Mutual Cas. Co. v. Oliver)[31] Some states require that an insurer show that its ability to defend was impaired by the late notice, while others hold such impairment immaterial. (Hoover Co. v. Maryland Cas. Co.)[32]

TIME PERMITTED FOR SUIT BY OR AGAINST THIRD PERSONS. The suit clause used in property policies limiting the time allowed an insured to bring suit against the insurer is not appropriate for the usual liability policy for two reasons. First, in a liability case the third party who has a claim against the insured has no right to sue the insurer directly in most cases. Second, the liability of the insurer to the third party claimant does not arise until the insurer, the insured, and the third party agree to a financial settlement or until a court has granted the third party a money judgment. This is made clear in liability policies by provisions similar to the following:

ACTION AGAINST COMPANY. No action shall lie against the Company . . . until the amount of the insured's obligation to pay shall have finally been determined either by judgment against the insured after actual trial or by written agreement of the insured, the claimant, and the Company.

Any person or organization or the legal representative thereof who has secured such judgment or written agreement shall thereafter be entitled to recover under this policy to the extent of the insurance afforded by this policy.

The simplified version of the personal auto policy reads:

In addition under the liability coverage no legal action may be brought against us until we agree in writing that the *covered person* has an obligation to pay or until the amount of that obligation has been finally determined by judgment after trial.

There is no provision with respect to the rights of third persons who have acquired judgments or have written agreements.

Under any of these provisions the insurer's obligation under a liability policy is contingent on one of two events occurring: (1) the outcome of a suit against the insured that was brought before the termination of the statutory period allowed for bringing suit, or (2) a settlement to which it has agreed. If timely suit is not brought, the insured is not liable and the insurer's potential obligation is lifted.

The reverse is true in subrogation cases. If the insurer has paid a sum to the insured under the policy arising out of a claim in which the insurer has subrogation rights to be enforced by a suit against the third party, the insurer must either achieve a settlement or bring suit against the third party before the termination of the statutory period. If neither event occurs, the insurer may be barred from bringing suit.

The time permitted for bringing suit varies, but in tort cases generally it is two years. Statutes of limitation for breach of contract run four or six years or sometimes longer. Some actions theoretically can be brought in either contract or tort. In medical malpractice cases, for instance, the physician has committed a tort on the person of the claimant and has also breached an implied contract to perform in a medically proper manner. In general, a claimant may waive the right to sue in tort and sue in contract. But, if the appropriate statute for bringing tort suits is two years and for bringing contract suits is six years, may the claimant sue in contract three years after treatment? Here theory and practicality collide and many courts have held that the two year statute applies. In order to solve this problem many states are

adopting specific statutes of limitations providing that persons generally over five or six years of age must bring malpractice suits within two
years after the act was committed or two years after the injury was or
should have been discovered, with an overall limit of five years after the
act. Persons under legal disability other than minority are given four
years after the disability is removed. Statutes of limitation are
discussed in Chapter 12.

Burden of Proof

The "burden of proof" refers to the apportionment between the
parties to litigation of the task of producing evidence, and denotes the
duty on a party of establishing the truth or a given issue by the
quantum of evidence which the law requires in the particular case.
Thus, in certain cases, it might be a "preponderance" of the evidence; in
others, "clear and convincing"; and in a criminal case, "beyond a
reasonable doubt."

In insurance law the general rule is that the burden is on an
insured to prove that the loss was proximately caused by the peril
insured against, or that the liability claim asserted against it was within
the coverage of the policy. With reference to a property policy, the
insured makes out a *prima facie* case by showing a loss of property
covered by the policy and caused by an insured peril, a demand upon
the insurer for payment, and a refusal to pay by the insurer. Where the
policy is on an all-risk basis the insured need only prove a loss to
property covered by the policy, the demand, and refusal. A *prima facie*
case is one which has been sufficiently established by a party's evidence
to justify a verdict in his or her favor provided the other party does not
rebut such evidence.

As a simple example in a suit against the insurer an insured who
has suffered a fire loss to a dwelling need only show that the dwelling
was named in the policy, that it was damaged by fire to the extent of a
certain amount of money, and that the insurer has refused to pay the
loss. At that point if no further evidence is introduced, the insured
would be entitled to a judgment for the amount of the claim against the
insurer. Of course the insured must introduce some evidence that the
loss was caused by the insured peril of fire. Proof which only shows
that the loss *might* have occurred in the manner alleged is not sufficient
if from the same proof the injury could, with equal probability, be
attributed to another, uninsured, cause. Thus when any one of several
causes may have brought about the loss, some insured and some not, it
is not for the jury to guess when there is no satisfactory proof for its
conclusion. The verdict must rest on probabilities and not mere

possibilities. However, the insured need not show that the suggested way is the *only* way the loss could have occurred.

In the case of an "all-risks" policy, the insured has a simpler task. Here the insured makes a *prima facie* case merely by proving loss or damage to the insured property, demand for payment, and refusal. As there are no named perils and all perils are covered (except those few specifically excluded), there is no need for the insured to prove how the loss actually occurred. This can be very important where the circumstances surrounding a loss are not too clear; for example, whether property was lost rather than stolen, or if it has just disappeared. As one court stated, under an all-risk policy the sole obligation of the insured is to provide the insurer in good faith with such information as it can concerning the time and the cause of loss. To require the insured to go further would convert an all-risk policy into a named peril policy.

Exceptions and Exclusions The general rule is that once the insured has proved a *prima facie* case, an insurer who defends on the ground that the loss was not covered under the policy (contending, for example, that the loss comes within an applicable exclusion) must establish every essential element necessary to constitute that defense. All ambiguities are resolved against the insurer. Thus an insurer must show that words of exclusion not only might mean what the insurer claims they mean, but that it is their only fair meaning. For example, if loss by riot is excluded but only two persons participated, rather than three as required by the common law definition of riot, then the exclusion is inapplicable. If only certain types of explosions are excluded, the clause will not be interpreted to exclude all types of explosions.

For "all-risks" policies, the rule is essentially the same. Thus for example where a policy covered "all risks" but had an exclusion of loss by "mysterious disappearance," the insurer denied liability on the ground that there were no forcible entry marks and therefore the disappearance had to be mysterious. The court did not agree and held that if the insured had to prove the negative of all exclusions, then instead of being an "all-risks" policy with certain losses excluded, it would become a named peril policy as the insured would have to prove the cause of loss in order to negate all exclusions.

The weight of the evidence required can be the deciding factor in a lawsuit, regardless of specific contract provisions, especially when the circumstances surrounding the event are unknown or unclear.

Liability Policies In general the burden of proof in a suit on a liability policy is essentially the same as on a property policy.

Of course, frequently the direct parties to the suit are not the insured and insurer as in a property policy, but an injured third party and the insured. The insurer then assumes the defense as it is committed to do under the policy.

In a liability case the plaintiff, to make a *prima facie* case, in general must show injury and that the injury was proximately caused by the negligence of the insured. If the plaintiff makes a *prima facie* case then the insured (and insurer) must demonstrate a defense, such as contributory negligence.

Presumptions A presumption is a fact that the law will accept as true without proof. There are two general types of presumptions— rebuttable and irrebuttable.

A rebuttable presumption is one which is assumed to be true until overcome by evidence showing that the presumption is in fact incorrect. Some are well known, such as the presumption of innocence in a criminal case. Other rebuttable presumptions are that a person is presumed to have acted lawfully (as in driving an automobile in accordance with the law); that a person has kept his or her premises in repair; that information contained in official records is correct; and that a certain legal status, such as marriage, once established, continued.

An irrebuttable presumption is one against which no evidence will be allowed. An example is the presumption that a child under seven years of age is incapable of negligence. Once the age of the child is established as under seven, no evidence of its negligence may be introduced. Another such presumption is that everyone knows the law.

In the same area of evidence is a rule known as *res ipsa loquitur*— the thing speaks for itself. Briefly this means that mere proof of certain types of occurrences warrants an inference of negligence. It is based on the assumption that certain types of events do not occur without negligence. The defendant must then prove absence of negligence.

Judicial Notice There are certain matters of such common or general knowledge that they require no proof. A classic example is that the sun rises in the east. Others include laws of nature, such as gravity, geographical facts, and well-known historical facts. If a court will take judicial notice of a fact, it need not be proven.

Evidence has an extra-contractual effect upon a proceeding involving an insurance policy and coverage may exist or be denied because of inability to prove or disprove a given element of the contract.

Exculpatory and Hold Harmless Clauses

Although these terms are sometimes used interchangeably, they should not be confused.

Exculpatory Clauses It is obvious that a person may not unilaterally relieve oneself of liability for the consequences of negligence. Whether one person may voluntarily agree not to hold another person liable for negligence is a separate problem. In general the law will enforce such an agreement, but not if the party surrendering legal rights has unequal bargaining power. The agreement would be against public policy, but the lack of equal bargaining power would have to be proved by the party asserting the defense.

An example of the latter is a requirement that a property owner agree to absolve a public utility from any liability arising from the negligence of its employees before the utility will supply electricity to the premises. This contract is against public policy and void as the parties are not bargaining on equal terms. However, the burden of proving that the contract is against public policy is on the one asserting the defense and the contract will be upheld unless there is evidence that the public interest is involved.

The effect of these agreements on collateral insurance contracts is obvious. It can govern which of two policies, or if either policy, may be answerable for a given loss or claim.

Hold Harmless Clauses   Simply stated, a hold harmless clause is an agreement to assume the liability of another, as contrasted to exculpatory clauses which relieve persons of liability for their own negligence. One party agrees to hold harmless (indemnify) another party for certain liabilities which may be imposed upon the latter party by law. Such assumption of liability can vary from the broad assumption of all liability arising out of given premises or operation whether caused by his or her own employees or the negligence of the other contracting party, down to the mere assumption of liability for negligence of one's own employees.

For example, the owner of land on which an extra-hazardous operation, such as blasting, is being conducted is strictly liable to third persons for injuries caused thereby even though the blasting is conducted by an independent contractor. An owner who hires an independent contractor to do the job may demand that the contractor specifically agree to indemnify (hold harmless) the owner for all liability arising out of the blasting. An injured third party may sue either the contractor or the owner, and if the owner is sued the owner is liable to the third party, but by virtue of the hold harmless clause the contractor must indemnify the owner.

The hold harmless agreement is therefore distinguishable from the exculpatory agreement. The latter exonerates the tortfeasor from liability. Thus, if in the blasting example for some reason the contractor had been able to exact an agreement from the owner to absolve the contractor from liability for damage that the blasting might cause to the owner's buildings, that would be an exculpatory agreement. The owner could not sue for such damages. Under the hold harmless agreement, however, the party liable is not absolved of liability to the outside third party, but the other party to the hold harmless agreement agrees to indemnify the party liable.

The acceptance of a hold harmless condition frequently indicates a weakness in the bargaining position of the assuming party. For that reason legislatures and courts look for ways to abrogate them. There are many statutes which prohibit such agreements in lease situations, construction contracts, etc. Frequently, however, these statutes specifically state that they do not affect the validity of any workers' compensation or other insurance agreements.

Both hold harmless and exculpatory clauses may be found in contracts involving the sale of goods, construction, and leases of property and have a definite extra-contractual effect upon the insurance contract.

The effect is not material with respect to property contracts, except that such an agreement by an insured with a third party may constitute a waiver of subrogation in violation of contract provisions. In certain cases, such as where a tenant agrees to purchase insurance in the owner's name but neglects to add the owner to the policy, the agreement, which is similar to a hold harmless agreement, will operate to protect the landlord under the tenant's policy.

Liability policies usually provide coverage for "incidental contracts" assuming liability by the insured. This takes care of major areas, such as leases, easements, sidetrack agreements, and elevator maintenance agreements. However, any other type of agreement is excluded unless contractual coverage is purchased. The wording of the hold harmless or exculpatory clause also will determine which party, and therefore which insurer, will be primarily and which will be secondarily liable.

PRINCIPAL EXTRA-CONTRACTUAL RIGHTS
OF INSURERS

General

The following sections will discuss some of the extra-contractual devices employed by insurers. This does not mean that such procedures may never be used by an insured, but merely that by their nature they most frequently are employed by insurers.

Other Insurance

The subject of other insurance clauses and their effects on various insurance contracts is complex. The following will illustrate in a general way how other insurance clauses vary liability under a contract both directly and in an extra-contractual manner.

When the Guiding Principles apply, the insurers in effect agree to disregard their contractual other insurance clauses and abide by those principles. However, there are many companies that are not signatory to the Guiding Principles and there are several situations not covered by them. Furthermore, the Guiding Principles are not legally binding, even on a signatory. (Hendrix v. Farmers Fire Ins. Co.)[33] For that reason, an understanding of the practical application of other insurance clauses is essential.

One type of other insurance clause provides that primary coverage is not affected by the existence of other excess or contingent insurance:

> OTHER INSURANCE. The insurance afforded by this policy is primary insurance, except when stated to apply in excess of or contingent upon the absence of other insurance. When this insurance is primary and the insured has other insurance which is stated to be applicable to the loss on an excess or contingent basis, the amount of the company's liability under this policy shall not be reduced by the existence of such other insurance.

There are three main types of other insurance clauses that are designed to eliminate or reduce coverage if other insurance is involved. They are as follows:

1. Other insurance is either not permitted, or the amount of other insurance is limited.
2. Liability under the policy is pro rata with other insurance whether collectible or not.
3. If there is other collectible insurance, the policy shall only cover that part of the loss, if any, that exceeds the limits of the other policy.

Insurers use these variants of other insurance clauses for many reasons: (1) where the intent is for the policy to be truly excess, there may be a definite rate consideration; (2) to reduce moral hazard by ensuring that the insured will not enjoy a double recovery; and (3) to protect against the effects of an other insurance clause in another policy.

The clause used in the standard fire policy and many other property policies is in conjunction with a pro rata clause and reads as follows:

> OTHER INSURANCE. Other insurance may be prohibited or the amount of insurance may be limited by endorsement attached hereto.

> PRO RATA LIABILITY. This Company shall not be liable for a greater proportion of any loss than the amount hereby insured shall bear to the whole insurance covering the property against the peril involved, whether collectible or not.

These clauses have uniformly been upheld. The homeowners policy previously contained a clause prohibiting other insurance on the dwelling building and was held to void coverage under the policy even though that penalty was not stated in the clause. The HO-76 program, under the property coverages, now has a straight pro rata clause applicable to the "total amount of insurance covering the loss." The prior homeowners also had an excess clause applying to all risk coverages in order to counteract the excess clauses of all-risk policies. Homeowners policies are usually written on a reduced rate basis and in order to make sure that it did not pick up the entire loss where there was an "all-risks" policy on the risk, it was believed necessary to make it excess. Had it been made pro rata it would have fallen under the general rule that when one policy is pro rata and the other is excess, the pro rata policy is primarily liable.

This, however, creates another problem. When both policies, the homeowners and the all-risk, contained an excess clause neither was by its terms a primary policy. However, since both policies cannot be excess, the provisions are mutually repugnant and cannot be applied. Therefore the general coverage of both policies applied and they prorated on the limits. (St. Paul F. & M. Ins. Co. v. Horace Mann Ins. Co.)[34] By virtue of that court interpretation, the homeowners policy wound up prorating on the risk. This will not apply under the HO-76 program, which is primary at all times.

The HO-76 has a peculiar other insurance clause applying to liability coverage reading:

> This insurance is excess over any other valid and collectible insurance except insurance written specifically to cover as excess over the limits of liability that apply in this policy.

It would appear that it is intended to abrogate the court-made rule that two policies with excess clauses are repugnant and should pro rate the loss, and reaffirms that in the presence of an excess coverage the homeowners will continue to be primary.

Another type of clause is found in the special multi-peril (SMP) policy. This clause provides for prorating with other property coverage that is "contributing" insurance, defined as any insurance written on the same plan, terms, and conditions; in other words, another SMP policy. If the other insurance is any insurance other than that defined as "contributing," then the SMP is excess. It uses the standard liability insurance "other insurance" provision making the SMP primary in most cases for liability losses.

It was foreseen that the SMP possibly would be called upon to contribute with certain specific types of policies, such as steam boiler policies. Contributing on the limits, with a very high SMP limit and relatively lower boiler limits, would upset the SMP rate structure. The industry had used a very complicated "joint loss clause" for many years to take care of this situation between fire and boiler policies. The matter was solved by the SMP borrowing the "other insurance" clause which is found in most "reporting form" fire policies where it was devised to take care of a similar problem. Essentially, this clause agrees to prorate with another SMP but will be excess as to any other type of policy.

Liability policies with the usual straight apportionment provisions do not give much trouble. One interesting situation involves insureds who are actively and passively negligent. For example, where the employee of a contractor was killed while digging a trench on property owned by a developer, it was held that the insurer insuring the "active negligent" contractor was solely liable and need not prorate with the insurer insuring the developer who was passively negligent.

In the more complicated liability clause, the usual problem arises when one policy has a so-called "excess" clause and the other policy has an "escape" clause. They read as follows:

Excess Clause

If other collectible insurance with another insurer is available to the insured covering a loss covered hereunder this insurance shall be in excess of and shall not contribute with such other insurance.

Escape or "No Liability" Clause

If other valid and collectible insurance exists protecting the insured against a loss covered by this policy, this policy shall be null and void unless the amount recoverable thereunder is not sufficient to completely protect the insured in which case this policy shall apply as excess over the other policy.

An "escape" clause, although not void as against public policy, is not favored by the courts. (Underground Constr. Co. v. Pacific Ind. Co.)[35] Many states still hold that when there is a conflict between either a pro rata or an excess clause on one policy and an escape clause on the other that the pro rata or the excess will be held to be primary and the escape clause excess. However, there has arisen what is known as the Lamb-Weston Rule of Oregon, which holds that in such a situation the mutually repugnant clauses will be disregarded and the liability of the insurers prorated on the basis of coverage in each policy. (Lamb-Weston Inc. v. Oregon Automobile Ins. Co.)[36] The rule applies to both excess and escape clauses. As the court said in State Farm Mutual

Insurance Co. v. U.S.F.&G., "the modern trend is not to engage in this type of semantical distinction when confronted with similar conflicting policy provisions each essentially designed to achieve the same result."[37]

In some cases, the application of a pro rata clause is impeded by statutory provisions. Thus the prevailing general rule is that the pro rata clause (whether straight pro rata, excess, or escape) does not apply to Uninsured Motorists (UM) coverage in a so-called "stacking" situation. It is not uncommon for an insured to be covered under two or more automobile insurance policies, each of which provides a statutory UM coverage of, say, $10,000. Assuming there are three such policies available to an insured, the total aggregate amount of coverage available would be $30,000. However, the statute only requires $10,000 and insurers frequently attempt to invoke the "pro rata clause" or the "other insurance" clause so that the insured will obtain no more than he or she would have obtained under one of the policies (the statutory $10,000 limit). The majority of courts hold that this approach is repugnant to the UM statutes and will not be enforced. (Cammell v. State Farm Mutual Auto Ins. Co.)[38]

Subrogation

The doctrine of subrogation was originally devised by courts of equity and rests on the maxim that no one should be enriched by another's loss. An insurer is generally entitled to subrogation, either by contract or in equity, for the amount of indemnity paid where someone else has caused the loss. While subrogation does not arise only by contract, the parties may contract with respect to it, or waive the right.

A subrogation action by an insurer is not a suit on the insurance contract as such, but is an independent action. It is usually stated that the subrogee (insurer) "steps into the shoes" of the subrogor (insured) and is entitled to the same rights and subject to the same defenses as apply to the insured. The subrogee gets no greater rights. For example, when a building collapsed and the jury found that the sole cause was windstorm, the insurer who paid the tenant's contents loss had no subrogation right against the landlord on the ground that he failed to keep the roof in repair, because lack of repairs was not the cause of the loss. (Texas Pacific Ind. Co. v. Building Materials Distributors, Inc.)[39]

Subrogation differs from assignment, which is purely contractual. An insured can assign a cause of action to the insurer as well as have it transferred by subrogation but the former is a voluntary act while the latter is involuntary and takes place by operation of law. The final result of both is practically the same except that in some states a cause of action for personal injury cannot be assigned but an insurer who pays for expenses arising out of personal injury may have a right of subrogation. By federal law when the United States furnishes medical services to veterans it can recover from the tortfeasor and the insurer of the tortfeasor cannot settle with the injured veteran and not bring the United States into the settlement, except at its peril. The courts frequently do not distinguish between assignment and subrogation as some of the following cases will demonstrate.

Even though subrogation arises by operation of law practically all insurance contracts (except life and health policies to which subrogation does not apply) contain a subrogation clause. The standard fire policy clause reads:

> This Company may require from the insured an assignment of all right of recovery against any party for loss to the extent that payment therefor is made by this Company.

The typical casualty policy reads:

> In the event of a payment under this policy, the company shall be subrogated to all the insured's rights of recovery therefor against any person or organization and the insured shall execute and deliver instruments and papers and do whatever else is necessary to secure such rights. The insured shall do nothing after loss to prejudice such rights.

It is also customary in many property and multiple-line policies to provide a limited waiver of subrogation provision. The provision in the HO-76 reads:

> Any *insured* may waive in writing before a loss all rights of recovery against any person. If not waived, we may require an assignment of rights of recovery for a loss to the extent that payment is made by us.

The general rule is that in the absence of express permission an insured cannot waive or otherwise impair the insurer's right of subrogation and if it does so it will void coverage under the policy. This is illustrated by a case where the insured property was destroyed by an explosion in a nearby railroad freight car. The insured, rather than accepting payment under the insurance policy, elected to sue the railroad. Following a successful recovery, the insured then tried to collect under the insurance policy and the court held that recovery against the railroad destroyed the insurer's right of subrogation and voided the policy. (Galvin v. State Farm F&C Co.)[40] However, where the insurer has settled with the insured, who then effects a settlement with and gives a full release to the tortfeasor who is unaware of the insurance settlement, the release given by the insured is a full defense to a subsequent subrogation suit by the insurer against the tortfeasor. The settlement by the tortfeasor in such cases must be in good faith and without knowledge of the insurer's rights. (Employers Mutual Liab. Ins. Co. v. American Protection Industries)[41]

It is a general rule that an insurer has no right of subrogation against a party who is an insured under the policy for any loss that might be paid under the policy. Thus, for example, if a home was jointly owned and insured by H and W, and H negligently set fire to the home, the insurer would be liable for the entire loss and would have no subrogation right against H because of being an insured under the policy. The problem in many cases is deciding whether a person is an insured under the policy. For example, a fire policy was issued covering a contractor and certain minor property (tools, etc.) of subcontractors. A subcontractor negligently started a fire and following payment of the contractor's loss the insurer took subrogation against the subcontractor. The subcontractor claimed there was no cause of action because he was an insured under the policy. The court in this case held that no part of the claim was for property owned by the subcontractor and it could not be said that he was an insured under the policy for such a limited interest. (Paul Tishman, Inc. v. Carney and Del Guidice, Ind.)[42]In a case which appears to be contra (Factory Ins. Assoc. v. Donco Corp.), the court held that the subcontractor, though not a named insured, was a coinsured under the policy.[43]

In Liberty Mutual Fire Ins. Co. v. Jefferson Family Fair, Inc., the lessor agreed to maintain insurance for the benefit of both the lessor and the lessee but the lessee was not named in the policy.[44] The lessee negligently set fire to the premises. After paying the loss, the insurer took subrogation against the lessee. The court observed that had the tenant been a named insured the insurer would have paid the loss regardless of its negligent origin. It further stated that although the lessee was not named there was no doubt that the insurance was intended for its benefit. On that point alone it could have held that there was no liability, as the general rule is that where parties agree for full coverage of property the agreement is for the benefit of both and the insurance proceeds will be held to constitute a satisfaction of claims for loss by one party against the other (Factory Ins. Assoc. v. Donco Corp., supra). However, the court went further to find that permission in the lease to vacate the premises after a fire "without any liability whatsoever" constituted a complete waiver of subrogation.

When bringing an action against the party responsible for the damage, an insurer, in pressing its subrogation rights, usually wants to stay in the background and have its insured maintain the action so that the jury's prejudice against insurance companies may be avoided. One of the devices used to accomplish this is a loan receipt executed by the insured when paid by the insurance carrier whereby the insured agrees to repay the amount received from the recovery he may make from the third party.

The wording of a typical loan receipt follows:

> Received from .... Insurance Company .... dollars, as a loan and repayable only to the extent of any net recovery we may make from any person or corporation on account of loss by fire to our property in or about ...., or from any insurance effected by such person or corporation.

> As security for such repayment, we hereby pledge to the .... Insurance Company the said recovery and deliver to it all documents necessary to show our interest in the property, and we agree to enter and prosecute suit against such person or corporation on account of the claim for the loss, with all due diligence, at the expense and under the exclusive direction and control of .... Insurance Company.

The insurer subrogated to the rights of its policyholder generally may not proceed against the third party who has settled with the policyholder in violation of the insurance company's subrogation rights unless the third party was aware of the insurer's interest. The insurer does have various remedies against its own insured in such a case. First, if the insurer has not yet paid under the policy, the insured's violation of the subrogation right may be a defense against the company's liability under the policy. Second, if payment under the policy has been made, the insurance company may start a separate action against its insured. Its causes of action may include (a) breach of contract (the insured in settling with the third party breached the subrogation provisions of the insurance contract); (b) quasi-contract and (c) constructive trust (where equity requires the insured to hold the recovery from the third party to which the insurance company is entitled for the benefit of the latter) and (d) injunction (where the insured may be restrained from receiving the proceeds from the settlement with the third party where such payment would be due to the insurance company).

Several policies such as the personal auto policy no longer rely on a common law right but contain a specific provision reading:

> If we make a payment under this policy and the person to or for whom payment is made recovers damages from another, that person shall hold in trust for us the proceeds of the recovery and shall reimburse us to the extent of our payment.

There are five rules that have been advanced to govern the respective rights of the insurer and the insured in the proceeds realized from the latter's claim against the responsible third party.

1. The insurer is entitled to the full amount recovered, whether or not it exceeds the amount paid by the insurer to the insured.

2. The insurer must be reimbursed first out of the recovery from the third party, with the insured getting what is left over.
3. The recovery from the third person must be prorated between the insurer and the insured in accordance with the proportion of the payment for the original loss by the insurer.
4. The insured is to be reimbursed for the loss not covered by insurance and the insurer s entitled to any remaining balance up to the insurer's interest, with any remainder going to the insured.
5. The insured is sole owner of the claim against the third party and only he is entitled to any amount recovered (thus in effect rejecting the principle of subrogation, as is the case in life insurance).

In branches of insurance allowing subrogation, rule four seems to have the most support.

A life and accident insurer is generally not subrogated to the claims of its insured unless it is so provided in the policy, a very infrequent occurrence.

There are three major differences between property insurance and life and accident insurance accounting for the contrasting rules as to subrogation rights. First, life and accident insurance policy proceeds are seldom sufficient to provide full indemnity, in contrast to property insurance. Second, the amount of the loss is not as readily evaluated in life and accident cases as in property cases, and third, life insurance is not merely an indemnity contract as is property insurance, but is also an investment.

The practice of including a subrogation clause is varied with respect to medical, surgical and hospitalization insurance. Medical and hospitalization insurance policies occasionally contain subrogation provisions although these are not always allowed because of the prohibitions against the assignment of causes of action for personal injuries.

Collateral Source Rule

The general rule is that a tortfeasor is liable for damages sustained as a result of his or her wrongful act. Frequently the injured party receives benefits for the injury in whole or in part from another source. These benefits are said to come to the injured party from a "collateral source" or a source other than the tortfeasor. In a suit by the injured party against the tortfeasor, the latter is generally not permitted to introduce evidence as to payments from the "collateral source" so as to reduce the amount for which he or she might be liable to the injured party.

The rationale for the rule was stated in Grayson v. Williams as "no reason in law, equity or good conscience can be advanced why a wrongdoer should benefit from part payment from a collateral source of damages caused by his wrongful act. If there must be a windfall certainly it is more just that the injured party should profit thereby, rather than the wrongdoer shall be relieved of his full responsibility for his wrongdoing."[45]

It is obvious, of course, that in the usual case it is not the wrongdoer who pays the damages but the wrongdoer's insurance company. The application of the rule can materially affect the amount that may be recovered under the policy. One major area where the question arises is with respect to medical payments. The usual case involves an injured party who receives medical payments under a liability policy and then sues the insured in tort and recovers under the liability portion of the policy. The question is whether the medical payments are from a "collateral source" and therefore deductible from the liability recovery. Most courts have held that it is not from a collateral source and therefore cannot be deducted, but there are a few cases to the contrary.

The rule is almost exclusively applicable in the area of liability policies. Property policies being policies of indemnification, it is usually held that the insured is entitled only to a single recovery and that payments received from a collateral source can be introduced in evidence. The cases that do hold that the "collateral source" rule, or a variation thereof, is applicable to property insurance policies involve payments by so-called "volunteers," defined as those who have no legal liability for the loss but for one reason or another reimburse the party sustaining the loss.

Usually collateral source problems in the property insurance field can be avoided by the insurer paying the loss and accepting an assignment of all of the insured's rights against other parties. However, this still does not preclude the possibility of double recovery in the pure "volunteer" situation where the insured actually has no rights against the party to which the insurer could be subrogated.

A somewhat common situation arises when two or more insurers are on the same risk and one of them pays more than its pro rata share of a loss. Some cases hold that this insurer is a "volunteer" as to such excess and cannot recover it from the other insurers, who are still liable for their own pro rata share. However, the majority of courts recognize that it is undesirable to reward an insurer who was slow in paying its obligations. These latter courts hold that an insurer who has accepted the burden of a full settlement is acting in the best interests of the insured and is not a volunteer and does not lose the right to recover from other insurers who are obligated for part of the loss. (St. Paul F&M Ins. Co. v. Allstate Ins. Co.)[46]

Some courts make a rather fine distinction in this area. Thus it has been held that if two or more insurers bind themselves to pay the entire loss insured against and one insurer pays the whole loss, the one so paying has a right of action against the coinsurers for a ratable proportion of the loss because of having paid a debt which is equally and concurrently due by the other insurers. However, if each insurer contracts to pay only a pro rata portion of the loss, none of the insurers has any right to contribution from the others and payment of the whole loss by one of them does not discharge the liability of the others because the contracts are independent of each other. Thus where there is a pro rata clause an insurer paying more than its proportion cannot recover the excess from the other insurer. (INA v. Fire Insurance Exch.)[47]

Workers' compensation payments are not subject to the collateral source role. This is because compensation statutes in many states permit the injured party to elect either to take compensation or proceed against the tortfeasor, or to do both. Where payments are made by the insurer it exercises its right of subrogation or lien on the proceeds of any recovery. Therefore the payments do not constitute payments from a collateral source, independent of the tortfeasor, since the insurer in most states either has a right of subrogation or lien on the claimant's right of action against the defendant.

With the multiplicity of sources from which a person may be recompensed for the same injury, there are moves to modify the rule to permit only one recovery.

Procedural Devices

Reservation of Rights and Nonwaiver Agreements Many times when there appears to be a breach of policy conditions by the insured, the insurer may nevertheless desire to investigate the claim without admitting liability or waiving any of its rights under the policy. The insurer can do one of three things:

1. investigate or defend the action under a reservation of rights;
2. investigate or defend under a nonwaiver agreement; or
3. refuse to defend, and institute a declaratory judgment action.

Rights may be reserved by a notice to the insured. It is a unilateral declaration that the insurer is proceeding but reserving all rights, and notice is given so that there can be no inference that merely because the insurer is proceeding to investigate the claim it is waiving any of its rights.

A nonwaiver agreement is similar to a reservation of rights notice except that it is a bilateral agreement between the parties rather than a unilateral declaration of nonwaiver by the insurer. The reason for the agreement is essentially the same as for the reservation of rights notice. Usually the insured agrees to give up certain rights in return for the insurer's agreement to proceed with the investigation or defense.

Declaratory Judgment Actions In place of a nonwaiver agreement, an insurer may bring a declaratory judgment action to determine whether it has any liability under the policy before undertaking the defense of a claim.

A declaratory judgment action when brought by an insurer usually seeks answers to such questions as whether its policy covers the alleged occurrence; whether it has a good defense to an action on the policy by the insured; whether it must undertake to defend the insured; and in general to establish the parameters of its liability, if any, before entering into a costly investigation and defense. It also is effective in demonstrating good faith if the insured should later sue and attempt to recover punitive damages.

Declaratory judgments were unknown at common law and are creatures of statute. Most state declaratory judgment statutes are based on the Federal Declaratory Judgment Law (28 USCA 400). The statutes generally provide that the courts shall have the power to declare rights, status, and other legal relationships regardless of whether further relief is or could be claimed. With respect to contracts the pertinent part of the statute reads:

> A person interested under . . . a written contract . . . may have determined any question of construction or validity arising under the instrument . . . and obtain a declaration of rights, status or other legal relations thereunder.

Nearly forty years ago Professor Borchard predicted that the declaratory judgment action would find its greatest usefulness in the field of casualty insurance and this prediction came true. It is used much more extensively in liability than in property coverages because it gives the parties a ruling in advance of litigation on whether the policy covers the situation and, possibly more important in the liability field, whether the insurer must provide a defense.

The outstanding merit of the action is that coverage can usually be determined in advance of the trial because declaratory judgments are heard by the judge alone without a jury. Therefore in most jurisdictions such actions can be heard months before a case could be heard by a jury. Further, in most jurisdictions the court will stay all proceedings in the liability case pending determination of the declaratory judgment action. This is particularly advantageous to the insurer because it prevents the injured person from obtaining a default judgment if the insurer is unwilling to waive its rights by appearing in the liability trial. In the declaratory judgment action all parties who have any interest in the insurance coverage, even though the interest may only be potential or contingent, may be joined as defendants and the decision in the case is *res judicata* (conclusive of their rights) as to all of them. The one possible disadvantage is that the burden of proof lies with the party seeking the declaratory judgment and as indicated under the section above sometimes this presents problems.

Parol Evidence Rule   The subject of parol or extrinsic evidence affecting a written contract was discussed generally in Chapter 3. It is reviewed here briefly and its application in insurance is discussed because it has an extra-contractual effect on the insurance contract. The parol evidence rule is that no evidence may be introduced, in an action on a written contract, of prior or contemporaneous agreements which would vary the terms of the written contract. It is based on the assumption that all prior agreements have been merged into and expressed in the written contract and therefore evidence of any such prior agreements is not permitted to be introduced in a suit on that contract to vary its terms.

Parol evidence cannot be introduced to show that the intentions of the parties were different from those expressed in the contract, except in the case of fraud, mistake, undue influence, or duress. Testimony of a party's understanding of a contract is inadmissible. Unambiguous words cannot be explained. The rule is that the written contract speaks for itself.

The rule has almost as many exceptions as it has applications. The rule assumes the existence of a valid legal contract. Therefore parol evidence may be introduced to show fraud which goes to the existence of the contract, or to show mutual mistake which also would demonstrate that the contract was not valid to begin with. Parol evidence can also be introduced to deny the existence of the contract or to prove that conditions were to be met before the writing was to become a contract. Such testimony does not vary the terms of the written contract but merely shows that it was never intended to be, or did not for some reason become, a valid contract.

Another exception to the parol evidence rule exists when the entire agreement has not been reduced to writing. Parol evidence may, under what is termed "partial integration," be admitted to supply the missing terms.

Also, a separate and independent valid contract between the

parties can be shown by parol, even if it affects the contract in question. This is similar to "partial integration," and such a collateral contract may be admitted, not to contradict the written contract, but to supplement it.

The parol evidence rule does not apply to valid subsequent oral agreements. In the absence of a statute which requires a written contract, such as the Statute of Frauds, the parties may vary the terms of a written agreement by a subsequent oral agreement and evidence of the variance may be introduced.

Where the terms of the contract have more than one interpretation, parol evidence may be introduced to show what parties intended when the contract was executed. There must be an ambiguity and this exception to the rule cannot be used to vary the plain meaning of the language. Ambiguity is often alleged in insurance cases in an attempt to vary the terms of the written contract. (This was treated in the section on Contract Construction.) Because insurance contracts are written and because all types of negotiations take place before, during, and after the execution of the contract, the parol evidence rule is frequently invoked in insurance cases. A few illustrative cases will indicate some of the problems in its application.

In Bersani v. General Accident Fire and Life Assurance Corp., the insurer sought to avoid a claim on the ground that a collateral contract between the parties provided that no claims would be made under the policy.[48] It seems that the insured needed insurance in order to obtain a mortgage, and to induce the insurer to issue the policy allegedly entered into a no-claim agreement. The insured claimed that under the parol evidence rule evidence of this collateral contract should not be admitted. The lower court held it admissible because it was not used to vary the terms of the contract but to show there was no contract at all. The appellate court stated that the rule is more than a rule of evidence—it is a rule of substantive law. The court further stated that parol evidence is admissible to show that a writing which purports to be a contract is not a contract but a sham to induce a third person to enter into a contract; but, where the parol evidence will show a collateral contract that is contrary to law and public policy, it will not be admitted and the parties will be confined to the terms of the written contract (insurance policy).

In a case involving cargo liability insurance, the insured claimed that the policy definition of gross receipts was ambiguous and parol evidence of the custom of the trade should be admitted. The court stated the general rule that when an express contract is plain and unambiguous, evidence of usage and custom of the trade is inadmissible to vary or contradict it. When the policy clearly spells out the definition of a term, parol evidence of trade practices or usage is not admissible. (Fireman's Fund Ins. Co. v. Mercer Marine Transit Corp.)[49]

Where a policy covered "tanks and structures" at 200 First Street and there were both inside and outside tanks, the court held that parol evidence could be introduced to clarify the ambiguity. The insurer said that "tanks" meant "tanks" and that there was no apparent ambiguity. The court, however, applied the general rule that when terms of a written contract have more than one interpretation, or where the provisions of the contract are uncertain, parol evidence is admissible to clarify the ambiguity and to show the intentions of the parties. (Atlas Lubricant Corp. v. Federal Ins. Co.)[50]

Specific Policy Provisions

Almost any word or phrase in the insurance contract may be the subject of interpretation, but there are certain areas in which questions constantly arise. Some policy provisions are not defined in the policy, and some applicable legal principles are not expressly mentioned in policies. These questions are then addressed to the courts.

The extra-contractual rights and obligations created by these provisions arise out of the rules adopted by the courts in interpreting them.

Direct Versus Indirect Loss   The standard fire policies of all states except Massachusetts, Minnesota, and California provide coverage only against "direct" loss by fire. What constitutes "direct loss" has been the subject of countless lawsuits and involves a rather complicated legal concept known as the doctrine of proximate cause.

There are many definitions of the doctrine of proximate cause and one of the simplest and clearest is:

> Proximate cause is a cause which in a natural and continuous sequence, unbroken by any new and independent cause, produces an event, and without which the event would not have happened.[51]

The insurance industry uses the word "direct" before "loss" in many property policies in an attempt to confine the cause to the immediate destroying peril. However, by and large, the courts have not recognized this limitation and they tend to equate "direct" with "proximate." They have also stated that the word "direct" means "immediate" as distinguished from "remote" or "incidental."

The courts recognize a difference between "loss" and "direct loss" but they are reluctant to hold that the term "direct loss" is restricted to loss directly caused by the designated peril. However, an insuring clause without the qualifying word "direct" may make the insurer liable for all known effects of a fire and include all loss which results even though other incidental agencies may be instrumental in adding to the loss. This distinction should be kept in mind when analyzing older insurance cases and when analyzing the fire policies of California, Massachusetts, and Minnesota which omit the requirements of *direct* loss. The concept of direct loss is easier to understand if it is restated in the terms of "immediate" versus "remote" or "direct" versus "indirect" rather than a vague term, such as "proximate cause." Certain tests are applied by the courts to determine whether the insured peril was the immediate or direct rather than the remote or indirect cause of the loss.

The first question is whether the peril must itself physically damage the insured property, which the addition of the word "direct" was intended to require. However, with very few exceptions the courts hold that "direct loss" does not mean that the insured property must suffer immediate physical damage from the insured peril. One such familiar type of loss is when a windstorm propels something against the insured property but the wind itself does not touch the property. The loss in such a case is a direct loss by the windstorm.

Similarly, for fire to be the proximate cause of the loss it is not necessary that the insured property actually be ignited or consumed. A recent case involved fire which damaged the party wall and in turn, required removal of the top two stories of the adjacent insured building. The court held this was a direct loss by fire even though the fire was outside of and did not actually burn the insured building. In another case, a TV antenna was knocked over by wind and punched a hole in the roof permitting rain water to enter. The court found a direct loss by windstorm. Another case involved a minor explosion in the fire box of a furnace which put out the fire in the furnace, causing the plumbing to freeze. The court held this was a direct loss by explosion although explosion never touched the plumbing.

The second test of remoteness involves distance. Most cases hold that the insured peril must occur on the insured or on adjacent premises. If fire destroys a transformer five miles away, probably most courts would say that the event was too remote to be the direct cause of loss. However, in several cases the courts have refused to restrict coverage to a chain of events originating on the insured or immediately adjoining premises. One case held that an occurrence of the insured peril at a point up to five miles from the insured premises was still a "direct" loss.

The third test is time. The general rule is that proximity in time is not a controlling factor. In one case, fire damaged a building, and a wall collapsing thirty-eight days later was held to be part of the loss. However, in another case, twenty-five days was held too remote. In still another case, wind blew the roof off a building, and twelve days later rain damage occurred. It was shown that persons to repair the roof were difficult to find, and the court held that the amount of time between cause and effect is not conclusive of a break in the chain of causation and that wind was the proximate cause of the rain damage in this case.

The fourth test is that of "remoteness in relationship," which combines or distills all the preceding tests. It involves the question for the jury, of whether the insured peril can in all fairness be said to have been a major cause of the loss and not just an incidental cause.

These tests can be summarized as follows:

1. Under most property damage policies the insurer is liable only for direct loss, which only means that the peril must be an immediate cause of loss as distinguished from a remote cause.
2. It is not necessary that the insured peril itself damage the insured property but it must have had sufficient strength to set in motion the forces which produced the loss.
3. If the loss resulting from the insured peril is too far away in terms of time, distance, or relationship, then it is a consequential or remote loss and is not covered.

Proximate cause is also involved in liability policies. It must be found that the negligence of the insured was the proximate cause of the loss before any liability arises under the policy. In negligence cases courts frequently apply what is called the "but for" rule, which asks whether the loss would not have been sustained "but for" the insured's negligent act. If the answer is "yes" then the insured's act was the proximate cause of the loss. Thus if *A* drove an auto onto a sidewalk and injured *B*, it is readily apparent that "but for" *A*'s action there would have been no injury to *B* and the act was the proximate cause of *B*'s injury.

There are instances where the acts of two parties coincide to cause the loss and the "but for" rule does not produce the proper result. Thus in a case where *A* and *B* collide at an intersection and *A*'s car is driven up onto the walk and injures *C*, it is apparent that both *A* and *B* are at fault. However, if the "but for" test is applied to *A*, the loss would not have occurred "but for" *B*'s negligence and *A* would not be at fault. The same reasoning applies to *B* and neither would be liable under the "but for" rule. In order to avoid this obviously incorrect result the courts have evolved the "substantial factor" rule whereby if a person's negligence is a substantial factor in bringing about an injury it will be held to be a proximate cause. The doctrine of proximate cause is also covered in Chapter 12.

Friendly Fire The standard fire policy expressly covers "fire" but does not define the term. Most cases of fire are clear but sometimes problems arise. The courts have evolved certain tests for the type of combustion covered by the policy. These may be summarized as follows:

1. There must be combustion, meaning a rapid and not a slow oxidation, such as rusting.
2. The combustion must be accompanied by a flame or a glow. Most courts hold that the amount of visibility or glow can be very small.
3. The fire or combustion must be hostile and not "friendly." A hostile fire is not confined to the place where it should be, such as in a furnace.

In general, to support a fire claim one must prove the loss was caused by a hostile flame. As stated, the flame may be very small but it cannot be miniscule. Thus, for example, where a policy covered fire but did not cover explosion and the lighting of a match caused an explosion, it was held that this was not sufficient fire to bring the entire loss under the fire coverage.

With reference to friendly fires the courts have usually required three elements to call it a friendly fire and not covered:

1. The fire must have been started intentionally.
2. It must be confined to the place where it was intended to be.
3. It must not be excessive.

In applying these tests the courts are not always uniform. Thus when a furnace overheats, as when automatic controls malfunction and the furnace is destroyed, some courts hold this to be a hostile fire so far as the loss to the furnace is concerned. (Basalo Mfg. Co. v. Firemen's Mutual Ins. Co.)[52] Similarly, a defective thermostat caused a stoker to overheat and melt part of furnace and also set fire to the building. The court held the fire to have been hostile and that not only was damage to the building covered, but also damage to the furnace. (Frings v. Farm Bureau Mut. Ins. Co.)[53] However, a majority of courts hold that overheated furnace fires are "friendly" and losses, including losses, for example, to charred or scorched woodwork in the area, are not covered under a fire policy. Also, destruction of property by accidentally throwing it into an incinerator has been held to be loss caused by a friendly fire and not covered.

A common type of loss is the scorching of furniture or rugs by cigarettes. In the case of carpets this can involve the question of replacing the whole carpet because of a rather small char spot. There is only one case directly on the point (Siverling v. Connecticut Fire Ins. Co.), and it held that the loss was covered.[54]

It should be stressed that the matter of "friendly" fire is material only in a named peril policy and has no application to an "all-risks" policy because there is no need in the latter case to prove that the "loss" arose from any peril, including "fire."

Some commentators have criticized the "friendly fire" doctrine but when considered from the practical viewpoint, it still serves a very useful purpose.

Similarly, an insured's negligence in starting a fire has no bearing on recovery under the policy. As long as the fire is not intentionally started, the fact that it arose from the insured's negligence will not avoid recovery.

Arson Arson by the insured is usually considered fraud and has always been accepted as a defense in a suit by the insured under a fire policy. The policy contains no express exclusion of loss by arson but as the court said in Fuselier v. U.S.F.&G.:

> There is no requirement that a fire insurance policy state that the insured may not recover if he burns his house. Our law does not allow one to profit from his wrongdoing. Arson or incendiarism has been recognized in Louisiana for many years as a defense to a claim on a fire insurance policy.[55]

This creates problems where property is jointly owned and one of the joint owners commits the arson without the knowledge or consent of the other. The traditional rule is that an innocent coinsured is also barred from recovery. (Klemens v. Badger Mutual Insurance Co.)[56] This is still the majority rule. It applies only where there is a tenancy by the entireties or a joint tenancy with right of survivorship. It does not apply to tenancies in common.

Another line of cases has now developed which focuses on factors other than property ownership, including

1. The severability of the insured's interest in the property
2. The innocence of the other party
3. The policy terms
4. The reasonable expectations of the insured

In one of the early cases holding the innocent spouse could recover, the New Jersey Supreme Court held that while the property was jointly held the arson was several and separate rather than joint and the husband's fraud could not be imputed to his innocent spouse.[57] Other courts have found that reasonable persons would not expect that the fraud of their coinsureds would be imputed to them in the absence of express policy terms. (Economy Fire & Casualty v. Warren)[58] The courts which permit the innocent spouse to recover are not consistent but most limit recovery to one-half the interest in the property.

Location of Property   The standard fire policy states that it covers the insured property "while located or contained as described in this policy . . . but not elsewhere." It is generally held that this statement constitutes a warranty and a breach will void coverage. Where a building was described in the policy as being on the south side of Rockford Avenue but the insured moved it to the north side without the knowledge or consent of the insurer, the policy was held void. The court said, "It is well settled that the description of the location of insured property is a warranty, the truth of which is a condition precedent to liability on the part of the insurer." (Antun v. New York Cent. Mut. Fire Ins. Co.)[59] In a similar case a dwelling described as being on Lot 1 in the policy was moved to Lot 7 after the policy was issued and without notice to the insurer. The insured claimed, after the loss, that the only question was whether the move increased the hazard. The court held that the insuring clause description, "but not elsewhere" could not be more explicit, and that there was no coverage. (North Carolina Blue Cross, et al. v. American Mfg. Mut. Ins. Co.)[60]

Requirements Concerning the Accidental Nature of Loss The question of whether or not the requirement of the fortuitous or accidental nature of the loss has been complied with should be decided from the standpoint of the person whose interest is protected by the policy. Such a person would be the insured in most cases, especially in property and accident insurance where the insured and the person sustaining the loss are the same, but also in liability insurance where the insured and victim are different. On the other hand, in life insurance it would be the beneficiary of the policy.

Most liability policies specifically exclude coverage for any person who intentionally causes bodily injury or property damage. These intentional act exclusions are the subject of innumerable court decisions. Intentional may refer to the act that produced the injury; the result obtained; or the intentional performance of an act with intent to cause bodily injury although neither the precise injury nor the severity of the damage was actually intended. The majority rule appears to be that when there is a specific intent to inflict some bodily injury the exclusion applies even if the resulting injury was different in kind, greater in degree or applied to a different person than the one the insured originally intended.

The rule that the loss must be fortuitous from the standpoint of the insured in liability insurance also has some exceptions. One such situation involves the statutory requirement for a liability coverage or for proof of financial responsibility, both of which are designed to protect the victims of accidents rather than insureds. However, in these cases the insurer might have the right for reimbursement from the insured who may have caused the victim's injury intentionally, and therefore would not be entitled to the protection of the policy.

There are situations where, even though the loss or injury was caused intentionally by an additional insured, it was fortuitous from the standpoint of the named insured or another additional insured whose liability is derived in a vicarious manner. Such persons, entitled to policy protection, might be the employer in the case of an assault by an employee, the parents vicariously liable for intentional acts of their child, or the innocent partner of another partner guilty of inflicting intentional injuries on the victim.

Another group of cases where the injury-causing act could not have been performed without legal "intent" holds that the implied or express prohibition against nonfortuitous losses is disregarded where the person committing it is not guilty of malice but is himself the victim of an innocent mistake. Examples of this type include "battery" by a young child resulting in an *unintended* serious injury; the insured being guilty of trespass by mistake; the insured being legally incapable of forming an intent by reason of being schizophrenic or deranged; the insured mistakenly believing that he is acting in self-defense; or where the insured is guilty of medical malpractice.

Coverage may be withdrawn from the insured for violating express provisions of policies by neglecting to take reasonable means to save the insured property from further damage or take other precautions to minimize the loss. This is in harmony with the generally recognized doctrine of avoidable consequences. Of course, should the insured take the necessary steps of protection if it is required by the policy, then it is only fair that the insurer should reimburse him for any additional expense involved therein.

Limits of Liability

Actual Cash Value In property insurance, recovery is usually limited by the policy to the actual cash value of the property, subject to the dollar amount of insurance stated in the policy. One area in which there is always a problem is how "actual cash value" is determined. The phrase "actual cash value" (ACV) imposes a limitation upon the amount recoverable but is not defined in the policy. The necessity for a judicial interpretation of the term creates the extra contractual rights and obligations.

Historically the most common approach for establishing ACV of both personal and real property has been replacement or reproduction cost less depreciation. Market value, if it can be readily determined, also has been applied as a test. However, for articles without a standard market value, that test can produce results inconsistent with the replacement cost method. For example, assume a suit of clothes cost $200 new and was damaged by fire after one year. If the fair market value test is applied, the suit would be valued at the value of secondhand clothing which might be $25, but the ACV might be, allowing for depreciation, at least $150 under the replacement cost method. If there is a coinsurance clause involved and the insured is badly underinsured, using the fair market value approach may permit the insured to escape a coinsurance penalty. (Jefferson Ins. Co. v. Fong Hong May)[61]

A third test which many courts now apply is the so-called "broad evidence" rule (also known as the McAnarney rule, from McAnarney v. Newark Ins. Co.), which states that the court will consider any and all evidence logically tending to the formulation of a correct estimate of the value of the insured property at the time of loss. At least twenty-one states now follow this rule.[62]

Each of these rules has its proponents and critics. In the final analysis, the purpose of any rule should be indemnity with neither over nor under compensation. In order to accomplish this and because there are many ways to establish the value or worth of property, the consensus has been that no rigid definition of ACV should be put in the policy. In actual practice it is usually fairly evident which test should be applied but on occasion an obviously incorrect conclusion is reached.

Over the past several years replacement cost coverage for buildings, and to a limited extent for personal property, has become available. This has eliminated many problems, with the notable exception of underinsured property that is subject to coinsurance, or buildings that are grossly overinsured compared with their true worth.

Insurable Interest. An insurable interest is any pecuniary interest in property which would be lessened by the happening of a peril against which the policy insures. It is not confined to ownership and extends to the insured's liability imposed by law, contract, or relationship of the parties. The following, among others, have insurable interests: agents, consignees, factors, trustees, common carriers, pledgees, builders, creditors, debtors, husbands and wives, joint tenants, lessors, and lessees. Some have insurable interests equivalent to the full value of the property, some to a lesser extent, and the sum total of the interests may exceed the total value of the property. No effort will be made here to analyze the subject of insurable interest, other than to indicate that court-made rules can affect the recovery under the policy.

Insurable interest is being used more and more to limit recovery to actual cost in cases where replacement cost less depreciation is relatively high. For example, a building purchased for $4,400 after a fire was then insured for $50,000 in a FAIR plan, and a second fire destroyed the building. The court limited recovery to the $4,400 paid rather than approximately $40,000 that would have been the replacement cost less depreciation figure, on the basis that $4,400 was the extent of the insured's insurable interest. (Chicago Title and Trust Co. v. U.S.F.&G.)[63]

Successive Losses. In the case of successive losses under a property policy the general rule, unless otherwise provided in the policy, is that the insurer is liable at most for the difference between the amount paid on the first loss and the policy limit. (Trull v. Roxbury Mut. Fire Ins. Co.)[64] Thus, for example, if there is a $10,000 policy on a building and a $5,000 loss, the amount of insurance is reduced to $5,000; and if there is another fire loss within the policy period of more than $5,000, the most that can be recovered would be $5,000.

However, the insurance industry, in almost all contracts, has incorporated a so-called "loss clause" which states, "Any loss hereunder shall not reduce the amount of this policy." The effect of this clause is to reinstate the amount of the loss, and under a policy with such a clause full recovery may be had for successive losses up to the face of the policy. (Palilla v. St. Paul F&M Ins. Co.)[65] The HO-76 policies do not contain such a provision. It is assumed that insurers will interpret them as though they did.

Liability Policies Most liability policies expressly confine the maximum limit of liability for one accident or occurrence to the amount stated, regardless of the number of insureds or injured persons. Thus, if a policy with three named insureds provides a limit of $10,000 per occurrence, the maximum liability is still $10,000; and if four persons are injured, the total limit is still $10,000.

Sometimes the problem arises of what constitutes one accident or one occurrence. In Truck Insurance Exchange v. Rohde, the insured negligently collided with the first in a group of motorcycles.[66] This collision caused the insured to spin and hit the second motorcycle and then the third. The insured's policy had $20,000 limits per person and $50,000 per occurrence. The insured claimed each collision was a separate event or occurrence and the $50,000 limit applied to each. The insurer claimed they were all part of the same occurrence and the $50,000 applied to the entire event. The court agreed with the insurer. In a similar case, a negligently operated truck struck a freight train and damaged fourteen cars containing property of fourteen different persons. The policy limit was $5,000 per accident. The insured on its own paid the parties $30,000, and sued its insurer for the amount over

$5,000, claiming the $5,000 limit applied to each person whose property was damaged. The court held that the $5,000 applied to the entire accident, regardless of the number of parties involved.

Proof of Loss The standard fire policy requires a signed and sworn proof of loss within sixty days after the loss. Many liability policies, such as the burglary policies, contain the following provision: "The insured shall . . . file detailed proof of loss, duly sworn to, within four months after the discovery of loss." The proof of loss informs the insurer of the particulars of the loss, gives the insurer an adequate opportunity for investigation to prevent fraud, and enables it to form an intelligent opinion of its rights and liabilities under the policy. The proof of loss should not be confused with the notice of loss, which is also required under many policies. The sole purpose of the notice of loss is to enable the insurer to take prompt action to protect its interests. (5A Appleman, Ins. L & P SEC Y 3481)

The general rule is that a proof of loss is a condition precedent to filing suit on the policy unless the insurer has waived the requirement. Although older cases require strict compliance, the trend is toward a standard of substantial compliance. The test of substantial compliance is whether the proof submitted by the insured fulfills the purpose of the proof of loss. Furnishing all details but failing to sign under oath has been said to be substantial compliance. (Sutter v. F.I. Exch.)[67] Complete investigation of the loss by the insurer with full knowledge of it from the day it occurred has been said to constitute a waiver of proof of loss. (Aetna Ins. Co. v. Solomon, *supra*)

Outright denial of the claim also constitutes a waiver. However, the denial must be made within the filing period. For example, where an insurer denied liability after the fire policy's sixty-day filing period the condition was not waived. (Pennington v. Aetna Ins. Co.)[68] Further, it must be an outright denial. Where the insured claimed its failure to furnish a proof of loss was waived because during the filing period the adjuster for the insured expressed an opinion that the loss was not covered by the fire policy but by a boiler policy, the court held this was not such a denial as to constitute a waiver. (Angelo State University v. International Ins. Co.)[69]

Where the insurer fully investigated the loss, had paid the mortgagee within sixty days without requiring a proof of loss, and had discussed the loss with the insured without indicating any intention to deny the loss, the insurer was held to have waived its right to require a formal proof of loss from the mortgagor as a condition precedent to payment. (Hawkeye-Security Ins. Co. v. Apadoca)[70] This is in line with the modern trend to alleviate the harsh effects of a policy condition when there is no apparent detriment to the insurer and the effect might otherwise be to deny recovery under the policy.

There is a difference of opinion concerning whether proof of loss is evidence. Under the majority view, it *is* evidence, although as with any other evidence it may be contradicted or explained. (Kinsey v. Trans-America Ins. Co.)[71] There is a line of cases, though, holding that the proof of loss is not evidence of the extent of the loss. (Tompkins v. Southern Lloyds Ins. Co.)[72]

Appraisal The standard fire policy provides that if the parties fail to agree on the ACV or on the amount of the loss, either party may demand appraisal in a specified manner. Appraisers determine the amount of damage to the items submitted for their consideration, but do not resolve questions of coverage or interpret provisions of the policy. These questions are reserved for the courts. An appraisal may be set aside by the courts if the award is so violative of the policy terms and controlling law as to indicate fraud, mistake, or misfeasance. (City Fuel and Supply Co. v. Millers Mut. Assur. Assoc.)[73]

Appraisal once demanded constitutes a condition precedent to suit on the policy. However, it can be waived. Thus, the denial of any liability by the insurer waives any right to demand appraisal as a condition of the policy. (Goodman v. Quaker City F&M Ins. Co.)[74] Further, the refusal by the insurer to appoint an appraiser on demand constitutes waiver.

There is some tendency to confuse appraisal with arbitration. Under the appraisal clause, only ACV and amount of loss can be determined. However, voluntary arbitration may be used to settle the entire liability under the policy, including the amount. Arbitration was not favored at common law because the courts viewed it as usurpation of the judicial function. However, over the years it has become accepted and arbitration provisions are even being written into some uninsured motorist and no-fault automobile coverages. In the year 1975 the American Arbitration Association arbitrated over 14,000 auto cases.

The awards of the two proceedings differ in effect. The award made under a fire policy appraisal clause cannot be made the subject of a court action. Suit must be brought upon the policy and the appraisal award is introduced to establish the amount of the loss. (Hartford Fire Ins. Co. v. Jones)[75] An arbitration award can be appealed directly to the courts.

In a state with a so-called valued policy law a total loss abrogates the appraisal clause. However, a question of whether there is a total loss can be submitted to appraisal.

Suit Against the Insurer

Property Insurance The standard fire policy and other first party contracts usually require the insured to commence suit against the insurer within a certain time, such as twelve months, or the right is lost. It is a condition subsequent that cuts off rights.

Liability Insurance Liability insurance policies contain a condition precedent to bringing suit on the policy. A typical clause reads:

> Action Against Company: No action shall lie against the company unless, as a condition precedent thereto . . . the amount of the insured's obligation to pay shall have been finally determined either by judgment against the insured after actual trial or by written agreement of the insured, the claimant and the company.

It further provides:

> No person or organization shall have the right under this policy to join the company as a party to any action against the insured to determine the insured's liability, nor shall the company be impleaded by the insured or his legal representative.

Generally claims are settled by agreement between the parties before the matter gets into the courts. However, if the matter goes to litigation, the insurer usually does not desire to become a direct party to the action although it will probably participate in the defense. There is a belief that if a jury knows that insurance is involved, they may put the burden on the insurance company regardless of the facts. In most states it is reversible error for counsel to bring out during the trial that there is insurance involved. In the light of almost universal insurance coverage there are many who question the value of this restriction.

A few states, notably Wisconsin and Louisiana, have so-called "direct action" statutes which permit the injured party to sue an insurer in many types of liability cases. This is also possible under court rules in some areas. The Federal Rules of Civil Procedure (FRCP) (Rule 14) permits either the plaintiff or the defendant to bring into a suit a third person "who is or may be liable to him" for all or part of the claim. This is known as impleader. The "no-action" provision of the policy does not bar the impleader. (Purcell v. U.S.)[76] A claim that the jury will be prejudiced by the appearance of the insurer in the suit will not bar impleader. (B — Amused Co. v. Millware Sporting Club, Inc.)[77] Many states have similar rules but they are infrequently employed. (Shingleton v. Bessey)[78]

Increase of Hazard The standard fire policy provides:

> This Company shall not be liable for loss occurring while the hazard is increased by any means within the control or knowledge of the insured.

Nonliability when the insured increases the hazard would be implied in a policy even if not expressly stated, but it is specifically included so that there will be no question of its application and because it applies the exclusion not only to acts of the insured, but also to acts of others of which he or she has knowledge.

The principal questions involved are: (1) whether this is a warranty so that any breach avoids the policy, (2) what constitutes an "increase of hazard," and (3) whether the insured knew about it.

The general rule apparently is that the clause is in the nature of a warranty and that an increase of hazard avoids the policy even though it might not in fact have contributed to the loss. Many states by statute provide that any warranty becomes a condition and permit recovery by the insured if the breach of condition did not contribute to the loss. (Hawkeye Chemical Co. v. St. Paul F&M Ins. Co.)[79]

The next question—what constitutes an increase in hazard—is very troublesome. It is usually a question of fact to be settled by a jury. Increase of hazard by definition is a substantial change in the physical condition of the property that affects the risk by materially increasing the probability of loss. The mere negligence of the insured or its employees does not constitute an increase in hazard. (Benton v. National Union Fire Ins. Co.)[80] A mere change of a casual or temporary nature is not enough. (Carr v. Iowa Mut. Tornado Assoc.)[81] A material misrepresentation, however, such as that the insured had had no fire losses when in fact it had suffered several losses constitutes an increase of hazard. Lack of the insured's intention to defraud has no bearing on the matter. (Security Mut. Cas. Co. v. Affiliated F&M Ins. Co.)[82] If an insurer learns of an increase in hazard and does nothing about it, this constitutes a waiver. (Garcy Corp. v. Home Ins. Co.)[83] However, a mere visit by the insured's agent to the premises, with nothing more, is not sufficient to raise an inference that the insurer, through the agent, gained such knowledge as would waive the provision. (Pearl Assur. Co., Ltd. v. Southern Wood Prod.)[84]

The older homeowners policies which used the fire policy as a base took care of the increase of hazard problem by a specific waiver. The HO-76 policy as an integrated policy without the fire policy as a base has neither an increase of hazard clause nor a waiver thereof. It can be argued that there is now an inference that an increase in hazard is a breach of an implied condition and if it contributed to a loss would void the policy.

The last requirement is that the insured must have known about it. Thus the act of a tenant (unknown to a landlord) which increased the hazard did not void the landlord's policy. (Fidelity-Phoenix Fire Ins. Co. v. Perry)[85]

PRINCIPAL EXTRA-CONTRACTUAL RIGHTS OF INSUREDS

Contract Interpretation

Doctrine of Reasonable Expectations   General rules of construction pertaining to contracts of adhesion are discussed in Chapter 5. A recent and widely accepted principle favoring insureds is the so-called doctrine of reasonable expectations:

> Insureds are entitled to the measure of protection necessary to fulfill their reasonable expectations and . . . (they) should not be subjected to "technical encumbrances or hidden pitfalls." (Gerhardt v. Continental Ins. Co.)[86]

Or, as stated elsewhere:

> The court interprets the form contract to mean what a reasonable buyer would expect it to mean, and thus protects the weaker party's expectation at the expense of the stronger's. (Gray v. Zurich Ins. Co.)[87]

The doctrine is based on the belief that an insured is entitled to the coverage under a policy that he or she might reasonably expect it to provide, and that, particularly in mass market contracts, exclusions or qualifications, to be effective, must be conspicuous, plain, and clear.

The doctrine probably had its first modern application in the case of Gray v. Zurich Ins. Co., *supra.* That case involved a suit against an insured for an assault and battery. The insurer refused to defend the suit because of the intentional act exclusion in the liability policy. The court held that the insurer was liable for the defense costs because the insured had a reasonable expectation that these costs were covered under the policy since the policy covered many other types of intentional acts. A companion case, Lowell v. Maryland Casualty Co., was decided the same day as Gray.[88] It also was based upon the intentional act exclusion. In the Lowell case, the assault and battery action actually had been defended and lost by the insured. This created an anomalous situation. That the insured lost the suit would seem to indicate that it was straight assault and battery and came within the policy exclusion. The court said, however, "because you didn't defend him, you not only have to pay the defense costs, but the judgment too," which amounted to an additional $1,500. So the company not only had to pay for the defense but also for a loss they didn't intend to cover in the first place.

The principle was soon embraced by the New Jersey Supreme Court in Gerhardt v. Continental Insurance Co., *supra*. A domestic servant was injured in the home and filed for workers' compensation payments, applicable in New Jersey to domestic employees. Lacking a workers' compensation policy, the employer called upon his homeowners insurer to defend the suit. The insurer declined on the basis of the usual workers' compensation exclusion in the personal liability section. The insured filed a successful declaratory judgment action. The New Jersey Supreme Court applied the reasonable expectation theory based on several parts of the policy including a broad insuring clause and a rather poorly worded exclusion clause at a location remote from the coverage provisions.

Although the principle is employed principally by insureds, it has worked to the benefit of insurers in some cases. Thus in California, where the doctrine originated, the appellate court in the case of Los Angeles Ins. Co. v. Firemens Ins. Co., where the insured was attempting to have automobile coverage included under his homeowners policy, said, ". . . nor do the reasonable expectations of the insured contemplate that his homeowners policy will provide such extended automobile coverage. . . ."[89]

There is some division of opinion on whether the principle can be applied only to an ambiguity in the contract, or whether it also applies to an unambiguous policy and entitles the insured to all coverage he or she can reasonably expect under the policy, except for exclusions that are "conspicuous, plain, and clear." It appears that the tendency is toward the latter, more liberal, approach.

Doctrine of Purpose Another widely accepted doctrine is what might be termed the doctrine of purpose, although no court has attached that name to it as yet. In some ways it is a return to the general rule of contract interpretation, namely, to ascertain the intent of the parties. In other respects, it resembles the reasonable expectation doctrine.

Briefly, the doctrine of purpose interprets the language of the policy, particularly exclusions in the light of the purpose. As one court stated, "The better approach is to examine the purpose of the exclusion in the policy and determine whether this is the type of risk against which the insurance company had not calculated its premium." (Royal Indemnity Co. v. Smith)[90]

Another court explained:

> In deciding whether the exclusions apply to particular facts, some courts have focused on the language of the exclusion, others have looked to the apparent reasons why insurance companies adopted the particular exclusionary language to determine whether in the light of

these reasons the policy was intended to exclude coverage in the circumstances of the particular case. (U.S. Fire Ins. Co. v. Schnabel)[91]

The courts in applying this doctrine asked:

1. What purpose was the policy provision or exclusion intended to serve?
2. Will the purpose be frustrated by permitting the insured to recover?

Not all courts are prepared to try to ascertain intent in this manner, and frequently the explanation of the purpose works in favor of the insurer. When a court understands the reason for an exclusion, it is more often willing to enforce it.

In the past few years at least three courts have reviewed the "visible marks" requirement of the burglary policy. Each court applied the doctrine of purpose where there were no "visible marks," as one would commonly understand the term, but nevertheless there was other physical evidence of a forcible entry. In finding the requirement inapplicable one court stated:

> The purpose of a burglary provision, such as the one at issue, is to enable the carrier to offer a less comprehensive policy to the insured at a correspondingly lower cost. In limiting coverage to forcible entry, physical evidence of which is required, the carrier protects itself from what commonly are known as "inside jobs" and from the frauds that would inevitably result if some physical evidence of break-in were not required.

The court then found that the purpose of the clause had been met by other evidence. (Weldcraft Equipment Co. v. Crum & Forster)[92]

Another case involved the assignment of a fire policy without the required insurer's consent. Upon dissolution of the named corporate insured the policy was assigned to its sole shareholder. The appellate court, in setting aside the insurer's defense of lack of consent stated:

> The object of policy provisions and legal rules which require consent of the insurer to any assignment of a fire insurance policy is "to prevent an increase of risk and hazard of loss by change of ownership without knowledge of the insurer." In this case that rationale is totally inapposite. The assignment of the policy to [the stockholder] did not increase the risk and hazard of loss, since [the . . . (stockholder)] did not, in reality, obtain any additional interest in the policy and insured premises above what it already had as sole shareholder in . . . [the corporate insured]. . . . There was no more risk and hazard of loss after the dissolution and assignment than there was before [the corporate insured] was dissolved.
>
> Once it is seen that there is no reason to apply the rule in the instant case it becomes clear that to do so would place form over substance and would conflict with the oft-expressed doctrine that forfeitures of

insurance policies are not favored in the law and are to be avoided whenever possible. (National American v. Jamison Agency)[93]

In a case favoring the insurer, the application of the care, custody, and control provision of the standard liability policy was in question. The insured claimed that certain property in his possession was covered and the court made the following observation:

> The policy is a liability policy and the obvious purpose of the exception is that the insured shall not be reimbursed for damages to his property or property in his care, custody or control unless an additional premium is paid.

The court also quoted the following from the Royal Insurance Co. v. Smith case, *supra:*

> Usually some form of insurance is available to cover injury to or destruction of the excluded property at a higher premium which is commensurate with the risk. The exclusion eliminates securing such coverage under a liability policy at a cheaper rate. (Baldwin d/b/a "D" Mfg. Co. v. Auto-Owners)[94]

This approach may well be applied more and more by the courts in the future.

Doctrine of Implied Warranty Many years ago *Vance on Insurance* advanced the concept of the application of a doctrine of implied warranty to insurance policies. The reasons were stated as:

> After all, the man on the street purchases his insurance policy in very much the same way he purchases his automobile or his reaper or other chattels. He knows no more about the making of a contract of insurance than he does about the making of an automobile, and he naturally relies upon the skill and good faith of those who hold themselves out to be experts in such matters, by advertising their wares for sale. It would seem to be the clear duty of the insurer, professing to draw an instrument protecting the applicant's property against certain defined perils, to exercise due diligence to supply a policy which will effect the purpose intended. Any damage caused to the applicant through the agent's mistakes or negligence in making inquiries that he should know to be pertinent should rest on the insurer. The situation seems to be strikingly analogous to that expressed in the familiar rule of the law of sales to the effect that a vendor supplying an article which he knows is to be used for a specific purpose impliedly warrants that the article furnished is suitable for that purpose.[95]

Actually Vance cites an article as far back as 1935 which suggested that the insurer issuing the policy should be held to an implied warranty that the policy furnishes the requested coverage.[96] This concept has been supported by at least one other writer on the subject.[97] The argument is that an implied warranty should be made applicable to adhesion-type contracts even if the "weaker" party can read and write.

Up to the present the doctrine has been adopted only by the Iowa Supreme Court, in the case of C & J Fertilizer Inc. v. Allied Mutual Insurance Co.[98] The following excerpt from the opinion is essentially the argument advanced by most proponents of the doctrine:

> Although implied warranties of fitness for intended purpose have traditionally been attached only to sales of tangible products, there is no reason why they should not be attached to "sales of promises" as well. Whether a product is tangible or intangible, its creator ordinarily has reason to know of the purposes for which the buyer intends to use it, and buyers ordinarily rely on the creator's skill or judgment in furnishing it. The reasonable consumer for example depends on an insurance agent and insurance company to sell him a policy that "works" for its intended purpose in much the same way that he depends on a television salesman and television manufacturer. In neither case is he likely to be competent to judge the fitness of the product himself; in both, he must rely on common knowledge and the creator's advertising and promotion.

There is no doubt that there will be a continuing effort to expand this doctrine of implied warranty on behalf of insureds.

Doctrine of Unconscionability   It has also been suggested that there should be a judicial, if not a statutory, adoption of a doctrine similar to the Uniform Commercial Code provision on unconscionability reading:

> (1) If the court as a matter of law finds the contract or any clause of the contract to have been unconscionable at the time it was made the court may refuse to enforce the contract, or it may enforce the remainder of the contract without the unconscionable clause, or it may so limit the application of any unconscionable result.[99]

Unconscionability has been found to exist where a party with superior bargaining power imposes unfair conditions on a weaker party, and has even been applied to contracts outside the UCC, such as leases. (Rego v. Decker)[100] It had not been adopted by any court in an insurance case until the C & J Fertilizer case, cited above. The court's comments on this are also illuminating:

> The situation before us plainly justifies application of the unconscionability doctrine:
>
>> Standardized contracts such as insurance policies, drafted by powerful commercial units and put before individuals on the "accept this or get nothing" basis, are carefully scrutinized by the courts for the purpose of avoiding enforcement of "unconscionable" clauses. (6A Corbin on Contracts Sec. 1376, p. 21.)

This is another doctrine which an insured's counsel may press upon the courts with increasing frequency.

Valued Policy Laws

Valued policy laws favor the insured. They are not to be confused with valued policies, which are policies that establish a fixed amount of liability on a particular property and in the event of loss to that item the stated amount is paid. Valued policy laws, or so-called total loss statutes, apply principally to fire policies. They were enacted by many states in the late 1800s and early 1900s, mainly to give insureds "what they had paid for." In general these laws provide that in case of total loss to an insured's property from certain specified perils (usually fire) the amount stated in the policy declarations is conclusively presumed to be the value of the structure at the time of loss and is payable in full without any deductions. If the value of the property is less than the amount stated in the policy, the insurer is precluded from arguing that a lesser sum should be paid. (Atlas Lubricant Corp. v. Federal Ins. Co.)[101]

Generally the valued policy statutes apply only to a total loss on real property, which was caused by the peril of fire, or, in a few states, windstorm. In Missouri the valued policy law applies to personal property as well as real property. Presently some nineteen states have valued policy laws of one type or another. They are principally smaller states, although the list includes Florida, Georgia, Ohio, and Texas.

The first question in a case under a valued policy law is whether total loss is involved. Thus, for example, does a building have to burn to the ground; or if it is destroyed to the point where a local building ordinance prohibits rebuilding, does this constitute a constructive total loss under the law? Most states hold that constructive total losses of this type come within the valued policy law.

The general rule is that policy provisions that are in conflict with the valued policy law are void. (Atlas Lubricant Corp. v. Federal Ins. Co., *supra*) Thus, for example, coinsurance clauses, pro rata clauses, the option to repair or replace, etc., are invalid in the event of a total loss. (Horn v. Atlas Ins. Co.—Sperling v. Liberty Mut. Ins. Co.)[102] A Texas case illustrates the principle. Policy A in the amount of $6,000 was written on a risk and a month later Policy B in the amount of $12,000 was written on the same risk. The Texas valued policy law provides that it applies ninety days after the policy is written. A loss occurred more than ninety days after Policy A was written, but less than ninety days after Policy B was written. Normally the two policies would have prorated the loss. However, the court held that Policy A ($6,000) had to pay to its full limit, and Policy B would then pick up any excess because of the general rule that the pro rata clause is inconsistent with the valued policy law and therefore was invalid in Policy A which was the only policy subject to the law. (Sneed v. Commercial Union)[103]

The valued policy law does not override policy provisions such as the suit clause, notice of loss, etc. (Altman v. Central Manufacturers Mut. Ins. Co.)[104] Furthermore, fraud will void a policy in a valued policy state even if the fraud consisted of a false statement under oath in a proof of loss concerning the value of personal property listed along with the real property. (Home Ins. Co. v. Hardin)[105]

Cancellation and Nonrenewal

Following is a review of the general rules previously discussed in this chapter, along with a discussion of the extent to which both cancellation and nonrenewal have been circumscribed by legislation.

Cancellation There are only two ways in which a valid policy of insurance may be canceled. First, under the terms of the policy, and second, under the terms of a subsequent oral or written agreement. (Wolverine Ins. Co. v. Taylor)[106]

Cancellation by Policy Terms. Most property insurance policies contain a cancellation clause such as:

> This policy shall be canceled at any time at the request of the insured. . . . This policy may be canceled at any time by this Company by giving to the insured a five days' written notice of cancellation with or without tender of the excess of paid premium.

The casualty policies contain a clause reading:

> Cancellation. This policy may be canceled by the named insured by surrender thereof to the company or any of its authorized agents or by mailing to the company written notice stating when thereafter the cancellation shall be effective. This policy may be canceled by the company by mailing to the named insured at the address shown in this policy, written notice stating when not less than ten days thereafter such cancellation shall be effective. The mailing of notice as aforesaid shall be sufficient proof of notice. The time of surrender or the effective date and hour of cancellation stated in the notice shall become the end of the policy period. Delivery of such written notice either by the named insured or by the company shall be equivalent to mailing.

Simplified policies such as the HO-76 and the personal auto policy contain a very involved cancellation clause. This is designed to comply with a majority of the state laws governing such cancellation. The HO-76 has adopted the casualty approach that proof of mailing is sufficient proof of notice. These policies also contain nonrenewal clauses restricting the insurer's right to not renew.

The effect of the property and liability clauses can be quite different. Under the property clause, the use of the words, "giving to the insured" has been interpreted to require that the insured actually receive the notice. (Nelson v. Phoenix of Hartford)[107] Therefore, while deposit in the United States mails of the notice of cancellation with sufficient postage and proper address is *prima facie* proof of delivery, it can be rebutted by proof of nondelivery. If the insured can prove nondelivery, the cancellation is ineffective. (Broadway v. All-Star Ins. Corp.)[108] There is some case law to the contrary which holds that denial of receipt does not create an issue of fact. (Annunziata v. Travelers Ins. Co.)[109] However, even this case stated that mailing is an issue of fact and evidence of the mailing is subject to the same evaluation as other proof. Where no certificate or other evidence of mailing was introduced, the court held that there was a lack of proof of giving notice of cancellation.

The problem of receipt of notice by the insured is not encountered under the liability clause because it makes proof of mailing of the notice sufficient. Even here the notice must be sent to all insureds to be fully effective. Thus where under a liability policy "L.G." was named as an additional insured and the notice of cancellation was sent to the principal insured but not to "L.G.," it was held to be ineffective as to "L.G." (Gasparro v. Sherer et al.)[110]

Strict compliance with all requirements of the notice provision is essential. Where the cancellation notice failed to advise the insured that the excess premium would be refunded on demand this was held to void the notice. (Strong v. Merchants Mut. Ins. Co.)[111]

Cancellation by Agreement. A subsequent oral or written agreement of the parties to cancel may be evidenced in several ways. A surrender of the policy by the insured to the insurer with the understanding that the policy is to be canceled constitutes a valid cancellation. (Melvin Cormier, Inc. v. American Employers Ins. Co.—Wolverine Ins. Co. v. Taylor, *supra*)[112] Whether cancellation by mutual agreement took place depends upon the intentions of the parties as evidenced by their acts, conduct, and words. There must be a meeting of minds.

One of the principal areas is "cancellation by substitution." In the typical case, an insured obtains an insurance policy on a risk and then at a later date purchases a second policy on the same risk from another insurer, with the intent that it replace the first one. If the intent to cancel is communicated to the first insurer a cancellation is effected. There are even a few courts that hold that intent need not be communicated to the first insurer because presumably it would agree. However, the weight of authority is that the mere purchase of a policy of insurance with intent to cancel an existing policy covering the same risk does not effect a cancellation of the existing policy unless the intent to cancel is communicated to the first insured. (Lambert v. Merchants Property Ins. Co.—State Farm F&C Co. v. Roberts—Tyner v. Cherokee Ins. Co.)[113] According to the majority, there can be no unilateral cancellation of the contract unless authorized in the contract itself, and a mutual agreement requires assent of both parties. If one party does not know about it there cannot be consent. (Lambert v. Merchants Property Ins. Co., *supra*)

Statutory Modification When underwriting results began to suffer in the mid-sixties, particularly in the automobile liability line, there was a wave of policy cancellations which created considerable public ill will. In an effort to remedy the situation, the major company rating organizations introduced in 1968 a program of voluntary restrictions on the right of insurers to cancel. However, this did not satisfy the public demand and shortly thereafter legislation was introduced in many states to limit cancellation and nonrenewal rights. Originally these statutes applied only to automobile liability policies, but now many also apply to property lines covering individual rather than commercial risks.

Currently, forty-nine jurisdictions have a law or regulation limiting cancellation and nonrenewal rights for automobile liability coverages. Generally these extend the notice of cancellation period from five days to twenty, thirty, or more days, and also limit the reasons for cancellation or nonrenewal. In addition there are some nineteen states that have limitations on cancellation and nonrenewal for all or parts of the property lines. These also extend the notice period and limit the reasons for cancellation or nonrenewal. These statutory provisions must be strictly followed or the attempted cancellation will be held invalid. This creates a powerful extra-contractual right in favor of the insured.

Duty to Defend

A liability policy contains two major insuring provisions. One provides that the insurer will pay all sums which the insured becomes legally obligated to pay as damages, and the other provides that the insurer will defend any suit alleging bodily injury or property damage and seeking damages payable under the contract. The duty to defend is separate and apart from the obligation to pay under the liability provision. There is no limit of liability applicable to the defense provision and the courts uniformly hold that the insurer must provide a proper defense regardless of cost. The obligation to defend is therefore broader than the duty to pay. It extends to any action, even if groundless, false, or fraudulent, in which facts are alleged within the coverage of the policy. In determining the existence or nonexistence of the duty, neither the outcome of the litigation nor the ultimate liability of the insurer is relevant. (State Farm F&C Co. v. Pildner)[114] When a complaint contains a count that may be subject to a policy defense (such as an intentional injury exclusion) and a separate negligence count (which is not) the insurer is obligated to defend. (De Luca v. Atlantic Mut. Ins. Co.)[115] The majority rule is that the allegations of the complaint constitute the sole test of the insurer's duty to defend. (National Cas. Co. v. INA)[116] Some states permit going outside the complaint and looking into the actual facts in specific cases to decide whether or not there is an obligation to defend. (Raday v. Board of Education)[117] Some states apply the "reasonable expectation" rule and permit looking at all the terms of the contract and finding whether the insured had a "reasonable expectation" that the insurer would defend. (Gray v. Zurich Ins. Co.)[118]

Requiring an insurer to defend when the complaint alleges facts indicating there might be a policy defense creates a conflict of interest problem. Usually the insurer requires a nonwaiver agreement before it proceeds with the defense. If it vigorously asserts lack of coverage, it may well be that it is not adequately representing the insured and yet it does not want to waive the policy defenses. In such a situation it has been held that the insurer should invite the insured to retain other counsel and if the insurer is in fact later found liable for the defense of the insured it should then pay the reasonable fees of insured's counsel.

One occasional problem is the obligation to defend after the policy limit has been exhausted through payment of prior claims. It has always been intended that the obligation to defend be coextensive with the liability under the policy and if claim payments exhaust the policy limits it was intended that the obligation to defend should cease.

This has infrequently been tested and in each case the courts have agreed with the insurer. The first case upholding this construction was decided in New Hampshire in 1939. (Lumbermen's Mutual v. McCarthy)[119]

Liability policies were revised in 1966 to specifically provide that "the company shall not be obligated to . . . defend any suit after the applicable limit of the company's liability has been exhausted by the payment of judgments or settlements." However, this provision does not permit the insurer to pay the policy limit into court and be discharged from further liability for defense. (Ursprung v. Safeco Ins. Co.)[120]

Chapter Notes

1. 514 P. 2d 223-AK.
2. 1975 F&C Cases 1078-PA.
3. 205 NW 2d 640-NE.
4. 320 A. 2d 688-ME.
5. USCA 5th Oct. 24, 1975.
6. 225A. 2d 328-NJ.
7. 203 NW 2d IA 1974.
8. 200 IL App. 20.
9. 323 NE 2d 521-IL.
10. 136 Super 468-NJ 1975.
11. 496 F. 2d 479-IL.
12. 378 F. Supp. 860-DC.
13. 74 F&C Cases 1415-DC.
14. 511 SW 2d 205-KY.
15. 75 F&C Cases 1052-TN.
16. 1974 F&C Cases 961-MO.
17. 237 CA App. 2d 435.
18. 299 So. 2d 192-MS 1974.
19. 102 CA Reptr. 868.
20. 314 A. 2d 420-IN 1975.
21. 231 A. 2d 740-PA 1967.
22. 257 291-MI.
23. 209 NW 2d 486-MI.
24. 526 P. 2d 169-AZ 1974.
25. 324 A. 2d 263-CT 1973.
26. 103 NJ Super 406.
27. 170 U.S. 133-1898.
28. 242 So. 2d 749.
29. 520 P. 2d 137-CO.
30. 530 P. 2d 74 OR.
31. 335 A. 2d 666-NH.
32. 75 F&C Cases 862-NY.
33. 74 F&C Cases 1466-NY.
34. 231 NW 2d 619-IO 1974.
35. 122 CA Reptr. 330.
36. 219 OR 110.
37. 490 F. 2d 407–WV 1974.
38. 86 Wash. 2d 264, 5437 2d 634-1975.
39. 74 F&C Cases 1225-TX.
40. 73 F&C Cases 771-MO.
41. 531 P. 2d 983-CO 1904.
42. 74 F&C Cases 190-NY.

43. 73 F&C Cases 828-MO.
44. 521 SW 2d 244-KY.
45. 256 F. 2d 61 WY 1958.
46. 543 P. 2d 147-AZ 1975.
47. 525 SW 2d 44 TX 1975.
48. 75 F&C Cases 943-NY.
49. 76 F&C Cases 1181-GA.
50. 293 So. 2d 550-LA 1974.
51. James H. Donaldson, *Casualty Claim Practice*, 3rd ed. (Homewood, IL: Richard D. Irwin, Inc., 1976), p. 31.
52. 263 NYS 2d 807-NY.
53. 133 NE 2d 407-OH 1955.
54. 180 A. 343 CT.
55. 301 So. 2d 681-LA.
56. 99 N.W. 2d 865-WI 1959.
57. 307 A. 2d 142-NJ.
58. 390 N.E. 2d 361-IL 1979.
59. 357 NYS 2d 865-NY.
60. 75 F&C Cases 962-NC.
61. 90 CA Reptr. 608 1970.
62. 159 NE 902-NY 1928.
63. 511 F. 2d 241-IL.
64. 57 MA 263.
65. 74 F&C Cases 1133 FL.
66. 303 P. 2d 659-WA 1956.
67. 509 P. 2d 418-OR.
68. 74 F&C Cases 1342 GA.
69. 491 SW 2d 700-TX.
70. 524 P. 2d 874-WY.
71. 74 F&C Cases 1077-OR.
72. 515 SW 2d 395-TX.
73. 149 NE 2d 652-IL 1958.
74. 241 F. 2d 432-MA 1957.
75. 108 So. 2d 571-MS.
76. 242 F. Supp. 789.
77. 168 F. Supp. 709.
78. 223 So. 2d 713-FL.
79. 510 F. 2d 322-IL.
80. 7 F&C Cases 496.
81. 7 F&C Cases 638.
82. 471 F. 2d 238-IL 1974.
83. 496 F. 2d 479-IL 1974.
84. 7 F&C Cases 1043.
85. 7 F&C Cases 751.
86. 225 A. 2d 328-NJ.
87. 65 CA App. 2d 263.
88. 12 F&C Cases 1260-CA 1966.
89. 106 CA Reptr. 540.

90. 173 SE 2d 738-GA.
91. 504 P. 2d 847-AK.
92. 312 A. 2d 68-PA 1974.
93. 74 F&C Cases 1461-SD.
94. 282 NE 2d 204-IL.
95. Sec. 89, at 540, 3d. ed., by Anderson 1951.
96. 35 Yale L.J. 203.
97. Slawson, *New Approach to Standard Forms*, 8 Trial 49 1972.
98. 227 NW 2d 169-IA 1975.
99. Uniform Commercial Code, Section 2-302.
100. 482 P. 2d 834-AK 1971.
101. 203 So. 2d 550-LA.
102. 241 KY 2263; 281 So. 2d 297-FL 1973.
103. 76 F&C Cases 1348-TN.
104. 93 NE 2d 28-OH 1949.
105. 75 F&C Cases 926-KY.
106. 75 F&C Cases 945-MS.
107. 318 So. 2d 839-MS.
108. 285 So. 2d 536-LA.
109. 75 F&C Cases 709-NY.
110. 74 F&C Cases 1228-NY.
111. 309 NE 2d 510-MA.
112. 280 So. 2d 355-LA.
113. 74 F&C Cases 245-TN; 75 F&C Cases 938-TN; 205 SE 2d 380-SC.
114. 321 NE 2d 600-OH.
115. 373 NYS 2d 630-NY.
116. 230 F. Supp. 617.
117. 328 A. 2d 17-NJ.
118. 65-CA 2d 263.
119. 90 NH 320.
120. 497 SW 2d 726-KY 1973.

Index

F

H

G

I

W